THE MANY FACES OF SUBUD

With love

Piantee

THE MANY FACES OF SUBUD

A Collection of Experiences

Riantee Lydia Rand

To order additional copies of this book, contact:
Xlibris Corporation
1-888-795-4274
www.Xlibris.com
Orders@Xlibris.com
28149

Contents

A necessary disclaimer 9

1: STORYTELLING *11*

How This Book Came About 11
   From Rasunah 16
About Being Helped, Helping and
Being Helpers 17
   Arifah (France) interviewed in Spokane (WA.) 19
   Conversation with Rasunah 21
   From Lillia 30
   Conversation with Lillia 31

2: SUBUD AND THE LATIHAN *45*
   Lillia 53
   Rasunah 55
   Carolye (Canada) interviewed in Mendocino 56
   Elna (U.S.A.) interviewed in LA. (CA.) 58
   Herbert (U.S.A.) interviewed in Spokane (WA.) 63

3: BEGINNING IN SUBUD *67*

Early Years in an Isolated Group—
The sixties in Aspen 75
   Mardiah (U.S.A.) interviewed in L.A. (CA.) 75
   Resmiwati (U.S.A.) interviewed in L.A. (CA.) 80

Saul (U.S.A.) interviewed in Santa Cruz (CA.) 86
Laura (U.S.A.) interviewed in Santa Cruz (CA.) 90
Redmond and Charles (U.S.A.) interviewed in LA. (CA.) 98
Lariswati (U.S.A.) interviewed in Spokane (WA.) 101

Other Beginnings 109
Harlan M. (U.S.A.) interviewed in Menucha (OR.) 109
Arifah (France) interviewed in Spokane (WA.) 112
Hamilton (U.S.A.) interviewed in Bali (Indonesia) 120
Conversation with Jim, Barbara & Marston (U.S.A.)

4: HABITS, TESTING, CRISIS or DELIVERANCE 130

About Changing Name and
Moving to a New Location 136
Carolye (Canada) interviewed in Mendocino (CA.) 139
Purification, Crisis, Metamorphosis,
Deliverance 145
Aaron (U.S.A.) interviewed in Spokane (WA.) 151
Ilaina (Mexico) interviewed in Spokane (WA.) 158
Rohanna S. (Peru) interviewed in Seattle (WA.) 161
Illene (U.S.A.) interviewed in Denver (CO.) 166
Hillary (U.S.A.) interviewed in Seattle (WA.) 170

5: DOCTORS IN THE SKY 180
Christian-Lucas (U.S.A.) interviewed in Menucha (OR.) 183
Lusana (U.S.A.) interviewed in Menucha (OR.) 189
Resmiwati (U.S.A.) interviewed in L.A. (CA.) 193
Saul (U.S.A.) interviewed in Santa Cruz (CA.) 196
Laura (Saul's wife) interviewed in Santa Cruz (CA.) 200
Laoma (U.S.A.) interviewed in Little River (CA.) 201

6: HEALERS AND HEALING 211
Lusijah (USA.) interviewed in Menucha (Oregon) 215
Solihin (England) interviewed in Menucha (OR.) 227

Heidi (English-Jamaican)
interviewed at Amanecer (Colombia) 238

Muchtar (Portugal) interviewed in Menucha (OR.) 243

Loretta & Alfonso (Mexico) as interpreted by
Arifah (France) at the World Congress in Spokane 246

7: SUBUD AND MY OWN TRUTH 251
Women in Subud talk about their spiritual journeys 251

Young Women Raised in Subud Families 257
Tatyana (French/American)
interviewed in Mendocino (CA.) 257

Petrice (Canadian) interviewed in Menucha (OR.) 265

Manuella (Hungarian-English)
interviewed in Mendocino (CA.) 267

Arianne (French/American)
interviewed in Mendocino (CA.) 270

Muftiah (U.S.A.) interviewed in Spokane (WA.) 276

Middle Years in Subud 280
Sabina (U.S.A.) interviewed in Mendocino (CA.) 280
Women on the Subject of
Having No Soul 284
Rohanna S. (Peruvian-American)
interviewed in Seattle (OR.) 284

Mardiah (U.S.A.) interviewed in Seattle (WA.) 286

Later Years in Subud 288
Lavinia (German-American)
interviewed in Menucha (OR.) 288

Arifah (French) interviewed in Spokane (WA.) 292

8: RELATIONSHIPS AND MARRIAGE 298
Illene (U.S.A.) interviewed in Denver (CO.) 307
Marston (U.S.A.) interviewed in Menucha (OR.) 311

Hamilton (U.S.A.) interviewed in Bali (Indonesia) 313
Elfrida (Canadian) interviewed in Bali (Indonesia) 315
Mardiah (U.S.A.) interviewed in Los Angeles. (CA.) 318
Lusana (U.S.A.) interviewed in Menucha (OR.) 319
Resmiwati (U.S.A.) interviewed in L.A. (CA.) 323
Osanna (Zambia) interviewed in Spokane (WA.) 327
Rashidah, (Indonesian) interviewed in Berkerley, (CA.) 329

Young Men Talk About Relationships 333
Matthew (U.S.A.) interviewed in Menucha (OR.) 333
Jaece (U.S.A.) interviewed in Menucha (OR.) 336
Rusdi (Colombia) interviewed in Mendocino (CA.) 337
Harlan G. USA. interviewed in Mendocino (CA.) 338

9: WORK IN THE WORLD & IN SUBUD 341
Aaron, (USA) interviewed in Spokane, (WA) 347
Elias (Brazil) interviewed in Mendocino (CA.) 349
Rusdi (Colombia) interviewed in Mendocino, (CA.) 350
N'Kanga (Zaire) interviewed in Spokane (WA.) 352
Laura (U.S.A.) interviewed in Santa Cruz, (CA.) 357
*Manuella (English-Hungarian)
interviewed in Mendocino (CA.)* 358
*Heidi (English-Jamaican)
interviewed in Amanecer, (Colombia)* 360

Becoming a Minister 362
Rohanna L. (Canada) interviewed at Menucha (OR.) 362
10: PROPHETS, VISIONS & INSPIRATION 369
*Leonard (French—English)
interviewed in Spokane (WA.)* 377
Sylvia (U.S.A.) from her own words. 394

EPILOGUE 397

GLOSSARY 401

A necessary disclaimer

This book was initially intended for people interested in Subud, or people who had already started on that path and wanted to know more about the experience of others on it. For those more familiar with Subud, the talks given by Muhammad Subuh Sumohadiwidjojo—otherwise known as Bapak, who was the first to receive this inner teaching, and of his daughter, Ibu Rahayu, would be more beneficial.

Subud is not a religion, nor a doctrine or technique, but is directly related to one's own experience when practicing the spiritual exercise, so each person can only talk about it from her or his own evidence. This collection of personal understandings and life experiences does not necessarily express the opinion of the larger Subud community. However, it is through direct experience that Subud members form their ideas, and these are not fixed, but constantly evolve with the practice of the latihan.

Because of this, it might also be that the conversations in this book, conducted over a period of more than ten years, no longer entirely reflect the views of those who were interviewed.

I must ask forgiveness of anyone who might be offended by anything appearing in this book.

1

STORYTELLING

HOW THIS BOOK CAME ABOUT

Subud is a direct and spontaneous spiritual experience, which allows people to receive a contact with the Great Life Force. It re-awakens their inner feeling and puts them in touch with their own guidance, eventually bringing to the surface their true nature which was previously obstructed by erroneous beliefs, ancestral patterns of behavior, culture, education and family malfunctions. There is a power within each individual that has the capacity to bring a healing to body and soul, and it can be awakened by the spiritual exercise of Subud. Many gain a deeper understanding of their own religious beliefs from the evidence they receive through the latihan. Others have become aware of their true talent and work. For myself, having experienced that the essence of all things resides in emptiness, I surrendered to that and became aware of the divine presence in myself and all around me. When I am totally present, the presence of God is felt and when groups of people come together in this state they generate an energy field of great intensity. There are now Subud groups in eighty countries, bringing together harmoniously people of many different religious and ethnic backgrounds.

This book is the result of the collaborative effort of three women who have practiced the latihan of Subud for decades. It compiles testimonies of Subud members from all over the world, on different topics. People interviewed were of different age groups, some newly "opened" in Subud, some older members, some second and third generation Subud. "The opening" is the occasion when a new member receives the latihan for the first time, after having gone through a three-month probationary period. This book started in 1989 when Lillia Davidson had the idea for it at about the same time I did. As we engage on our conscious spiritual journey we often begin to notice this kind of synchronicity, and the more we notice the more it happens. Lillia and I were in two different places, she at the Subud World Congress in Australia, and I at home. The idea was to write a history of our Subud group in Aspen, Colorado from its beginnings in the mid-sixties, and to follow early members through their different journeys.

While Lillia was away I became absorbed in recording the humorous and odd aspects, the trials and tribulations, along with the unusual freedom enjoyed in those days by groups of isolated members, as we called groups like ours that had little or no influence from mainstream Subud. Our Aspen group was entirely composed of seekers and iconoclasts, dissatisfied with the choices society offered and looking for better alternatives; not part of the original wave of pioneers who helped bring Subud to the West, they belonged to the next generation which, more often than not, had come to Subud through the mind-expanding drug consciousness of the sixties.

When Lillia came back from Australia we realized that we had been working on the same idea. We decided to work together. Lillia had a picture of the-Great-Story-Teller-in-the-Sky listening carefully to stories bearing witness to the joys and trials of life in the flesh. Everyone made his or her story most captivating in an effort to enchant Him. We are part of the experiment of free will and have come here to have an experience that can only happen in a world like ours—and of this we testify to the divine. I understood that my own story, as I told it, helped me break boundaries; becoming aware of my personal myth gave me the incentive to improve on the way I lived.

We were a few years into our collaboration when Rasunah Katz joined us. Unaware that Lillia and I were engaged in this work, Rasunah came to say that the two of us were to collaborate on a writing project. This was revealed to her during latihan and she believed the subject of the book would be about feminine spirituality. I told her about my collaboration with Lillia: her receiving might have been about joining us. I added that we could use some new energy for a project, which at that point was dormant. She did give the project new juice, organized meetings, thought of questions to be tested, suggested interviews. Later, during a meeting, Lillia informed us that her participation could no longer be in the writing part of the project, maybe more in making pictures. I didn't understand what she meant until I had a dream in which she made me a gift of her self through a mural she painted on the wall of the house I lived in.

The colors were earthy and sunny, gold, sienna, rust, and ochre with a few faded patches of emerald and turquoise. The mural seemed to radiate an extraordinary light that made the room vibrant with the colors of the sunset. It filled me with delight. At first I only noticed the top of the mural, but when I looked again I saw the bottom and got the whole picture. A voice in the dream told me that there was an extraordinary gift in Lillia's art. Through this mural I was able to understand Lillia's true nature; she showed me the colors of her true self, helping me understand her story from an inner place. Color, as much as sound, is part of a story.

The three of us met regularly for a while and eventually I ended up working alone on the book while Lillia fed me pictures, dreams and ideas, while Rasunah gave me support and motivation. They kept restoring my faith. The process of creating this book was like the making of a life, the result of collaboration at times, personal work at others, ultimately in God's Hand. The not-yet-written-book seemed to dwell in a realm into which I was allowed to peek just for an instant, just long enough to meet the spirit of writing and translate its whispers into language. To meet with this spirit I went into a wilderness, at times remaining there through barrenness and doubts until it consented to take me on the book-making journey. This became my vision quest. Times of great inspiration pushed me through my usual limitations.

Difficulties arose when old insecurities and issues surfaced, especially in partnership with others. The book, held like a mirror in front of me, revealed flaws I didn't always like to see. When threatened I wanted to control the work instead of trusting it and letting it flow. How could I get it all done without order and control? However, what I tried to control I killed. On the other hand, long periods of aridity brought guilt about what I was not doing. So, what was I to do? I came to understand that finding the balance between surrender and perseverance was what my work was about. As long as I held the belief that things were valuable only if they were difficult, this prevented them from being easy. As with the experience of the latihan, it was when I let go of control and started trusting, that the flow was re-established. As I worked, indications were given, ideas were clarified through dreams, visions and sudden flashes of intuition—during which clear sentences rang in my ears. I looked at everything I encountered under a new light and with a new intensity.

I realized that I carried with me every story I heard and each one filled me with new meaning. No two stories are the same; the telling brings understanding and bridges isolation. Every story has more than one version. Each version offers another way to experience it. Stories are alive and grow each time they are told, incorporating a piece of every teller. The best stories have many meanings that change with our capacity to understand. That is why the words of Bapak seem to acquire new significance over the years.

Some stories are meant to be recited aloud, the sound of the language being an essential part of the effect. Muslims often say that when they hear the Koran being chanted in a mosque they feel enveloped in a divine dimension of sound, which reminds them of the angel Gabriel enveloping Muhammad in a powerful embrace on Mount Hira. Even non-Muslims like myself can be shaken by the sound of a *sura*. It is as though Muhammad created an entirely new literary form that does not need to be understood to be effective. When Jews study the Torah they do not simply run their eyes over the words; instead they savor each word God himself is supposed to have used when he revealed Himself to Moses on Mount Sinai.

Sacred texts are meant, through sound as well as words, to yield a strong sense of the divine. It is said that nothing is greater than the primal sound; it is the essence of life, the word of the worlds. God speaks to us through it. Out of this divine voice all other sounds flow and linger in the material planes as echoes of the original melody. They are heard as the music of God and can be translated in speech, then writing.

Light and sound are the two aspects through which God appears in the lower worlds. The Holy Spirit can manifest as light, which is a reflection of the atoms of God moving in space, or as sound, which is the audible life current that carries our souls back to God.

For me, writing comes from listening to something that gradually surfaces from my deeper self. I become a channel for this inner voice. The drive to write stems from the desire to achieve the best possible translation of the divine language, this mysterious tongue that constantly creates new understanding. Trading stories with others reminds me that despite great distances we share beliefs, insights, joy and misfortunes and that life is a process of purification. Often I don't know why I have been touched so deeply by a story, I can only recognize that a secret chord has been struck.

Creation is never finished. We are always in the process of becoming. The three of us decided not to force things but to let the stories progress, take their own course. We didn't always choose the most extraordinary tales nor did we dismiss the stories of those who no longer practice the latihan at this time. We "tested" (testing is simply to pose a question in the latihan and be ready to receive the answer in movements, sounds and pictures) along the way when it was needed. But mostly, we listened. When Varindra Vittachi (a well-known journalist and an early Subud member and helper) asked Bapak how it was that so many people in Subud felt the need to write about Subud, Bapak gave a dismissive wave of his hand and answered, "Purification!" So, this book can be considered a purification exercise that may be helpful to others in their own process. Often, I use the pronoun 'we' when I talk about a tendency that is common to most humans. It is a generalization, and of course, there are many exceptions. May I be forgiven if I offend anyone through my efforts.

STORY IS MEANT TO SET THE INNER BACK IN MOTION

From Rasunah

I have chosen this book, in which I join my sisters Riantee and Lillia, as a way to ask questions so we can weave together a story that began long ago, one that continues to be re-created as we travel together on the spiritual path of Subud. Ours is a story of sharing long hikes into the wilderness with many young children around us, a story of failed attempts and starting over, creating and recreating relationships. It is also a story of building trust, of deepening communication and concern for each other and the world.

A week before I approached Riantee about this book I had a dream. I was on a long journey; the path was sometimes very treacherous. I was caring for a perfect being about twelve inches tall, very thin with long lines and a small domed head. He was old and wise looking, completely naked, apparently neither male nor female, but I always referred to this being as Him. As we traveled along we came upon a barbed wire fence and I helped him go under the fence on his back. The feeling around him was quiet, peaceful and knowing.

When I awoke from this dream I felt refreshed as though something new would be coming; it felt momentous. There was a flooding of ideas, inspiration returned, and the energy to write again mysteriously opened up. The being in my dream, that exquisite thing, became a symbol for inner change, the wise voice, the naked intuitive self. I am beginning to hear this voice clearly and to differentiate it from the outer voice, which says, "Do this, do that." That one impedes change.

For each of us, things seem to simmer deep within this place of knowing, this wise being, and as we peel away the layers, the tears, the hurt, the denial, the anger, the shame, patience arises. It's a time of waiting which may allow something new to come in for we have begun on our journey of recognition.

For years I wrote furiously and with abandon, seemingly without purpose. I didn't feel I had a choice. I simply wrote because I had to, writing was the juice of my life, my savior. The repetition of words and phrases, the whole rhythm of poetry moved me and expanded my consciousness, making me feel alive, connected to the natural world of my childhood. It kept me available to the mysteries of life. For me poetry was another language, a place where I could be free, where I could rock against my deep origins, where I could drift like sediment over the earth. Poetry contained me, and I was to breathe it for the next fifteen years. Then I lost it soon after being opened in Subud.

I see this book as a way to share in our own unique way, to record the words of others with neutrality, without criticism or praise. I see this book as a flowing river. In its course stones rise and shine, then recede into the deep water, becoming one with it.

ABOUT BEING HELPED, HELPING AND BEING HELPERS

To begin with Bapak chose helpers because he could no longer be present in all the places where new people were being opened. They were Bapak's helpers and their task was to be witnesses, during the opening ceremony, of the sincere wish of the new member to worship God.

Later, people who were experienced enough in the latihan (spiritual exercise) of Subud to answer questions, who could adjust to the members' needs, who proved to be of good character and loved by the membership, would be chosen, if they were willing, through testing.

Bapak said about testing that it is for the purpose of obtaining an answer from the Great Life Force, as far as possible free from the influence of one's thoughts and desires. When a helper or a member carries out testing in Subud it is similar to doing the latihan. The difference is that when testing, the person first has a question to ask before doing the latihan, to which he or she receives an answer, in whatever form he or she is able to receive. It is necessary first to understand the meaning of the question, then to immediately let go of these thoughts until there is no trace of them left in the inner feeling, only the feeling of surrender.

So testing is an extension of the latihan directed towards the exploration of specific topics. The wording of the question is very important. General testing is conducted with the whole Subud group and the helpers. The member wishing to test a question as well as a few helpers available for the testing attends the personal testing. It can also be done individually.

A helper is a member who understands that it is necessary to come to decisions without relying on desires, heart and mind. Bapak asked helpers to be aware that it is God's will for humans to be able to receive the bettering of their inner being and to follow the right way of life for them. He added that helpers can help others by becoming examples, but for this they have to possess a character that likes both receiving and giving. A helper often makes more progress in his/her spiritual development by becoming a helper.

Bapak explained to us that helpers are not leaders and that there is no difference between them. They are equally high and equally low whether working on the regional, national, international or local level. Helpers are only intermediaries, responsible for the development of new members, and they are meant to look after the membership, be in harmony with one another and appreciate each other.

MINE IS THE STORY OF A PIONEER, A WEED EATER

Arifah (France) interviewed in Spokane (WA.)

Translated from French

Wisdom does not lie in the constant struggle to bring the sacred into daily life but in recognizing that there is no daily life, life is committed and whole. We are on sacred ground.

I was opened in London at Coombe Springs. I stayed two years in London. That is how I became a helper. All the latihans and openings were happening in a building with nine sides, the famous enneagram of Gurdjieff. I was in the kitchen one day and Bapak came through. He said to me, "What are you doing here?" I answered, "Well I am taking care of the food because everybody will come to eat after the openings."

"Not at all, you don't stay here. The openings are about to start, you must go there."

I answered, "No, I can't be present at other people's openings."

But the young Indonesian who was with Bapak said to me, "You cannot say no to Bapak."

Bapak then turned to me and said, "You are a helper, you should go." And I answered that I was not a helper at all. Then he seemed puzzled, and the young man insisted that I must go.

When I arrived in the latihan room Bapak's wife Ibu said to me, "Well, you were long enough! We were waiting for all the helpers to be here to start the openings."

Most people there knew nothing about Subud. We barely knew how to start the latihan. There were no guidelines then; we were pioneers. Bapak told us: "I have appointed you to serve."

We should be serving our brothers and sisters and that's why we are appointed helpers. Now that Bapak is dead there is no hierarchy. He said that our personal life didn't matter as long as we were an example, that Subud was a pure gift of God. Members and helpers now have hundreds of books and talks, but they still don't really know enough. There was even a fairly new member who didn't know who Bapak was. She was opened months and months ago and asked, "Bapak, who is that?"

Bapak's wife, Ibu, said, "I don't speak English very well, what I tell you I don't tell you twice."

Anyway. To get back to Coombe Springs. John Bennett said to me one day, "Well my dear, you are on the list to clean the garden today."

"This is a spiritual school," I answered, "and I certainly will not do that." But I did. Another day I had to cook breakfast for all the people.

The man who became my husband was into Gurdjieff so in the evenings I went and watched their classes. I watched this beautiful dance. Bennett caught sight of me one night and he said, "You shouldn't do that, you shouldn't watch those sacred dances." It was sacrilegious obviously, but I didn't know anything about spirituality. I was not a searcher. Spirituality just fell into my lap.

Many start the training and don't come back because they go into the world to look for different lessons. Some say that Subud is too hard. Others have this or that problem, they don't receive well enough, they are bored etc. Those are only pretexts, in fact they haven't been touched yet in any part of them because they didn't want to surrender, accept what is. And that is essential, as soon as you start the latihan.

The latihan is not just divine grace; it is a school that has no end. Some people barely start the school and they want to leave it. Too bad because there are many temptations out there, many schools of the nafsu (lower forces.)

I tell helpers in France to keep a relationship with those who leave Subud. Either write or phone every so often. Not to talk about Subud, but to chat in general. I often invite members who

have left to come and eat, watch a movie with us. I send them the
Subud paper. When I change address I let them know. Sometimes
their children get interested in Subud through this.

I sort out things. I try to clear the way for others. So here,
mine is the story of a pioneer, a 'weed eater.'

THE PROCESS CONTINUES TO WORK IN
ITS OWN UNIQUE WAY

Conversation with Rasunah

*"Ten percent of those coming to us will prove to be
steady membership."*

Bapak

I've known you and Lillia for some twenty years and remember
wondering what you were up to when you went off to do a latihan.
I was never very interested for myself however. Lillia, another
woman friend and I once rode to the city together. We were talking
about writing, creativity and things like that and Lillia thought to
herself (so she told me later), "These two women will never be
interested in Subud."

The way it happened for me is that first of all Sam, my
husband, got interested in the latihan through his closeness to
Lillia. This was way before I was interested myself. He described
this to someone, how he was doing the latihan by himself during
this time of intense friendship with Lillia.

Later when I began to sit outside the Greenwood church in
Elk where we still do latihan, as soon as I heard the latihan—
that very first time—I knew that it was for me. I had no doubts
that I was going to continue with this. I even felt that I was in
latihan out there, outside this church; it felt so close to me. It
reminded me of the times when we all went together to the Pomo
reservation for sacred dances. The whole Indian connection that
was so close to me came back. It felt like the latihan was very
connected, very much in the same spirit.

And there was never any doubt in your mind about it later?
Not at all. I never even wanted to ask questions. I noticed
that people being opened nowadays rarely do ask questions; they
just do it.

*It must be a new tendency because people like me who were
opened in the sixties and the seventies were full of questions. The
new generation of people coming into Subud doesn't seem to have
the need to understand with the mind as much; they just know
what it is from an inner place and that is sufficient.*

I think that young people at this time are much more evolved.
It's like Diane, (a newly opened member) who only now is starting
to have a few questions about testing. Before that she had never
talked to any helper about concerns or questions she had, not
even to you. It's like she knew already.

*Her case is similar to yours inasmuch as you and she were
around Subud for years before it dawned on you that it might be
something you wanted.*

There was so much mystery around it, and Subud people
were very discreet about it. You and Lillia would get ready to go
to the latihan hall and there were things that intrigued me. Like
you would say, "Let's grab a bite to eat before latihan." So I
thought to myself, "So, you have to eat a lot before going into
latihan. It must be very strenuous." But somehow you don't ask
about those things because you sense that it is a very unique
thing and it moves in its own way so that asking too much is
probably not the way to do it. It feels so private.

This was true until I got opened, but after a while I read
everything I could find. One thing I have come to understand is
how important the opening is to people. I felt my opening very
dramatically. I felt a load lifting off my shoulders and my eyes
started to flutter, yet I couldn't open them or close them. They
would just flutter and I saw this incredible golden light. It felt so
unique. I'll always remember that. I always had faith in that,
even though for a long time in latihan I didn't feel like I was
getting anything.

But I was patient. I would come faithfully twice a week and

many times would stand there for half an hour and feel that nothing was happening. But then, looking back, I see that so much was happening in my outer life! I believe now the process was working.

I saw signs of it working in your outer life immediately after you were opened.

Yes, in fact, I feel so apologetic to you and Lillia. I am so grateful because I feel I was probably difficult about certain things, going through purification and all that, but you were so patient with it and always made it possible for me to come back.

I see this with new members now, there are times when people don't come back because their process is so accelerated and they are afraid in some way.

And sometimes they feel embarrassed.

Yes. Because it's a beginning of consciousness and you are aware that those things are happening, yet you have no control. The process will spin out as far as it needs to and then it's gone. It's only after a lot of painful lessons that I realized that. Now I am not afraid. I feel that whatever comes, it will also go away.

Not only does it go away but also it takes away something that was an obstacle.

Absolutely.

Every time we have a jarring experience, every time we are a pain to others, it's because something is being worked on, some issue we have, some place where we are stuck. When we are fluid it works itself out, unless we resist. Resistance and trying to control can bring about a crisis.

Yes, you can stop the process, or slow it down. You can really stop the purification. That's why I feel the opening to be so important, because in a sense what I felt during the opening is that there was a lifting. And I have witnessed it during other people's opening also. Especially when I attend to an opening, I feel this incredible thing go up and then inside me and then out again. So when people tell us, "I don't think I was really opened," it's very important to work with them on that. Because everyone has doubts. Even though I said I felt it myself right away, doubts arose.

I probably came with my doubts to Lillia, because I remember that she reassured me. "I know you were opened," she said. "I felt the opening." And that is a really important thing to be able to say when the person is having doubts.

In what way would you suggest that one might work with people when they feel that way?

Do special latihan, do helper's latihan with them. There is an example of a member in Elk. I think what might happen is that new members, when they hear other people's latihan, start comparing. It should be explained clearly that every person has his or her own latihan and that it could never be like someone else's. The helper should help the person go through the doubts, which I feel you and Lillia did for me very well. I am trying to be constantly aware of that.

So how long was it before you became a helper?

Seven years.

Did you feel ready at that point; did you know it was time?

No, not at all. When Lillia brought that up I was saying, "No way." I was sure I was supposed to be a committee person. I was sure I was supposed to do this or that, but not be a helper. I was running away from it. And then when the helpers from Marin came to test and the testing showed that it would be okay for me to be a helper, I remember how one of them took my hand and said, "See, you don't have anything to do with it." And I felt relieved.

I feel a great loyalty to you and Lillia. My tendency is to step back because you have been helpers forever and I really respect the way you do things, also because I myself feel a little less confident in doing things, but that's changing.

Yes it has changed. You are taking your place as a group helper. Every helper has a different thing to bring, something that is valuable in its own special way. In fact, whenever a new person asks about Subud, we could test who has the most compatible personality in order to serve that person best, because when it doesn't work out, the new person doesn't come back.

As we know, it has happened in other groups. Also the longer I am opened the longer I feel the responsibility to make Subud part of my life, for my daily life to be Subud, because of the words we say in the opening and because of what Bapak explained, that we have the responsibility to carry this forward into the world and not keep it just for ourselves and our group of friends.

In our group some members are not comfortable doing the latihan in people's home as you know, and it's interesting that we cannot find a neutral place. Maybe it's not the right time.

Or else there is something else, an obstacle. Every time we tried to rent or buy a place, the group became divided.

It brings up control issues in everyone. But the church in Elk has always been there as a neutral place once a week, so those members could go there. There is something else obviously. I remember having to swallow my pride when I got into confrontations and misunderstandings with people, but I would swallow it and continue going to latihan.

Doing the latihan together is the only thing that can change that.

To change the subject. You were still writing poetry when you first got opened, what happened to that?

I wrote only for the first three years and after that it was gone completely. I remember telling Lillia about it and she told me the story about how a dancer who was opened in Subud totally stopped dancing after her opening. But much later she started dancing again from an inner place.

I started reading my poems during Subud events, and then my writing became different, so I thought, "Oh okay. A different content, a different way of writing." But slowly it went away.

Do you feel that it may come back?

Like I said, I am open to it, but I don't have any attachment and it's not going to come from my will.

What about your career as a social worker?

I feel like I really help people, I am good at it. Sometimes I feel that something wonderful happens when I am with someone totally at the end of his or her rope. I'll get very quiet. Though I am off work now, I feel that when I go back there has to be more of that. I can't just rush through my day and do the administrative stuff, because that's nothing.

I feel that I am close enough to my real work because a lot of it is being with people, talking to people. Whenever I have asked about my true work in testing it always seems to have to do with voice.

And your voice when you talk is very quiet, very calming.

A lot of people say that.

Do you see a big difference in your personality since you got opened in Subud?

Yes, it's like night and day. I was a very impatient person before Subud, very impulsive. My mind was always going round and round, like a typical Gemini. Now I am lucky to have anything in there at all.

Patience is definitely one of the things the latihan teaches.

Yes, and not to be afraid. Because I do think that it's pretty unusual what happens and we should not be afraid of the unusual, trust it instead.

I remember being amazed how the latihan affects your children. I even asked about it in testing. Of course my oldest son, Aaron, is in Subud, so he has his own path with it and he has come through a lot of changes, but I see it in Ethan and Eva, my other children, and they are not even interested, but they may be affected in ways of which they are not aware.

How about your husband, Sam?

Sam receives so much of his spirituality through the creative process. But even our relationship since Subud has totally changed. Night and day. I always loved Sam and admired him and everything, but it's so much better now. I just feel so much calmer in the relationship and so much more there. I used to be flighty and looking everywhere, for what . . . I don't know.

Maybe you were looking for drama, romantic drama, fantasy.

That's why I understand women who do that, because I used to do it myself, endlessly. A rich fantasy life.

I believe that the high, passionate, ecstatic fantasy women have about men, and men about women, is often a misplaced search for God.

I really think so.

Originally, the medieval romance tales were metaphors. The romance really represented the search for union with God, and the white lady with whom the knight had a platonic relationship was his soul, interceding between himself and his God. So in fact, what he was in love with was the feminine part of him, just as the longing of the lady for the inaccessible knight was a longing for her masculine part.

Yes, as a matter of fact, throughout all those fantasies, whenever the reality came a little too close, I would move back because that wasn't really what I wanted. Deep down, I knew that wasn't it. Once I found Subud and the latihan it never happened again.

You found a better way to God and it put things into perspective. And this power works on people around us as well, not only on our family, our children, but also on the people we encounter in our daily life.

Diane for instance. She was married to my nephew, never asked me much about Subud, but for years was aware of it in my life. I believe she was gaining some awareness just from being around people who were opened. Once she got opened, it was as though she had been in Subud forever and she already felt the latihan very strongly.

But tell me. How do you see Subud working in the future?

I really see it helping the world. When I read articles about the Congo and what's happening in Russia and different countries where Subud has just arrived, I see that it gives people hope at least. We were talking to some people last night and they were going on and on about the hopelessness of the world and I finally had to say, "You know, I really hope and believe that there is some kind of balance always working in the world. Think about all the good people who are doing things and working for the good of humanity. If we don't carry hope, if we are so afraid and talk only about the negative, the bad news, we are really doing an injustice."

We are doing worse than an injustice, we are holding this bad energy and making it manifest in the world. We are energizing the fear.

Yes and I can see how Subud works to bring harmony in us individually, then in our family, then in our group, then in the world. I feel that we have done terrific work as a group and I never want to leave it. Even Sam, who is not in Subud, feels that this is a really good community and if we were to leave it I am not sure we would ever find the same thing elsewhere. So I think a lot of work has been done in this way right here.

Do you think that Subud is good for everyone or do you believe that different people do best with different ways?

I think that some people don't need it at all. And some people do fine with their own path. I kind of judge it by looking at Sam. I feel that he probably will never get into Subud as much as I would like that to happen, but his method for being a person who is in the here and now works very well for him. To me that is being spiritual, to be alive in each moment of your life. And I see my children like Eva, who is a very big person that way, and Ethan also. I don't think that Subud is for everyone necessarily, although I hope that anyone who wants it will come in contact with it. But I think there are many other ways.

A lot of Subud people I have talked to feel that they have been called into Subud. So I guess that some people are called there, and some are called elsewhere. Some people tell me they have resisted it for ten to fifteen years before finally getting opened, even though during those years Subud would come back to them again and again through different encounters, different situations, the loaning of books, etc.

Yes, that's right. There are great stories about that. And just the unique way that it has moved here. I never in my life would have thought I would get into something like that. I was raised a Catholic and I was so turned off I couldn't imagine, in my twenties, being interested in spiritual or religious pursuits. And here, look at this incredible transformation.

In the beginning I didn't use words such as God or things like that, but now I feel free to describe it in many different ways including God, or life force, depending on whom I am talking to. It has a unique way of spreading in the world, and I feel like one of those people who have been called, because of the dreams mostly. Like the one just before I was opened, and then the one about my son Aaron who came and sat on the edge of my bed to tell me all about Subud just before he got opened, as if he knew everything about it. This was before I even knew that he was interested in Subud at all.

So because of those things you could call coincidences but are really warnings, previews of what's to come, I feel that I was called into Subud.

What's your understanding then about people who get opened and leave Subud soon after? Do you feel that a responsibility, on the part of the helper, hasn't been taken?

Yes, I did at first. I had that experience with someone in Fort Bragg. I felt tremendously sorry that maybe I talked about Subud too freely in those days. I have learned since that it may be better not to talk so much about it. I learned that very slowly, but I was so excited at first I wanted it for everyone. I felt that it was for everyone.

Now I understand that it isn't, and I totally understand why we are told not to proselytize. Some people have to go through a long process before Subud is right for them, and if they jump too quickly it gets confusing.

Probably this is why Bapak advised us not to talk much about it until people ask. Maybe you have to let it call you, and when you talk about it too much you push it on others before their time is ripe.

Yes, I learned that. But I also feel that once you get opened, the process can continue to work in its own unique way whether the person comes to latihan or not. As long as those people remain comfortable within and not worried about things, that's okay.

It has often happened, in my helper's life, that I open someone knowing intuitively that they will not stay in Subud. I open them because they ask; I talk to them about Subud but don't mention my foreboding because I don't want to discourage them. Later I don't feel right because I was not able to warn them about what I saw happening.

I feel that in the end it has nothing to do with us. Even if that's all that person gets, that's what God wants for that person for some reason. It may be about something that will happen in the next life.

We are told that we have a responsibility as a helper, but even though these responsibilities are clearly defined in a small manual, in the end you have to define your own, for yourself, all the time.

SPIRITUAL HISTORIANS

From Lillia

At home in a direct language from the heart of things, she has come through many battles, limpid behind the ancient sadness of the innocent eyes: these are my eyes. Here is the world seen through those eyes. Here is my heart at this moment in time, on this day.

When the impetus to write down Subud stories started up again, with Rasunah's new input, I happened to come early to Lydia's (now Riantee)'s house for latihan. Rasunah and Riantee were meeting about this project. Would I like to be included this time again? Yes, but can I write?

When I tested later about it I understood that I should be "in the pages" of the book. I could keep a notebook, take notes. I looked through my files and found early material, Lydia's introduction, the interviews she had finished and passed on to me four years before. The work had begun to take form through her efforts of writing it down, or wrestling with it on paper.

The picture, during latihan, of telling our story to the-great-story-teller-in-the-sky came back to me. It reminded me about an experience I had of feeling like I was always telling my story, complete with all the worries, the friends and relations, all of it moving along with me. It was especially vivid during Bapak's visit or during congresses. As the congress moved along through days and nights my story would evolve and become lighter. It changed in the way I cried, in movement, in mystery and surrender. I came home having told it all, ready to carry on, write it down, communicate it.

The questions I want to ask myself in order to tell the story are narrowed down to a few things. How did it come about—this spiritual life in Subud? From what place? What book did I read? Where was I? How was I seduced? It seems that I was seduced. The latihan started like an affair, a friend that I found, a confidante in this whole thing. It did start as an affair, but it's still going on . . . a very long affair. By now there are so many loved ones included, children, brothers and sisters, even grandchildren, whole generations involved in this long love story.

It is time to try to write all of it down. Visiting Melinda and Leonard Lassalle in Mont Ventoux in France, I sat upstairs in the room where I slept, did latihan, and read books which reminded me that everything for me started back in Aspen in 1966. I had just returned from France then, read some book and started my affair with Subud in a meadow. That was twenty-five years ago. It was a mysterious, calming moment, which brought me back, connected me with my travels, my loves, my family, and recognizing all those cycles made me think that I could write something down, I could describe some visions.

TO ME THE LATIHAN WAS EVERYTHING

Conversation with Lillia

We are born unencumbered, free of expectations and ambitions, regrets and embarrassment, free of fears and worries, each of us touched by God.

Going back to 1966. I was in Aspen making Irish coffees with Redmond Gleeson, then Marty. The bar was about ten feet long and it was crowded in there. Later I took off with Charles and Lydia Rand for Paris, and spent two and half months there. We all were friends way before we were opened in Subud.

I came back and landed in New York where a friend picked me up. I had to go up to Vermont to pick up my child Sarah who had been staying with my parents; then go back to Aspen where my husband was. I didn't want to. I kept going back down to the harbor to see if I could possibly catch a boat back to Europe. I was feeling so poetic. Definitely on a search for truth. I had started some Gurdjieff studies. *In Search of the Miraculous* and *Beelzebub's Tales to his Grandson,* along with Ouspensky's books were like my Bibles; I was also doing some writing on the subject.

Anyway, the thing that brought me back to Aspen was this little voice—either it was an inner voice or I really heard someone say that Penny Gleeson (now Mardiah) was doing something spiritual in "the meadow," something in which I would be very interested. This sparked me off. The voice was very clear and it was obvious that I should go back to that meadow. It was something that made sense to me.

When I went back I found that it was Subud that was waiting for me, in the form of Kitty Trevelyn, a helper from England visiting her daughter, Elisabeth. I was sure that I wanted to be in Subud. It was not the first I had heard of it. I had been told of people doing the latihan in some abandoned coke ovens up there in Elisabeth's meadow, maybe two years before that. I was not interested at all then, but all of a sudden it was one of the most important things to me. Everything else took second place, my family, my life, everything. I was in such a state. I was ready for anything.

I remember Kitty confronting me about that. I was saying that I could easily hitchhike around the world at that point, just put my thumb out and go whichever way the wind would have me go. But Kitty said no, you couldn't do that. She tested whether I could be opened and the answer was yes. She was living in a caravan up there in Steve and Elisabeth Greenfield's meadow, and we did latihan in those big coke ovens. Ondine, a helper from Denver and Margaret, an older member, also my friends Elisabeth and Mardiah (Penny) Gleeson were there. It was October 1967.

I remember that as such an intense transformative period in your life. To me it was like you had been opened in New York before coming back to Aspen.

It definitely felt like I had been opened that summer, on the island of Formentera. Actually that island gave me a different perspective. I was getting a new set of values about things. New words were being understood. I was beginning to write. Caring, taking care of things was becoming important. I was getting some real guidance about that. Everything I read was of utmost importance.

Then, getting back to the super-civilized world of New York City, driving on freeways, everything was such a contrast. A real culture shock. It was then that my Subud life started in a way. After about a month I was in a serious crisis. I felt so uprooted. I didn't know the word crisis, hadn't heard it before that, but I was in one.

After my marriage broke up with Doug, I went back to New York with my daughter Sara. I was still on a search for truth. I remember that I was carrying around *Beelzebub's Tales to his Grandson* when I met a Subud man named Walter on a New York bus. "What book are you reading?" he asked. When I told him he said, "You know, that book is taboo in Subud." I was never able to finish it after that, even though Gurdjieff said you should read things three times. I was prepared to read it three times, but I dropped it instead. This made quite an impression on me.

Later I heard from Sylvia (previously Elisabeth) that the Gurdjieff people in Coombe Springs were always walking with their heads together, always engaged in serious talks, whereas the Subud people were kind of light and airy and well . . . mindless. Yes, mindless, floating around. She made this physical description of two kinds of people, two kinds of ways. This still holds true and makes a lot of sense to me. You know, there is a possibility for mindlessness in Subud, rather than a constant study with the mind, which is my tendency. I still do that.

But in those years it happened so fast to me, the mindlessness and the formlessness. It threw me into a crisis. I was not ready for it to happen to me. Those kinds of things don't happen quite that way to me anymore, because it scared me so much that now I take great care in my search for truth. I really did plunge, a great plunge. I was aware of it being like a birth. The chief problem was that only a few people's voices could come through, because my own voices were so loud. You were there and I knew you were a friend and that you were rare. Subud people I also could listen to. But I saw most people, including my husband, run away from me in total terror.

Lots of friends from my social life, which was sort of a drug scene, fell away, either because they were afraid or because what was happening to me was too strange. What we were doing in Aspen in those days was skiing, working at night and beginning families. Most of the clarity came through Sylvia. She was telling me to surrender and those words melted me. I was struck by them.

I remember in latihan having very distinct visual things, like seeing building blocks being pulled out from the bottom so everything collapsed in order to be rebuilt. It was a picture of rebuilding my life on solid ground, because down at the bottom there were some blocks that were really incorrect and it was very important to replace them. I knew I had a long way to go. I also had the feeling of falling prey to the material forces, going way back. I knew I had to go way back there, but it was like being hurled through space.

I remember when you told me that you had to relearn everything. You said something like, "If only I could feed myself and my child in the right way, this would probably save me." You wanted to go back to the roots of things.

Without being aware of what was happening or having anyone tell me, the Subud process was taking place and the latihan was at work on my inner. This is always amazing to me. In the twenty years that followed reading about it and comparing it with my personal experiences, I realized what had happened to me. I kind of liked the idea that so little was known with my mind. This way it was like carving a path, and I hope that it's always that way for people rather than coming in having read all about Subud, having heard Subud people talk about it: finding their own way through it, the understanding coming with the experience of it. We had to be taken apart and put back together again within our ancestries. We had to start our life over and it was all so unexpected.

Fortunately at that time, in Colorado, we were able to live in the woods and to have a very slow and simple kind of existence. Everything was a discovery. Finding out about our own resources, hauling water, building fires, etc. It was like until then a lie had gone on as far as what life was really about. And now the truth of it was being revealed.

I remember being so relieved when I came out of the crisis to find that there was another word for it: deliverance. That time of deliverance was intense. I kept going back to that experience in terms of the balance between male and female within me.

I also remember that you described some rather horrendous, wild, outrageous, psychic and wise experiences. I believed at the time that you were on your way to self-realization.

When I was taking the plane back from New York, I remember being lifted right out of myself. Some master surgeons, some physicians, and care-giving people were talking about me saying, "She needs help." They were looking after me. I think they were from the realm of the angels.

I was going through magazines on that plane, looking at pictures of people and seeing the source of the photographs. I saw the origin of things; saw the death of people and how they would come to their end. All this was happening fast, so fast.

It takes years to sort it out. But now I have received those kinds of experiences from the latihan. Having caught up with all of that I know that it was an experience of the after-life or the

Great Life. The thing is, I was frightened by it, and so I wanted to run. My own fears, and I still have some, stood in the way. I was being seen from above.

During that time I looked at you as an enlightened being and wished I would have those strong experiences myself. I couldn't understand the fear. I thought to myself, "I would love to be going through that." I trusted that your experiences came from a higher source and couldn't see a reason to fear.

But I felt like I was out in space, in orbit. I was looked at from above, watched. When you get the idea that you are always watched over, it's a little unnerving because all your walls and boundaries disappear. You thought that your thoughts were hidden and secure, and suddenly everything is in the open.

I believe that they are actually forces that want you to do all right, forces that are watching over you in a caring way. I was convinced that I had a friend in the latihan who wanted things to turn out well, who was working for the good of humankind. I had been so rebellious before. I challenged everything, challenged the idea that things could be working in that way. I didn't especially believe in God. I did as a child, in a childlike way. I believed that God and Jesus were good sorts, but never had the faith that something really big was at work.

When I was first opened I had the feeling that a lot of the garbage was thrown off almost by the shovel full. I was thrown over backwards and sort of hanging there, being unloaded, and unloading a lot.

What about the people around you, your Subud group?

Most of us were in our twenties. We had a great communication and much in common. We visited and shared a lot. Actually our life was ideal. We had lots of free time. We had little children so we organized playgroups. We walked in the forest, endlessly philosophizing and analyzing. We were students of nature, of life, constantly making discoveries about the world and ourselves and sharing them with excitement. Life was full of joy, I mean, each day we were looking forward to what we would learn.

I remember you and I walking and talking. I will always have this funny picture of something that kept happening to us. We would talk on and on and end up sitting under a tree or somewhere to contemplate while continuing to talk, solving all the problems and dilemmas of the world situation. When we felt it was time to go, we'd get up and more often than not would find that either we had been sitting in some sort of pine resin that stuck all over our clothes, or in a pile of animal shit or some kind of yuk. We would laugh and exclaim, "There we are again! Isn't this telling us something? We have been sitting in shit all this time . . . philosophical shit." But we loved it. There was a thread of wanting to find out everything about life and to stay alive in it. And this is still the thing with us. And Subud came right in there and filled the space we were making.

I don't know if you remember the following incident. It was before either of us had heard about Subud. Charles, my husband and I left for France for the summer. We all had been searching. Before we left, you and I promised each other that if one of us "found it" she would have to inform the other immediately. When we met again you had a Cheshire cat smile on your face and said, "I found it." So I answered, "Okay, I'm ready. I have to find out about it."

Yes, we had a lot of trust in each other. It was underlying our relationship. You didn't question what I found. You said, "If you say so, that's it." And you went and got opened.

Actually there were no helpers in Aspen and I had to wait for Ondine to come and open me. I wanted to get opened right away. On a visit to San Francisco I had gone to see Martha (now Mardiah) Tarantino who was a helper in that city, to talk about being opened. Things were not moving fast enough for me in Aspen. Martha told me that I couldn't skip the three months probation. So I went back to Aspen and waited.

Mardiah (then Penny) Gleeson was the first of our group of friends to get opened. Charles, my husband, and Redmond, (then Martin) Mardiah's husband, were great friends. They watched the whole thing, but stayed on the fence. They wanted to give it time and see if it was for real or if we were just fooling around. They were not going to get caught up in this spiritual stuff before they found out more about it. They did some serious watching before they decided to get opened. It took Redmond quite a few months, if I remember right, and Charles a few years. That was the most unusual thing about our group. All the women were opened first. The husbands who were more skeptical went in with much more caution, when they went in at all.

I remember though that Charles would always watch out for you. He made sure you got to latihan on time. He would often drop you there because you were not driving in those days. It was like his duty.

At this point my life fell apart, and my marriage took an abrupt turn. I remember that Steve Greenfield, who had been in Subud way before we all did, came to our door one day and Doug, my husband, fled as if he had seen a ghost. "This is just getting to be too much," he said. His life was blown apart from the moment I came back from New York, after Europe, and got opened in this weird thing called Subud. I was like a maniac to him, seeing things from the invisible realm. He made himself very clear: he didn't like what was happening with this movement. To this day he still feels this way, unless he has changed since we last talked.

Maybe it always is that way with Subud. Some people are repelled and some people are drawn to it right away. But to answer a question you had earlier I hardly remember anything about the relationship between members, about people from outside, etc. My personal life was taking all my attention. From my perspective I began to get more people interested in the movement, people like Roy who became my second husband. I felt that Roy was a perfect candidate for it.

I remember that most of us would talk quite a lot about Subud to everybody in those days, and we pulled in a lot of people. We wanted the whole world to do the latihan. We were quite enthusiastic.

It was not like that for me in my life. The latihan worked more through my marriages. I was still not very together in my outer life. The only consistent thing was doing the latihan. I brought my partners into Subud, first Roy and then Efron.

How was the latihan for you during those years? How is it now?

To me it was everything, the main focus in my life. If I look back I could say that I am the same person that I was then, but that I have grown. I love more deeply. I feel more deeply. Three of my children are opened, so the experience has grown that way also. I am still in touch with friends who are not in Subud. My friends are the same, only the experiences are deeper with them through the latihan. It has definitely been the focus of my life.

Tell us more about your life in Aspen.

I lived *in* the woods and all I cared about was the latihan.

You lived a beautiful simple life as I remember, washing the clothes in the stream, drying your baby's diapers on the grass in the meadow, living in a tent, then in a school bus.

Yes, I remember that laundry was very important, my main thing. I was washing and washing. I am still washing, because I am a laundry lady these days. It's a symbol of purification. I walked around with my kids on my back. I drove broken-down cars. I lived way out in the mountains, rarely going to town, hunting for wild mushrooms, living off the land somewhat. I started a whole new diet too, partly because of being poor, partly because my husband, Roy, had a Health Food store.

After I got opened, food took on a new significance. I started making bread and going to town to sell it or trade it for groceries at the Health Food store. That's how I met Roy in fact. So I would make bread, and take it down to get supplies for the family. I moved out of Aspen and to Ashcroft, into a two-hundred-year-old cabin. In many ways everything was changing. I had dropped my social life. I became more isolated, didn't keep the same pace as others, didn't see the same people.

I remember. It was indeed a different pace because before that you were quite outgoing, sports oriented, very athletic.

I kept skiing but in a different way. I did cross-country skiing. One thing I had lost was any financial know-how after my first marriage fell apart, and also any competitiveness. Nevertheless skiing was part of my life. I had to ski to get to where I lived in the winter out of necessity. It was either skiing the path or hiking the path. Just like in Scandinavia, trucking laundry, carrying supplies on our backs, etc.

Did you read the Pewartas or any Subud literature in those days? Did you have much contact with bigger groups?

For years the only thing I read was *Concerning Subud* by John Bennett. Then after a while I started reading Pewartas. But mostly things were happening inwardly. We would go and do a latihan with the big group in Denver whenever we could.

Then Prio came to Aspen. By that time we had quite a large group. It was a pretty grass root kind of group though. We were people who loved the mountains and had come there to get away from something or other. We were pretty intellectual, searchers, students of philosophies, religious experiences and spirituality. We discussed everything in the domain of ideas. Then I started to live in isolated places and hardly joined the discussions anymore.

For the last twenty-seven years Lillia has lived in Northern California, in Elk, Little River and Mendocino. She is no longer a laundress but has developed her skills as a potter and painter on pottery. She also does healing, working with polarity. She has many grandchildren.

*   *   *

A decade later, in 2005, I asked Rasunah and Lillia to talk about what was happening now for them.

Rasunah, quite a number of years have gone by since our last interview. How have things changed for you? I know that you have become more and more active in the organization, became Regional helper for two terms . . .

I completed the first term and dropped out of the second for family reasons. I received a lot of purification during that time for myself, so in that way it was very good, but it was a hard job and continues to be so for a lot of people who are doing that work. There is a big controversy right now about Subud helpers who make mistakes, but I believe everybody makes mistakes. I make mistakes all the time. It's hard to do what members would like you to do, while staying within your own receiving and seeing that some of those problems are group problems that could be solved by the group. I was able to stay with my own receiving which is to be quiet, not that I was not participating, but it was the right way for me to be in a place of quiet. I felt good about all the members, very loving and I always received a lot from them.

When you say that group problems should be resolved within the group, do you think the group would have a better chance with the help of a mediator?

Yes, most of the problems are outer things that can be discussed. We have had that in our group, and we had the whole group decide rather than just the helpers. Of course testing is very important and valid for personal testing on the subject.

Another thing that has happened to me is that I am more able to be in that space of receiving all the time, so that questions are coming up and they get answered in a more natural way.

At one point testing is no longer necessary except for spiritual matters because all your decisions are made from that place.

Yes. I am more comfortable with less testing. When I was doing that helper work I thought I would do better as a committee person. Now I am doing a little bit of committee work and it feels good.

So would you say that the latihan and testing are more integrated into your life?

Yes much more and I am so grateful for that. Sometimes what I receive seems so unexpected that I say, "What is this?" but I know I am getting whatever I am suppose to get and it's going to be different from whatever anyone else get. It's a good understanding for me to have. The other thing that has really changed is that I used to feel that more involvement with the organization would be good for us as a group, but actually I have come to feel that we all bring to the organizations our particular gifts and I trust that.

So you are more accepting of differences?
I would say yes.
*Lillia has arrived and has been listening. I ask her what she
thinks about all that.*
Lillia—I can relate to everything Rasunah said. I am kind of
neutral myself. What's going on that level doesn't grab me as
much. I feel more interested in the international Subud work; I'd
like to be involved with Susila Dharma, that's what grabs me
more. As for our group, I don't feel that we are separate because
of our location, although we are influenced by our location.

Rasunah—That's a very good word separate. It's something
that came up for me too. I don't feel anymore that any problem is
separate or the problem of an individual. It feels more like we
are all in it together. So if we have a member, say, is touching
other members in latihan, I would rather get together and talk
about it. We are all part of a process, and it's not just one person
who is making a mistake, we are all trying hard and making
mistakes at the same time.

*In a way the individual is a reflection of the group, which is
a reflection of the national, the national of the international,
and Subud a reflection of the world. What's happening to an
individual might be troublesome but look but at what's happening
in the world.*

Rasunah—If we all could see problems as 'our problem
together' things would be easier. We are not single in what we do.

Lillia—Beside, growth comes from mistakes. How else do we
get it? If I wake up and get a little pain here, a little pinch there,
I say, "Oh no. That doesn't feel good." But then it transforms
because when you pay attention to things, that's how they change,
and it's part of the growth.

*Especially if we can look at those mistakes and use them as
tools, stepping-stones to our higher self. A mistake or fault is nearly
always a stepping-stone.*

Lillia—I don't even know if we can grow that much without
them. We don't learn from a smooth path, we stumble, we stub

our toe. Then we go back and say "I have to do that again this time and do it differently."

Rasunah—It's like planting a seed. Now when I make a mistake I know it immediately. Much more than before. A couple of time recently I have made mistakes with people and it hits me so hard. Maybe it's being more conscious. Earlier we could get away with mistakes.

And we were successful at hiding them from ourselves. We no longer get away with that. Now Lillia would you also say that the latihan is more integrated into your life, that you don't have to step aside to test, but get your answers as you go along?

Lillia—I would say so although testing is always a surprise. Never what I thought it would be.

Rasunah—Yes, it seems like there are more surprises in latihan as I go along. During latihan I felt this definite touch on my hip and it stopped my latihan. The problem of people touching people in latihan came up for me then, so even though there was not a person involved I felt, "Oh that's how it is for people when someone touch them. It was like I was given a little insight and later I had to speak to that issue.

Lillia—You experienced it with the distance of the latihan. There are always surprises in latihan. To me that is a mark of the latihan, the unexpected or the surprise. I trust it because it is not what the mind expected.

You asked what changed for me. Whenever I make a statement about something it changes immediately so that's one thing I have learned: not to be too sure and not to make definite statements. The things that are growing and changing are family, and feeling less impassioned about stuff, in a more neutral way that I have ever been. I am more hesitant to speak. Maybe I know more but I say less.

Maybe it's a sign of getting older.

Rasunah—The mechanism that has me do or say something has changed. I could think to say something and then feel, "You know I don't really need to."

Lillia—Not that things are less important but there is bigger neutrality,

Sometimes we may see that speaking it is not necessarily the way to straighten things. Sometimes it's better to say nothing and let the process work on the inner level.

Rasunah—A great big change for me is that at the beginning I used to interpret every little thing. What somebody said or did, the significance of things etc. That need to interpret or judge fell away.

Getting older reduces the stirring up of emotions, so does the latihan.

Rasunah—I attribute almost everything to the latihan. For me there is nothing that works that well, but of course I haven't experienced many other practices.

Lillia—For me it's easier to see how it works for you and changes you, than to see it for myself. I can think, "Oh it's wonderful what has been happening to Rasunah."

Rasunah—This is interesting Lillia. Because for me you were an example and it came all the way around. Let me show you how it worked. Year ago you taught me something about generosity with children. We were on a camping trip and you showed me something about sharing, about how we were all in it together and it was essential not to think of yourself and your family only. And then recently I was doing something for everyone in our group, including everyone and this newer member told me, "You taught me how to be generous. You showed me how not to exclude that one person. So it came full circle. You taught me, and I gave the newer member what you gave me.

It was a small experience but it always stood out.

Probably because it was something important for you to learn at that time. So the gifts get passed around.

Rasunah, then Lillia. Thank God for sisters.

2

SUBUD AND THE LATIHAN

*"We should not say the latihan kejiwaan of Subud.
It makes it sound as if it is only in Subud that you can
receive God's grace, the guidance of God, or the revelation
of God. Which is not the case. The fact is that anyone who
surrenders to God with patience, acceptance and sincerity
can receive the latihan kejiwaan. It is not the copyright of
Subud. Nobody can lay claim to God."*

Bapak

Through the latihan people renew their contact with the Power
of God. The Subud membership is aware that it is a direct spiritual
experience reawakening the inner life of those who practice it.
The information below is given to explain Subud for those who
are inquiring.

The central feature of Subud is the latihan kejiwaan, or
spiritual exercise, held for half an hour up to an hour, two or
three times a week. Men and women practice in separate rooms.
Subud has little doctrinal teaching except for the belief in divine
power and higher centers of consciousness. The implication is
that people practicing the latihan align themselves with those
higher centers. It is available to any person of seventeen and
older who has a sincere wish to worship God and wants to receive
this contact.

Members who do this latihan allow what they believe to be the Power of God, to direct them. The latihan prompts one to make movements and sounds that arise spontaneously from within. These often take the form of singing, chanting, shouting, moving, dancing, crying, laughing, etc. Participants may experience powerful feelings of rapture, joy and release, or various forms of psychological and physical healing. During latihan, one lets go of one's thoughts and emotions in order to follow what surfaces. It is a form of cleansing that allows individuals to develop and trust their inner guidance; gradually, they are released from the past and able to let go of emotional resistance to what is.

Muhammad Subuh Sumohadiwidjojo, referred to as Bapak, or father, a name that indicates love and respect, received Subud in central Java during 1924. As the story goes Bapak—who had been a student of Sufism, was coming back from a walk one night when he suddenly saw an unusually bright light in the sky. The light descended upon him and filled his whole body, causing it to vibrate. Thinking he was dying he rushed home and lay down, waiting for whatever would happen next. Then the light went away and he felt compelled to get up and do his Muslim prayers as he was in the habit of doing before going to sleep, only this time he was filled by a such a powerful force that he couldn't do anything but follow the movements that it indicated. He felt totally calm, conscious and surrendered to this power.

For many years after that he received this spontaneous impulse—which later became known as the latihan—and every night he was made to get up and pray. As this inner action deepened it brought many profound experiences. Eventually it became clear to Bapak that he was receiving a gift from God, also that this deep and complete metamorphosis within his being was accessible to everyone and that he had the duty of making it available to all who asked for it with sincerity. He was not, however, to try to spread it by his own will.

In 1933 it was revealed to him that what he had received should be formalized as the Subud movement. Through his inner receiving he was told that people from all over the world would come to him.

His wisdom became much valued by all who came in contact with him and people from other parts of Indonesia began to seek him out. Eventually Bapak received that this gift was meant for the whole of humankind. In the past, individuals wanting to study the mysteries had to search a long time before finding some special teacher of unusual quality and power, but no one's presence was necessary for the action of the latihan to take place. Humans no longer needed prophets, priests or other spiritual leaders to serve as intermediaries between themselves and God; it seemed that now was the time for a direct contact with the divine.

Restricted to Indonesia until the 1950s, the movement then spread to Europe and America, at first principally among followers of the Russian-born mystical philosopher Georgy Ivanovitch Gurdjieff, who had now died. These people brought Bapak to England in 1956 and 1957. After that Subud quickly spread throughout the world to more than seventy-five countries.

The latihan as we now know it is a spiritual exercise that is universal and accessible to all, even those who don't have a belief in God. It is not a teaching, nor a technique, nor a religion but is in harmony with all the different religions of the world. It helps individuals to regain the original awareness and more subtle feelings that are gradually lost when a child is enticed more and more by the outer world, away from its true nature.

Bapak explained that at this time, the outer world is mainly a creation of the thinking mind backed up by the sensory perceptions. Because the mind and the senses are instruments of the material world and generally not infused with spirit, this condition has brought most humans into contact with the material world in a way that now threatens to overpower them. This has created an imbalance so that in the spiritual realm, many people are still like infants.

The words of what is now known as the 'opening' ceremony, during which new members stand quietly with their eyes closed in the presence of those who bear witness to their desire to worship

God, are like triggers for codes stored inside the body. What has been learned from imitation, association, comparison is replaced by a consciousness of the present moment that creates a clear space of infinite possibilities.

I have, myself, become more aware of how it feels to be alive in the spirit, more present, attentive and receptive. In the latihan, we receive according to our nature and evolve in harmony with our own inner being. What might be right for one individual might be wrong for the other, so following our own nature rather than acting from a desire to be loved and accepted is essential.

The latihan appears to seek out those who are open to it and will benefit from it. Many people believe that they were called into Subud, that Subud had found them in the most uncanny, synchronistic way. Some describe suddenly having a heightened sensitivity to beauty, to certain places and to other people involved with Subud. Things leap at them with a vividness of color and sharpness of shape they hadn't experienced before. Everything seems magnified and they become aware of coincidences and synchronicity in their lives. It is as though some spiritual force were operating in everything they do.

Subud is an abbreviation of the Sanskrit words Susila Budhi Dharma. These words together mean the life of humans, rightly lived, with the whole of all their spiritual powers, in conformance to the Will of God.

Bapak has defined Susila, Budhi and Dharma for us:

Susila literally means right living or right action. It defines the qualities necessary for the true character of a person to become apparent, for the conduct and actions that are truly human to arise. Often, these qualities are not noticeable in a person's early life, but at some point or another an action begins that transforms the person.

Susila also includes the concept that we should be of service to our fellow creatures here on earth, and this means not only our fellow human beings but also everything else that lives, even inanimate objects. We are here to fulfill a great responsibility and not just to use everything on the earth for our own benefit, taking for granted that we exist only for our own advantage.

Budhi means the inner nature or spiritual powers of man. In humans, like in all other creatures, there dwells an inner force drawing them towards their proper path, the path that leads to God. Budhi refers to the powers that are latent in humankind but are not usually developed, powers that are deeper than the working of the senses, emotions and thinking.

Dharma means God's law or the Will of God: sincerity, trust and surrender awakened in humans by the Will of God. It is not just a commandment given long ago that's no longer valid. It can be made alive right now. There is a way in which everything we do can be the fulfillment of God's Will for us. In Subud we submit ourselves to be trained by the wisest and most constant power in the world—the Universal Spirit. We surrender to this training, trusting that God knows what is possible, not only from our body, our mind and heart, but also from our latent powers, so that we can do our very best whilst on this earth.

Ibu Rahayu, Bapak's daughter, tells us that when we are first 'opened' in Subud, a contact is made between God's power and the essence of God that is within us. But there are other things within us besides God's essence, forces that give form to our being, allowing us to live as creatures of this earth. As we take care of our basic needs we are shown that on the earth everything is dependent on everything else for survival.

This interconnectedness also involves eating and being eaten. Our relationship with food is a fundamental one. For instance, if we eat just to satisfy our desires, wastefully or in a rush, we desecrate the vegetable or animal forces within our food. It is not the eating of animals that is against the duty of humans towards their fellow creatures, but the fact that the humans eat the meat in an unsacred way. Whether animal or vegetable, some of that life is destroyed when we eat it, and in this way we are shown that we depend on other lives for our own life on earth. Acknowledging this fact, we can eat food so as to be able to fulfill our earthly duty, stating our gratefulness. Food energies blend with our own, finding the place where they already exist within and the food is ennobled by our eating it. I once heard Bapak say that humans were the food of angels.

Ibu Rahayu, and also Bapak, talks about forces that are like so many other souls within us, growing alongside our human soul as it grows. They have great power and we don't suddenly become free from their pressure, so what we receive is not always straight from God. However, as they develop in order to reach their higher place, these forces become harmonious with each other and with us. This—depending on our state—may however be a lengthy process.

Ibu Rahayu describes three stages in the latihan, each of which—depending on our state—may take a long time to complete. The first is an awakening: parts of our bodies, then parts of our soul, awaken until every part is brought to life.

The second stage is a preparation during which every part of our being is made ready to receive God's grace. During this stage we come to recognize the different forces that reside within us so that we may use them instead of them using us.

The third stage is when the roles become reversed. We are able to put the forces that were in charge of us in their right place. They rise to a higher level and start working for us and with us, no longer hindering our way to God. Then we are ready to receive the true gifts.

In this stage there is understanding and awareness that take the form of wisdom in the thinking. When we die we will find that we are not indebted to these lower forces; because of this wisdom, we will be able to return them to their true realm.

People I talked to often have reported the feeling of finally moving onward in life after being opened, guided by mysterious circumstances and waking up to who they really are. The latihan helps give inner content to the outer events of their lives, but at times, people may become disappointed because, after doing the latihan for a long time, they hardly feel any improvement in their being. During the exercise they feel surrendered and at peace, but in taking care of the needs of their lives they are swept away, and it's impossible to distinguish which is from their higher self and which is from their lower emotions. However, once we are in touch with the inner dimension it remains available to us at any time. We don't need to search for it outside ourselves; it accompanies us in everything we do if we pay attention.

Bapak described how people, during most of their lives, are preoccupied with controlling their situation in the world to maintain their security and welfare. Their inner is easily influenced and affected by conditions of life that change faster and faster from generation to generation, especially since the intellectual powers of humankind have developed and made amazing progress in the field of science. Consequently, humans have become dominated by their over-active minds, so that their desires, thoughts and emotions are constantly at work. The opportunity for the inner feeling to be quiet scarcely exists at all.

Abandoning the way of thoughts and desires to attain spiritual consciousness allows us to come into contact with the Great Life Force, and a vibration is experienced within. Following this, we may reach a state in which we can no longer use our will to achieve what we want because our passions have left us. All we can do is surrender—that is, letting go of emotional resistance so a space is created for grace and love to enter. We accept not just the good, but also the higher good, which includes the bad.

When the inner feeling is filled with the Life Force, without the interference of the thinking mind and the emotions, we are able to wake up to what's really going on in our souls. The inner vibration begins to set us free from our emotional habits, fixations and prejudices. Surrender does not transform what's out there, it transforms us so that our whole world is transformed.

The way I understand it is that we are not a blank slate upon which something new can be written. A great deal was already written on the slate at the moment of conception, then more and more came to be scribbled on our new being, before and after birth. We carry in us, particularly in our physical bodies, traces of our past lives and, through heredity, the past lives of our parents and ancestors as well. We also have deep-seated habits shared by our culture, although usually we are not conscious of this. The practice of the latihan frees us from the past so that the slate can become blank.

During my years in Subud, I've learned that nothing is known for certain. What I know now may change in the next moment. No matter what story Bapak told us at one time, another year, another crowd and the story would be different. Truth is relative. The fact that the story we hear evolves as we do also comes into the equation.

A Subud scholar who researched the matter and discovered that those Sanskrit words didn't mean exactly what Bapak said they did, contested even the meaning of the words, Susila Budhi and Dharma. According to the story, the scholar was lovingly challenged by a woman helper of many years who argued that she had had a receiving about God's language being so vast and expansive that there was no equivalent in any language. Bapak's rendition was "good enough" however.

Over the years I have witnessed members, especially among younger generations, being put off by one rendition or another. I myself was only able to understand and appreciate the full wisdom of his words much later, often in the light that another translator of God's words shone for me. It was not necessarily someone in Subud, but under that new light I would have a flash of understanding, "So, that's what Bapak was talking about!"

Slowly I came to experience the reality of Bapak's explanations—that it is not through great efforts and work that I receive the latihan. It is effortless, playful even. All I have to do is come from a place of trust—like a child traveling from one fully experienced moment to the next. If I stop questioning the how and why of everything, if I trust my process and accept what is as a stepping-stone, obstacles can become tools.

The more I love and appreciate others the more energy flows into me. Loving is a state of being, a way to relate to a world which is forgiving, nurturing and supportive. It has the capacity to lift others. However I have to love and forgive myself before I can love anyone else; when I begin to see the sacredness in myself and others, I understand that life must be honored in all forms because everything on this earth is interconnected and interdependent.

Listening to the stories of those around me is important and as people tell them, I can give them energy, listening with my inner, appreciating their wholeness and the jewel within. As I allow the flow of energy to happen, they acquire more presence, a greater sense of clarity in their telling, greater insight into their truth. Often, as they tell that truth and examine it with sincerity, they begin noticing the emergence of patterns that are uniquely theirs. It's as though the latihan were a key to unlock stored knowledge, a way for information to flood into our being.

In very subtle ways the latihan changes my perception, and I start drawing to myself everything I need to learn. Every person I meet, book I read or journey I take, patiently makes up a whole.

Once we are on our path, there is no longer any chance meeting.

LEARNING TO SAY NO

Lillia

In latihan, I was once a crumbling wall because way down at the bottom some of the foundations had been removed. I would have to go back to that bottom and rebuild.

Visually, this image is still strong today; it is inside my story. In latihan I was once a Japanese woman serving tea, strictly formal on the outside while crying continually inside.

Long ago I had a vision while riding on an airplane. I was a seer flying beyond the boundaries of body, landmass, or time and space. I saw an earth-formed swastika coming out of the ground.

Another time while on a plane crossing the United States, I was the patient of angel-doctors working to heal me. They called me "She" and referred to me as "Her." They filled me with information.

When we started on this project, we gave each other the assignment of dreaming the title of our book. That very week I dreamt the phrase, "You Have to Learn to Say No." Riantee said that it would work for my section of the book.

My title came from a conversation I had in dreaming with my teacher-seer. He told me I had to learn to say no in order to be able to see in a psychic way. This meant that it was not sufficient for me to receive the yes side of a vision, but that all of it had to be revealed, including that to which we had to say no.

In the dream I seemed to be looking at the earth from above and it was rising up like a wall in the form of a swastika. I closed my eyes, but my guide made me open them. The latihan opens the eyes of our jiwa. As the seer I could say no to some visions; only the eye of our jiwa can see it all.

Today, I witness putting off writing as the day calls me outside. Deal with the kitty's vomit first. Then help Sara, my daughter, and Habibie, her son, clean the rabbit cage. I hold Habibie horizontally on my shoulder and brace his bottom on my hand so he looks skyward. We make up a song: "Look up to the sky, Mother why? We look to the sky, wonder why, Habibie and I."

I am thinking that the latihan is working all the time, working in these everyday morning rituals. The same is true when I sit down to write about a spiritual experience, which happened during group latihan in Elk. It was in 1983 or so. We were doing latihan in the parsonage of the Methodist church. I was clinging to the body of Christ on the cross; the wounded body was in my arms. I said, "Let me share the pain." He answered, "There is none. Give me yours." I said, "If I give away my pain, my passions, my life, my suffering then I won't have anything left. I won't be able to walk the earth." He answered, "Try it. Just give me your suffering."

So I began to give things up one by one, passion by passion. They were like children, I cried for the loss of each one. When it seemed like they were all gone, another one would come from another corner of my body, until they had all passed on and I was limp, washed of everything.

I asked: "What can I do? How can I thank you?" He answered: "Just don't forget me." The experience stayed with me. I could go back to it anytime. I could forget or not forget; it was up to me. When it was over I slipped down the body, down his hip, down his knees, down his bleeding feet, down the timber that had been cut for this purpose. My body, now very light, began to experience itself filling up, and the woman I was became a laundress carrying a basket which filled steadily and emptied as I walked.

The latihan is always making a story and it remains mysterious in the way it comes. Bapak said that the latihan is not just for this lifetime but also for the hereafter. It is boundless, a gift for traveling beyond my body, to the places where people are that I intend to help. After the World Congress in Australia and many crying latihans, I felt totally unencumbered by worry for the first time, an experience of total trust and freedom.

POETRY AND DREAMS

Rasunah

On June 2, 1985, after a series of dreams, I was opened in Subud and quite dramatically I stopped writing. Poetry had been a huge part of my life and I was perplexed, questioning in agony, lost and without direction. Looking back at it I would say that I was in crisis. I was undergoing many subtle but deep changes in my relationships, in my place of work. A sort of quaking, an upheaval was taking place. My dreams about writing were part of the life re-direction that was beginning to take place.

I remember telling Lillia about these dreams, searching for the meaning of each symbol as though it might help me resolve the puzzle of my writer's block. I took solace in Lillia's story about a ballet dancer who stopped dancing after she was opened in Subud, and then started again from a different place.

Soon after, these early dreams were replaced by dreams that I have come to understand as dreams of surrender. There was always a great body of water, waves threatening to engulf me, an attempt to flee and then, as I gave up, an acceptance. My hands would fly above my head. I would let myself go into the gigantic wave, falling back through eons of time, surrendering to God. I was always surprised to come out on the other side, alive, awakened, and deeply grateful.

Over time I forgot about writing, I felt peaceful, without ego, happy. The latihan was becoming my subtle teacher, endlessly difficult, always intriguing. Slowly, writing has returned to my life, but the credo that describes it has expanded from Henry Miller to the Koran which foretells, "You will be called upon to account for all the permitted pleasures in life you did not enjoy while on earth," or to the Inuit people saying, "It is holy poetry, holy singing we are after," or even to my own notes, "It is in the not knowing that we exist most purely."

Poetry has now become only a part of the flow, neither less nor more important than the cycle of seasons. The poetry that comes to me now is designed to lift the veil of illusion, it emanates from instinct, from the wild unconscious. It rises to consciousness, trying to make sense and give purpose to life. At its best, it joins with the life force, telling me what comes next, preparing me for changes. It does this by remembering the past, seeing the beloved reality.

I AM THE KIND OF PERSON WHO HAS ALWAYS BEEN DRAWN TO THE SPIRITUAL

Carolye (Canada) interviewed in Mendocino

"Purification is a stripping away of all kinds of things that have been buried in the inner feeling for a long time. People who experience a period of purification usually feel as if they are able to find a new understanding, whereas this is something that has been buried for a long time within them."

Bapak

I am the kind of person who has always been very drawn to the spiritual. I dragged my mother to church when I was five years old. When I was ten or eleven I had myself baptized, went through catechism, etc. I really wanted to be involved in something spiritual but it didn't take me long to realize that the Catholic Church was not offering what I wanted. When I was growing up there were not many options. So after a while I checked out born-again Christians but that didn't go over great. I dabbled in a couple of other things and came to the point that many people arrive at: What now?

I was left with this longing that wouldn't settle. By that time I was about fifteen and had been very good friends with a Subud family. Delia was my best friend. Her mother had told me a little bit about Subud, and the more I found out about it, the more it became a political decision for me to join. I was a teenager and upset about some of the religious things going on in the world, feeling political about it. Besides, the fact that there was no one in charge, no hierarchy, no rule, no establishment interested me on the spiritual level also. I felt deeply compelled to be opened by the time that I was sixteen nearing seventeen. I felt that it was right for me and there was no stopping me. It's in my nature to be like that. When I get my mind set on something there is no talking me out of it.

So I knew I wanted to be opened but the helpers really made me go through the whole rigmarole. They lengthened my probation period, so instead of lasting three months it became six or seven months. They wanted to make sure that I was really into it and that it was not just a passing phase. But I knew so strongly that if they had made me wait three years, I would have done it.

Finally I was opened and it was exactly what I wanted. I never left Subud, I never stopped doing the latihan, I never had any doubts and it has been almost twelve years. It was like a magnet drawing me. It was like nothing I experienced before. The first time I did latihan it was like developing different senses, being able to smell for the first time, to hear, etc. People who are in their thirties and have more life experience probably already have a sense of what's that's all about, but for me at seventeen it was brand new, like nothing I ever felt. My opening was not full of movements and sounds but it was a clear opening in my life.

I felt a lot of really deep changes right away. I had actually been suicidal for years prior to being opened. Many times I came to the brink. But everything came to a turning point. I was in my last year of high school. School and I didn't get along very well. I knew that once I graduated I could finally leave my family home—which had been a prison for me. So there was a light at the end of the tunnel and I never went back to the same depression and hopelessness. My family life, accumulated for years, had made me feel totally worthless as a person, and the latihan, in a slow way, gave me back a sense of who I really was.

What changed was that I went to stay with a Subud family. It was not very easy the first couple of years after I got opened. But then wonderful things happened, I met my husband, my life changed completely. I would never go back to childhood again, never, not for an hour; but some things were hard. I felt that there was a lot of purification that needed to happen as result of ancestry, family, depression, etc.

The next couple of years I had a lot of health problems. It could have been the climate of the area, it was damp and cold, but on the other hand there was something else at work. I had continual bad colds; instead of three days I would have them for three weeks. I would just get over one and catch another. Then there was always something else, bad indigestion, etc. I feel that this was an inner purification.

THE BENEFITS OF THE LATIHAN

Elna (U.S.A.) interviewed in LA. (CA.)

The closer I come to the light, the more shadow I discover in myself. The more I love and the more I am aware of my limited capacity.

When I was seventeen and living at home, my brother wrote to me a lot about Colorado and how beautiful it was out there. I began to realize that there was a lot more to be seen beside suburbia, so I followed him out there. For a living, we sold leather shirts we made, driving from Denver up to Aspen and Vail. Along with us came a girl who had gone to school in Carbondale, so we stopped at the Health Food store in that town. There was a man working there who had something different and very special about him we all felt. He wore his hair up on the top of his head and had a great big long beard.

A month or so later I ended up moving up there. The man with his hair pilled up on top of his head had become my boy friend. His name was Roy. We were together for a couple of years, and all of Roy's friends I met and felt close to were in Subud.

I was there for about two months when I started getting strong feelings about going home to my family. When I arrived at my parents' house they had just gotten the news that my brother had died in a motorcycle accident. So I was with them for this most difficult of times.

When I got back to Colorado I really felt different. Nobody had known me or was familiar with my early life, so I felt I was starting something totally new and separated from my family. I met you and Charles, Lillia and Efron and their children, also Rohanna, Laura and Saul, Margaret, Illene and her mother Ondine. Later I met the people in the Denver group. I remember going to Margaret Albouy's house and she talked to me about the latihan. There was a strong feeling, something wiser, deeper and older, about which I felt good. You Riantee, and later Lillia, were the ones who talked to me the most though. I met you through Roy before I met Lillia.

I was opened that September. My brother had died in June. At that time Prio was visiting the group. There were quite a few other visitors. I remember speeding with Roy in his car trying to get to latihan in Aspen from Carbondale in time. The roads were narrow, winding and dangerous, and I remember feeling that I didn't want to go to latihan. In fact I just wanted to go the other direction. It seemed that my resistance had been there forever. A tearing down experience, forever, forever.

I really didn't feel very much when I got opened, just some sensation in my right hand. That was about the size of my receiving. I think that the latihan is still growing very slowly for me. Although I can say that I have experienced some beautiful, strong receivings. Much more now than at the beginning. But at one point I even dropped out of Subud.

Even when I moved to California I don't remember that it was that good either. I never went to latihan more than once a week, if that much actually. I am not going to put my latihan down. It's just that now I feel the latihan working in my life. It probably was then also, but it took some strange forms. Like I would think, "Why am I thinking about dresses during latihan?" Much later I found out that clothes are my life's work, making dresses. I was much more worried about what people thought of me then, whether people were watching me, whether something was happening for me or not. It was just junk, ways to put yourself down, separate yourself.

In California I got married to Edward who also was in Subud. I had met him through Roy and we had traveled down together. We moved to the Mendocino area with the Davidson and Rand families. We thought of buying orchards and going into the fruit business.

That didn't work and eventually Edward and I moved to Santa Rosa. The group was in Sebastopol, but it was not that strong a group, or at least it did not feel that way to me. I don't even remember the people. It was sort of scattered. So we just dropped out for about three years. It probably had more to do with my marriage breaking apart.

One day there was a phone call. By then I had been to Europe and back and I felt more horrible than I had ever felt in my whole life. That phone call was from a man wanting to find out whether my husband and I still wanted to be in the Subud directory or not. And that is what brought me back to the latihan. I began going on a regular basis to the Santa Rosa group. At that time there was a very strong group in downtown Santa Rosa. That also made a difference because I was working downtown and it was easy for me to get there.

I met lots of good people and made myself go to latihan twice a week, even though it was a struggle. Not an easy period, but things began to look up. I decided to go to College, and at the same time I started to feel the latihan working for me. Little by little I felt it affected my life, affected the way I was learning. I knew for example, that it was through the latihan that I had become more interested in studying. I learned in a different way. My outer life had more meaning, was more significant. At the same time I felt more responsible. I started to grow on all different levels and became aware of that.

During that period, (I was opened in 1972 and that is 1982 or 83,) I was listening to one of Bapak's tapes when something hit me strongly. It was the fact that we don't need to be depressed. Bapak was really telling us to get on with it, and I got the message. I sat down to think. I had been in Subud for more than ten years and nothing in my life had been as important to me. It finally dawned on me what a blessing the latihan was. I think I wrote to you, Riantee, and to Lillia about it. It was a revelation, maybe, an intellectual one in a sense. But it also went deep into the feelings. It might have hit the feelings first and then became intellectualized. After that, things took off. My commitment was renewed.

I graduated from school two years later, decided to leave America and travel to Europe. I had written to Ibu Rahayu and she advised that my work should be fashion and color. So one of my reasons for going to Europe was to look into those areas. I first went to the Subud camp in Italy, the kids' camp. I was a counselor there, which was a lovely experience. I really felt my heart opening. It was my first real experience of living in Subud as a family for five weeks, eating together two to three times a day, everything together. It was wonderful.

Later I went to live in Paris. It was a period of unrest for me. I found myself spending all my time going to latihan because I felt I needed it so badly to cleanse myself. I saw Subud in operation in other countries beside mine, and how different it was for young people coming into Subud at that point; also I became aware of the variety of visions.

Anyway, I spent three months in Paris, and since for me it was kind of difficult being there I decided to go to the international conference center that Subud was building in England, Anugraha. I must mention that I had many great experiences with the people in Paris, in terms of the humane quality of Europeans, which opened me up to the humaneness in myself. Incroyable! Everyone there was hospitable and helpful to me.

I went to Anugraha with a couple of the French brothers from the Paris group. We took the bus, then the boat, and we were there three days after Christmas. I met Hameed Francis and his wife Istafiah, a wonderful couple. I was staying at the Subud house in Central London but soon afterwards I moved in with them. I worked for them as a nanny to their children. I also worked with Hameed setting up things on his computer.

At this point in my life I strongly experienced the results of the latihan. I began to be totally convinced of the validity and truth of the latihan, also that to follow it was all that really mattered. I felt I was definitely on the right track, that God was always protecting me and moving me in the right direction . . . My destiny was instilled in me.

I also understood the beauty of relating to the family that I was born into, even though they never wanted Subud in their life. I felt the power of my ancestry, felt more in touch with my ancestors, had more understanding of my line of ancestry.

After a time many Subud people would say to me, "I think you are going to go to Indonesia!" Istafiah put a batik in my room and said, "I feel that you'll be going to Indonesia." Also, while I was in France, I had met a woman called Lisa whom I stayed with and she had just been to Indonesia. So I said to myself, "Yes, I am going to Indonesia," and began in this way to put the seed in my mind. I even made preparations to go for Ramadhan. This plan had never entered my mind when I left America.

Anyway, I went to Scotland to visit my ancestors and decided to pray to them so they'd show me the right direction. I was having breakfast and being quiet one morning when my cousin's wife sat down across from me. "You know," she said, "I just had a feeling that you should go back to America and take care of everything there before you go to Indonesia."

So I flew back to America, sold my belongings and went to Indonesia with a clear conscience. Everything was in order. I stayed for seven weeks. It was the year before Bapak died, and we had latihans with Bapak. I would say that the best experience I had with Bapak was when all of us visitors sang in front of him. Because I wasn't prepared at all, it was terribly embarrassing and humiliating for me, but at one point I sensed that Bapak was looking at me and I experienced myself as a child, so innocent and lovely. I felt very happy and warm, like nothing else mattered.

I had to go back to the States after seven weeks (which was a blessed time and I won't ever forget it,) so I decided to enroll in school. I met Mardiningsih Arquette and reconnected with Mardiah a sister from the Aspen days. They helped me find the right school and I started a yearlong course in fashion design. From there my work began to take root. Now I see the results of the latihan everyday. In fact the latihan is more what's happening than anything else. So that's it . . . that's it. I've said it all.

Elna is now married and has two children.

LOTS OF COINCIDENCES

Herbert (U.S.A.) interviewed in Spokane (WA.)

The space of becoming around all beings and inside of which they can grow, expand and take flight is sacred. In each true meeting there is an invisible presence. It's that presence that is looking for us, that presence we are looking for.

I was in San Francisco when Bapak first arrived in this country. I had a friend named George who had a bookstore and I used to hang around there. Then my wife and I moved over to Berkeley. We had three children, two of mine and one of hers from a previous marriage. One day I got a postcard from George saying that a remarkable man called John Bennett was going to give a talk there.

I had read one of Bennett's books that George had loaned me. I had heard a little bit about Gurdjieff but I wasn't very much into it. However, I liked George who was a very hardheaded skeptical type. Even though he had a bookstore full of magical spiritual literature, he didn't read any himself. Since he was so much into this Bennett thing I thought there might be something to it. So I went to the talk.

I became aware of a series of coincidences, the first of which was that the event took place in a wing of the Zen temple where the Japanese Go Club used to meet. I had been a go player there. In the same auditorium I had gone to see the movies of Toshiro Mifuni.

Bennett rambled on, comparing the different ways he had investigated. His way of depicting the innermost self was to draw a circle on a board with fuzzy lines around the outside and a point in the center. He said those fuzzy lines were all of our consciousness, emotions and everything. The central point of contact was so far inside of us that we were completely unaware of it.

That didn't exactly fascinate me but at a certain point, I guess it was about half way through, I had a funny feeling, like two little antennae sprouting out of the top of my head, floating over the audience and up on the stage where they slipped into Bennett's head. I said to myself, "That is very strange!" And of course, it stopped immediately. A while later I heard him say, "If any of you want to get that contact with your innermost self put down your name and address and you will be notified." He never mentioned God throughout this whole talk.

So I put down my name and got a postcard a couple of days later. I went to this hotel in a nice neighborhood on Pacific Avenue. There were a lot of people being shuffled around from one room to another. I went with a friend who was a librarian at U.C. Berkeley and we were patiently waiting around. After about an hour this guy in a very snappy cowboy style outfit, a very sharp and aggressive type, stood up and said, "If this is the way they organize things, I don't want anything to do with it." And he left. But we stayed.

When our turn came, about ten of us went down the hall and into a room. Before we went in a man stepped out of a doorway nearby, and I got a funny impression when I saw him. It was as if I were looking in through a doorway into empty space, where there was a complete absence of any emotions, issues, likes or dislike, just empty space. I was looking at Bapak, but I didn't know that.

So we got into the room, Bennett was there and this other man was there. He started to talk in a foreign language and Bennett translated, "Bapak is here to witness your wish to worship the One Almighty God and so, surrender yourself completely to the Will of God."

I was thinking, "This is the first I hear about God, much less about surrender." But it occurred to me that I was there and I might as well find out what this was and if God did exist, which was an open question for me. If He did I was perfectly willing to surrender to Him. Then they asked us to close our eyes.

The rest of the time I was madly trying to keep my eyes shut because there were noises and I wanted to take a look. But I thought, "I better do this the way they advise me." In the middle of it all something apparently happened. But it didn't seem like anything very much, and as soon as I noticed it went away. It was a physical experience, not inside my head. When they said, "finish," I turned around and there was the same man opening up a little gold cigarette case. He avoided my stare.

So even though I didn't move or anything for the first year, something told me that this was my last chance. So I stayed. And here I am at the International Congress in Spokane decades later.

*　　*　　*

Eight years later:

I never had any doubts about doing this for the rest of my life. The character I usually think that I am has been gradually purified in the forty-six years—from March 1958 to now, February 2005—so that now when Ilaina and I read talks by Bapak and Ibu Rahayu they are full of wonderful truths and realities. I have now been married to Ilaina for eight years, we had a big wedding in Puebla, Mexico on September 29, 1996. We lived in San Diego for five and half years and now live in Los Angeles.

3

BEGINNING IN SUBUD

"Facts are accumulated by effort, but truth reveals itself effortlessly."

Dr. David Hawkins

Life appears to me as a hoop; not the snake biting its tail that represents the infinite, but an ascending spiral that brings about new levels of awareness from which we can look at the same experiences from a different perspective and gain a new understanding. This might be the form my personal purification takes. I seem to return to my beginnings, even more so when I think I have left them far behind. I might feel totally different about life now from how I felt years ago, but my true nature was in place from the day I was born. It just got covered over as I grew up and took on different personas. My spiritual life is a process of uncovering, cleansing and freeing myself from outer influences and forces so I can get back to this true self; it is also a process of learning to work with those forces.

Friends from the past that I left behind because I judged them "stuck," would reappear in my life, handing me a key. Our original connection was re-established when my judgment vanishes; our essential self hadn't changed.

I witness a dance. What I had started long ago is going on now. This dance reminds me of the patterns the sun makes on the bottom of a pool as I swim under water. A gigantic network of configurations that result from ripples of water interacting with one another. Woven light, dancing, links connecting and moving on to connect with other links; the connecting network of light eventually going back to the original link, having gone through many changes and transformations. No beginning, no end. Just reaching farther and coming back to start new patterns.

People I have questioned for this book often show me how the dance goes. They hold the understanding I need at the time. They mention a name, a place, a belief long forgotten and I am made to see that my past still walks with me, although it doesn't influence me quite as much as it used to. I begin to understand how I am guided, how everything I encounter comes into my life for a reason, that the divine spirit has a way of doing what is exactly right for the person concerned.

I joined Subud in 1964, like many who were opened at that time, as a result of a search. However my passion for searching was not immediately assuaged. Before Subud I was used to attaching story to everything I came across and looking for the meaning of every story. Then I analyzed the meaning and built theories about human behavior. I found boxes in which to store everything and everyone including myself. I labeled those boxes, thus keeping a temporary condition in place, making it solid. I looked for the reason behind everything. I journeyed through a forest of highly significant symbols. I thought I was using the superb instrument of my mind; in fact it was using me.

This was my disease: I believed I was my mind. A continuous mind activity kept me imprisoned in the world of form, and because thought is material—part of the realm of the manifested—I couldn't be conscious of the God essence in myself, in all things and all creatures.

Infatuated with concepts, theories, I fitted everything into systems and that made life exciting. I was thrilled with my explorations. But intellectualizing doesn't provide a guide to truth; there was emptiness at the center of myself, a residue of dissatisfaction. I was so identified with my mind I didn't know I was its slave; and the mind loves so much to sink its teeth into all that meaty stuff. I could never find the 'off' button.

I assumed that I was shaped by the people who influenced me, that the circumstances of my life made me who I was. I believed with the existentialists that existence precedes essence. I was made out of what I knew, shaped by what I did. My face was the face of all the others who had been important to me. I lived, like many others, in the somnolence of the tongue, in a language that claimed to represent but only described because the spirit had gone out of it. I aspired to be a writer but used words in a way that was not truly mine, subjected to the small deaths of society living. I had lost the reality of my oneness with all that is. I was lost to myself and I lost my words until much later, when I let them rise from the quiet inspiration at the center of my self.

When the latihan came into my life, my passion for figuring people out didn't die. In fact I still have it and probably will keep some form of it. I came to realize, however, that what I think I know about someone often prevents me from truly listening and knowing that person, just as what I say about myself might prevent me from being myself.

To truly listen to someone is to love them. When I listen to myself in the moment, the constant activity of the mind seeking salvation from the pain ceases. The pain is one primordial one: the loss of awareness of who I am beyond name and form and the sense of threat, of abandonment and incompleteness that goes with it.

When I sincerely listen I become conscious of being and my body is flooded with consciousness. I feel my body parts as fields of energy and experience the state of connectedness with God, the joy of being, the love for myself as soul and part of the whole.

Over the years I witnessed the obstructions blocking my inner receiving being peeled off one layer after another. For instance, when dealing with fear: my biggest and most paralyzing fear, deeply buried, might surface and precipitate a minor crisis. Then this suffering is over, to my great relief. I think it's gone forever. But at some later date it will reappear, this time in a milder form. This goes on until I reach a place where the fear is still there, but as a usable tool for living rather than an impediment. I become the watcher and the fear is fuel for consciousness. When this transmutation of suffering into consciousness happens, the split in me is healed for a while: I become whole.

To begin with, the subtlety of the latihan, for someone looking for spectacular enlightenment and extraordinary manifestations, was somewhat disappointing. In the immediate, I hardly noticed anything. After a while however, a new perception slowly illuminated everything with love and compassion. Little by little my systems were dismantled or fell apart. My beliefs were removed one by one. I still had theories and ideas but no sooner were they expressed than they shed their first layer, like an onion, exposing the next and making me cry. I could no longer hold on to anything, nor could I believe that I knew anything. The structures on which I had built my life collapsed and I was in a constant state of dissolution. Once I even lost my words; I couldn't make sense of what people around me were saying. Without words I was nothing.

At times I would become so oppressed I was unable to get up in the morning. I looked at life with discouragement. It seemed to me that during most of it we struggled to gain back what we had possessed at the beginning and lost in the process of growing up. When we finally regained that original state, we were ready to die. What a fate!

But I found that often, when I was a step away from despair, I was a step away from a state of grace. All my concepts transformed and vanished when I tried to grasp on to them, leaving me with nothing to hold on to: I couldn't find anything solid to step on: I didn't fit in any of the old images of myself; and that, oddly enough, was a relief because there was no longer the experience of an individual self separated from others. To me, surrendering was letting go of resistance to what is, and I understood compassion as the acceptance of what I have in common with all other creatures: mortality and deathless dimension.

Everything I had held as true melted away. I was filled with love and trusted that I was loved. A presence, forever supportive and encouraging was with me everywhere I went. Under the watchfulness of the divine eye, I experienced an immense silence in my mind. That which was witnessed and that which witnessed were one and the same. I became aware of the tremendous task we were given, as humans, when we were put on earth. I felt honored to have been given this most difficult mission, and trusted to have the capacity to accomplish it. I believe that we all have that capacity if we trust that we do.

From some of the lost Dead Sea Scrolls that are now surfacing I understand that the wisdom of the Heavens was given to the people of this Earth in a complete and intact form over 6000 years ago. Every human who walks this Earth is said to be a highly evolved being who has successfully achieved a life in the Heavens and has come to this earth to accomplish something that can only be accomplished here. We, as humans, are here to love and to find a love greater than the love of the Angels of the Heavens, and any time we find a way to love ourselves out of the suffering of the world, this love is honored and mirrored by all the angels. They have learned new ways to love through the experiences they can't have as angels, but that we, humans, are having here.

Often, through what appeared to be a coincidence, I ran into something that confirmed what I had unconsciously known all along. And in this way, as I journeyed from who I appeared to be towards who I really was, many sides of me died, others were born or reborn. Through the difficult times a voice within kept saying, "Don't give up. Don't always look straight ahead. It's often at the edge of vision that the divine is revealed."

I was from a generation that believed it could change the world and do it fast. Many people who joined Subud in those days had roamed the planet to find an alternative to the 'materialistic Western approach.' But our search had remained unsuccessful. We had followed gurus, studied different doctrines and philosophies, investigated oriental religions and tribal cultures, eventually 'dropped out,' turning to art, poetry, music, beads, long hair, psychedelics and fast wisdom. The psychedelics, as teachers, taught us much, but after years of short ecstasies we were still questioning, "Why must we always come down? There must be a way to feel the divine without ingesting some substance, a way that could be repeated at will."

So we continued our search: Buddhism, Zen, Hinduism, Sufism, eventually Gurdjieff and Ouspensky, but we were not satisfied with the headiness and rigidity of their techniques for self-awareness. However, Gurdjieff's prediction towards the end of his life caught our attention: I am not long for this world, but do not grieve. Someone much greater than I, is preparing to come to the West and continue the work. Look for him in India, not in your British India but in the India of the Dutch. Then we also heard that John Bennett, a former disciple of Gurdjieff, had made a certain technique available in the West.

In the beginning, many of us found Subud through friends. We had little understanding of what the latihan was really about. Some even believed that it was a way to get high naturally. Lillia and I were absolutely confident that there was something to be found and that eventually we would run across it. And when Lillia met me with the words: "I found it," I didn't question, I just started my probation period. Any doubts I might have had were erased by the miracle of a close friend's psychological recovery after she was started doing latihan. Three months later I was opened and never stopped doing the latihan, although I sometimes had misgivings about the institution of Subud. I avoided big groups; discouraged by what I took to be a lack of wisdom in Subud people I met, in the apparently slow progress I was making myself. But I trusted in the power of the latihan.

I witnessed the progress in others close to me before I saw it in myself, but I sensed some amazing power at work within. Things didn't change right away. Most of us continued smoking a little marijuana and after latihan engaged in long philosophical discussions about life, death, human nature and God. Our favorite subject had become Subud and the latihan, of which we knew so little. We compared our receivings, shared the visions we had during latihan. The time after latihan often became a showcase for 'experiences' and those who didn't get much of anything felt deprived or spiritually retarded. However, each in turn had their time of glory.

Because we always searched for undiscovered 'truths,' awaiting messages from God, dreams were highly regarded and analyzed. Dramatic dreams or visions were greatly admired. I remember a particularly impressive dream I had about mistaking Jesus for my soul mate. I walked towards him and he allowed me to put my head on his shoulder. Since he was much taller than me, my head rested on his chest where I could feel the beat of his immense heart. I became enamored and was going to kiss him passionately, but he said, "No, you are making a mistake, that's not what this is about." I accepted that and relaxed into an affectionate sisterly embrace. I started feeling my heart expanding. It became bigger and bigger until it was so huge I was nothing but a heart. Every part of me was heart. I experienced being the immense heart of Jesus.

In another dream I was a child growing up in front of Bapak. I felt so accepted—nothing in the world could hinder my total trust in him. He explained that our religion was for the heart and it was good to assimilate our given religion before exploring others. I had rejected Christianity early on but I felt myself as a Christian at that time. The latihan had given substance to my Christianity. Eventually I felt other religions as part of my spiritual make-up as well.

In our small group of beginners we read everything we could about Subud, avidly devouring the Indonesian Subud magazine, which was called the *Pewarta*, as soon as it arrived. We interpreted everything according to who we were at the time. We believed that part of being in Subud was to lead a pure and frugal life, to get back to the land, grow our own food, bake our own bread, wear flowing clothes and no make-up. We gave up psychedelics, which, after waking us up, were putting us to sleep.

A terrifying experience made me quit smoking marijuana. I visited Dante's inferno, a horrendous hell in which my mind was prisoner with no way out. It no longer belonged to me; I had no control over it. And there was no savior in sight. I was petrified, not so much of dying but of having lost my soul. I promised God I would never touch the stuff again if I were rescued. And I was.

When our small group made forays into bigger groups, we noticed that many older Subud people were not at all living in the 'prescribed' way. It was an enormous disappointment to realize that even those who had been in Subud for a long time had faults and flaws. Was the latihan not working or did it take that long to make a difference?

I tortured myself with judgment until I realized that any judgment on someone else was a judgment on myself coming from a place where I couldn't yet forgive myself. And forgiveness was to offer no resistance to life!

I had expected to be totally purified in no time at all, and I became worried that the latihan was not working on me. Had it all been an illusion? Subud publications often offended me. I felt there was a patronizing, patriarchal, righteous bend that encouraged hierarchy. Many times I thought of leaving Subud, but couldn't give up the latihan. Eventually I came to the conclusion that since my guidance came through the latihan, I would understand tomorrow what I didn't today. I stopped resisting and accepted what was. I didn't need to continue reading what offended me. I didn't have to live close to a big group or follow anyone's directives. The guidance I needed I would get for myself.

So I began to rely more on my own receiving.

EARLY YEARS IN AN ISOLATED
GROUP—*The sixties in Aspen*

IT WAS BIGGER THAN MY KNOWING

Mardiah (U.S.A.) interviewed in L.A. (CA.)

*Each meeting holds a piece of our puzzle; when a true
encounter happens, a piece of our being is revealed. Little
at a time, pieces come together like themes of our destiny.
Without knowing it we often deliver to the people we meet
the key to our enigma.*

My husband and I met in Aspen, Colorado. I moved there in
1961. We were ski bums. Every off-season, in the fall and spring,
we would take a trip away from Aspen because there was no
work there. We would often go to Mexico for the warm climate. In
the spring of 1966 we took a trip and stayed in Mazatlan. Within
a month we were out of cash and had to wait for more money to
be wired to us. We traveled with friends and both our campers
had broken down and needed to get fixed.

At that time we had lived in Aspen for five years, first being
hippies and trying many drugs, then getting married and giving
birth to a baby who was just a few months old. I was ready for a
change in my life. I was no longer excited or satisfied with things
the way they were.

This friend, a kind of hippie guy named Teddy (he'd work
fairs and circuses but also spent a lot of time in Aspen,) was in
Mazatlan at the same time as us and he needed a ride to L.A. to
see a friend we all knew from Aspen.

Redmond, my husband, had always hated L.A. Although he
had never spent any time there, he considered it an awful place
to be. But somehow, he agreed to take Teddy to that city.

The car got fixed. We drove to L.A. where we sought out
Steve L., Teddy's friend. He lived in a little apartment in Venice.
We dropped Teddy off, said hello-good-bye to both, and then

went to stay at the house of friends who had recently moved to Malibu from Aspen. They wanted us to see some of L.A. so they drove us around. We were on the Sunset Strip when this guy stepped out in front of our car and waved us to a stop. It was Steve, whom we had seen the day before and said goodbye to. We drove to his apartment. He had just been to the Renaissance Fair and had picked up some wood rose seeds. He was trying to get a psychedelic high out of those, so we all sat down in the apartment and tried to experience a new kind of high. But nothing happened.

We were getting sort of restless and were ready to leave when I noticed this pamphlet on a table. It was some kind of Subud News article. I picked it up and said, "What's this?" Steve answered, "Oh! It's this incredible new thing that I have gotten into. It's really an amazing trip. You should go down there, right downtown on Hope Street and see for yourself. It's really something else." And he went on to describe this experience he had of being on fire. He was just completely blown away by this. He had even drawn a picture of it. As he was talking something was happening to me, and I knew, I just knew, that what he was describing was what I had been looking for.

Steve told me that you didn't have to take any drug to experience this, so I thought to myself, "Of course, on psychedelics one experiences a parallel state of being rather than the ordinary state, so I know that this state exists, but I also know that there is a greater way to experience it. Why would you have to take a substance to experience that?" I just knew that what Steve was talking about was real.

Redmond thought it was baloney. He just wanted to get out of L.A. as soon as possible, so I couldn't go but Steve told us that there was Subud in Aspen and he described the people who were in it: a couple we had met without knowing they were in Subud. The man was a little guy, Steve G., and his partner was a tall English girl, Elisabeth. They were young but not part of the crowd of ski bums we used to hang out with. They lived off in a little shepherd's cabin in a great meadow and kept to themselves.

They lived without electricity; back to nature people into a simple life style. I wasn't too upset about not going to Hope Street since I could investigate right away when I got back to Aspen. Which is exactly what I did. I immediately contacted Elisabeth and told her I was interested in Subud. She informed me about the three months period of waiting. She did the latihan with this older lady who was married to a man who was not in Subud. Her name was Margaret. The latihan took place in this abandoned coke kiln down from the meadow where Elisabeth and Steve lived. I sat outside the kiln and listened to the latihan to see how it felt. I also read a lot of literature that they gave me. As much as they had. I think I over-studied Subud.

I was very, very excited, but my life didn't change all at once. I remember taking an acid trip during my period of probation. I was looking at a Pewarta at the time and the literature became three-dimensional. I had experiences at that time, which really kept me on the track even though I was still doing psychedelic, and grass. I was made aware that this latihan was a real power, a real substance. So I stayed with this process, sitting outside the latihan and doing just that.

At one point Elisabeth's mother, Katherine Trevelyan, was coming to visit. Steve and Elisabeth worked together on this funny old wagon, rounded up a rod and put a chimney stack in there, moved a burning stove, made a desk, a cubby hole for storage, opened a door and a window, and there it was. They had made this neat little house on wheels for the mother. Katherine arrived, and I was just under the three months probation period when she did. She was a helper. Neither Elisabeth nor Margaret were helpers, although they had been doing the latihan for a long time. Katherine felt it was okay for me to get opened because she was there and it was an opportunity.

I was opened just about a couple of weeks before my probation ended, in the little brick domed building. It was a very awesome opening, although I could also remember experiencing a lot of self-doubts. I felt that maybe everybody else was experiencing the latihan and I was not, but at the same time I was really made to move and there was no straying from it. It was the type of experience that made me feel like I had to keep going with it because there was nothing else. It was bigger that my knowing.

*   *   *

Mardiah, eight to ten years have gone by since we had that conversation. Since then you served a term as National Helper, you are now the chairwoman of Subud LA. It seems like you have become more and more active in the organization; so how are things different for you?

Frankly I am no longer aware of how it was then, but what's changed is the realization that I needed discipline. For my outer behavior I couldn't just rely on the latihan to lead me on my path because I am a very lazy person, just an ordinary flawed person, and it's very easy for me to rationalize wrong behavior and be under the influence of forces that are not the higher ones. I do feel freer from that influence and it's easier for me to separate from it. It's not that I wasn't aware of those forces before but I was not taking action to be separate from them. What I have done is to be more willing to give space for my latihan to be in charge.

You have to make that effort, it's almost like a prihatin, fasting from the forces, and I have been able to do that. It's not that I am different, I am still the same person and I have the latihan as before, but I am willing to give more space to it.

For myself I feel that the latihan has penetrated my understanding more. I could go back and look at everything I have believed to be true and have a totally different understanding now of how the spiritual works within. It's a stage Bapak and Ibu have described at different times. Do you feel that for yourself?

Yes I do. My perception is that through effort and willingness the life force is flowing, whereas before there were obstructions because I was not willing to surrender, not all the time, so I was not able to receive the benefits.

How was it for you to serve as a National Helper?

It was a tremendous gift because it was an affirmation of myself, an appreciation. I had been given the strength to do the job and in exchange I was very willing to serve.

You told me during that time that you once received in testing that to serve is to be out of the way.

It is your witnessing that allows the receiving to be from God when you are empty and surrendered.

How is the chairwoman's job different?

To be a chairperson is very challenging and totally different from anything I have done before in Subud, or in my life for that matter. I can stand up and be a leader, make decisions, but it takes a lot of courage for me to do that because I don't naturally have the ability. I have been an entrepreneur in the past but I have been very careful to use the skills of other people to help me. To have to answer to a lot of people is a challenge; you have to take responsibility for the building (Subud House,) and the feelings of people as you take decisions. I had great confusion about what was correct or not correct to do. "Is it my place to take that decision?" or "Is it my will?" or "How do I move forward in my job without creating dissention?"

As I evolved in the job, I have become more willful, more confident in my way of doing things. That to me is showing my own confidence in myself, how I work, how I receive to work. What I bring to the job is a more housewify expression than most other chairpersons. I like to change the furniture and clear the space, try different things with it, play around with how to arrange things to make it the most comfortable and useful, and get to know what's there by looking and sorting. Very hands on. Now I have confidence in that, whereas before I would think that "they" were the experts out there, and I just a little person.

I came to realize that I relied on my husband too much for practical matters, and I am beginning to find out how to do it myself. I like to work with people even though I avoid people, and of course I want people to love me and agree with me. But they don't, so I get very upset. There can be ninety-nine people agreeing with me, but it takes just one disagreeing for me to take it as total opposition. So it forces me to work on myself. It helps me grow and accept who I am.

I see the LA. chairmanship as a big job because it is a huge part of the Subud world and it has a tremendous influence. If we are to bring Subud out to the world I want to do my best to represent the LA. group as an open, accepting, not exclusive one. There should be joy in building Subud, which, in my mind, has been stagnant. I am not working to get the group active in using the building, but to get the outside world active in using it, because then the Subud people will want it back.

I have fights with Subud people and often find that the forces sweep up the dearest, sweetest people. I am sure I am also swept by those forces, because they are so strong when you deal with that stuff. That's why those kinds of jobs are such a challenge, there is huge purification going on. You may think you are doing such a great service when in fact it's your own purification going on.

I DIDN'T HEAR ABOUT SUBUD, I SAW

Resmiwati (U.S.A.) interviewed in L.A. (CA.)

The pallid reason of mankind swept by the joyful madness of God opens a door that lets it in with laughter and tears.

I didn't hear about Subud . . . I saw. I came back to Aspen in 1967 after a few months in Hawaii and walked into Lillia's house (she was then Linda.) Something was different in her eyes. Mardiah, (then Penelope,) was there too, and I could see that there was a drastic change in her also.

I had been feeling that there was something missing in my life. It led me to search, I didn't know for what, but at the time I entered that house on Main Street I had given up. I had absolutely given up what I wanted because there was no way that I knew how to get it.

Ever since I was nine years old I asked the question, "Oh my God, what did I do to get here? This is awful this suffering, this is terrible." In my teens I tried to understand. I was reading Gurdjieff when I was thirteen or fourteen. I would read avidly any book I could put my hands on to try to find an answer, the great masters of the Far East, anything . . . What's interesting to me is that we all came from that place, our whole Aspen group.

I was about nineteen when I realized that there was nothing I could do to get what I was looking for. It was not in my power. Any tool I had could not be of use, it would be like saying, "God, I am sure that there is something I can do to make you grace me." Right! It was impossible.

That's when I threw every book out of my house and gave up. When people told me about their beliefs I was furious. I didn't want to hear it. I was so full of everybody else's belief system that there was not one little tiny space in me for anything else.

A couple of years later I went to Hawaii. I was depressed. I looked at my marriage and it was not what I wanted. Everything I looked at in my life made me say, "Is this it?" My interpretation of things was that they were just shit. That is when someone took me on my first acid trip.

It was really incredible. I did it in a controlled way, guiding the trip. I didn't do it just to get high, oh no. I knew exactly where I was going to be the first hour, the second hour, etc. I was going to be by myself.

What happened is that I started too late and was on a motorcycle when the acid came on. I was trying to get to the top of this mountain to sit there and dig the sunset. I don't know how I made it up there because I was on high wires. The thing that was significant about the acid is that it opened up a different perspective for me. I was able to see that there was more than I ever thought was possible within me, that there were other states available to human beings that were incredible. It was like every one of my senses was opened up to the hilt, but I had to give up my thoughts.

I used the drug only for a period of a few months. I took it to stop smoking, and if I had a question in mind I took it to find the answer. The last time I took any drugs I said to myself, "This is great, but now I know I have to do it without a crutch." I didn't know how and I knew it was not going to come from anything I knew. It was nothing I could do on my own.

So I got back to Aspen, and two days after I went to Lillia's house. She opened the door and there was something in her eyes, something about her that made me say, "My God, what have you people been doing? There is something very different about you?" Lillia kind of giggled and answered, "Well if you want to know, come with me next time when I go to latihan." That's when I thought of asking her the question, "Wait a minute, is there anything I have to do to have this?" because I knew that if she said yes it was not what I was looking for.

What I was looking for was a connection because I was not at all connected. That was what had been missing from my life. Lillia answered that there was nothing I needed to do. In fact I had to give up doing anything except the latihan. And then I knew that this had to be it.

We all had something in common: we came from a totally different place than most people at the time. We had a special vision and were renegades. I certainly was not going to be in a nine to five job like my dad. I needed to go out in the world and find out a few things. We were dropouts, didn't want to accept any of the values we were handed, took nothing for granted.

Something else interesting is that I didn't know how to think anything through. I assumed that if you didn't know where you were at, you had to get out and change location. What I didn't realize was that the place had nothing to do with it. I got very worried, after I was opened, that something might happen no matter where I was and I would have to stay with it instead of moving on.

I had always believed I could only be involved in anything for a certain amount of time, in my relationship with my husband Paul for instance. I would start a certain kind of thinking that led to anxiety, a frustration with the way things were.

My solution had always been to leave. "You've got to get out," I would tell myself. When I lived with Paul we moved at least seventeen times. Even when we had twins, Raymond and Lucas, we moved a lot. We kept saying, "Oh, this is it," or, "This can't be it," thinking that our discomfort was really about the place, about the world.

As I kept doing the latihan, I experienced the vibration moving me more and more, and the latihan was around a lot more in my life and outside of it. It was not about the world anymore.

Now it's about the world again, but in a whole new way. It's like the terror we all experience that it's not safe out there: the thoughts that produce those emotions just don't seem to come anymore, there is trust. And there is no way that I can ever understand how this happened. My fears are gone. It's like I am lifted in the world now, more so than ever in my life.

To get back to the time of my opening. At the time, in Aspen, we were doing latihan in two places: Steve and Elisabeth's cabin in the meadow, or the kilns, which were in the woods not far from there. You had to sit outside if you were a probationer—in the woods right—and listen to these sounds coming out of this coke kiln that would echo. Whoo, whoo, whoo. And I kept imagining all sorts of beings behind me in the trees, oh God!

At one point we changed location because Aspen had a beautiful music school and we could rent it for latihan. My opening happened in the music school. I had asked to be opened before the three months probation was over because I just had to be inside that room with the others. I thought, why not? I know everything already, *(she laughs)* . . . But the result of the testing made it clear that I was not to be opened before my time, that I had to finish my probation.

So I did and when I got opened you were there as Lydia. Ondine and Illene Lawyer were there. Lillia Davidson, Mardiah Gleeson, Margaret Albouy and another Margaret from Denver were there also. When they read me the opening I was trying to listen to the words but none of it made any sense to me. I didn't know what any of those words meant, but it sounded okay . . .

My biggest fear was that I was going to look like a jerk and that nothing would happen to me. When they told me to close my eyes, to be willing to follow whatever I received and their latihan started, I remained standing there, totally unable to stop these thoughts, "Oh, I am not going to feel anything. This is stupid, what am I doing here, and what is this?"

All of a sudden, I started crying. It wasn't really like I started to cry. It was like the crying started. Almost like it was from different parts of my body. It was not from my eyes, my thoughts, my emotions. It was from this incredible place where I didn't even feel sad. It didn't make me sad that I was crying, but I was crying.

It was really deep. I didn't feel that there was anybody around me who felt sad. In fact everybody was happy about it. I could feel them saying, "This is good, this is good. You'll never be able to laugh until you can cry completely." That was what I was looking for.

I was aware of that vibration right from the beginning, right between my breasts. I felt like I was being pushed backward. I believed that if I opened my eyes I would see myself walking, but when I actually opened my eyes I was standing. My body was not moving, but this vibration was going, Woom, woom, like that.

The first thing that happened after I got opened was that I was unable to handle the frustration in my marriage with Paul. I had just found out about testing, so I went to see the helpers and asked if they would test whether or not I should stay married to Paul. They answered that they could not test anything like that. Instead, they tested what my attitude toward Paul was, and how would God have it be. As it was, I started to throw up . . . After the question, how would God have it be, I had the experience of holding a small boy in my arms. The sad thing about it was that although I had the inner experience of it, I was not able to do it in my life. So I left Paul and came back, and left again and came back again, trying to make it work. The last time I came back I got pregnant.

I had had the feeling that I was coming back for something other that just being with Paul. So I got pregnant and it was great. It was so incredible. My child was due in August, and two babies came out in June. Twins. There is so much about that experience that was a blessing in disguise, but I should write a book because this is another story.

It was so great that the latihan was available when the kids were young. We could really use it because of the testing. For instance, the doctor told me that Lucas had cerebral palsy and he had to have braces because his legs were all crooked when he started walking. I knew that it was not true. I just knew it. An experienced helper was visiting from England at the time, Katherine, and she tested with me what was the source of Lucas' disability. The whole group participated in the testing as we always did in those days. Katherine received that Lucas just had a limp inside his leg. Whether or not he brought this with him when he was born, or if it was something he just was starting was not ascertained, but she knew for sure that it was not cerebral palsy and it would straighten out.

She asked what to do and the answer was that I should do the latihan by his crib for three months every night. In three months his legs came right together, perfectly straight, and of course we found out that he didn't have cerebral palsy.

Those kinds of things were very powerful. The benefits of the latihan? The main benefit has always been that no matter how bad the circumstances in my life are (and they have been trying and bad, painful and confusing enough as to make me unable to handle a lot of things,) I always gain from finding the true meaning of the experience within myself. There is a certainty. No matter how bad it is I will always have that. It's the most important thing in the world.

THE LATIHAN DOESN'T GO AWAY

Saul (U.S.A.) interviewed in Santa Cruz (CA.)

*In the past all the answers were in the sacred books
and people could let the words come through the door of
everyday life: everyone came from God and returned there.
At this time our landscape expands so fast, the growth is
out of hand and we must make room for the divine, find
our own way to God. We must trust our own path, against
all odds.*

My first experience in Subud happened in the summer of
1965 in Los Angeles. I had stopped there to see friends and they
invited me to come to a Subud meeting downtown, in the Hope
Street Hall. I went with them and they directed me to a helper.
We talked about Subud. He gave me the details and told me to
go sit outside the latihan. So I did, and his instructions to me
were to try to get quiet.

I was sitting outside the latihan and I felt kind of a warmth
come over me. I unbuttoned my shirt but the heat seemed to
intensify. Then I became aware of a light that was like a spotlight,
only no matter where I moved it was still there, and I seemed to
become warmer yet. At one point I became aware of something
on my back that was like a weight, and it grew heavier, almost to
the point of doubling me over on my chair. Then I started to rock
violently and I felt like the thing was being torn from my back.
This thing, whatever it was, sort of flew off me, I don't really know
how.

To this day I don't understand what it was about, except to
say that it was, 'The monkey on my back.' I became so light after
that weight was off my back that I felt like I was levitating. It was
a feeling I had never experienced in my life, so light. Then, I
suddenly became aware of the noise of the men leaving the latihan
room and putting on their coats. There were lots of voices. I came

back to the physical world and was aware that I had a big smile on my face. I felt very different and when I walked up to my friend Victor, who was the fellow who got me to the Subud house, he said to me, "You look like the Cheshire cat." And we laughed.

Anyway, the next day it was super hot so I was sitting out in the yard, still spacing out from the experience that I had the night before. I was watching two butterflies that were flying together and circling. They flew right in front of me, then went directly toward my head and one landed on each of my shoulders. It blew me away.

I soon left L.A, and went back to Colorado. Within a day or two I ran into Redmond, then Marty, and he started asking me how I was. At one point he said, "Something has happened to you," or "What has happened to you?" and we got into that conversation about Subud. I told him there was this guy in town, someone named Steve, who knew all about it and he said, "Well, we have to find him."

So we started looking around for the man. We inquired and someone told us, "Oh yeah, I know him." So Redmond and I found this guy who was supposed to be Steve G. in town. We approached him and said that we wanted to know about Subud. He denied knowing anything about it, so we thought that maybe it was not the right guy. Then we found out where this Steve was supposed to live and we went to his house. Well, it was the same guy. So he said, "Yeah well, blah blah blah, I do the latihan and if you guys want to come we can set up a time for you to sit outside." That's what we did. We started going to his house and sitting outside at a time when he did latihan in some old coke kilns, huge, cone-shaped, made of bricks.

In the meantime, Penny or Melissa, (Mardiah is her name now,) was already hooked into this practice and had talked some lady friends of hers into it (you, Lydia now Riantee, and Linda now Lillia,) as well as some other women. Pretty soon a women's group had started. Redmond and I went to Denver to get opened and we had a men's group also.

I stayed in Aspen for another seven years but the experiences that had the most impact on me were those in L.A. I had one experience there when I left my body. We were visiting L.A. during Ramadan and it seemed like there was latihan all the time, plus the fasting and stuff . . . One day, I was doing latihan and I started leaving my body. It was like I wasn't really paying attention to what was happening and the next thing I knew I was already out of my body. I went up above everybody else and I was looking down and watching what was happening below. When I intellectualized it however, it became a mental process and I came back down. That was really wild. I felt totally spaced out for a couple of weeks after that.

I had no doubt that the latihan worked because from the very first night I had that experience. Later I talked to Prio about those experiences, and when I told him what happened when I was sitting outside the latihan he said, "Well, obviously you got opened at the time, right on the spot, probably because you were already so open and needing to be practicing the latihan. The fact that you had to go down to Denver and be opened more formally was just a confirmation."

It was the same for me as for a lot of the people that were our age in the sixties. We were seekers. We were looking for a path to fulfill the need for spiritual enlightenment or whatever. I just happened to stumble into Subud, and there were a lot of other people who went in other directions. I think that what interested me about Subud was the unorthodoxy of it. There were no parameters, at least in our group. It was like, hey, you just went in there and started opening yourself up and all that stuff would come to you. That to me was really attractive because it was wisdom without doctrine.

It definitely changed my life. Before my first experience in LA, I was a wild person. I took massive amounts of drugs and drank too much and did all that stuff, but I was so struck by the experience of the latihan that I realized there was a higher level of being you could not get to with your intellect. You could get there by opening yourself up in other ways. That was happening to me and a lot of other people in Subud.

I stopped doing the kind of drugs I had been doing and the amount I had been taking. I was not really trying to alter my consciousness anymore. I still smoked a little pot and I still had some booze and stuff like that, but I wasn't using drugs as a way to open myself up and see how far I could get, how much I could work with. Through the latihan I got as close to God as I thought I needed to get at that point in time, so the whole necessity of expanding my awareness through drugs was unnecessary.

I actually lived in Aspen for ten years. What I saw in Aspen was the birth of a group. Well I mean, it was like seeing a flower open, going through the joy of it. It's like we were pioneers. We were full of vitality, doing a lot of things together just like a big family. But at one point the vitality sort of died out in the group. People started moving away and the group fell apart. There was not a lot of energy left. I don't know, that was maybe just my perspective, something I was going through myself.

I had been in the restaurant business for ten years and out of the blue I became interested in doing carpentry. It so happened that in Carmel Valley there was a Subud construction business starting, Stone, Post and Flowers. Someone I knew was going to Carmel Valley and they said that if I wanted to go to California to let them know. So I asked my wife what she thought about moving to California. She felt that maybe it would be a nice change, and so, next thing we knew we were on the road.

We went to Mexico for some months and my third child was born. I took about a year off to get the whole scene going in the right direction, and then I decided that I wanted to get into building. I went to work for the Subud building enterprise. The group had high energy. I was working with people who were in Subud, and everybody I knew was in Subud. It was really good.

I felt like I was in a community of very committed people, and the energy level was very high. We did a lot for each other. There was some weird stuff going down, but we were all committed to making this Subud project work. However, these funny things happening on the side brought an end of to the Subud business. There was some pretty bad stuff associated with that.

Subud people moved out of Carmel Valley then, and that was the demise of the Carmel Valley group. Some people lost a lot of money. Some people lost their jobs, and some people were blown away by the fact that something, which was supposed to have so much purity, could still have people in it who were corrupt. It was not the way they thought it was supposed to be. It was tragic actually, but we stayed around because we liked it in the Valley where we were raising our children and we didn't want to blast them out of there to some place where they didn't know any kids.

Then it got to the point where the Subud house was to be sold and there no longer was a Subud Carmel Valley. From being one of the highest energy, high impact groups in California it went to being dead.

I wouldn't say the latihan now is as big an influence on me as it was before, I don't do the latihan actively twice a week like I did before, but the spiritual exercise and my connection to God is like a tool for me when I need it. I don't think that the latihan will ever go away. The guidance is with me. When I travel like this and go visit old Subud friends I love to do the latihan. It's always present to be tapped into.

I THOUGHT NO RULES OR REGULATIONS WAS WHAT SUBUD WAS ABOUT

Laura (U.S.A.) interviewed in Santa Cruz (CA.)

"Bapak's function is that of a school servant who sets out the books, opens the doors, cleans the room and arranges tables and chairs. When you are in the classroom the teacher will come in and give the lessons, and the teacher is not Bapak but God himself. Bapak is not a teacher, but only a servant of God."

Bapak

When I joined Subud I was in an isolated group, I moved to a much bigger group later. I think what made a huge difference to me is that there were no rules, no regulations when I first started Subud. I thought that's what it was about. I found out later, upon coming to California, that there were all kinds of restrictions in spite of the fact that Subud had been defined as having no rules. People interpreted the latihan and said for instance that if you clapped, you were calling demons, that you shouldn't lie down because of this, because of that, etc.

Those kinds of restrictions can really stifle and inhibit. I realized then how free it had been before. In a small group, it was okay to just follow the latihan without thinking much about what was correct or not.

Without those inhibitions we learn from our own experience, which is actually the only valid reality. When I was introduced to Subud I was about nineteen and I was living with my sister in an apartment in Aspen. A friend of Margaret Albouy, who was at that time one of the two Subud women members in Aspen Colorado, came from across the hall with a book, *Concerning Subud*. I sat down, read it and said to myself, "This is interesting stuff, that sounds pretty good to me." Then I forgot about it, or I guess I didn't know that it was available in Aspen at the time. It sounded more like something that was happening elsewhere in California.

So I put it aside, but now and then it would come up. I would meet someone who would say this or that about this new movement, Subud. A lot of people said that they wished they could be part of it, but they didn't want to change their life style. They didn't want to change their ways and they thought they would have to.

What finally happened was that I went to the post office one day. I had received this big soggy cardboard box. It was just about falling apart it was so wet, also huge, about two feet by one foot or so, tied together with strings keeping it from totally coming apart. "What in the world could this be?" I said to myself, and I took it home. When I opened it, it turned out to be a box full of very ripe peyote buttons. I still, to this day, don't know who sent it. I never found out.

My sister and I sliced the peyote and dried it. It was hanging on strings all over the place because there were hundreds of those buttons. When it was dry, we took it over to two friends who were notorious dope heads, and we decided to have a big group of people over. We would just use all this peyote until it was gone. It took us three days to go through it all, but we did it.

It was then that I met Saul, who later became my husband. It was on the second day that he came over and took some peyote with us. In the course of the evening I looked at him and this light was shining out of his forehead. It was like coming out of his third eye. I thought he was Christ. I really did. I had never seen that in a human being before and I felt there was something really different about this guy. So I went home with him that evening and I have lived with him ever since *(she laughs.)* I had known him just one day right! That's pretty amazing when you think of it. Incredible.

I wonder if he even remembers this . . . He didn't know all this was going on. That light coming right out of his third eye. It was very powerful. I was quite stunned. Then, I found out that he was in Subud and I thought, "Ah so," I connected the two things. It seemed to me that Subud was the reason for that light. I guess it was only a little while after this that we went to L.A. to visit friends in Subud, Lariswati and Victor. We stayed with them. I sat outside the latihan there and felt a great deal of warmth and lightness.

I remember walking down the street after one latihan and seeing a very solemn young woman standing there, on the street corner, really into herself in a deep, dark place, and this smile came over me. I had been fed by the energy I picked up in latihan so I looked at her and smiled. This helped her, and me too. I could see that there was something in the latihan, something so powerful. That was pretty much when my probation started I guess.

When we went back to Aspen I contacted Margaret Albouy, and we talked about drugs and drug experiences. She was telling me that drugs had been a frequent experience for people in Aspen, it seemed like people were searching for something else outside the accepted traditional ways of religion, so they looked in that direction.

I felt all along, throughout my young adult life, that I really needed something else, some real connection with the spirit, something that would not be external to me but which came from within and answered my need. During my probation period everyone always asked me, "Do you have any questions about Subud?" But I never did, and I still don't. To me it has always been just the experience.

We were a group mostly made of young people recently opened. We just wanted the experience and no restrictions. There was nothing with which to compare and judge our experience, and no one to set up rules of behavior. That was the attraction. I don't think we missed anything from not having all that information, all those directives. In this way, we found out for ourselves and it was much more powerful and real. And actually I don't think we were doing much that was wrong or unorthodox— except smoking a little grass here and there.

In my own case it was a terrifying experience that made me stop smoking marijuana. I already had two daughters and I was starting to notice that, instead of the ecstatic, freeing, enlightening experience I had always had before, using marijuana often brought on fear and anxiety about my children. Mostly I worried about their physical welfare, feeling that I was failing them and that something drastic would happen to them while my attention was taken away. But it was difficult for me to give up what I considered a sacred tool, an ally that helped me see clearly and be visionary.

One day, an atheist friend who was visiting me from France, asked:

"How can you attribute such qualities to a weed?"

"Well it makes me feel so good and loving towards others. It puts me into a non-judgmental space. How could it be bad when it gives me such wonderful insights and makes me feel closer to God?"

"You know," my friend answered, "the Devil is very seductive. He often tells the one he is trying to win over that he is God, or that he comes from God. He knows how to show only godly qualities when he wants to."

I looked at her in total disbelief, "God? The Devil? I thought those terms would never pass your lips, that they were ridiculous and repugnant to you." She answered that she was actually surprised to have used those metaphors. The impact was even stronger because of her surprise. It was like she had been made to speak.

I had to flirt with the devil one last time however and when I did, I went into a place of such darkness, coldness and isolation, I thought I would never be able to come back to the world of my fellow humans and experience their warmth ever again. I felt that I could never be whole again on this earth. The fear and anxiety was so intense I believed I would lose my mind, be lost in darkness forever. I desperately prayed, asking to be brought back to the world of the living, promising I would never touch the stuff again. And it happened; I came back whole.

For me I guess, what made me stop was the testing about drugs with Bapak in L.A. He announced that we were going to do some testing about drugs and it was like a nightmare. Having no guidance, we often had to find out the hard way.

When I was doing my probation, the Aspen group was doing the latihan in a coke kiln, so I guess the probationers from that period were the kiln babies. I was not opened in the kiln though, but at Margaret's house.

The charcoal kilns everyone from Aspen mentions were made out of bricks, about fifteen feet tall and shaped like beehives, about fifteen feet in diameter so there was plenty of room for a small group to do latihan. The only light came from the opening of the entrance and a hole at the top of the cone. The probationers sat in a meadow surrounded by Aspen trees outside the kiln.

There is another way in which the latihan seemed to work strongly for me. I had never used birth control and I had been sexually promiscuous for about three years. I don't know why, I never thought I would get pregnant. Two weeks after I lived with

Saul I became pregnant. At the time, it seemed to me that my first child had been waiting around until she could be born in the best of conditions. I think she was very wise waiting on the sideline until the time was ripe!

My memories of doing the latihan in Aspen are of having no organization, no rules, not even a schedule really. We were pretty open about when and where and how we did the latihan. My experience at the time of my opening was very subtle and it continues to be like that for me. I wasn't sure whether anything had happened and I have found out since that it's pretty common. It was actually after Margaret came back from seeing Prio in Denver that I think I really got opened. For some reason I was really zapped then and knew for sure. A big part of the obstacle to my receiving was that I was using drugs. The life force couldn't make it through; something wasn't being penetrated.

After that things really started to happen. I had strong experiences. I realized then that there were different sorts of experiences in Subud and that it might be to my benefit to go see Bapak, to hang out with people who had been doing the latihan for a long time and were really good channels for the life force. That made sense to me.

I remember that at one point, three other women and myself got in a car and went to Chicago to see Bapak. I had two children, Elvina and Richmond. Richmond was four months old, and we all got into this van and drove across country. It was such an interesting experience. Not always easy, but a strong experience. Later we moved to Carmel Valley and I experienced a large group with all its advantages and disadvantages.

It's often easier for people to notice the working of the latihan in their lives than during the latihan itself; they might not necessarily get much during latihan, but they see their lives changing, their vision of the world changing, they take a different route, not really knowing why. Was it like that for you?

Drastically so. During latihan I thought, "Well I don't know what that's all about." I skipped and sang and was quite content with that. I wasn't really an intellectual person at that time. Now the story continues to unfold, and at this time in California there is a real maturing coming into the latihan. I notice it in a new way now since I have left Subud for several years. There were many disappointments for all of us at some time or other.

It was never my own latihan that I questioned. It was what was going on in the group. Things that were tested that were totally incorrect. How could it be that people who were supposedly receiving from God could be so flawed still?

In answer to someone's question, Ibu Rahayu once explained that it can happen that something tested by helpers could turn out to be wrong because we are not yet totally free of nafsu (passions and desires,) not yet a clean and direct channel to receive from God. So we do our best.

Anyway, at the end of the Carmel Valley group, when things were really falling apart and we couldn't afford to keep the Subud house, there came a time of great change and transition. A lot of people were moving into Monterey. The group there was becoming stronger, so they wanted us to be centered out there. However, in Carmel Valley we owned this wonderful property and were wondering why not continue to use it? So we did this testing about what to do and what I got was myself on a path. I was walking along the path and the path stopped, and there was nothing to say for it. Not that there was a good reason for the path ending there or anything. It was just what it was, a path ending. And indeed it has been true; it ended there. To me, what came to an end was participating in the group in the way I had. That really stopped.

The experience of Subud and the latihan still profoundly guided my life, but what I did then was channel my energy into art school, becoming an artist, which is what I had 'received' as my work years before. You can say that I still loved Subud. I might have been in fact living it more than ever while not doing the latihan.

The latihan is not just the latihan, it is your life, and once opened, you are always opened. I remember Ondine saying (I really loved what she said,) that she could not understand people who had totally given their lives over to this thing called Subud, dedicated their lives to going to all these meetings. "I always thought that the latihan was supposed to serve your life, not the opposite," she added. So, it's a balance. But I guess some people need to do that for their life.

We need those devoted people since we are not doing that organizational part ourselves. Someone needs to do it if there is to be Subud in the world. People have work that is different at different times in their lives. We should be thankful to those who do Subud work just as they should be thankful because through that work they get what they need. They grow with it.

That's true and it's right for them. Coming back here to Mendocino has been really important for me because I hadn't done latihan for years. You are in the best possible world; you stay clear of all the difficult stuff by always remaining in small groups.

It may be that, when there is no difficulty, the growth is slower, that being a bunch of friends having fun just doing latihan together lets us get away with avoiding the difficulties that might be necessary for our growth. When there is not much organization and everything remains spontaneous it might be that we cannot get very big.

But I continue to think that it may be the answer. I know you could never live anywhere but in rural areas and it's right for you. My daughter Elvina says that she would only get opened by the people who came from our small early group. It's the people that she trusts and they feel like a center to her, not unlike the center that she has within herself. To me it seems like it has come full circle. I think that maybe I could go back to a group now. I was thinking last night that the place from which I would go back to the latihan is so different now.

When I was in our small group in Aspen I didn't want to be part of a big group, but now I feel that it would be on my terms no matter where. I would know what is right and good for me and wouldn't bend to meet someone's expectations, trying to measure up to some outside idea. It's true that in a group there are a lot of forces that come in and try to confuse the issues, but I am so much stronger now.

MEN FOREVER ON THE FENCE

Redmond and Charles (U.S.A.) interviewed in LA. (CA.)

*"The mind is caught dealing with what's unreal while
the inner spirit deals with reality."*

Bapak

*Redmond and Charles were reluctant about being interviewed.
Redmond would not advance an opinion except in jest. I teased him
about not wanting the truth about himself to be revealed. He agreed
that it's in his nature not to let himself be subjected to inspection.*

*Charles and Redmond were together when I questioned them.
What they have in common is their need for privacy and their
disrespect for established authority. They are distrustful of groups,
critical of humans and modern society flaws and foibles. Redmond
refuses to be serious about anything; Charles has always chosen to
live in isolated natural settings and prizes independence and self-
sufficiency above all.*

*Nevertheless I got a few facts from Redmond when I didn't
have my tape recorder for he was unwilling to speak into it. I have
had to put those facts down from memory. Redmond said he was
opened in December 1965, some months after his wife. He observed
from afar before making that commitment.*

*When he decided to get opened, he and his friend Norman
(now Saul) drove over Independence Pass to Denver because there
were no helpers in Aspen. On the way back Redmond and Norman,
who was nicknamed Spider at the time, smoked some dope (no one
had told them they were not supposed to.) Spider asked Redmond,
"Did you feel anything during the latihan?" and Redmond after
taking a toke answered, "No, but I sure do now!"*

*Redmond tells me that it was common practice to come to
latihan stoned, or after having had a couple of beers. No one was
aware of experiencing any obstruction because of it. The
psychedelics, up till that moment, had been everyone's way to open
up to spirituality.*

He says that he resisted being part of a Subud group, just as he always resisted being part of any kind of group, and probably always will. The groupie mentality irritates him and he doesn't think that Subud is free of it. From his point of view hierarchies were established from the beginning according to who was the closest to Bapak and Ibu, who had lived in Indonesia, who had had the honor of receiving Bapak and his retinue in their homes, etc.

Redmond joked about the 'hall-of-famers' (the oldest, supposedly wisest members), the perpetual crisis cases, the groupies, the Regional, National and International Helpers taking themselves so seriously, the inner politics of chairmen and committee members, etc. He was greatly relieved when his friend Charles got 'opened' in Topanga Canyon in 1970 after more than five years of sitting on the fence. He had someone to joke with, someone who shared his blasphemous sense of humor.

Charles remembers that he encouraged his wife to join Subud, made sure she got to latihan on time, drove her there before she learned how to drive. But he had no interest in it for himself. He said he was not particularly impressed with the Subud organization.

What Charles remembers most about the early Subud days is that his friend Spider (Norman, then Saul) was outraged, during latihan, about another member whose farts smelled of garlic. This man considered garlic a potent healing food and he ate quantities daily.

He also recalls the time when a man who had been in Subud for a while, Steve, went into crisis and how his arrogant behavior was deflated. He became cursed with absolute indecision in the face of every minor choice he had to make. Later, after Steve came back from a visit to Indonesia, he thought that the spirit of the man whose blood had saved him from sure death possessed him. (He had a transfusion after a serious attack of typhoid fever.) How he ranted and raved until the group arranged for him to live in an apartment above the house where Charles lived with his wife. The helper who was sent from L.A. to keep an eye on Steve was of little help, Charles recalls. As far as he could tell the helper was also in crisis.

Charles also remembers a certain latihan on an isolated

*orchard farm on the Colorado plateau above Paonia where a
Subud brother was care-taking. Steve was out of the heavier crisis
state by then, but still malfunctioning. He was doing the latihan
in a barn with a few brothers and yelling at the top of his lungs,
"God help me, God help me." A non-Subud member happened to
be walking by and yelled back, "Help yourself, you fucker." And
everyone burst out laughing.*

*Finally Steve, after one of his 'receivings,' sent a letter to Bapak
asking him one single question: "Could my name be Henry?"
From what Charles and Redmond recall, the letter that came back
from Indonesia in answer contained an initial, which wasn't H.
Nevertheless, Steve called himself Henry from then on.*

*Charles recalls doing latihan in the strangest places: the
beehive-shaped coke kilns with the caved in roof, mosquito ridden
in the summer; the tent in the high meadow, the forest at times,
different members' cabins and houses; a music school; and finally
the one room cabin with the gigantic stove right in town where
passers-by could hear the pretty hectic goings on. In those days we
had some fairly rowdy and loud members in the group, many
crisis cases coming through.*

*Charles kept imitating people saying, "I have received this, I
have received that . . ." which became an excuse for all their
idiosyncrasies.*

*In 1966 the small but fast growing group was in bad need of
a man and a woman helper. The only thing the group could figure
out to do was to send all the members' names to Bapak. The answer
was not long in coming and to everyone's bewilderment two new
members, a man and a woman, were chosen by Bapak to be helpers,
instead of the more experienced, stable members. Redmond was
one of them. So new members could be opened in Aspen. And they
were . . . by the dozen!*

*When I asked Redmond what had been the benefits of Subud
for him he answered:*

"Subud has made me a better human being, more opened to
my fellow human beings except for those who live across the way
from us, and those on the other side, those in far-away weird

countries, and those of different shape and color and anyone different from me . . .

When I asked him to tell me about his beginning in Subud he answered:

In the beginning there was a word . . .

Redmond's wife had come in the room to get us for lunch, and she said:

I think you might be the one in crisis, you have been in crisis for twenty-five years.

To which Redmond answered: that's the effect Subud had on us old members.

Years later, there was a gathering in L.A. during which Ibu Rahayu for the first time did 'testing' with men and women in the same room. Soon after, I had this dream:

Ibu Rahayu had given us new directives. Now the awareness testing was to be done, not just with men and women in the same room, witnessing each other, but at the same time in mixed groups.

Men and women were waiting for someone to take the lead and start the testing. Ibu had designated a group of seven women, waving her hand vaguely and saying that anyone of us could do the job. I didn't mind doing it, but I didn't want to be the first. All seven women felt the same so that everyone waited, until finally a man took the lead, the most unlikely man in my eyes, a jester, never taking spiritual matters seriously and often a bit sacrilegious in his sense of humor. It was Redmond.

I was sure that the testing would be sort of a joke with him leading. In fact, he led with reverence and in total silence. The testing questions were not expressed out loud but everyone could hear them.

A LONG STORY IN SUBUD

Lariswati (U.S.A.) interviewed in Spokane (WA.)

The conflict within must be lived gently for it is the training of the soul; things that are oppressive cannot be

*wrenched out of the self, for along with them, we would
tear out our heart.*

*It was during the International Congress in Spokane that I
asked Lariswati to tell me her story. I had known her since the
early Aspen days. Her husband at the time, Victor, had lived in
that town and they made a habit of going back to visit fairly
regularly.*

*We talked, sitting by the river during one of the mild Spokane
evenings, watching an exceptional sunset while some children played
by the bank and people in small groups strolled or sat around to
talk surrounded by the golden light. As she started her story I recalled
these words from Bapak, Life is to our true self what our dreams are
to our physical reality: the dream of our true self.*

My coming to Subud is a long story. In my life at that time I
had been searching, ever since high school. I was brought up
Protestant. I was dating a man called Peter Filipelli and he was
Catholic. After high school he went to university and we started
seriously dating so I studied catechism. I had arguments with
the priest about everything. This didn't do it for me.

I thought I would find what I was looking for in travels, so I
started traveling, but I found that wherever I was, I was still with
myself. Then I thought I would find it in fame and fortune so I
pursued an acting career doing TV and commercials. I worked
in three movies, but I hated that scene.

I was dating a musician at the time, Richie, who played with
the Shelleyman Band, and my girlfriend was dating the bass
player. They wanted us to come to San Francisco to watch them
play. But I didn't want to go near that city. Well one night, Sandra
and I both felt compelled to go to San Francisco. So we packed,
unpacked and repacked and finally ended up in the Triumph
sports car, driving to San Francisco. One of my shoes was missing,
nothing matched, but the guys were glad to see us. At one point
I said, "You know Richie, I have a friend who went to law school
here, and he really loves this town. Why don't we invite him to
the club to be our guest?" He said, great.

I tried calling information but there was nothing under that name. Richie had to rehearse that afternoon at the Black Heart. You walked out the door of our hotel and into the Black Heart, so I went down to look in the phone book because I didn't trust information. No Filipelli. I thought he might have changed his name to Phillips. Nothing.

After the rehearsal, we were walking that ten feet back to our hotel when Richie asked if I had been able to get in touch with my friend. I said I hadn't, but as I looked up there he was, in front of us, Peter himself. I yelled, "Flip Filipelli." That is how we called him in those days. "What a coincidence!" He and Harun Tarantino had been at the restaurant of the hotel where we were staying, but we never ate at that restaurant. They had ordered but then decided to leave and go across the street to eat. It was at that moment that we met them. They accepted the invitation to the club.

When Richie was playing his tenor sax I didn't want anyone to talk, but Peter was asking all kinds of questions. I got madder and madder and when he insisted I said, "Do you really want to know what I think? Well. I think that people can't face the fact that there is no soul and that when they are dead they are really dead. That's why they keep searching. It's a crutch."

And suddenly in my head, there was this great big quiet, right there in the jazz club. It frightened me to death and I started to cry. He asked what was the matter and I said, "Please, get me out of here. I just lost my mind."

He answered, "You haven't lost your mind, you just found yourself."

"Sure, sure, sure, get me out of here," was my answer.

"I asked you earlier if you ever read anything about Subud, have you?" he asked.

I had never read anything, but I said, "Oh, I might. Who is the book by?" (*She laughs.*)

He went on to say he would bring me a book and wanted me to read it, but not to pay too close attention to anything it said. He had things to do but would come by the club at some point.

All the rest of that night—like we went out to get something to eat, then walked across the Golden Gate Bridge to watch the sunrise—I was a witness to what was happening. It was as though it wasn't me it was happening to. I couldn't fathom what was going on and the next day I was still out of it. I told Richie, "Look, that guy is going to come by with some book for me but I can't make it down to the club. Please apologize for me."

Everyone got dressed to go to the club and suddenly I started feeling better. I got dressed and arrived just as Peter did. That's when he gave me the book. So I went up to my hotel room and read the first page. It was Bennett's book and that feeling came over me again only this time I knew what it was.

We contacted the Subud group and I was tested. They received that I had been spontaneously opened. They opened me officially, but I guess I was opened when I was sitting next to Filippelli the first time, even though with my mind I didn't know. He must have been feeling the latihan as he talked and my soul was asking for help.

I knew Lariswati had been friendly with Ibu, Bapak's first wife. I asked her, "How did you meet Ibu?"

The first time it was in Mexico. After one of Bapak's visits we did testing in Hope Street. Then Bapak and his group went to Mexico City and a friend of mine said, "Let's drive down there." So we did. I had been opened about three years at that time and I wanted to get my real name. We were at a private home in Puebla and I was trying to come up with ten names beginning with L. Finally, the tenth name I put down was Lucia. Latihan was going on and I didn't get a chance to give my list, but someone passed me on the stairs and said, "Lucia."

I didn't have much more contact with Ibu then, but my latihan was very strong right from the beginning. When my friend and I came back from Mexico in my car we saw a man lying on the road right by Ralph's market on Sunset Boulevard. She was driving and slowed down the car. I told her to stop. The guy might need some help. She answered, "Don't be ridiculous, it's just some drunk. He had a fight or something, besides, I am smoking a joint." Soon after, I was arrested for hit and run.

Bapak came back and stayed at the Lakes' house. I went there but couldn't get to see him. Ibu came out by herself when I was waiting and asked, "Who are you?" "I am Lucia," was my answer. She told me to come with her. She took me into her bedroom and she said, "I want you to unpack my suitcase." The suitcase was locked.

"I can't," I answered." It's locked."

"Why did you lock it?"

"I didn't."

"Then open it."

"I can't."

"Why did you lock it?"

Then I realized she was falsely accusing me, just like I had been accused of the hit and run. I had been found guilty of the hit and run and was facing up to ten years or something like that. That's why I wanted to see Bapak or Ibu. I wanted to do a last latihan before my final sentencing.

Anyway, Ibu made me so angry that I got up from the floor and stomped to the kitchen yelling, "What is she doing? She is accusing me when I didn't do anything." Anyway. I finally got to see Bapak and he told me that when I would go for the sentencing the next day I was to look the judge right in the eyes and visualize Bapak's face. He added that I would be back to continue serving Ibu by one o'clock. I did what he said and got away with a small fine. That was when I got to know Ibu, and every time Bapak came back I was right there serving her.

I told Lariswati about another suitcase story Olivia had recounted about Ibu trying to make her fit more stuff into a suitcase that was already too full and asking her to close it. Insisting upon it although it was impossible. Ibu obviously had something about testing people with suitcases! I asked: "Was Ibu often willful and capricious like that?"

Yes. She wanted every piece of her hair collected. She didn't want any left in the sink or on the floor, and then she would save it all. I never understood that. It was maybe because of witchcraft. Probably, in Indonesia, if someone gets hold of a piece of your hair they have all kinds of powers over you.

Anyway, I was always faithful to the latihan, never had any doubts. The latihan always has been the miracle in my life through bad marriages and divorces, through all the drama of life.

The first time I went to Cilandak was during the revolution. We had heard that everyone had to leave Indonesia to go to Australia or New Zealand. But I got a cable from Ibu telling me to come to Indonesia because the other sisters had run away and she needed someone to do latihan with. So I went. I had sent a cable to say I was coming and the cable arrived three weeks after I was already there.

So I arrived at the airport and nobody was waiting for me. There were roadblocks everywhere. I got hold of a taxi and the driver said his father would know where I wanted to go. So I got in and he took me down some streets and finally to his father who listened to me. There was another Cilandak with a slightly different pronunciation that was a mental hospital. I kept saying, "No, no, Subud, Subud." Eventually he understood and got me there.

When I arrived Prio and Bapak walked up to me, and Bapak took me to a room with mosquito netting, even fixed my bed for me. They had been expecting me. That's when Bapak, Prio and Sudarto were sitting up all night in the compound. They did that for a hundred days. So I felt very protected.

Before I knew I was going to Indonesia I had a dream. In the dream I was in a strange place, with these strange things happening and I had this pain in my ear lobe. I was on a plane. Suddenly the plane started to shake and fall apart. I was falling, luggage was flying around me, and the plane started to crash. As I told the dream to my husband, Victor, I said, "One thing for sure, I'll never get my ears pierced."

But I forgot the dream and while in Cilandak I kept begging Haminah to take me to the place where I could get my ears pierced. She kept saying tomorrow, which there, means sometime in the future. But I kept at her and finally got it done. Soon after,

I got a terrible ear infection. Everyone in the compound was trying to put hands on me to ease the pain in my ears, but Bapak said no one was to touch me. Then he wrote his name on a piece of paper and told me to burn the piece of paper, put the ashes in a glass and drink it. And the pain went away; it was wonderful. I was lying there between sleep and waking in the morning and all of a sudden remembered my earring dream. I said,

"Oh my God, I pierced my ears!"

I kept asking Bapak if I should leave but he kept telling me that I could stay as long as I wished. I had to decide for myself when to go home. I got a letter from Victor saying, "Remember baby, it's your 33rd birthday. Time to be crucified." He didn't remember the dream of course, but this letter got me really worried.

I hadn't booked my ticket home. So I went over to Usman in a panic and he talked to Bapak. He came back telling me that Bapak said I could take a boat home, but also that I could stay as long as I wanted, that Victor could join me and we could get married on the compound.

Another incidence was when Prio and Brodjo took me into town and we were going to visit Dr. Subrodjo. I think he was the Minister of Religion in Indonesia at the time. We pulled out up in front of his house and I said, "Oh, I have been here before." I described the high red ceilings and bookcases going up but they told me I couldn't possibly have been there, that I never was in the country before. How would I know those things? Then I remembered that this had occurred in a dream. All the details matched the reality though. These kinds of coincidences and synchronicities kept happening.

Bapak told me I should write my stories but I never did. Then Ibu asked me to write to her and I never did. When I would see her after a long time she would point to me at the airport and say, "You didn't write." Then Sharif wanted me to write the story about Rochanawati, Bapak's stepdaughter, but I know I won't.

Tell me about it.

I never got to meet Rochanawati. The day I arrived she had retired into her room. It was the beginning of Ramadan and at that time they were building Bapak's house. There was a partial roof already up. Tuti, Bapak's granddaughter, and I used to go up there and sing songs. She was eighteen, very shy and wanted to learn American songs. The other night she actually started singing the songs here in Spokane. She remembers those songs. She said she never forgets anything. Anyway, on the roof one night, she said to me, "You know, those who are pure of heart get to see Muhammad on the first day of the New Year."

The sun was setting on the day of the New Year and I was sitting there. Everyone coming in asked if Rochanawati was going to be joining us. Without thinking, from the top of my head I answered, "I don't think so. I think she is reaching the peak of her crisis." I didn't know what I was saying.

I was the only foreign person there so I had a table upstairs right outside my room where I was eating my meals. While I was sitting there, Tuti came out and she said, "Lucia, can you go get Bapak quickly. I started down, but Bapak was already coming up the stairs. Rochanawati had just passed away and everybody started rushing to get everything ready. The youngest children were crying on the upstairs porch of the guesthouse. That's where Bapak and Ibu were still living at the time, and I didn't know what was going on.

So, I tried to sit down and feel quiet next to the children who were crying. As I got very quiet the most beautiful fragrance floated by, like delicate flowers and eucalyptus oils and the children stopped crying. Then the fragrance went away.

That night everyone was up all night building the bamboo hut to cleanse the body. I went up on the roof of Bapak's house by myself, and the same fragrance floated by me again. I walked to all four corners trying to smell where it came from but I couldn't figure it out.

I was walking back to my room and had to pass the dump, which was right outside of Sudarto's house. There I smelled the fragrance again. I slept like a log, better than I had ever slept before. When I got up in the morning I went to Usman and asked to book reservations on the day of my birthday.

At that point I knew that it was the fragrance of Rochanawati that I had smelled, and everyone I talked to knew right away. Just yesterday Tuti was telling Sharif, (her husband and the World Subud Association Chairman at the time of the interview), the story and she actually remembered it better than I did.

After that I was walking back when I met Bapak and he asked, "So, what have you decided?"

"Well, I booked reservations on my birthday," I answered.

"Good," he replied. He asked the exact time I would be on the plane and for me to know that Bapak would be praying for me. Whether the prayer would be for easy passing or what, I was left in the dark about it.

The flight to Singapore was uneventful but as we were taking off for the next leg of the journey the tower signaled for the plane to stop. The luggage door hadn't closed. Had the tower not seen it, it could have been like in my dream: the air getting it, the plane shaking, and the luggage and everything falling off. Victor said he never saw anyone so happy to get home.

I hadn't been to a World Congress since Cilandak and it is wonderful that by the grace of God I can be here . . . even though I am complaining about not getting enough sleep.

OTHER BEGINNINGS

SEARCHING FOR GREATNESS

Harlan M. (U.S.A.) interviewed in Menucha (OR.)

"The boundary between life and death will disappear. It will simply be a transition from not being to being. You will find that in the not being you are. By contrast, very often in your ordinary state of being, you are not. Because you are not aware of yourself, you are not aware of your life. So even though you live, actually you don't exist."

Bapak

It started out in 1957. I lived in Chicago and I got bored with my existence in the city. I began to feel sort of mechanical and lifeless, so I decided to go out searching for greatness and to move to the South West. I quit my job, got in my car, and drove to Tucson, Arizona. When I got there I looked around and said, "Well, this is where I am supposed to be, but what am I supposed to do now? Well, okay, let's find something to join that is kind of fun."

So I joined the Tucson Space Club. In November of 1958 I went to a meeting of the Space Club and was met by a member who said to me, "Ben, have you heard about Subud?"

"What's Subud?" I asked.

"Well it will awaken the Christ consciousness in you," she answered.

"I wonder what on earth she means by the Christ consciousness," I thought.

She told me that I would have to sign a little piece of paper and in three months they would go ahead and give me the contact in this thing called Subud. So I said, "Oh okay!" And like a dutiful little boy that I was, I went ahead and signed the piece of paper.

In December of that year, a helper came from Los Angeles to speak to us about Subud. He came in this room that was full of people who all were members of either an ism or following an IST: Sufism, spiritualism, theologist, scientologist, etc. If it ended in IST, they were there! And they all had their own little thing that they wanted Subud to prove. And if Subud would prove their particular thing they would join, if not, forget it.

So the helper sat there in the midst of this room full of fifty basically hostile people and held his own magnificently. I was sitting close to him, wanting to send him strength and help him in doing this. I didn't know what a helper was, and didn't even suspect there was such a thing but finally I asked, "Mr. So and So, you have given us thorough explanations but can you give us a physical description of what happens when people do this thing that you call the latihan?"

So he gave me a physical description of people sitting, and then standing around in a circle and somebody saying, "begin," and everybody starting to move spontaneously, nobody directing them. So I said to myself, "This sounds like something that might be really worthwhile because nobody is telling you what to do except God."

Another month or two went by and several helpers came to Tucson to open the people. One of them said, "Now, I want you to know that if any of you come out of curiosity it won't do you any good because you won't receive anything." So I went out by myself and questioned myself, "Am I going into that just out of curiosity?" and the answer was no. I asked a question, "Almighty God, do you really want me to join this thing called Subud?" I got really quiet and deep inside myself where I was used to finding answers; I heard a yes. So I joined Subud.

So you were already pretty much in touch with your spiritual side, your inner self?

I think so. One of the reasons was that I had an experience when I was seventeen years old. I saw what would happen to me several days in a row, several weeks before it happened. And you know there are no atheists among the apostles after going through an experience like that!

I went through my search. I got involved in spiritualism. I read Gurdjieff and Ouspensky, and by the time I got into Subud I had gone back to being a more or less regular Episcopalian. But then the latihan came. Somebody said "Begin," and I felt like a little boy. I sat on the floor and started playing, and singing a song to myself, and then I started crawling around on my hands and knees. I wanted to sing out loud but I stopped myself. As soon as I stopped myself, somebody sang the notes I was going to sing. That is how my latihan started. I thought, "Oh don't stop that! Sing when you need to when you are in latihan." They haven't been able to shut me up ever since then . . .

I have always been interested in music. As a boy I sang well and had true pitch.

Ever since I was thirty-three years old Subud has been more

than half of my life. I am in my seventies now. In my own way I have been faithful to the latihan. I am sure all of us would say that. I have messed around with a few other things, things I shouldn't have messed around with maybe, but I never really got away from the latihan.

I can't imagine what my life would be like without the latihan, but I have no way of knowing. God's power is unlimited and guides everybody, those who receive the latihan and those who don't.

I was made a helper within the first year. They sent a letter off to Bapak saying, "Here is somebody who can travel around, who is free and can help people in other places." So Bapak said, "That will do."

Bapak made me a helper in a similar way, before I was ready.

I want to answer a question you asked me earlier about the Subud organization. I think that any organization always depends on the sincerity, the dedication, the devotion and the energy of the people who run it. It also depends on the willingness to forgive people for their mistakes. There will always be mistakes, it's inevitable, but if you let mistakes harden your heart the game is lost.

I AM NOT GOING INTO ANY ROOM TO GET OPENED

Arifah (France) interviewed in Spokane (WA.)

Translated from French

"Money has a life and a desire to be used in a better way, its usefulness being for the purpose of people living better lives. All the people. We must understand the heart of money and talk to it, ask it what it wants. Ask ourselves: how do I give life to people?"

Dr. Hattori

My spiritual story really starts when I was twelve, on the day of my First Communion. It was traditional in the Lourdes region in France, for young girls to leave the room during the family banquet that happened after the ceremony, and escape toward to the chapel where the communion service had taken place in the morning. There, the young girls offered the flowers they had received to the Virgin Mary. They made this gift of flowers, each one in turn. Like others I went to see the Virgin and prayed to her for my parents and my godmother. Suddenly, as I opened my eyes, I saw the statue leaning towards me and smiling. I got scared. I left running. I didn't know what had happened to me.

I didn't know what it was all about and I never told anyone, until I met my first husband. I met him while I was studying in Paris. He was a refugee from Austria who had fled from the Nazis during the war. He was very intelligent, fifteen years older than me. Needless to say I was in total admiration. We became close friends. For me he was like my father but with many more diplomas: he had been to five universities. During all the years of my studies I would see this man, then lose sight of him, then he would show up again, then I would lose him again. I admired him so much that eventually this admiration transformed into romantic love.

When I went to Paris to finish my studies he said to me, "You know nothing about life. You have been totally protected by your parents." It was true. I didn't know what money or work was, nor what a salary meant. At my parents' place everything was produced right there. They had a great big farm. We made our own bread, our own wine. We lived on the edge of a river that came from the mountains. There was salmon and all kinds of fish. I was the last of seven children. My mother had adopted four from her brother because his wife had died giving birth. So we were eleven children at the table every day, plus all the farm hands and workers for the plantation. My mother, my aunt, my godmother, etc spoiled me to death.

When I arrived in Paris to stay with another aunt I really didn't know anything about life obviously. I finished my schooling and took a first job as an employee of the Agip. My Austrian friend and his family started a small enterprise. He told me that

I needed a balance because I was in danger in this life. There was no question of marriage yet.

One day he said that to help me he would send me to London where I would see a certain Mr. Bennett. He gave me the address and a plane ticket. I must tell you that the conditions were such that even that was like a miracle in those days.

So I went to London. It was in 1957. We were still feeling hardship after the war. I arrived at Coombe Springs all alone like a big girl. John Bennett was there in his garden. He had been given this enormous mansion with big lawns.

Bennett said to me, "So you are Miss So and So. Mr. Togonin talked to me about you, and he told me you were ready. You will get opened at three o'clock."

"Ah," I answered, "but Mr. Togonin didn't talk to me about that! You are going to open me? He didn't say anything about that."

"Well," answered Bennett, "don't worry. Take a nap, take a bath and then you will go to the room and I will call my wife."

I told myself, "What? I am not going into any room and getting opened. I will take my ticket and go back to Paris in the same way I came."

I was about to do this when a very nice lady—I remember her very well, she must still be alive in Canada, a fairly large woman—asked me, "Where are you going?"

I said to her, "As you see me I am about to go back to Paris because they want to open me at three o'clock." Can you imagine that, to open me?

She laughed so hard! Then she took my hand, gave me a hug and said, "That's wonderful, you don't know anything obviously, stay and come with me I'll tell you all about the opening of Subud." She talked me into it.

I went into the room that was indicated to me by Bennett and saw three women in this dark room. They asked me if I had taken a bath, if my clothes were clean, then told me to take my shoes off and close my eyes. I thought to myself, "Forget it. I certainly won't do that. I want to know what they are going to do to me." I didn't close my eyes but when they said "Begin," whether I wanted it or not my eyes closed and I fell on my knees. I cried for what seemed to me like hours and I didn't know why I cried. After a while very nice women came to me and I saw a door being opened and they took me out.

Much later my own family took my daughter away from me because they said I was part of a sect. I nearly died of grief, but I trusted God. Two years later I received the address of where she was. They went to court and lost. My sister had my daughter and the court declared that there was no stealing between members of a family!

My daughter had become a communist. When I went to the police about it they laughed at me: it was a communist district. The Caviar Left they call it because most of them had plenty of money. My faith was a threat to all of them.

Subud people are often subject to persecution, especially in some countries. They are like the early Christians, threatening. That is because Subud is saying the truth. We are spoiled; we forget how much others suffer in this world. Someone from the third world said to me once, "In France you will suffer because you are rich and you don't have wars. You have everything you need, but you are spoiled and not grateful." Now we are starting to suffer, but God will protect those who worship him.

Do you know that story about how the Almighty made a young Subud boy invisible when the soldiers were coming to get everyone in the village to kill them? He was left behind although he was right there with the others. Bapak said God made him invisible.

There are many stories like that in Subud. Do you know the one about when Bapak was traveling with the Indonesian ladies to give a conference in England? You know how it was: Bapak walked first with Sharif following him and then came his wife, daughters and grand daughters, etc., all dressed up. In the hotel lobby they crossed the path of an Arab Sheik who stopped in front of Bapak, totally astonished. They recognized each other as Muslims, had a whispered conversation and the Arab asked, "How is it that you have such beautiful women?"

Then, right on the spot, he wrote Bapak a check for twenty four hundred pounds saying, "Here, this is for you because you have such beautiful ladies." Subud really needed that money because we were getting ready to start Anugraha and all that. Sharif took the check and thanked the Sheik.

When they got back to Cilandak they couldn't find the check. It seemed to be lost. So Bapak laughed, "It came, and then it went." Everybody else was upset but not him. Much later Bapak went back to London and ran into the Sheik again. They saluted each other and the Sheik asked if the check had been useful. Bapak answered that he hadn't been able to cash it because it had gotten lost. So the Sheik said, "Oh, you should have told me." And he wrote a bigger check.

When money wants to come to someone, it comes no matter what. I notice that even with my accounts. They often tell me I have much more than I calculated I had, this when I need it for spiritual matters. Even though I keep close track. The mistakes are always in my favor. Money comes. It will come to those who have the right attitude. It wants to come to good people to raise itself to a better level. Miraculous things often happened when Bapak was around or during big Subud events.

Bapak said that often, the lower forces will try to prevent people from getting to the places where a strong purification would happen for them. It was not unusual to encounter major obstacles on the way to see Bapak.

Sure enough! We were three women driving from Aspen, Colorado to L.A. for an International Congress. I had just learned how to drive a few months before and was still very uncertain, but my friends insisted that I should take a turn driving since we had decided not to stop at night. I was six months pregnant with my first child and sound asleep when one of my friends woke me up, handed me a pill to keep me awake and asked to take my turn at the wheel.

I hadn't been driving much more than fifteen minutes, believing we were on a straight road through the desert, when I suddenly, at eighty miles an hour, came upon a sign warning about a hairpin curve. Too late. I was already in the curve and trying to hold the car through it, but I lost control and we went flying through the air, did a complete somersault, landed on the car's nose and started rolling down.

We had actually taken the wrong road and we were in the Grand Canyon, rolling down a gentle slope towards the abyss, but a tree, (the only one in the area) stopped us at the edge of the cliff.

We were in a state of shock as we pried ourselves out of the car (accordion shaped from the impact of the somersault and the tree) and climbed back on to the road. The friend who had been sitting in the back was bleeding profusely from a cut on her scalp, It was dark and cold and we were somewhat delirious, walking in the direction of the last lights we had seen about twenty five miles back. It was better than going toward the unknown ahead of us, we believed.

We had bandaged up our wounded friend with a towel and the bleeding seemed to slow down. We all felt exhausted. My friends wanted to stop and lie down to rest, but I knew we shouldn't because it was too cold and if we fell asleep we would be a danger of hypothermia.

Finally a truck full of Native Americans rescued us and took us to the nearest hospital. After the rangers went to the site and saw the condition of the car, they talked the hospital authorities into keeping us a few days to check about possible internal injuries. But, except for that scalp wound on our friend that needed about fifteen stitches, there was nothing wrong and my baby was well. We got to L.A. just in time for the start of the congress.

It was some years later, during one of Bapak's visits to L.A. that another miraculous event took place to show us how protected we are when we stand in a place of trust and fearlessness. After the talk I was walking with five other women through a gigantic parking lot to get to our car. We were pretty exhilarated from the evening, happy, laughing. We walked two by two because there was not enough room for all of us between the rows of cars. I was in the second row. At one point I noticed a young man walking toward us but didn't pay much attention. When he got to the two friends who were ahead of us he stopped them and said something I couldn't hear. I was in this silly, giggly mood and I pushed them past him laughing and saying, "Tell him we don't want any."

We walked by him and left him there, open mouthed, looking back at us. It was only when we got into our car that the two friends who had walked in front asked, "Did you hear what he said to us?" We hadn't. "He had a gun pointing at us and warned, 'Hand me your purses or I'll shoot you.'" I recalled how dejected he looked when we walked past him and couldn't stop laughing. It might have been his last attempt at burglary!

I have another story, which happened when Bapak sent my husband and I me to live in Australia. They had seven Subud houses in all of Australia. The group we were in had been functioning for thirteen years but there was nothing established, no house, nothing. They did latihan in the Union House, a place where communists met. During latihan I received that I should not do my latihan there anymore. I told my husband about it and he answered that he received the same thing.

It meant that we had to look for some other place. So we phoned all the nice people who had welcomed us at the airport to tell them that we wouldn't be at latihan because we had received not to do it at that place. We added that if they wanted us to, we would find another place. "Well," they said. "You can find us a house if you want." We had both received that at 11:15 the next Saturday we would sign the contract to rent a house. It was very precise.

And that's exactly how it happened. My husband looked in the newspaper. The owner gave us an appointment. At 11:15 on Saturday we signed the papers. Everybody had agreed to go ahead after I had told them about my receiving.

Later Bapak advised us to buy that house. But we didn't. We had to accept the committee's decision. We had no power ourselves. So we kept renting this house instead of buying it and we started five small enterprises. Every week we had to pay the rent for the house and often we didn't have it. That Saturday we had absolutely no money. We all emptied our pockets. We took everything there was in the cash of the enterprises and we just made the rent. But we had nothing to eat from Saturday night until Monday.

A man said, "Well, if we could make a big sandwich for each of us we could hold out until Monday."

"How much do we need for that, about ten dollars, right? Do you have gas in your car?" I asked.

"Yes," he answered.

"Can you take us to the beach?" I asked. And he agreed.

We had been working hard for the enterprises, volunteering all the way. We needed one day off. Sydney's beaches are wonderful under moonlight. We were seven or eight and we stopped at the first beach. There were lampposts all along. I thanked God for having had enough gas and thanked our friend for being so nice as to take us using his last gas. I added jokingly that we would soon receive ten dollars so we could each have a sandwich. While talking I took a bunch of sand and let it run through my hand and suddenly, here was a ten-dollar bill all folded up into a tiny small shape. The beach is six kilometers long there. Nobody could believe that just at this spot there would be this ten-dollar bill.

One time in Sydney I had a vision, during latihan, of forty thousand dollars floating into my opened hands. I believed it probably was some sort of purification because the group didn't really need forty thousand dollars. They didn't want to buy a house and we all lived okay with the profits from our small enterprises at that point. Personally, an American brother had offered my husband and me a small hotel to manage so we had money coming from that. In general we were doing okay.

Then we learned that our national treasurer had committed suicide in Sydney Harbor because he was accused of stealing forty thousand dollars. It made me think of my receiving. He supposedly had opened an account to build a Subud house and put all the money he got from fundraisers and enterprises into it, but the money was not in the account and he was accused at the yearly assembly.

Later my husband offered to reorganize the whole system of enterprises and committee. Bapak said it was good to do it that way. We followed his guidance. While we were cleaning up the office and reorganizing the files I found a bankbook from a savings account. We discovered that all the money was there, all the forty thousand plus interest in some other account we didn't know about. We went to the bank the next day and sure enough, the money was there. Why the treasurer did not tell us about it we will never know.

You always have signs all along, guiding you, if you are willing to see them. We don't have to fear poverty, God will provide guidance and help.

WHETHER TO TURN LEFT TO LATIHAN OR RIGHT TO GO SCORE

Hamilton (U.S.A.) interviewed in Bali (Indonesia)

There is no such thing as a man who is good and a man who is right. The only one who is good and the only one who is right is God Almighty."

Bapak

I first heard about Subud when I lived in Formentera through somebody named Jerry whom I never saw again. He had told a friend of mine, Pietro, about something called Subud. We didn't think much about it but then one day, maybe six months later; Pietro was leaving Formentera to go to Paris to visit his mother. As he left he said he would maybe see Krishnamurti and for no reason that I could think of I said, "And check into Subud also." He said okay and that was that. I heard later that he was opened in Subud but I personally didn't see him again.

By this time I was living in London and a friend of mine came by to visit me. He said to me one day, "I am going to Subud tomorrow, would you like to come along and talk to someone?" I should add that on the way from Spain to England, on the train to Paris, I had read *Concerning Subud* by Bennett. I can't remember how I came upon it. Someone must have given it to me. What you said earlier is true. Many feel that Subud chooses them rather than them choosing Subud. Many of the people who were on the island of Formentera with me at the time are in Subud now. And it's not that we told each other and then joined. We did it separately.

Anyway I went with my friend, spoke to some helpers, signed my name and became a probationer as they called it then. But I left London after a month and went back to Spain. I thought there would not be Subud groups in Spain under Franco. In fact there was one in Barcelona but I didn't know it for it was underground. So I forgot about Subud for a few months, went back to the US. for a one month visit to do a little business. The last word a friend of mine said before I left was, "Don't get caught in the big P.X. (the big shopping center for the US. army abroad)" and I answered, "It will never happen." I never though I would live in America again.

In that month two things happened to me: I met the woman I married and I got opened in Subud. I lived in New Jersey and decided to see if there was a Subud group around. I looked in the telephone book and there it was. I told the helpers I had started my probation seven months earlier in England and asked if I had to wait another two months. They tested, even though I hadn't done everything a probationer should do, and the answer was yes. So I got opened. My opening was kind of quiet. The group was composed of nine or ten men and none of them had been in Subud less than ten years. Their latihans were very quiet. I kept feeling inhibited. Everybody was so quiet in there!

Then I went to New York. There I could make noise . . . I thought I was in the middle of Marat-Sade then! What kept me in Subud was not some powerful experience but mostly it was Bapak. In the early years there is so much imagination! I was involved with a lot of that. A very spacey time full of crisis. My mind would do all kinds of comparing: Zen Buddhism is better. This is bullshit here. This is this. This is that. The mind would do all kinds of things, but having been in Bapak's presence my mind couldn't get rid of him and the feeling that came with him, the specialness and the strength of the force that came with him. That's what kept me there.

I also want to tell you about a little episode that was very powerful for me. It was in 1967. After returning from Europe I rented an apartment in Newark, New Jersey, right across the river from Manhattan with my new young wife. I had gotten introduced to heroin (available by prescription at that time) while living in London and hanging out with musicians. I was using it fairly regularly. I would travel into Manhattan to score. At that time I was always either looking for or trying not to look for heroin. Thus, I did not feel free.

During that period I was opened in Subud, but continued to use heroin. I would drive through the Holland tunnel and would not know until I was through the tunnel whether I would turn left to go to latihan or turn right and head to the Lower East Side to get the heroin.

After perhaps a month of this, I went into the rented latihan space in New York for a group latihan. I was put quickly into a very dark unpleasant state and the words came to me over and over, "If you continue with the drugs this will be the state of your soul." I hated this feeling so much and wanted it to stop, but it just kept coming. After latihan ended, I went home and smashed my glass hypodermic to pieces and aside from one solitary incident later, I never used heroin again.

COMING TO SUBUD THROUGH THE FOURTH WAY

Conversation with Jim, Barbara & Marston (U.S.A.) Interviewed in Menucha (OR.)

"We are part of a universe in which everything is connected to everything, all its secrets are thus available to us if we know where and how to look."

Dr. David R. Hawkins

You are all gathered here because, during the opening circle of this gathering, Jim asked for people who had come to Subud through the Gurdjieff work to please meet with him. Were any of you previously connected or have you just met?

We've just met.

So, how did you make the leap?

(To that question I got more than one answer. Someone answered that they leapt from TM, adding, "quite a leap!" Someone else said it was more like falling into a leap, a third admitted that he was just there to listen in and hadn't made the leap entirely. When I directed my questions to Jim, who had called for this group to come together, he started to tell his story.

I was doing Gurdjieff work in San Francisco in 1974 and met some students of Bennett. We became good friends and compared notes about practices and exercises, pulling out all our secrets and sharing them. They told me about the latihan and said Mr. Bennett had opened them.

Do I understand that he continued opening people after having left Subud?

Jim—Yes.

Marston—It's really all conjecture because before Bennett's death he supposedly wrote a letter asking forgiveness of Bapak, adding that he never really meant to leave and never really left. Who knows the truth of all that?

Bapak said the following in a talk he gave in Vancouver on July 18th 1981:

"One that Bapak happens to remember is our brother John Bennett, who, long before he died, wrote to Bapak and accused Bapak of having come between him and his practice of the work which he had received from his teacher, Gurdjieff. But later, when he had an operation and was close to his death, he wrote again to Bapak expressing his regret at having deviated from Subud and expressing the opinion that actually the latihan kejiwaan of Subud is the only way whereby the jiwa of man can be brought to life and that is the reality of all his experience in the kejiwaan. In another talk, Bapak also said he still had this letter.

Jim—Anyway, I heard about the latihan at that time. Later I met someone in Cloverdale, California who was the editor of the newspaper there, a guy called Hanafi Russell.

Yes I know him well. He was a good friend, but I haven't seen him in years. It's interesting how there seems to be a web constantly being woven around us, connecting us and everything we do. Especially in the spiritual realm. It's like the universe doesn't want us to forget this and it winks at us to remind us.

(Hanafi, the Subud brother we were talking about has died since this conversation, from a sudden heart attack.)

Jim—It's the cosmic joke. Anyway, I was looking for a job. I was a hippie trying to find a little bit of work and Hanafi had put out an ad for a job. I went to apply. He didn't hire me but we talked a lot about spirituality. He inquired why I was applying for this job and why I even was in Cloverdale since I was living in Hopland at the time and it was quite a commute to get from Hopland to Cloverdale. I answered that I was doing Gurdjieff work and that's why I was there.

The Gurdjieff group was in San Francisco but there were plenty of people around Sonoma county and in the Cloverdale area, among them Robert Duropp who was a friend of mine at the time. A name from the past, a fascinating guy. I haven't read his book yet but want to.

Anyway after talking to Hanafi I went to a couple of latihans and sat outside in the Santa Rosa group. I had my back against the wall and listened to these wonderful latihans. Then I had to go back to San Francisco and didn't continue with this connection. I immersed myself more in Gurdjieff work, also studied Buddhism and Sufi practices for many years.

You must have gotten pretty advanced.

Oh very. Anyway, I moved to the Northwest two or three of years ago and one of the first things I did was study a course in Theology. I was studying midwifery and could take anything I wanted to complete the course. I didn't think twice about it and went straight to the Vancouver School of Theology at the University of British Columbia. I developed a friendship with another student, Rohanna Laing.

I was sure you were going to mention her the minute you talked about theology. She also is a friend and I interviewed her last year in Menucha. It's like somebody else is organizing my supposedly random interviews and making connections that are none of my doing.

Jim—That's very interesting, there must be a plan to it all. Anyway, we decided to buy a bottle of wine for a party we were organizing at the University. We only did something as simple as driving to Safeway but I had this overwhelming impression that angels, guarded, protected us. Rohanna was floating down the road, totally absorbed in her own self, and cars were wheeling past us within inches. Getting into the parking lot was a miracle; we were nearly hit three or four times by cars coming in the other direction.

I was stunned into some kind of higher state, and thinking, "Holly cow, we are really protected here." I was not going to say a word because that might have broken the spell. We had survived hell in this one drive, and we still had to get back home from the university after the party.

Later we were talking and Rohanna said, "You know, I think I am always in latihan." And I thought, "Oh my gosh, it has come back to me." I hadn't talked with anyone about latihan for years. She was very open with me and spoke genuinely about her experience. I resolved immediately to be opened. I felt it had come full circle. Actually, sitting outside the latihan hall in Cloverdale those two times, created a memory for me. All Rohanna had to do was trigger it.

Was your opening very memorable?

Jim—Yes, it was as though I was being showered with my own energy and a strong vibration was going through me. I am sure that it was my own life energy. I had this beautiful sense of being rained upon by it. I haven't had this experience since but I've had others.

Strong experiences only happen here and there. We don't seem to be ready to handle them full time yet, or maybe it's a way to keep us interested.

Jim—But I have an impatience about them. What has been happening since is more like seeing how my inner state changes. Objectively, there is nothing. I haven't had another metaphor given to me. The metaphor is just in living. Ever since my opening there has been a progressive shift. I find myself slowing down in my latihan more and more. There was a time when I was aware of the bottom of my feet, more than I had ever been in my life. That's the sort of thing. More aware of my body, more and more aware of the deep flow of myself. Coming out of latihan is always very special to me. I cherished the time before and after latihan.

Marston—How would you relate your experience with Gurdjieff with the Subud experience? Are they very different, are there similarities?

Jim—They are very different and they complement each other at the same time. I think that my latihan is more like my own physical experience, but I haven't learned yet how to work with other people in Subud. I haven't figured out how to give something like that to my Subud experience other than just doing the latihan.

While doing Gurdjieff work I would occasionally have these amazing moments of clarity when things would become incredibly significant and the light would shine. Those are memorable experiences and I have touched a little of that in latihan. I would say that this is where the two experiences come close. Maybe next year I will be able to tell you more about that. However the clarity I receive in my latihan is different. It could be also a question of whom I am at this time in my life, more balanced. The feeling is stronger.

A good question though. I don't mean to make it a cover term but there is a lot to it. I think I am more aware now of what I am doing. If I am scared, if I am joyful, if I am in one state or another I am more truly in it.

Marston—Before the latihan it was maybe more from your head.

Jim—Yes, you are right, more from my head.

Now addressing Barbara: How about you? Do you also have an experience of moving from Gurdjieff to Subud?

Barbara—I got involved with Subud out of necessity. There was no Gurdjieff group where I was and it made this big void in my life. I decided that I would have my baby and then I would get involved with Subud because there was Subud where I lived. Then within five years, I would take my son with me and live in Freemont. But when the five years were up I realized that I couldn't do that.

Marston—How did you find out about Subud? How did you know that you had this choice?

Barbara—Well I had a friend. She and I had known each other since we were twelve and we had followed each other through the years. She lived for a while in Whiteson and was opened in Subud there because the people we had known as teenagers were all involved in Subud. She seems to always be a step ahead of me. When I left to go to Whiteson she said, "Okay. Subud is for you now, not the Fourth Way."

Would you explain the Fourth Way?

Jim—The Fourth Way is Ouspensky work, but it's used pretty loosely to describe the Gurdjieff work also. It came from the book *In Search of the Miraculous*, but also from the book called *The Fourth Way*. Most Gurdjieff groups would call it the Middle Way really.

In what way would you say that Subud and the Fourth Way are similar or dissimilar?

Barbara—All I can say is that in the first six months of Subud I felt like I got more than I had in the four years I did the Fourth Way.

Was your opening a strong experience?

Barbara—My opening was slow. I didn't feel anything particularly. I heard people around me and I thought they were crazy, and that I also was crazy for being there with them. But it grew and grew and grew until there was no mistaking it. It was stronger than doing the Gurdjieff work.

How about you Marston, do you have anything to say about leaping?

Marston—Finding Subud was really a miracle for me. I was running a theater company at the time and I read a book called *The Technique of Silence* by Richmond Sheppard who was a Subud member at the time. In the back of this book was his biography and when I read it, it was like something intriguing was calling.

I was an admirer of Richmond, but didn't take in the part about Subud. This was in LA and I wanted to bring Richmond for a workshop because he had studied with Marcel Marceau and he was very well known.

So I called him and asked if we could arrange for him to give a workshop and performance for my company. He accepted and we had lunch together. There was this strong community feeling as we all sat around the table. Suddenly he said, "I've got to make a phone call. I have to look up this group because I do this thing called latihan and I've got to contact the group."

Since he was the honored expert, anything he did was of great interest to everybody. If he had said, "I got to go do a Gurdjieff thing," we might all be in Gurdjieff today but he said "latihan." So we went to get a phone book for him. In those days not many Subud groups were listed but this one was. So he went and every time he came back from latihan he would say, "Oh it was so great," with such sincerity, we were more and more curious about it.

He is such an actor, and so enthusiastic. More and more people in our group would ask him what it was exactly he did, and he would describe it. Here we were, all mimes, and he was talking about singing and movements and doing the silent thing and spontaneity, etc. To us who did a lot of improvisation it sounded like this incredible gift. We asked, "How do we do this?" and he answered, "You will have to talk to people called helpers and find out about it."

I heard all this but I was managing this company and was up to my ears in it. Never enough time, always too much work, so I thought to myself, "Don't go off on the spiritual path, you really don't need this." So, almost the whole company got opened except me, the director.

One Thursday, they asked me if I wanted to go with them and sit outside. A deep part of me told me to stop resisting. I went. In those days probationers sat outside of the hall. It was in a nursery school behind a Quaker meeting hall and men did the latihan with those little chairs around. Someone said to me, "Take a chair and go lean against the wall over there."

So I leaned against the wall. There was a doctor and this other guy next to me, leaning against the wall also, listening to the latihan in the night. I thought, "This is really weird. What is this and who are those people?" "Just be quiet and listen," they had said to me, so I was quiet but my mind wasn't.

This reminds me of a story, which took place when we did latihan inside this brick kiln, located at the edge of a meadow surrounded by fir and aspen trees, in Aspen, Colorado. The probationers would have to sit or lie in the meadow while we went inside this dark, beehive shaped structure with an opening on the top.

During the summer there were a lot of mosquitoes in the kiln so we would pass around the mosquito repellent and rub it on before going in for latihan. One of the members told us that when she was an applicant, she believed it was some kind of magic potion we were putting on our bodies and that we were going inside the kiln to change shape.

Marston—Lots of imagination in those days!

Anyway, after latihan two helpers met with me. One was a famous architect named Antoine Predock and another was a fellow called Simon. I never heard anybody give such a good explanation of Subud. It was to the point, perfect for me because all they talked about was the simple act of submission to God. They hardly said anything else, neither about Bapak, nor about the organization. I went back home and said to myself, "This is it."

So I continued to sit outside the latihan. After about four times I started feeling the vibration very strongly. I know that sitting outside the latihan you get opened before you are opened. Three months later I got officially opened and became very active in Subud. I have been ever since.

4

HABITS, TESTING, CRISIS or DELIVERANCE

"Consciousness can indeed be investigated. If in actuality the subjective and objective are one and the same as some research has shown, then we can find the answers to all questions by merely looking within humans themselves."

Dr. David R. Hawkins

Most humans are creatures of habit who often choose the paths of least resistance. Procrastination and inaction are central elements of personal routine, unchallenging therefore safe. Content to live entire lives repeating thought patterns and actions in imitation of ancestry, family and community, most people follow paths that have been traced generations before them. Change is undesirable and everything truly new threatens the established ways and beliefs. Whatever creates movement is immediately suspicious because it's going to disturb inaction. To effect change in ourselves we need to have the courage to endure the temporary discomfort of growth, but too often, without verifying that the prevailing ideas and convictions of our society fit our inner nature, we accept blindly what we have been told. Many religions teach that God loves unquestioning faith and that knowledge is dangerous. Many settle for faith instead of personal experience, faith in government, in justice, in society. Some believe they hold the truth and say that they would die for their beliefs— beliefs they consider to be universal. But do they ever try to imagine what those beliefs would be if they were born in Africa, India, Peru or Afghanistan? It would be interesting for them to imagine what convictions they would die for then.

Even when we think that we are not going for all that hogwash, that we are finding alternatives, resisting, protesting, changing things, etc. we spend a lot of our energy reacting against the dominant paradigm rather than finding our own distinctive way of action. I was caught in this reactive pattern of "going against," until I practiced the latihan for a while and understood that only personal experience can create wisdom: there lay the answers for the mystery of my life. This realization was augmented by the excitement of having been given through testing the tools to inquire into the nature of things. I could investigate different possibilities in order to pick the best for me, resolve conflicts, or at least understand the reasons for what I was going through. The process of individuation had begun.

Habit being our most entrenched addiction, many people in Subud got into the habit of testing. We tested about everything— even what color should be worn for the day—until Bapak became aware of this (for it was widespread) and warned us to use testing with discrimination. He advised to test only about matters we could not decide with our mind, or about spiritual matters, but not to use testing as a fortune telling tool.

Ibu Rahayu had told us that the whole of our life could become an education to live in accordance with God's will. So we can use testing to feel how it is when different forces guide us for instance, and practice what we receive in latihan. To be attentive to our inner feelings as we work or interact with our family, friends or colleagues is a form of casual testing. But too much intentional testing would be like bothering God every time we want to do something and asking the Divine to decide on our most mundane activities when our task is to develop that capacity of decision for ourselves.

Spiritual progress is for you, Ibu advises, not for others; the things that can impress others are from the mind. The supernatural powers we may obtain from the lower forces cannot be taken with us after we die. In Subud there is no extraordinary power that can be seen outwardly or demonstrated. Everything is real and can be experienced as a reality in our ordinary lives. Our soul has to develop hands and feet, ears and nose, heart and lungs, etc. In testing, it's the body of our soul that is receiving the answers.

The kind of testing Bapak did with us was more like an investigation of the life force's subtle movements through different parts of our bodies, also of our inner nature, of national characteristics, etc. We looked into the nature of humans tens of thousands of years ago, into the nature of different substances; we felt how it was to be in the company of angels. We tested about true culture, about the strength of our worship, about our promise to God at birth, about the purpose of human existence on earth; we experienced God's love for us, the difference between being bound by cultural beliefs and being truly guided. We learned how to pray for our ancestors, how to cry or laugh for no reason—thus understanding the essence of emotion. Most of those things pertained to a reality that was inaccessible to our physical senses.

Testing is conducted from a place of surrender and trust that gives us direct access to all time, all knowledge, and all abilities. We receive the truth through the awakened eyes of our feet, our hands, etc. We become free from what has been. Moving through the wilderness of a forgotten dream we dance, we sing our answers and speak our truth, receiving the solution we need, the knowledge we seek. We are like strings awaiting the loving touch of the virtuoso, instruments on which the master creates ecstatic harmonies of improvised devotion. In rhythm with the Great Heartbeat we drum splendid realms of possibilities. We stretch into unrehearsed movements that expand our limits and dissolve our outlines, minds no longer clouded with preconceptions.

Testing for me has been a way to stay in touch with my higher self, my deeper inner wisdom. It developed my self-confidence. It gave me faith in myself as I discovered that my inner had the answers to any question I may have, that God had given me the tools to deal with any situation I was faced with, that I had access to high levels of information, the capacity to experience all the possibilities of this earth, but also beyond this earth. More than remote viewing, it was a way to check my relationship to the Divine.

After a while, many Subud members become aware that testing personal questions in order to resolve problems, not only gives a deeper understanding of different aspects of the difficulty, but also, a broad range of possible solutions.

During Subud gatherings and congresses, testing is used to help make business and organizational decisions, to appoint members to different positions. The investigation of emotional, psychological, political, spiritual subjects is also conducted. Some members are opposed to what they call "mixing," which refers to any other practice that would interfere with the latihan. There are many interpretations of what mixing is, ranging from calling on dark powers, shamanism, practicing spiritualism, witchcraft, voodooism, meditating, visualizing, mantra chanting, channeling and even doing psychotherapy. Ibu Rahayu explained that what is considered to be mixing is any practice other than the latihan that would be consciously used in conjunction with or during the latihan.

Testing is also used to find out if it is time to change one's name. Changing one's name is a significant part of the Subud experience. The name given to us at birth seldom is our suitable soul name, it can be a burden, an obstacle to becoming our true self, in some cases a prison. The sound of our true name awakens our inner self and can strengthen places where we have weaknesses, and pull us out of ruts in which we are stuck and repeat the same mistakes over and over. It can move us out of imitation patterns. Little at a time it might free us of our faults. Some people have experienced a great feeling of liberation after changing their names.

Bapak's clarification is that we come to Subud because we are tired of the old house in which we have lived up to that time. The 'house' is dark, crumbling, unsafe, the roof is leaking, the floors are damp, the ventilation deficient. So we want a new 'house'; that's when we feel the need to change our name. The name change may happen more than once, whenever we are finished with one cycle and are ready for another. It was Bapak (and later Ibu Rahayu,) who tested and gave people an initial— the first sound that meets our inner and resonates within when people call our name. They asked the members seeking their true name to make a list of the names starting with this initial that come into their consciousness. From this list Bapak or Ibu would choose by testing.

People in Subud also use testing to find out what is the best place for them to be for their development, if they should move away from where they now live and where to. They may have many places in mind and use testing to find which one is the correct one. Inner growth may result from being in the right place at the right time, and may bring physical as well as spiritual benefits.

In testing it is important to be clear about the question we state; however the wording is not as important as the intention. It is the sincerity and the willingness to accept the answer that counts most. It is best not to test if we do not have the willingness to follow the guidance we will receive should it go against our desires. A testing session might deal with some blockage we have in receiving freely from God, blocks to our personal wisdom. We may wish to experience different emotions, first without the spiritual distance created by the latihan, then with it. We might find out how we express our femininity, our masculinity, what is the difference between force and power, how we misuse our power, how would God have us use it. We can experience how harmony within us will bring harmony to the world; feel how it is when we are filled with the love of God, when the life force flows through all our senses. We might benefit from knowing how we feel inside when we are in front of someone telling a lie, or someone who means us well. We may feel the awakening of different parts of our body during a session of awareness testing. We might also want to become aware of how we receive a yes or a no without apparent movement, in our little finger, in our teeth, in our toes, tongue, etc.

The answers might come in words, or in movements and sounds, it might just be a stretching of the body, a sudden rush opening a dammed up place and allowing clarity to come in, a flash of understanding that doesn't come from the mind or heart but from an inner place.

Here are some examples of answers received and interpreted during testing sessions:

"God's will is to feel the joy of life and share it with others. Your God-given mission is to be happy and share your happiness.

To listen is to love.

The way to release your blockage is to let yourself bubble like a spring.

God loves you unconditionally, in movement, in transition, changing, journeying, playing.

When you move without fear you are as big as the universe, and still expanding beyond that.

My creativity: an insect with antennas taking in things from the outside world; a worm that wraps itself into a cocoon to move into dream time until the time comes to grow wings and fly into a new level of life.

The different parts, throat, eyes, legs, arms, heart, breast and sexual organs have their origin in the inner body.

Suffering is resistance—you find God through surrender and acceptance.

Don't turn away from pain, give attention to the feelings around it; but don't create a story about it.

There might never be peace on earth for it would take every human being peaceful; the earth is a testing ground.

True worship is to be 'out of the way.'

Personal power is the power of God.

God is not interested in my projects and accomplishments, only in how I develop my soul through the things I do.

What I have in common with all other beings on this earth is my mortality, as well as my immortality; for me this realization is the peace of God.

I am totally responsible for everything that I do."

Often, in order to bring clarity to an apparently insoluble problem, or when there is confusion about what is the right direction, the right way, path or attitude in a particularly difficult or emotionally charged situation, four questions are most helpful: What is my attitude towards such and such? How would God have it be? What is the obstacle to it? What can I do to remove this obstacle?

Rather than asking what is our right work or talent it might be more useful to experience how we feel when we do our right work.

Through testing I have learned that masses of people who die in terrible circumstances and conditions often have made a contract before birth accepting this sacrifice. When there is some dark, devastating, event on this planet, it is balanced by a huge opening for more light to come in and raise the consciousness of populations.

There always are surprises in testing, sometimes awe-inspiring, or at other times difficult to accept. The answers occasionally come through poetic images and inspired metaphors, psychic revelations, but mostly they are ordinary, down to earth, obvious, sensible answers. Most people I have talked to end up feeling that after a number of years, the testing goes on all the time, every day, in every aspect of life, just as the latihan is manifested in everything they do, in a matter of fact sort of way.

ABOUT CHANGING NAME AND MOVING TO A NEW LOCATION

In the course of my Subud life I often was asked whether Lydia was my Subud name and when I answered that it was my given name, many inquired as to why I never changed it. I simply answered that I didn't feel like it, that I liked the name and it felt right to me. I loved the way the tongue rose to the palate just in the back of the teeth to form the liquid sound of the first syllable, then retreated slightly back to sharply end the second one. It didn't burden me, didn't bind me to any ancestor; it left me free to be who I was. I experienced it as a neutral name for me, and most people liked it. It was not too common. Mainly, a rebellious part of me refused to do what most Subud members did; I was going to be different.

At one point I became curious enough to ask Bapak for an initial, convinced that it would be L. for Lydia, but in fact it was an H. I never went any further with it because, among other things, my husband didn't like any of the names I came up with using that initial. I was not strongly motivated and realized that something in my name didn't want to let me go.

Some fifteen years later, I was testing with a couple of new members as to whether it was time to send for an initial when another helper suggested that I test for myself also. I was curious and decided to do it, but as soon as the question about changing name was stated I began sobbing uncontrollably, struck with grief, this until a clear voice rang in my head, "Your name is an ancient promise." And that was all.

It took me a long time to be able to manage the grief and resume the crying. I had no idea what the sentence really meant and what connection it had to my inability to change my name, but I was determined to let it go at that.

Years went by and the only reminder of the episode was that any time someone asked me whether my name was a Subud one I would burst into tears. I had the vague sense that it had to do with my mother because she was the one who chose my name, but I didn't really know why or in what way.

Finally, I was at the congress in Amanacer when the question of name change was raised in a conversation I was having with some Argentinean helpers. When I tried to explain why I didn't have a Subud name I burst into tears again. Someone suggested doing testing on the subject. Most of the helpers had a very busy schedule of testing to which I was reluctant to add, so I tested on my own, just before the latihan started.

I saw pictures: a deep well, three women in white robes standing by it, one of them my mother, but very young, her hair up in a style I never knew her to use. From the right came a gigantic man wearing a terrifying disproportionate wooden mask. As this giant—decked out in heavy ceremonial garb—walked toward the two women, I froze. I heard a voice shouting an order, "You must kill your mother," or, "You will kill your mother."

It felt as though a dam broke within me and the flow of tears that poured out during the long latihan took me over, washing and cleansing me. There was elation in those tears; there was relief and gratefulness. Something momentous was happening but I didn't understand what or why. I didn't even know for sure whether I was one of the three women in the vision, but I sensed I was.

Later, I did more testing with a group of helpers from many different countries. I think we asked what was the significance of this flow of emotion around my name and I saw my mother, a young woman again, coming towards me, holding a heart in her hands, a real heart, with blood and cut arteries and all. She held it out to me as a gift saying, "I release you."

Every one of the six or seven helpers that were present received the notion that I had been held by a promise but was now released by my mother. A few got a picture of a heart. We all agreed that it was time for me to ask for an initial and believed we could test ourselves for it. I asked Ibu Rahayu in a note if we should; she answered by giving me an initial. This is how I became Riantee.

I had been Riantee for quite a few months when I had this dream about my name:

I am in an exotic place with a group of Subud people. Mardiah, Rohanna S. and I are standing in a huge hall. I have just received four names Bapak gave me from which to choose. (Apparently there was a debate as to whether I should keep Riantee for a name or not.) Someone hands me the piece of paper with the four names and they are all very ordinary French names I have negative associations with.

Those names are unacceptable to me. But there is another piece of paper that is passed around with yet more names for me, The-One-Who-Looks-in-God's-Direction, The-One-Who-Points-To-God's-Direction, The-One-Who-Follows-God. Too difficult for people of my culture to use those long names; they may be for later in my life. I am wondering if I could find out what they are in their original language. The dream leaves me with the dilemma.

A BIG PART IN FINDING WHO I WAS . . .

Carolye (Canada) interviewed in Mendocino (CA.)

"If you follow a human teacher, your own nature disappears and you are no longer yourself. If you follow the teaching of Almighty God, that is, something where you are in touch, you are following that which is within you, your own nature."

Bapak

A big part in finding who I was, was the fact that after four months I found my true name. I never disliked my old name, but I felt compelled to change it.

It's only after I changed it and used it for a while that I could see how much the old name had been a prison for me and burdened me. My old name is the female version of my dad's name—I used to be called Michelle and his name is Michael—and he was so difficult during my childhood that to be able to be free of that was a great relief. It was one of the most powerful things that happened in my life, changing my name. Like in the opening, something in me shifted permanently for the better.

Later, when I decided to find out about my true work and my true talent, it took many sessions of testing which involved many questions every time. To tell you the truth there were only two questions that were helpful, which were the first questions I ever asked: "How does it feel when I do the motions of my true talent?" and the last question: "Should Carolye study languages at this time?" The first one was very helpful because several years later I realized that I was doing something giving me the same feeling I had had during that testing. "So this is it." I thought. "Here is that feeling again!" The last question was also helpful because when I received the answer that I should study languages, I also got the feeling that I should be willing to see where it led me. It was an opened door I should enter without expectation. Because I was willing to study languages I went back to school, which led me to taking writing classes, and these showed me eventually that I wanted to write. Going to school is what I felt it was really about.

So it was not about languages but about language. Often people expect to have a big illumination about their true talent. Like the voice of God telling them, "You are an artist," or "God wants you to write," or "Science needs your talent, etc." But it's seldom like that because talent usually is a much broader concept: a talent with people for instance, a talent with plants, animals or a talent for understanding energy, how things work, how people work, etc. The direction people take eventually shows them in what way this talent can be narrowed down to a specific kind of work that will earn them a living. People are often disappointed because they feel that what they received was too vague but in fact they are given a direction.

Yes it's true, and that's why I also had that special feeling when I tested about doing my true work in other circumstances. When the answer was confusing I said to myself, "This is also good work for me. This is also an option."

We have different work at different times. Varindra said that it was essential to recognize one's role, play it and when it was done to be willing to leave it because there is nothing more pathetic than an actor clinging to his role after the theater is closed.

Isn't motherhood your most important work right now?

Yes. I always knew I wanted children. By the time I hit puberty I knew that, as certainly as I wanted to get opened. I met my husband not even a year after I was opened. It was very much one of those Subud things that fall into place because it's right. It was extremely easy to start that relationship.

Roland had decided that he was going to be celibate until he met the woman he wanted to marry. So within a couple of weeks it was pretty clear for him that we were a good match. For me, after a month or two, I couldn't conceive of a future without him. Already we talked about our children, the house we would buy one day, our future.

Because of circumstances we started living together from the day we met. Harlan G. had introduced me to Roland and his mother after a concert. We all went back to Mendocino and we stayed at Roland's house for a night. The next day he said, "Why don't you stay for a week?" I stayed for a week and his mother said, "Why don't you stay for a month," and after that month Roland said, "You are going to stay right?"

Children didn't happen easily. I had two miscarriages before I had my first child. The first miscarriage happened early on and was not too physically taxing, but emotionally I was drained. I processed it for many months afterwards.

Roland all along felt that he wanted to wait longer, and for a number of years he had been saying next year, next year. It was a huge commitment and it was hard for him to make it.

The first time I miscarried I had spent a week believing that I was pregnant and becoming more certain all the time. By the time the week was over I knew I was. Roland had been away and when he came home I told him. His life had been so stressful, he was so overwhelmed with responsibilities that he answered from a deep gut place, "I sure hope you are not," and was obviously so deeply miserable. The next day I miscarried.

The second time I had bothered Roland so much that we agreed I was not to mention it once for the whole duration of Ramadan. On the last day of Ramadan we would talk about it to see if he had come to some kind of clarity about it. So, the last morning of Ramadan he woke up at dawn to do latihan. When he came home I asked eagerly, "So have you thought about it?" He had done some testing and he answered, "I am willing to sort of consider the possibility of perhaps being able to consider the idea at some point in the future that is not too far off." As loaded as you can get. But the testing had been positive. Three days later I found I was six weeks pregnant!!!

When I was eleven weeks pregnant, everything seemed to indicate that the timing had been perfect. When I miscarried that time I was absolutely devastated. I was certain I could not have a child after that. When I think about my life now if I didn't have kids it would be pretty empty, incomplete.

Professionals told us that I had to wait six months before trying to get pregnant again but five months later, at the time of the Subud World Congress in Spokane, I knew without a doubt that I was pregnant. Again I was devastated when I found out I was wrong. In the middle of the congress I ran down to the Safeway and went to the bathroom to have a pregnancy test I was so anxious to find out. How could I have been so sure and actually feel this presence around me, this spirit hovering? I now feel that it was Maxwell getting ready to come through. It was our anniversary at that time and we spent a miserable day.

That evening Ibu Rahayu gave a long talk to the youth and the whole time I felt like she was looking straight at me and addressing me. Then she asked if anybody had any questions and I didn't have a question but I raised my hand first. What came out of my mouth was, "Is it possible to do testing with the helpers and have the answer be entirely wrong?" Everybody laughed and she answered, "It is possible because we try our best, but any of us can all be wrong at one time or another. We have to forgive ourselves and others."

It's interesting that when Bapak or Ibu give a talk, people in the room often feel that it is addressed directly to them. Since those talks are spontaneously received they pertain to the needs of the group, and the needs of individuals in the group may have at that time. In your particular case it could be that many people in the group had been going through the same sort of thing you were going through, not about babies necessarily, but about receiving a message in testing that is wrongly interpreted.

Yes, that's true. Anyway, three weeks later I was pregnant with Maxwell. The first week of motherhood with my first child was above and beyond everything. Maybe it's because it was the first time. You are so blown away. I would give up all my life experiences just for that first week. I felt that I was receiving from the spiritual realm everything I did or said. Everything was so right! Pure ecstasy.

As far as the future of Subud is concerned I feel like we are not yet big enough for the latihan. Our personalities don't let the latihan come through totally. We can't put them out of the way. We can't let go of ego and often enter into the power struggle. Also there is a problem with this generation and this culture. Things are moving so fast and there is so little time. People my age don't have time to think of their spiritual life. Also there is little time for new members, they don't feel supported and they leave disappointed.

Something I would like to talk about with other Subud members is their experience in moving to different places according to what the testing shows. When Roland and I were in Argentina, we tested about where we should move to next. We had been living in California since our marriage. There were a number of places we were considering. So we went down the list and tested all of them and this led us to the conclusion that the interior of Canada was the best place for us. I had the feeling that we would be flourishing there. Roland had the feeling that it would be challenging, at least at first, but also very positive. Worthwhile.

It's interesting because some of the places we tested like Hawaii, (How would it feel for Roland and his family to move to Hawaii?) felt so wonderful and easy but nothing like the feeling received during the previous question: "How is it for Roland and his family to live in the place God wills for them to live in?" Easy does not mean right I guess.

It felt like a huge leap of faith to head out to the interior of Canada with a U-HAUL and a two-year-old to an area that I never had been to, even though I am Canadian.

A lot of Subud people do those gutsy moves even to faraway foreign countries, just on that faith.

Gutsy or stupid. I never realized how much faith this was going to require, but the first couple of months were just excellent. We were living in this little town called Roslyn and I can't quite believe how many opportunities came our way. It was a streak of luck, one thing after another, connections to people, connection to work. We were both doing a major career shift, which is tricky.

Then we went back to California to pick up the rest of our stuff and Roland had a couple of loose ends to tie up. We were gone for about a month and during that time it seemed like the message was, "Well, if you decided not to be in California then really don't be there." Every connection we had was cut short, work, etc. The most incredible instances of bad luck. Such a horrible trip and an enormous financial loss during that month.

By the time we arrived back in Roslyn we were really in recovery mode. And so it was harder because the money we depended on totally fell through, even more so than we could imagine. That changed things drastically. Still opportunities have always come to us in the ten months we have been there, little jobs and connections for my poetry, for Roland's photography, etc. but we were extremely poor, scraping drawers for change on occasion and pregnant with my second child on top of that.

Now I see that even though it was very hard, there have been lots of benefits that couldn't have happened anywhere else. I couldn't work because I was pregnant and had all the time to work on children's books. Now that I had the time I realized that I was going to make that my career work for the next few years. Had we been anywhere else I would have been able to find work in spite of being pregnant, and would have been totally distracted.

Also, had we been anywhere else Roland would have been able to get work in spite of the fact that he was illegal at that point (we are in the process of legalization.) He would have been able to get carpentry work under the table, but we heard so many times from so many people not to even try it in Roslyn because there were so many border officials living there and people talked. So he was forced to spend all of his time setting up his photography, which he had wanted to do for years but never had the time. And now he has his photography business all set up.

It may be that the place that is best for you to move to at the time accomplishes something in your life but is only temporary, and it brings you to the next step in the same way that your talent points you to your right work.

I have met a couple that has been through this. They had tested about a move and after many months of hardship, and only in retrospect were they able to see why they were brought to that certain place. For instance, this woman moved to Indonesia, a place indicated through testing, for a year with her new husband. She experienced extreme hardship there because she was extremely sick, bedridden almost the whole time. How could that seem like a positive thing?

She realized later that because she was in her forties when she got married and her husband in his fifties, they were both very established in their lives and set in their ways. They would never have been able to bring their lives together harmoniously had they not gone to a foreign country, which was, for neither of them, their own territory. She became so helpless that she had to depend on him for the most basic needs. Now they are really solid.

From the outside it may not appear that testing about a place is a good thing to do, because people who do, end up with all this hardship, but I think that from the inside you can tell that despite the hardship you needed to be there.

PURIFICATION, CRISIS, METAMORPHOSIS, DELIVERANCE

In a talk he gave in 1969, Bapak said that purification is the stripping away of all kinds of things that have been buried in the inner feeling for a long time. People who experience a period of purification usually feel as if they are able to find a new understanding, whereas this is something that has lain buried for a long time within them. When people undergo this period of purification it is usually a heavy experience for them. States of purification are certain to occur as long as people are following the latihan kejiwaan of Subud. He added that this is what is necessary for the self of each of us, so that the various imaginings and ideas buried in the inner feeling, which cause us to behave less than well, can be done away with, and the development of your true jiwa can proceed quickly.

Many people in Subud still refer to a time of purification as crisis, but others prefer to call it transition, metamorphosis or deliverance. What follows is a result of my personal observations, understandings and receivings, as well as some personal experiences and the experiences of others close to me.

Physical, emotional, psychological and spiritual crisis are actually passages, transitions, a painful time of emptiness between something that is leaving and something new coming through. Old structures have collapsed and the new ones are not yet in place.

A crisis often takes people on its own journey and dictates its own timing. Decisions during that time are not taken from the rational or logical mind. At times, a person might become painfully aware of past mistakes and be emotionally paralyzed. Each decision to be made seems to be a potential for new mistakes. Or else both sides of things are equally convincing because judgment is suspended and a choice is impossible.

Eventually most people come to the other side having gained a new dimension, unless the unconscious wish to remain in the crisis—because it's a state in which they feel close to God and receive visions and revelations—keeps them in this timeless place, unaware of responsibilities.

Mankind is made up of all kinds of people and we cannot expect everyone to be committed to growth in the same way we are. Subud may not be for everyone, or there might be a certain time when it is more favorable for an individual to be opened in Subud. To get opened prematurely, when an individual is too psychically fragile, might precipitate a spiritual crisis, that is why testing is conducted before opening someone.

The practice of the latihan makes us more aware of the working of the forces within us, but we might not have a full understanding yet of the way they work and this might be threatening to those in a fragile psychic state. As our channel becomes less obstructed, the life force is allowed to flow more freely through us and whatever issue has not been dealt with, or cleared, in our ancestral or personal history might surface in the most unexpected and sometimes disturbing ways. If this process is stifled or repressed because of fear, it will form chaos in the body and mind.

We do not exist just in one form, but most of us don't remain connected to our other identities. As we practice the latihan, those spiritual identities begin to make themselves known to us, it's as though the sounds and movements we make during the latihan awaken something that was stored deep inside.

As we continue this practice, we begin to develop the inner body of our soul and ascend the scale of vibration, entering different frequency levels. This may be unsettling for some who are very strongly attached to a certain belief system, a certain form, one image of themselves. When, after working very hard towards some accomplishment like fame or fortune, we realize that there is no salvation in what we achieve, possess or attain, we might go into depression and world-weariness. What's the use of anything we think, not realizing that when we are a step away from total despair, we are often just a step away from self-realization: through becoming totally vulnerable we can discover our true essential invulnerability.

An enlightened state might, at times, appear to be a crisis state. A friend in crisis told me that she could see intelligence as a frequency manifested in geometrical shapes that reached the planet through sound. Another person saw that in the beginning of times there were only circles, which later evolved into lines, squares, etc. until hieroglyphic patterns appeared that had different meanings for different categories of people and became language to some. During those times, the intensity of ecstatic transition can bring a feeling of impending death.

I met individuals who assured me that during their transition crisis they could breathe under water, travel in the past or future, consult the Akashic records, and become aware of life's manifestation in mathematical formulas. Some were system busters: they would see right through the smoke screen of anyone they had dealings with. They couldn't help but tell the truth of what they saw, uncovering the lie that helped others live, and become unwelcoming mirrors pointing to weaknesses and faults. Others had trouble accepting them, finding them troublesome, odd, difficult, and threatening.

Most of the time the usual drama of life can go on without affecting people in crisis; it's as though they were immune. This is because they are not available for the mundane. They seem unconcerned by the difficulties they create for others and this is unsettling for many of their family and friends. To them, happiness or unhappiness is one because they are aware that only the illusion of time separates them.

Often, we are identified with some form of negativity and don't want to let it go, we deny, ignore or sabotage the positive in our life. Our fear is that if we face who we truly are, we will be forced to change. This can take phobic proportions because change, for some individuals, involves too many difficulties. So they stop the process, holding on to what makes them unhappy rather than facing the unknown. At this point they might stop doing the latihan, refusing the trigger that forces them to deal with their unfinished business and create their reality in accordance with God's will. This might throw them into a transitional crisis.

We might notice the constant frequency of change as soon as we dare step out of the house we had imprisoned ourselves in for security, and this may start with our very first latihan. When we take that step, stand in front of God and surrender, we become aware of a guidance uplifting us. It brings a greater comprehension and disengages us from the paradigms that have dictated our lives and defined our world in very limiting terms. It might take a crisis to accomplish this for some, but for others, it's through a very long and patient practice of the latihan that change comes about. Bapak warned us to watch out so that we don't end up doing the latihan of our habits. When we understand that our choice of thoughts, of words, creates our circumstances, we can no longer remain in the victim identity habit and the huge changes this may precipitate can be quite unsettling.

Either we accept change and commit to it, or else we are scared of it and resist, and that can throw us into a chaotic state. I have noticed that whenever people resist, their spiritual crisis lasts much longer and it even can become a permanent condition, a condition they become attached to once it's familiar enough; beside irrational behavior is what others expect.

Change can precipitate crisis, but often crisis anticipates a great change in one's life. True change is the most difficult thing for us, humans, for we often mistake immobility for stability and security.

On the spiritual level we are all one body and we have a collective pain body—it's the place in each and all of us where ancestral, cultural and universal pain is stored, often awakened during the menstrual flow. When terrible, perverted things happen, like the holocaust, they don't totally disappear when they are over, they remain in the collective pain body. They linger on, and those who are undergoing a transformation have the power to see them. They come back heart-sickened. The fear is so great, and the confusion about life on earth so total, that faith and trust vanish for a while. They cannot believe what anybody tells them anymore, convinced that there is no possibility for trust on this earth.

A person I knew who was in crisis had a vision of millions and millions of people suddenly leaving the planet in one afternoon. This might not have been as great a tragedy as she saw it to be, had she been able to understand this from a place of surrender. But she periodically would lose faith in herself and believe she was at the wrong place, at the wrong time, the only one going against current, picked because of it to be persecuted or killed by those from above who constantly discussed her flaws. She might have been passing from one of her identities to another, but the turmoil within about the visions didn't let her find her inner place of knowledge.

The fact is that we cannot fight darkness, just like we cannot fight unconsciousness. If we do, the polar opposites embed themselves and we become identified with one of the polarities. Continuing with the latihan when we undergo a transformation is essential, and the Subud community might have to lend a helping hand, letting the people in crisis know they are not alone, that testing and special latihans are available to help them through. As we let our purification take its course and surrender, we'll become more acutely aware of everything and everyone around us, also of the whole planet.

The earth and the different forces that reside on the earth are always seeking purification, and as we strive to make our molecules more perfect, we help them. The earth is a being capable of understanding our human dilemma; the forces are entities willing to work with us. When we begin to communicate and work with the energies that make up the earth we create a bridge between earth and sky and become an energy flow for change. Listening to the silence inside ourselves we catch messages from every living being and become aware of how generous plants are to humankind, how willingly they give of themselves when they are used in the right way. To some, they disclose what their properties are and how to heal the body with them.

During a testing session, a woman helper received that the pollution on the planet is a reflection of a psychic pollution, that plants and animals are a mirror of our time, that they reflect all our fears, all our joys. They know what is happening to the earth at a deep level. It is a preconception that man is the most evolved creature on earth. Everything is evolved in its own realm. There is even intelligence within an amoeba.

Our human life seems to be about finding that middle way between total involvement with our inner life and exclusive involvement with outer life, an understanding that will help us use them both to keep our balance on the tightrope. A transformative crisis might be needed to accomplish that.

And of course, this book maybe the reflection of my own personal crisis, going on right now!

YOUR OUTER DIRECTION CONFLICTS WITH WHERE YOUR INNER WANTS TO GO

Aaron (U.S.A.) interviewed in Spokane (WA.)

"This power of life we have within us can span between heaven and hell, whereas the nafsu can only exist in hell— that is, in this world."

Bapak

I think it was originally a loss of love, a loss of my sense of spiritual self that brought me to Subud. I had the feeling that I originally was born whole. I had a very happy childhood during which a deep spiritual connection to the earth was developed, and even without having a doctrine or a religion, I had a very strong sense of spirit, which was connected to Subud.

Actually, at an early age, although I was not in Subud (nor anyone in my family,) we were friends of very old Subud families, the Rands and the Davidsons, also Kendrick Petty. A bunch of other Subud people opened in the sixties lived around us and came in and out of our lives. We went on camping trips together, hiking, backpacking. My first puppy love, at thirteen, was a girl in a Subud family and then, in college, during my freshman year, I met a young woman a little older than myself who was in Subud.

When we broke up I went through a few very difficult years trying to find myself. I was pushing the threshold of pain and was going through a very hard time. I made a lot of spiritual connections when I was at Sonoma State University. I tried Hatha yoga, I tried meditation, I tried fasting, etc. An epitome of spiritual awakenings. I ended up really surrendering to an amazing life force. Since then I use that as a gauge.

Ever since I got into Subud I hit that high, (and even higher,) about twice a week. I don't even think twice about it now. But then it was like an awakening for me. About ten years went by. I was in the process of breaking up with my girl friend of seven years. At that time I had a wonderful outer life, but my inner life had dwindled. I had become much more pulled by the material forces. After a while I just couldn't take it anymore and decided I'd better get back to my roots and find myself. In the process of going back to art school and taking classes, I got ready to break up with the woman I had been living with.

I felt the urge to call the original girl friend who (I could say) initiated me to Subud. She gave me a number in San Francisco and I called that number. I did the probation period and decided to go through with it. I got opened, and ever since then it has been different—I mean my path would have been different had I not joined.

I know that I lured you by saying that I was an expert on crises when you told me you were working on the chapter on crisis, but I may have led you on. I feel like I have been in crisis both in Subud and before Subud for a big part of my young adulthood, but I don't know if it was aggravated by Subud.

I think that Subud leads you to a path that is a more correct path for you and that only hindsight can really show in what way. After you have been on the path you can look back and say, yes that was a good path, but when you are on it, sometimes your outer direction conflicts with where your inner wants to go. I would say that this can precipitate a crisis. I am definitely not past this.

The first few years in Subud were a kind of re-wiring of myself. In that re-wiring there is something scary. There can be a drastic change, and change might be perceived universally as difficult, especially as you get older, it requires a lot of faith.

I think that a lot of my experience is related to my attitude toward how I should be as a man, and this usually involves relating to women. I was basically fairly young when I got acquainted with Subud and I did it through the love of a woman.

So maybe there is a strong female connection for me, and a lot of times it's through my relations with women that I will learn a lot about who I am. I think that has been very powerful, more than ever now.

That is the change I am dealing with now: it's sort of hard to accept the fact that I may not actually need women the way I thought I did, that my relationship with women may not mean what I thought it did. That picture is being readjusted and in that there is fear. Why do you feel this way? Is there something wrong? Is it just change, is that change going to be equally as valuable as the way you used to operate? Between one door closing and another opening there is an in-between stage and that is the crisis. That is when it takes faith to make the jump. All your structures are taken away from you and nothing has replaced them yet.

I also have experienced some physical loss. I had a bad knee injury in 1981. I wrecked my knee in a soccer match, and this happened right around the time I was breaking up with a woman I loved. I think it was the day after she told me she was getting married. She never did end up getting married, the whole thing was a disaster for her, but it was also a disaster for me, and the next day I hurt myself. Maybe there is no correlation, but I think there might be.

Ten years later I was with another woman who might not have been good for me, but I didn't realize this at the time. My knee told me because it went out totally. I wrecked it and it was so painful I ended up not being able to walk. It impaired my ability to do the things I was used to doing. It was an actual outer manifestation of a change that was necessary.

I feel that my Subud inner life is very quiet. It's difficult for us to know the language of the inner because, in this Western society, we know a language of hard facts. It's hard for us to give that up. We, as workingmen in America, are yet to find the language of the inner. I find that the hard facts are constantly being reinforced in language, and if you don't use those tools you can't really get very far in the material world. It's an interesting challenge to breach the spiritual—the sense of quiet, the notion of the sublime—while using your animal force to get on in the work arena. This can bring on a crisis also.

Here we are in Spokane and I should be looking at you as I talk, but this water in front of us is mesmerizing. I must say the Tenth World Congress is happening in a beautiful surrounding. It's wonderful to be here. I feel much more centered here than I have been in other places. In my moments of clarity I keep an eye out for a life partner. Yes, I definitely am looking for one. Do you have an idea about what direction to look? Maybe that is what I have to give up, having an idea, any idea about it. I have been confronted with few possibilities during this congress.

There are two thousand beautiful women here today so there is a lot to choose from, but that is actually misleading because there are only very few. I like to kid around and say that there are actually three or four that are perfect for me, but I don't know who they are and that's the challenge. More of a challenge than it sounds actually, because in fact, it may be that there are not any, or that there is only one. At one point the possibilities narrow down to nothing. It's odd that the older you get, the less attractive you get, the pickier you get. It should be the opposite but that is the reality. But of course, looks are not what's important here, feelings, inner feelings are what count.

You asked me what are the symptoms of a crisis and I would say that recently, my crisis is a sense that I somehow missed the boat. I have a terrible rejection issue. I get the notion that my heart is freezing and that it's not going to work again. This manifests by my going into depression. In the last year I went through a very deep depression. For me it was unheard of.

I think it came from being really opened and taking something in from someone else. A lot of people would say that I am not taking responsibility for my own self and that might be true. When I give up everything, everybody, every notion of time or dream or desire, what I am finally faced with is choosing to accept the situation like it is. It's just me, alone in the world.

How am I in that state? Do I want to be happy and accept, be grateful, or do I want to still compare, judge, push myself and be hard on myself to try to achieve what my will thinks I should manifest. What I have finally discovered is that my will just can't do it.

I owe a big part of this to Subud. In a way you could say Subud hinders you from exercising your will, but at another level you can easily see how Subud gets your will to be less of a powerful influence so other doors are able to open. When I couldn't exercise my will to get what I wanted I surrendered and this took the form of a depression. It was like giving up on life. I believed I would never marry, never achieve much greatness, didn't see myself having been much of a prize for anyone. Still, in the end, I was going to be happy for what I had.

Even if I have nothing, the bottom line is the path, the Will of God. You can be happy no matter what happens, if my arm is taken away, my leg taken away, my heart taken away, I am still going to try to be the best that I can be with that handicap. In this way you reach a deeper and deeper surrender and that's probably what crises are about. I have been told that you don't say crises anymore, you call them metamorphoses. A metamorphosis is supposedly very painful for the insect.

For me it was very painful and actually mind-numbing even, for a period, nearly suicidal—although I have much too strong a life force to be able to even consider that. However I was as close to that as I would ever care to be, with a sense of being completely helpless. Everything you do seems worthless, or rather you can't do anything at all. And there is no escape. You are at the mercy of the One Almighty. It's both wonderful and tremendously difficult to be there. I think that I have achieved that several times in my life.

This last year around Christmas time I reached an all time low. At the beginning of the year I made a resolution that I was going to be happy with my life, accept and embrace the qualities that I possess and work with that. I would stop telling myself that I should be somewhere else, doing something else. I think the big crisis is to try to bridge two worlds, or live in two worlds at the same time.

I haven't really found the answer yet and I still would like to, but in the meantime I have taken the pressure off by embracing the work, which nurtures me most.

I want to get back to relationships. After I broke up my long relationship I had a long-distance relationship with a woman who was in Subud when I met her, but not receiving well. We had a strong connection during the congress in Denver and it felt very positive, but as the relationship progressed I realized that she wasn't anything I had thought in terms of the spiritual. I was willing to accommodate.

Part of me is very accommodating in a relationship, I try very hard to make things work even when the odds are against it. I don't know what it is in me, but it's like I love the challenge and try to rise to it. The more challenging the more I try to become heroic.

Anyway, I ended up having to make a choice between Ramadan and her. Since she chose to have an affair with somebody else I chose Ramadan. It turned out that her affair was a very minor thing and after some time she called me. We ended up getting back together. She was no longer in Subud and I tried to bring her back, but she ended up taking me out of it much more than I wanted to. We broke up in the end.

I was left with this very difficult awareness that my faith had been severely tested. I felt like I had made such a bad mistake with that person, given so much and gotten so very little back. I started getting worried about the path of Subud. I began to think that maybe I should just do the worldly stuff and develop my character more through that.

I was really in crisis at that point, obsessed with the idea of what direction to go. It came to a head when I understood that it was the realization that I was not really doing that much artwork—more involved in construction—that killed her interest in me. She wanted an artist type. After that, for several years, my latihans had a reserve quality to them. I believed I had to keep one foot in the material or outer life. I don't think it's the way to be in Subud, if you are going to do it, you have to have faith.

I can't be fooling around and receive anyway. If I make a commitment to Subud, in that I receive clear guidance and benefits for my life, if I do it half way, I end up with half of that. That's not a good way to be. I think that what this congress is teaching me is that I can't hang on to an idea in terms of a mate, a life partner, a family. I think that I am very surrendered in the moment as to what is going to happen ultimately. I am flexible and believe that this period is about being patient and waiting for the right time.

I am happy with all I do physically in my outer life, but I have not received any strong connection to anybody here. I am very much surrendered to what happens but . . . I hope something happens this next week—or before I get too old.

I am thirty-three, Jesus Christ's age when he died. Sometimes I feel that I might have to be put on the cross. I went into this congress thinking I didn't want anything to change because I liked the way my life was going. I have met eight new women this year, all platonic and nourishing. I have the best women friends and in a way I want it to stay that way, remain grounded and levelheaded.

I received the most powerful latihan during one of the youth latihan. It was like a clear river, just like the one we see in front of us here today. I was cruising along on that little boat and then all of a sudden it was like Mt. Fuji rising right out of the water. I went, "Oh man! Not again, not so soon, I have been enjoying the river ride, now I have to climb that?"

The tricky part is that I am numb to it even though I am aware of it. I am thinking, "Am I really going to rise, do I really have it in me?" I am aware that it's coming up, it's going to be in my life, it might just be the next mountain or it might be a whole range in back of it, but I am made aware that my life is not going to be about just cruising and kicking back.

At this time Aaron owns a house in San Francisco that he remodeled exquisitely. He is also building another house for himself on a ridge in the Mendocino area, he is married and father of a little boy.

THE MIRACLE OF SURRENDER

Ilaina (Mexico) interviewed in Spokane (WA.)

(Translated from Spanish)

I was opened in Subud in 1964. Before that I had an enormous amount of worry about finding God. I was a very good Christian, I had much faith, but I wanted something more. One day I was walking along in such despair about this—it was a beautiful day, the sun shining brightly—that I said to God, "Senor, if you don't help me, I will get lost trying to find you." I was crying, feeling like a little girl, all lost.

Soon after that I was eating in a restaurant when I felt someone looking at me very intensely. I turned around and saw this older man. He was like as if he was illuminated. It was this very special hour when the sun was setting right behind him. He asked me if I would mind him joining me. I said why not, and we started talking. I told him that I felt very disoriented. He turned out to be an astrologer who had studied Sufism, chiromancy and palm reading in ways mostly lost to the world in Germany.

He asked me if I wanted to have a consultation. He was much more than an astrologer, he also had studied many philosophies, and he talked about fascinating things. In the end I told him that I was not interested in a consultation because I felt there was something more than that for me. "I think I know what you are looking for," he answered. Only then did he talk about Subud.

So this is how I was introduced to Subud. He gave me directions on how to get to a group. For three months I had to go to Mexico City and meet people who gave me explanations about the latihan of Subud. After three months I was opened.

Even before my opening I started feeling the latihan. It was as though this man I talked to in the restaurant had opened me. Even at the time I felt a movement within, and I said to myself, "Something is strange here. Maybe I am not well." My head was spinning.

Still, when I got opened I was surprised by everything. My first big experience was when I saw a light, and two forces, the negative and the positive. I was at work when it started to happen and I got a very bad headache that I couldn't get rid of. I finally had to leave and go home to lie down. When I got home it seemed like I was on a tormented sea. "There is no ocean here, what's happening?" I thought. Then I felt a force that rose. It was the color of lava, very black, but with other colors within that black. And suddenly a light appeared. The two forces were coming right out of my head and they joined like this *(gesture)* then they fell down and I kept hearing the sound of the sea through it all.

I don't know how long it lasted. I had lost the notion of time. When I felt the negative force I fell down. All the colors came into my body, and all my destructive, unhealthy thoughts went away. After this I always had faith in the latihan. Whether it's raining or blowing I go to latihan.

I had terrible things happen in my life, terrible crises. Crisis often takes the form of sickness for me. Not too long ago I was coming out of latihan and walking home when I felt a very big pain. A blood clot had burst and my feet swelled up like balloons. The pain became so intense I thought I was going to die. I took some homeopathic medicine, and went into spontaneous latihan. From eleven o'clock at night until five in the morning I was in latihan. The pain was so intense that if I hadn't felt the presence of God, of Bapak and of Christ, I wouldn't have been able to stand it. I was writhing on the ground with pain.

I couldn't get up for twenty-eight days. When I finally went to see a doctor, he told me that had I come earlier, they probably would have amputated my foot because there were traces of gangrene in there. But now it seemed to be healing, so he would try to avoid the amputation. I would have to take medicine and have much rest.

I was very disturbed at the thought that I might lose my foot; besides, I couldn't do anything by myself because I couldn't walk. But nobody around me seemed to understand that. They thought I was making it up, that the disturbance was psychological.

This lasted for three years. I was on crutches and used a wheelchair to get around. I was losing the sensitivity in my feet from not using them. It was a terrible time and my family was not helping much. They said I was crazy. I was able to stand it because God and the latihan were giving me strength. Little by little I started being able to walk.

I understand now that through all this I have liberated a lot of my ancestors who were stuck. Two years ago, some ancestors came in a vision to thank me for the help I gave them by accepting the pain. What I was told is that if someone resists his or her own process because of fear or anger, a sickness comes. And I had been putting obstacles in the way of my healing. Had I submitted I would have been able to rise sooner, but instead I was obstructing the way. I dreamt this, also that I was supposed to surrender to God.

My first husband, who died, was one of the founders of the Subud project in Mexico, so we went to live there. An extraordinary thing happened to me while I was there. One day I felt something moving in one of my eyes. "What's wrong with me," I kept thinking. Then suddenly everything went black. I received that it was a blood clot again, and that if I didn't do anything soon I would die. I told my husband and he wanted me to go to the hospital immediately. I refused because I was afraid they would operate on me.

Instead I asked God for forgiveness, repenting for whatever in my doing had brought that on. "Tell me, please tell me what to do?" I asked. A while later I opened a book of Bapak's talks right at the page where it mentioned testing about the eyes. I thought I should try that test and after doing it I fell asleep. During my sleep another Ilaina came out of my chest and sat in front of me. It was my jiwa. She said, "By surrendering in this way you will be able to see the light again." When I woke up I could see in that eye and didn't have to go to the hospital.

However that purification lasted four years, during which time Arifah was my only friend. Most people can't understand those times of crisis; the group believes that you are not all there! People would always see Arifah, the French lady, going around with this nut they believed I was. They thought she was crazy also. People who have too much faith threaten others I guess. Now I have just married my second husband, Herbert, a scholar, and people wonder how I could get such an intelligent man.

I must tell you another miraculous story. One day I was very broke. As I walked down the street I was wondering how I would get the money to pay my bills. I felt the pressure of the material forces all around me and asked God to help me. A woman in the street asked me if I could direct her to the university. She didn't know the area at all and needed to see a certain dentist very badly. I had some time on my hands, so I decided to help her out and take her there. On the way she told me this story:

"A small truck drove by my house today and in the truck there was a bull. They were taking the animal somewhere. The driver didn't realize that a small crate had fallen out of the truck in the street as he rounded a curve. I yelled for the truck to stop but he didn't hear me, so I went to pick up the wooden box and opened it. In it there were gold bars."

As we got to where she wanted to go she handed me a gold bar saying, "Take this. God gave it to you, but don't tell anyone because if you did your life could be in danger." She added that she had arranged to go to that dentist to sell him the gold. She also gave me two hundred pesos so I could take a taxi and get to my house fast without being stopped by anyone. Then she disappeared.

I had received the money I needed to pay my debts and I was very grateful to God for that.

I DIDN'T THINK I WAS WORTH IT

Rohanna S. (Peru) interviewed in Seattle (WA.)

*The form a true being takes is not due to any teaching
but a joyful explosion of body towards God.*

I have been in Subud for twenty years. I was looking for something that made sense and I tried some yoga. When I was twenty-five someone talked to me about Subud. They said that in Subud you don't use your thinking mind. I answered, "Well, that's yoga." I was afraid that Subud would interfere with what I was learning. "It will be your own teaching and somehow you just have to trust it," I was told. Then I forgot about it.

Later however, when I became disappointed in the yoga teacher because he wanted to sleep with me I said to myself, "This is not what I thought it was. Maybe I should try that other thing."

The man who later became my husband introduced me to Subud. We were not married yet, but he would tell me what was happening to him. He had been active for about five or six years and he told me that Subud was the way for him. So one day I said, "Okay, I'll try it." In those days in Lima the rule about probation was not enforced so I got opened immediately without ever doing a probation period.

During my first latihan I had a lot of passions coming up. I felt like my dirty clothes were being taken off, that they were being rubbed and scrubbed against the helpers. That made me feel shy you know, to have my dirty clothes washed in front of everyone. I didn't like it, but they told me not to worry, that it was okay.

That first time the latihan was very strong. I felt like I was flying. I was running from one side of the room to the other. I felt like I was going to bump into the window and launch myself or smack myself against it. WHAM! I was going mad, I needed to keep myself in check, but I couldn't, and WHAM again! People were very worried.

I hadn't read much about Subud before getting opened. My mind had been fully trained: my ancestors always insisted on knowing everything there was to know, they didn't trust anything they couldn't touch. They were very rational. So, that was the state of my mind, but my soul was looking for something else because things around me didn't make any sense. I had to do something. I had tried yoga, I had tried marijuana, I was down to nothing and had to do something fast. So I jumped.

Before I went to South America I lived in Mexico and hung out with a group of people who were heavily into drugs. I remember feeling that if I stayed in Mexico I would not survive. I said to God, "You must get me out of here." It was the following day I think, that I was offered a trip to Chile. I was sent to a castle in Santiago to work on a movie. I had been in the movie-making business, but dropped out when I got into yoga in Santiago. I felt I had been used, and that it was not helping me in any way. I was desperate and Subud came at the right time.

I didn't trust my guidance immediately. I probably don't even trust it now. I don't trust a thing. What kept me in Subud for twenty years is faith I suppose. I believe in surrender. I am just learning now to surrender and follow. I couldn't do that before, it was impossible. I was totally immersed in my own thinking! How could I let go?

I didn't ask for a lot. Just that I didn't become a whore, or an alcoholic, or a druggy, just that I didn't kill myself. The latihan was a rescuer. The helpers were my friends and they were not trying to teach me anything. What would they have to teach anyway since we had the latihan?

Now I can see that I have evolved, that it has been a growing process. But when you are in the water, swimming, you can't see the bank. It took me all these years to be released and accept that I can be loved whether I am good or bad; that I can be loved and I can love, not the dependent kind of love but just love; to accept that love, and let it be. I couldn't love before, it was not possible. Just that is huge to me! I started noticing those changes about three years ago. I took a trip to Indonesia and that is when it started to happen.

I would say that we are being purified all the time, and we all have been purified a lot. Life is more than a purification though. The minute you purify something it gets clean and comes alive. Then you have to do something with that life. Before the purification there might be life but you don't know it. Once you know that there is life, it means that the process of purification has started and you are in God's vibration, accepting it, whether painful or not, without judgment. Life is good.

I didn't know it, but I was in crisis before I went to Indonesia. I had had six or seven years of thinking I couldn't make it, and mostly, I didn't think I was worthy. I had a dependent relationship and I wasn't happy in it. I don't think he was happy either. He was kind enough to let it be so I could work with him.

I didn't know what was going on. I didn't know that it was a crisis I was going through, but I was in pain and it was awful. I mean pain that was excruciating. It had to come out though, but I don't know how anyone survives such things. Now I can tell when somebody is going through this. It's like you are totally worthless, and really, you are worthless until you can accept to go along with God, because only then can God go with you.

I have been faithful to my husband. Sometimes I wonder you know, but I don't think I can throw what I have away. My husband and I had a period in which we were practically divorced. We were living in the same house but we didn't talk. We had a business together, we took care of the things at home, but I had my life and he had his. I never was with another man though, nor he with another woman. We just lived very separate lives.

When I was in Indonesia I asked Sudarto about this and he said, "Get up in the morning at 4:30 or 5 o'clock, do your prayers, then get back to bed and be a couple, make love as a couple." When I went home I did that, and amazingly enough we started talking. My relationship with my husband is not the dream love affair, it has never been, but it's sufficient. He is kind and we get along.

To me sex is up there (showing the sky.) It's everywhere. I had an experience when I stopped sleeping with my husband. I started to have sex spontaneously. I would pull into myself and have an orgasm on my own, sometimes during latihan. At times it was very strong and it went on for hours, I didn't know what it was about.

For years this went on, sometimes I was in the theater, or in the car driving . . . and Oho!!! Once I was coming out of the market, I had finished doing my shopping and the light, the temperature, the people, the moment, all was perfect. I was in love. All of a sudden, from a crack in the universe so to speak, something opened and I felt like the atoms were making love to each other, that the whole universe was moving with love . . .

Rohanna's description brought back an experience I had when I was ready to have my first baby. I told her the story. I was about two weeks away from delivery when my husband and I went to pick up my parents arriving from France, at the airport in Denver. Denver was about four hours from Aspen over a high pass. We were early and decided to do some shopping. I was trying on boots in a store when my waters broke. I ran out of the store in total distress and embarrassment. My panic, as I reached our van, was met by a gentle caress, a warm breeze on my skin that took away all my fears.

The meeting of skin and air became a merging. The temperature was just right. I felt like I was swimming in a warm, benevolent pool. Losing all sense of having outlines, my body melted into something resembling love. As all my senses turned to liquid, my spirits rose in exultation. Everything was perfect, just as it should be. Things happening at the exact moment they should. The light fell with affectionate care on everyone.

It was as though I could see through the eyes of the creator for an instant and all those tired people doing their shopping at the end of the day, all those overweight suburban mothers with curlers in their hair, berating their kids for their bad behavior, all those noisy, quarreling children, every single being was absolutely beautiful and perfect. Everyone housed a treasure inside of him or her: love was in his or her heart. The people walking by looked at me with friendly smiles on bright faces. I was touched so deeply I cried . . . and my tears gently pushed me into the flow of things. I entered the cosmic dance in which everyone, everything makes love . . . and we had to drive back over the pass to Aspen as fast as we could so I could have my baby there.

Yes I know that feeling. It's like an orgasm, a gigantic orgasm. I was looking at people, they were full of love. That's the life force I think. People were doing their shopping, and on one level everything was casual, but whoa!!! Interesting, that your experience and mine were so similar. Down to the details.

Through the practice of the latihan I have gained more acceptance of others and myself. I think I was sexist. I think I was afraid. And I definitely judged people. The practice of the latihan is just beginning to be integrated in my daily life. I am just beginning to be strong enough to believe that I can do it. It's not happening all the time, sometimes I am here, and it's there, or sometimes my inner is not with me on the outside. I don't bring it out with me because it's not strong enough to come out. I spent most of my life in my mind, so I do a lot of thinking.

I hope that some day I will be able to be without the prejudice in there *(tapping her chest,)* or that I can stop being half asleep; that I can deal with the constant fear, the world's prejudices and people's manipulations. We need to know our motivation and have strong motivations. It's not enough to say I want this, because maybe what I want is not good for me. But if I am sure I want that thing, then, whatever I have to go through to get it, I'll have to accept it.

IT WAS THE BEST THING FOR ME, DIGGING, DIGGING

Illene (U.S.A.) interviewed in Denver (CO.)

My mother was in Subud and got opened in 1959 when I was eleven. She did the latihan with some women at home, and I thought that the people in the Subud group were very, very strange, except for Leila and Raisa—Leila was the helper who opened my mother and a very close friend of hers. She was a lovely person and I was comfortable with her, also with Raisa, but some of the other people you know! In those days, there was not much group life besides latihan. Every once in a while there would be a potluck dinner, and we would go to those people who to me seemed rather odd. The whole thing didn't have much appeal for me as a child, besides, mother would go out two nights a week, which is always annoying to children.

I didn't peek on the latihan as some other children did. I was not really interested in Subud until I left home, until I could come to it on my own. My mother told me about it and got a Subud name for me when I was seventeen, which I was not a bit interested in using. My mother is very wise, she didn't push it.

My name before was Suzi. My father never liked my new name. He thought Subud people were even stranger than I did. I am sure there was a certain element of conflict, because my mother was doing something he was not doing and was not a bit interested in doing. Because he is a lawyer, his mind is totally into the rational vision. Of course, my mother is an intellectual too, but she was always interested in the spiritual aspect also.

I went off to college and I tried to solve all the problems of the world by myself. I remember my mother saying to me, "Illene, you can't do this, you will have to surrender this to God." I would answer, "Mother, that's quitting, that's giving up." I remember our discussions very well.

Well, I was so exhausted from being involved in the Peace Movement, from all the insane people who were involved in the Peace Movement who were just crazy people, that I finally realized I couldn't do it. I wasn't going to be able to stop the war, I wasn't going to be able to do much of anything and I was spiritually exhausted. I knew I was.

I went home for Christmas. It was the winter of 1969. I saw the snow in Colorado and I said, "That's it. I am moving here. I am staying in the mountains." At that point my parents were living in Denver. I told my mother, "I have to go to the mountains." She answered, "Great, we'll go too." Friends of theirs (who had been friends of the family forever,) had some land very close to your own in Carbondale, near Aspen. They had one of the first houses on the Roaring Fork. They were going to Mexico for two weeks and they said we could housesit.

At Christmas I asked my mother if I could borrow a book on Subud. That was the first time I was really interested. When I read it, I was so exhausted and relieved, I knew then it was right. By the time we took the Smith's house, in January, I already was receiving the latihan spontaneously. As soon as I decided that it was what I wanted I was opened, but I was certainly receiving the latihan before that. I would wake up in the middle of the night and do the latihan.

I said to my mother, "Well, I guess I'll be opened." It took me a while to say that out loud. By that time we had rented that little tiny house in Redstone. I don't remember if you were there that winter. It was a small A-frame cottage that was way up high towards Redstone. It was lovely. We spent the winter there and I skied all winter. I ran the little day-care center for the Sunlight area, so I had a free Season Pass. This is how I healed from the insanity and got opened at the first regional congress, which was held in Aspen that April.

Prio was there. Someone asked Prio if I could be opened without probationing and he said of course, because children of Subud members could. I remember Sylvia, one of the Subud members saying, "But Illene, we need you to baby-sit that weekend." I was the official baby-sitter for the group and I still had to cook for everybody. I remember making Paella for forty-five people. It was fun, it was wonderful.

As soon as I was opened I realized that it was where my knowledge would come from. There had always been things I knew that none of my friends knew, things I was the only one to know. The day of my opening, I realized that it had been coming from the latihan; from then on it was alive.

I went through a huge crisis. What it did for me was to take away fear. It took away all anxiety about anything in life. That was a great blessing because I have never been afraid of anything since. Well, I do have one fear actually, as a mother, the idea of having one of my children die is still frightening to me. That's a fear that's not gone and I suppose it will never go.

I think that what triggered the crisis was going to Cilandak during Ramadan, doing latihan—you know those two hour latihans—and later fasting during Lent. So it was two major fasts in one year. It was a spiritual overload, which sort of pushed me over the edge. I was flying, I was not walking.

My parents went to Brazil and left me alone in the house. Because I had been fasting so much I was not eating in a normal way I got very ungrounded. Nobody knew what to do for me except Steve G., because he had been through it himself—in fact he is still in it. I went to stay with him and his wife at some point because a teenage son of my parents' friends had come to stay in our house with me and he was a very disturbed teenager. He stole my father's car and that freaked me out so badly I didn't want to be in the house or around him. He left at one point, but I was afraid he'd come back. So I went to stay with Steve and Sylvia. Steve made me work in his garden, it was the best thing for me, digging, digging . . .

If I deal with someone in crisis I will know what's the best thing for him or her to do. Do you know that I used to drive my car around in circles. I would start out for Aspen and then say to myself, "Oh, I don't know that this is the right thing to do," so I would turn around and go part way back then ask myself, "Is this the right thing to do?"

I told Illene of my experience with Steve G. I was driving to Aspen from Castle Creek. It was very cold, the ground covered with a few feet of snow. I found Steve hitchhiking on the road, dressed lightly, and not wearing gloves. I picked him up and asked him where he wanted to go. He said to Aspen. We had just gone maybe half a mile when he suddenly got up, grabbed my arm and yelled, "Stop right here!" Startled, I stopped.

He explained that he had made a mistake, that I had to take him back to the place where he had left his skis and he would go back home. The road to his cabin was not ploughed and he had to cross-country ski through meadows and woods to get there. The urgency was so great that I obliged. I got half way there when he tried to stop me again. This time I didn't stop right away and he grabbed the wheel. I ended up taking him back and forth four or five times until I got angry and yelled at him, then forcibly took him home to Aspen with me. I thought he would harm himself if I left him in this isolated place. That's when we asked for a man helper from L.A. to come and take care of him: and Harlan M. was sent to us.

It's horrible to be like that, because you don't know your front from your back, you don't know what you are doing, you can't make any decision with your head because you think you have to receive. I finally came out of it, it was gradual you know, coming out of it. I don't remember how many months it took. It lasted all summer when my parents were gone, and obviously I had to get myself together a bit when my father got back. Then I decided to go to work in Denver and that was a gradual grounding.

THIS GUY, HE HAS ALWAYS BEEN IN CRISIS

Hillary (U.S.A.) interviewed in Seattle (WA.)

I started putting this book together with Lillia. We meant to explore the development of Subud members in isolated situations, far from the guidance and rules of more established groups, and to begin with interviewed people who had been in our Aspen group in the sixties. Then we realized that the book was larger than that.

After that we didn't plan but let the book progress on its own momentum. People interviewed were contacted spontaneously at different gatherings. When Rasunah and I were attending the National Congress in Seattle in 1993, we agreed that it was important to interview Hillary, a young man who had tested for a position in the Subud Youth. His story made a full circle, taking me right back to the origin of the Aspen group. The synchronicity in all this is too obvious to ignore.

I lived in a lot of different places because my father was a businessman. All over New England, then for the past three years in Missouri and Montana, which is where I learned about Subud through a sort of Sage, the kind of person Taoists talk about, one of the few highly developed persons I have met in Subud. His name is Antonio. He has no last name, just Antonio.

How I met him was walking out of the University of Montana's dining hall one day, and on to a porch area with tables. I have always been drawn to certain attractive looking older men, the attractiveness being that they look like Taoist saints. Anyway, this guy was sitting there alone at a table so I asked, "Can I sit here?" He was wearing a California Angels' hat and I had no idea who I was talking to. I thought maybe it was a janitor because he was not dressed like a professor. He didn't look dirty or anything, but more like a working person type.

Anyhow, we started talking. I was trying to ask him politely what he did, and he didn't respond to my trite politeness because there was nothing real to respond to.

So, there he was, eating his food and responding, but not to my questions. He was talking to me from a true self, and everything I said seemed to sort of fall flat. I felt, on the one hand that something painful was going on, but on the other hand it was the greatest blessing in the world.

I couldn't believe I found this blessing from a person who was still alive. At the time I was reading Krishnamurti. Being with this man made me feel the same way. To read those things in a book is pretty cool, but finding it in a person really surprised me. When he pulled out a cigarette after lunch I felt that it was not right so I said, "Don't you kind of feel, as you smoke, the pain of what it's doing to your lungs, to your body?" He answered, "I wouldn't worry about it," and he offered me a cigarette, which I didn't take that time.

I asked him where he was from and he said, "Sometimes I feel like I just fell out of the sky." I thought, "Okay, this guy might be a little flaky, maybe I don't buy this." He asked me what I did and I said, "Well, I spend a lot of time in the woods hiking around and stuff, also playing drums." That's just about all I did, as well as smoking a lot of pot. He asked me if I would play racquetball with him the next day and we actually ended up talking for about two hours. I told him my whole life story and he just listened to me, making interesting comments here and there. Like one thing he said was, "What other names do you use?" I felt like saying, "Well, actually, I don't really have any nicknames," and he was sort of looking at me like, "Well?"

And all of a sudden, my half-dead face came to life, all this color came to it. I looked very alive. At least he said so. I suddenly realized, Whoa, I could actually have other names. And I felt so expanded just because of the question he asked me. Then I fell out of understanding what was happening and didn't know what I was doing there. He would communicate back to me in a way that was clearly much more than casual, although he was using casual conversation, casual words. I would say it could have been from God.

A few days later I went to play racquetball with him and on the course I felt like the space we were in together was sacred. The word reincarnation comes to mind because it was like that . . . this eternal world we were in. I say reincarnation because I felt myself moving beyond what I yet knew. It was like more of me was allowed to exist, kind of like getting opened.

So this is my whole advice for Subud people: they should do things together, men and men should play sports together. Since they don't have sex together they should interact in other ways. When you are talking, if you are fortunate, you can also have an experience with a person, but it's much more natural to do physical things together. In the span of time we have been friends, he and I have played tennis together, ping-pong together, lately he has been teaching me to use the pottery wheel. We worked together at this restaurant where he took the orders and I was a short order cook, a sort of cowboy bar in Montana.

He is like a spiritual father. What's happening is that I "know" him, and I know other people who "know" him and who have gotten close to him in the same way I did. It's amazing because a lot of sons end up having a posture like their father, or a mannerism, or certain codes of dress and other things. So much of me has sort of become his son, it seems like what Bapak talks about when he describes ancestral purification. The amount of assistance I have gotten from him makes me feel like, "Why do I get the most wonderful thing in the world?"

I don't identify with many of the young people I talk to. I don't identify myself with Subud youth because I don't really feel like I am part of this thing—I am part of like, a much bigger thing. Bapak says that movement is how the purification takes place. That's what Antonio has been to me, movement.

Another Subud guy in town also found out about Subud through him. He is in his forties and has nicknamed Antonio the taskmaster. Now this guy has been opened. For periods of time he comes to latihan, but basically he's got like a wall around him, or at least, heavy curtains. He has a family, a kid, and it's like he doesn't want to taste the truth because it would shake up his whole world. Yet, at the same time, in his conscious explanation of himself and who he is, he is dying to open up. But he won't do anything about it. So, he has sort of pushed Antonio out of his life, just avoids him. Every time I see the guy he is a little bit fatter and less happy. But let's not go on about this . . .

At this point, things Hillary had described about Antonio started to come together into a picture that was somewhat familiar, as though this man Antonio was coming alive and I knew him well. But I didn't know where I knew him from, from what part of my life, or if it even was from this life. So I asked Hillary for his last name again, also where he was from.

He doesn't have a last name, he is Mister Antonio. He is from New York City.

This answer brought on another question, for at this point the picture had become clearer. I asked if Antonio had ever lived in Aspen, Colorado and Hillary answered that he had. "Oh my God!" I exclaimed, "I am sure that Antonio used to be Steve G., later Henry, the first member of our Aspen group."

So you know him. I don't usually meet anybody who knows him, he is so crazy. The people who do know him say, "Oh yeah! This guy, he has always been in crisis." Anybody who has a strong spiritual life in Subud is discounted as being in crisis.

People in crisis are often great teachers and catalysts for others, but you don't have to be in crisis to have a spiritual life.

Yes you do. I found out that crisis is another word for spiritual life. Those are people who really receive for themselves. Other people who are not in crisis are basically followers who live in neat little boxes. So crisis is just a word that means much.

How did you know Antonio?

I knew him well in Aspen in the sixties. I knew him when he was a carver and I drove him around at the beginning of his crisis.

That's so neat. So even back then he used to carve things. Anyway, I got opened about three months after I met him, January of '91. The first time, during my opening, I felt moved very strongly, not as strongly as I was three months later though. I definitely saw a progression and I felt the latihan working in my daily life also. From the first few weeks I noticed.

What's happening to me is like the rules of the whole universe have been changed, like everything that humankind has known, all the spiritual truths that people live by no longer have any meaning. It's like if I go for certain truths I might hope to get enlightened, right? But that's not it. It's not even just me that is changing, it's also things out there. Things that have to do with my fate and everything else that's happening in the world—they all have a completely different significance now. So to me, anything I previously knew means absolutely nothing anymore.

Subud is just the latihan. It's not the people in Subud. It's kind of interesting because I had this experience: I was testing what my talent was and I received this thing between my hands, like two things feeling each other. What I was doing last night had the same kind of feeling. I was sitting with Simon—this guy who has been a major cause of problems you might say—talking to the National Helpers. And the National Helpers have been a major problem to Simon. I was sitting between Simon and a National Helper and it was the same kind of experience, like both those guys have the same kind of problems as I do, the same kind of freak-out shit. It was like I was both those guys. I am here and I am there at the same time. How do you treat things like that? You just say thank you God, because at least I feel like I am in the whirlpool.

There is a Native American tradition called "the clown." The clown basically mimics people and turns up faces. Hopefully people will laugh, but if they take themselves seriously they get pissed off. In those cultures people have the right to do whatever they need to do. That's like Antonio. With him and his girl friend called Coyote, it's a similar sort of thing. He is so up-front I am embarrassed to take myself seriously.

This guy lives on welfare, but for Christmas he gave his girl friend and me some expensive gifts. He buys me steak dinners often. I buy him steak dinners too, but it's like, my parents support me and he is on welfare. But this makes no difference to him. That's how I always thought it should be. He dresses like he could be anybody. Sometimes he can't afford a meal, but he always looks sharp as anything.

As I become more aware of things in Subud, of what's going on, I thank God for Antonio. Like, him and Manyko are the first people I have been able to relate to for quite a while. During my very first latihan I felt, "Thank you for Antonio, thank you God."

Yes, the power of God is working through him. He hasn't been to any congress for a while I think. He attended one five or six years ago, but since then there is always something in the way. It seems to me that God has arranged it all. Like for instance, even at the beginning, when I was telling him about myself, he was sort of amazed because everything I was telling him, even down to where I am from—around Long Island—also my years of sailing, it was like he had had the very same experiences. Our bodies are similar and our characters fit together so well.

Hillary, you have been trying for the position of chairman of Subud Youth. Do you believe you could do a lot of good if you were in that position?

If I had had more experience in the world I think I would be able to do it. But I am only twenty-one and I have no experience outside of school basically, sort of a young person's school experience. I feel that Antonio has learned through

having done so many things, has gathered experiences, and
has come to know what can really happen between two people.
Being here, at this congress, it's like interacting with people
who have the reputation for being spiritual, but like seeing them
only doing small talk. It seems like when I am at one of my
parents' dinner parties. The way I deal with that is that I find
God tells me what it means.

I feel about Bapak the way I feel about Antonio. He's the
best friend a person can have. I feel the same way about
Krishnamurti. Those people are like my parents, they have huge
roles in my life. I feel that Bapak is an individual who advises
other people to be individuals. Many young people feel
rebelliousness towards Bapak, yet I hear them telling stories about
themselves being kids and loving to be close to him. But they
didn't know it at the time.

I feel very glad to have people I can talk to and who help me
develop. I don't feel like I am a follower of anyone, even if people
might say, "What about Antonio?" He is just like a parent. People
may have a trip about me following someone else, but God sends
you what you need, in whatever form will be the most beneficial,
so . . .

If there is one way that Subud might grow best in the world,
it would be if people stayed with the most real thing within them,
even more so for the National and International Helpers. Basically,
since Bapak founded Subud, everyone was willing to accept that
he received this thing from God and that they were all equals
under his guidance. But the reality is that there are people in
Subud who, I believe, are not so different from Bapak, they are
pretty much complete people, yet I come to congresses to seek
them out, and in the past few years I've met only a small handful
who really have let go of their mind and who operate from
somewhere else.

Like Bapak who I'm told couldn't remember one moment
when he moved on to the next.

When I meet new members from Missoula, I'd like it if we
could all sit around like Bapak and his friends and followers

used to do. Bapak up on the stage could feel their inner and the whole room was like humming with their vibration. When a room is filled with spiritual giants people start coming to Subud. Now, what's happening instead, is that when I send a friend to the helpers, he goes there and he sees a bunch of well-to-do, pale people. So he feels that Subud must make people boring. But really, I know it's no big deal, because that friend is taken care of even as we are speaking.

As I transcribed this conversation with Hillary I came to understand once more that the way we see others has a lot to do with where we are ourselves in our journey of purification, and that Steve-Henry-Antonio is a catalyst for many.

In previous chapters Lillia, Saul, Redmond, Charles, Mardiah and Laura all referred to him in one way or another. Illene and others also talked about him. He obviously made a big impression on people. Before I met him, he had been described to me as an artist from New York, a strange and reclusive character who sculpted wood and marble and had very strict rules of behavior for himself and his wife. She was originally from England, raised by a Subud mother who had been opened at Coombe Springs.

As the story went, Elisabeth was more gregarious than Steve, but he didn't like her close friendships with other women because he believed that women together became gossipy. An old, tired story I believed and I had just found out how it started.

In the old days women used to get together either to do laundry, shelling peas, cracking nuts, quilting, or any other task that could be accomplished while talking. It was their social time and they talked about things of common interest: the happy and sad events in the villagers' life; who was born; who was getting married and to whom; who was sick, dying or in trouble and needing help. It was not malicious talk, it came out of a need to inform and understand, and it had a healing purpose. Women talked about how they could help those in need, what could be done and they would work out a schedule. If nothing could be done then they would pray for those in need. This special time together was called the godsibb or godsip.

The story goes on to tell how the men became jealous of this intimacy women developed between them, because it took their wives' interest away from them and the home. They, themselves, didn't have anything like that. So they started calling it gossip derogatively and forbade their wives to work with other women.

I do not know what is true or not in all the stories that circulated about Steve-Henry-Antonio. Many found him difficult, forceful and arrogant, controlling, having a tendency to tell people what they should do or not do. Too often he told people what they didn't want to hear. He was always trying to make people share what they had with others, but many were not ready to do that.

For some, he was a saintly hermit, generous with those who didn't have anything, offering refuge to those in trouble, words of wisdom to those confused. He lived a very pure and simple life, close to nature, using his creativity for non-commercial pursuits. To those like Hillary, he was a truly enlightened human being.

What is the truth of Steve-Henri-Antonio?

At the time I knew him his wife went along with everything he believed. There was little arguing possible with Steve, one either agreed with him or left him alone. A wise fool, showing one truth about himself one day, the opposite the next, he insisted on teaching people to let go of their preconceptions, prejudices and erroneous beliefs. He said that in a land of quicksand you can only stay on top if you believe that you don't need firm ground to walk on. But many wouldn't be taught.

When his wife started questioning whether she wanted to live in the isolation he chose and reached out to her women friends it made things difficult. He decided to go to Cilandak for the World Congress. He didn't believe in doctors or conventional medicine and didn't get the required shots.

He came back as Henry, with typhoid fever. He refused to be treated or taken to the hospital in spite of his wife's plea. He would fight the sickness on his own! Only when he was totally delirious and limp was she able to take him to the local hospital. Doctors couldn't believe that she had waited that long. They immediately gave him a total blood transfusion, which saved his life, but when *he recovered he complained that he was haunted by the donor's dysfunction, his nightmares, his personality.*

When he was completely well his wife went back to England and didn't come back. It was after her departure that Henry went through the crisis mentioned in Illene's interview. When he became functional he left town and was only heard about very occasionally.

Many stories went around about him, at times he was described as a cowboy from Montana, other times as a hippie craftsman who made wooden toys and sold them at fairs, other times yet as a con-man, or a guru-like figure, etc. Those characters were high in color, straight out of novels, movies or plays.

Still the question remains: who is Steve-Henry-Antonio?

5

DOCTORS IN THE SKY

*"Human life is not nullified by death. There is no life
and death in the life of the inner self, it continues uniformly
as one existence. Both life and death are the same in God's
sight, they are both living appearances of one soul."*

Dr. Hattori

Lillia introduced the concept of doctors-in-the-sky. Her story
of flying across country and having a sense of medicine people
surrounding her to discuss her case, led me to converse with
people who had experience with sickness. Apparently nothing
was wrong with Lillia physically, but her inner body was out of
balance, probably due to some obstruction those higher doctors
commented upon and were getting ready to remove. It felt to her
as if invisible "higher level beings" were examining her and
deciding to operate.

Many of the people I interviewed reported similar
experiences, especially during a severe physical ailment. Some
had psychic operations performed on them; others received
accelerated guidance during the course of their sickness. All
had the experience of being looked after, cared for and worked
on by invisible but all too present healers.

A young man who played the piano divinely during the
entertainment night at Menucha (a Subud retreat) told the story

of how he became seriously ill after being opened in Subud. He was going to be confined in his home for an extended period of time and was terribly depressed so his parents, in an effort to help, brought in a piano for him to learn to play. When he put his hands on the piano he felt a force guiding them and he began playing as though he had played all his life. Without having to take any lessons he became a virtuoso.

Disease may be a way to break through a reality we are too attached to, a reality based on restriction, limitation, denial or judgment. We are shown that we have a choice and a responsibility in the way we experience reality. Because of this we are forced to embody the expanded perspective of the inner self, and this transforms the ego self which was holding the collective beliefs in place. There is a release of the way we normally perceive, and then our outer reality slowly shifts to reflect the inner change.

A minor sickness may be a way to gently push us off the position of judgment from which we operate and which demands to be constantly defended, for this is exhausting and depletes us of energy.

Many types of illnesses are caused by the ego's continuous resistance, which creates restrictions and blockages in the flow of energy through the body. The pain body—which consists of trapped life-energy that has split off from our energy field—becomes autonomous and lodges itself in the mind and body where it generates a negative energy field that totally occupies the person. When we are not present in the moment a residue of pain is produced and all emotional pain from the past merges with it. The pain body can become like an entity, dormant for long periods of time, but anything can trigger it so it grows to be vicious, violent and self-destructive.

It is unconsciousness that produced it, but exposed to the light it becomes light. When the sick person develops into a watcher, his or her sustained conscious attention brings about the transmutation and the pain becomes the fuel for consciousness; the split is healed and the person becomes whole.

The pain body also has a collective aspect: it is suffering that has accumulated in the human psyche for thousands of years through disease, war, murder, revenge, torture, madness and cataclysms. Certain races have a heavier collective pain body than others.

Without consciousness, we are perpetually forced to relive our emotional pain and this triggers the collective pain. If shame, guilt, fear and anger remain the ruling factors in our lives, hopelessness, frustration and apathy settle in. Sickness may create the impetus that is needed to align ourselves with the divine Power and we might then be closer to enlightenment because we are more strongly motivated to wake up.

Until we have the courage to try new things and deal with the difficulties of life, confront our fears and character flaws, and look at obstacles as opportunities we remain in survival mode and take on rigid positions. A sickness may force us to become more flexible and not see the world as so black and white.

During the time of a major sickness everything is accelerated. We attract the lessons we need for our growth and healing. The synchronicity of events around us is precipitated to such an extent that we become aware of a guiding force assisting us at all times. Guide, doctor, healer or messenger from the spirit world, some presence at our side helps us to accomplish the changes.

A spirit being may also come to people undergoing a spiritual crisis, after a tragedy, trauma, or any devastating event in their lives. The doctor-in-the-sky operates on their psyche and removes the malignant growths that stand in the way of their spiritual healing.

From one of Varindra Vittachi's books, (he was a famous journalist and writer from Sri Lanka who was close to Bapak) I learned that there are five kinds of physical sicknesses:

1—The ordinary and minor ailments often helped by the latihan.
2—The hereditary defects and weaknesses for which latihan can be performed, and if it is God's will, they will be relieved.

3—A sickness that comes as a warning that one's life is not being lived in the right way.

4—A sickness given as a result of continuing one's wrong way of living, too much thinking and worrying for instance. The latihan performed for this asks for forgiveness and the strength to change one's patterns of life.

5—A sickness given to summon one to death, and the latihan in that case helps in accepting God's will.

I remember that when I first came into Subud there was much publicity about the miraculous healing of the actress Eva Bartok who was cured of a terminal illness when Bapak came to her bedside and did latihan with her. It was given as an example of what could happen—not that Subud is a cure for physical sickness, but that it could certainly be a way to heal us by dissolving the limiting myth of separation and duality.

THE GUIDING PRESENCE IN ILLNESS

Christian-Lucas (U.S.A.) interviewed in Menucha (OR.)

Integrity of being, sincerity of approach, curiosity for life, but also for death, leads us to ourselves and to the God within. Both life and death are one and the same in God's eyes.

I talk to Christian, sitting on the back stairs of the cafeteria at Menucha. The blazing foliage of the trees across the way is like the last surge of a dying fire, the salute of a finishing season and the reminder that a new seed has been planted deep inside. It's going to remain dormant until it is ready to germinate.

Although there is no water in this landscape it feels like a stream is rushing by. I realize that this feeling is not coming from the surroundings but from Christian himself, limpid as clear water with a streaming forward. His purity has nothing to do with morality; it is presence in its primary element as we sit on the bank of the water of our death, solitary but surrendered and trusting. Any time we sit quietly, mind and heart empty, our presence becomes the presence of God, always there to keep us company.

Christian warns me that he has gone through an incredibly powerful physical process, that he had come to the end of it and he is not sure he wants to open himself up again.

"It's like I have been through a war. I don't wish to go back and look at the remains," *he said.*

I ask him to talk about simple things like how he has come to Subud, how he has become so light and clear.

I came to Subud through some friends I was connected with and who I loved dearly. My aunt was actually opened in Subud about thirty years ago, so it was already introduced to my family. For twenty years or so I had some contact with Subud through this aunt. I went through my candidacy period and was opened here in Portland. Then I became an isolated member in Iowa for a while, but ended up coming back home.

Three years ago I was diagnosed with a malignant brain tumor. At the time I was just devastated. I couldn't believe it. I had seizures for four years prior to the diagnosis and I had the awareness all along that those were symptoms of something very serious. But hard as it was, I still trusted God to lead me through this test. I came to Portland and started doing an alternative treatment program. Along with it I did the latihan religiously.

Last spring I went through a strong spiritual experience. I began to have those stirrings during the night. I'd wake up and feel an energy going through me. Originally I was really scared of it and tried to stop it, but after a time I began to get used to it and give in to it.

I would get up around 1:30 a.m. every night and start doing the latihan for hours. I would enter an altered state and knew just what I needed to do, but without conscious thoughts. I would just do these things. It got to a point where—it actually sounds crazy when I say that, but I love the fact that in Subud we are allowed to express those things—there was a physical presence with me.

I actually experienced operations being performed on my body, operations happening without any surgeon being physically present. I could hardly believe this, but there were times when I was aware of places in my arms where the blood would rush. It was actually a fearful feeling—this blood rolling along the bottom of my arms. Things came out of my stomach and things would be pumped into my heart. Previous to all this I felt like someone was holding me down, I was being restrained somehow. When I finally surrendered I stopped feeling constricted and just started doing latihan, taking care of my spiritual life, not thinking about all of this.

Fortunately I was not alone. I always had people with me, not necessarily in the room but they were in the house at all times. I received a lot of ancestral stuff, ancestral connections. I had strong support from the group. I went through twelve days of this. I could not eat anything during the day and at about nine o'clock I would be done with my day. Then at one o'clock it would start all over again. During those times I had receivings on different things, various questions I had, to which I received the answers.

As I experienced these operations I went through a time when I had in mind that I had to die somehow. I wasn't very afraid of the actual death process. At that point a friend came over who was a nurse: she was a very spiritual person. All along I knew exactly the people I needed to have with me to complete the circle. It was a continuous process. I would be done with that person and then the next would show up for me. I had the presence of mind to ask them to be a part of this process if they would.

I went through a really intense breathing process and this nurse was there to complete things for me. I would reach incredible levels. I actually reached places when I thought it was too much and I would pray, "Oh my God, I can't go on like this." And then I would reach another level and this incredible light would come and purify everything that was inside of me. Then I would start with another layer and this was repeated until I finally got to the end of it.

This woman was with me throughout this time of being centered around my ancestral purification. There was also something inside talking to me about being able to express myself and tell my truth, the truth of what was happening to me. I would get to these levels and all of a sudden I would say, "Talk, talk," and we'd both break into laughter.

So all through this time of heavy purification there would be these beautiful connections. I was going toward this completion that would truly allow me to become my inner self, also allow my inner to speak and become whole. When I finished that particular sequence of events I was so fragile, so vulnerable and opened that it was hard for me to leave the house.

Through a period of three years I was pretty well confined to the house and focused on my healing, changing my diet, doing colonics and daily enemas, a really intense physical cleansing. In the summer, with the two Subud sisters that were with me at the time, we decided that I would make a pilgrimage to Spokane to the congress. So we did and I ended up staying there, even staying an additional week in Montana. My point for saying this is that because I hadn't been out of the house for so long this was a gift. I was given so much all along and I know for sure that God had something for me because of all the guidance I was given.

How do you feel now?

Since that particular experience I have not had any diagnostic to see if the tumor was gone, but for four years I had been experiencing very intense physical sensations and seizures and now I don't have any seizures.

Do you feel that it's better not to check with the medical profession, especially since you feel you are going through intense purification, because there is so much fear involved with the diagnoses of conventional medicine?

That's the way I feel. I still take an anti-seizure drug and I don't think that it's hurting me in any way. Even though when I enter the medical framework I get much worse, for the most part I feel healed and incredibly blessed. I am anxious about my next test (*he laughs,*) let it not be too big a one.

How long had you been opened before you were diagnosed?

Years before, but I had been an isolated member so I had not done latihan very regularly until three years ago when I came up here. The friend who brought me is the man in the green shirt over there.

Oh Marius! I had arranged to interview him next. It often seems to me as if these interviews have a life of their own.

When I went to the Male Clinic to have a biopsy, Marius received that it was important for him to be with me. Had he not been there I don't know if I would have survived. His presence allowed me to trust the process, trust God, and he wrote a prayer for me. It became like a mantra that took me through that first initial period that is so scary, probably the worst.

I have been with friends when they were diagnosed with cancer. All the fears come at you at once, and everyone has a suggestion. All the possibilities of cures are thrown at you. It's like an assault. You have to make a choice very quickly, you are told. And it's your life you are dealing with.

It's having the right presence with you that allows you to be quiet enough to trust. For me it's kind of hard right now because I trusted God so implicitly and knew that I was given this experience for a reason—I mean it's the worst thing that ever happened to me but still . . . Now,

I don't know what to do next, and I don't have that guidance that overrides my thoughts. It's anticlimactic. I feel good again. I feel strong again, but I ask, "Oh my God, what do I do now? Where do I go now?" To experience a miracle is proof that we can accept it. But what comes after the miracle?

I talked about all this to my osteopaths at the time, and they both thought that I had gone crazy. One of them was a true believer and I was amazed that a miracle to him was so far removed from being possible. But I have received it and it's important for me to claim it. I want to be able to talk about it. It's my story; I received in the deepest way. I have to tell it.

The parallel journey of healing, when one chooses to embark

on it, is like a prihatin (fasting, observing a spiritual fast.) One enters it alone, leaving all one knows behind and putting oneself with total trust in God's hands. The guidance comes, very intense, so much so that many timid souls are not willing to go through with it, preferring to have the symptoms under control as soon as possible and the sickness out of the way so they can go back to their habitual life. As the symptoms are suppressed they often are pushed deeper and probably will have to be dealt with later in more serious circumstances. But if one is willing to follow the astonishing guidance, to open to the guardian angels that are constantly sent to people during an illness, the truth of the sickness will be revealed and the inner shift that is necessary will happen.

I took a little break from typing and went for a walk up the mountain, under the falling snow. The snow has always been a miracle to me, a proof of God's presence in everyday life. This walk was a prayer of gratitude for all the daily miracles I usually ignore, the presence I fail to see, the gifts I forget I am given, the treasures I take for granted.

Christian's story is important to me as a parable. Many of us ask, sometimes with great insistence, for our lives to be given meaning, for God to make his presence felt in an obvious way, for our guides and guardians to appear, in short to be given a vision, a strong experience that would do away with all our doubts, a guidance so powerful there would be no way to ignore it, and no choice but to follow it.

We ask for the full force of the power of God to displace us from what we consider our insignificant little life and to give us the great inspiration of the Divine. When we are given it in one form or another however, we take fright. Enlightenment is a great risk. When it appears we beg God to take it away quickly or to give it to us little at a time, with an eyedropper.

We start complaining again as soon as it's over, when we have to go back to our ordinary life. We fit the wings that were given to us into a small box in order to keep them as souvenirs. We go on with our life but secretly we ask, "Oh God, I don't know what to do *next. Please give me more inspiration. I can't live without divine inspiration."*

I have been guilty of all of this myself and I am thankful that I haven't been sent a serious illness as a test of my willingness to be guided through. I realize now that the inspiration has to come from me, daily, the inspiration to see the beauty that is given to me and be grateful, the inspiration to keep hope even in the midst of a bad world situation, to trust that I possessed all the tools I needed from the very beginning.

Life will only give me back what I give it. I have to give myself my daily bread, my nourishment. Then only will God feed me.

I am loved when I am the source of my love.

(Since this interview Christian became Lucas. He got married, a marriage he had postponed when he was diagnosed with inoperable brain tumor. In the five years since the diagnosis he had two children. He went on regular hikes, became strong and healthy and was the co-chair of Subud Youth.

Before going to the National Congress, which took place in Maryland, he told his family and friends that he felt he was going on to some new work, important work. Later he told someone close, "I feel really strong. I am sorry I am leaving."

He had been feeling a little tired at the beginning of the congress and when he didn't show up for one of the meetings his friend Lewis said it was very unlike Lucas. He went to his room and found him dead in the bed where he had been napping. Later his wife found a love letter he had slipped into her purse, probably sometime during the day.)

WHAT BRINGS ONE TO SICKNESS

Lusana (U.S.A.) interviewed in Menucha (OR.)

Some, prisoners of a shadow, remain captive in their father's house, beguiled by their mother's garden. Their

truth, discovered during the healing journey, is a treasure
that even death will not take away. The cancer, like a
jewel in her breast.

The cancer made me completely aware. An opportunity, a
wake-up call. Something inside your body is telling you that it's
all wrong somewhere, that you are not doing it right. For me it
was having to look at things, do all kinds of therapy and inner
work, lots of latihan while asking: "Whatever is there, come up
and show yourself."

So you go into it and have to look at that part of your life that
brought you there and prevents you from moving on. The strongest
awareness for me was fear, how fear permeates every part of my
life. I was afraid of being right, afraid of being wrong, afraid of
disappointment. Fear in most cases dominates everything you
do.

So, little by little you let go of that. But the other problem is
not knowing how to love yourself. I still don't do that very well,
but I do recognize and feel the energy of love, not of being in
love, but love coming into my being and opening up doors so I
can journey

You went on a journey of recovery?

Yes I did. I had a tendency to give my power away throughout
my life. I bowed to people that I felt had an inner knowledge bigger
than mine. Whatever they said I'd say, "That's okay, that's it."

As women, in our society, we are trained to bow to authority
and give precedence to another voice beside our own.

Yes. I came to the crux of it when the cancer was discovered
in my breast. A helper who had always been the person I went
to for guidance received that I should have the operation,
because of course the doctors wanted to take the cancer out
while it was small. The night before the operation I got a call
from somebody else I totally respected, saying he received that
I shouldn't have the operation. I had given him authority and I
trusted him. Then the woman helper said that from her personal

receiving she understood that if I didn't have the operation I would die.

On the way to the operation I stopped to do a latihan with a Subud sister whom I love, and after latihan she said, "Don't you think we should call Rahayu about this?" She called and Rahayu said no operation. I just about flipped out. Terror totally filled me. I was so afraid I was going to die. But something within said no. I just about went crazy with indecision, knowing that the last receiving came from Ibu Rahayu.

Anyway, we did a latihan and I received this spiritual force that came in and stayed with me, and along with it came a voice, "You won't have to have the operation as long as you remain very diligent and I will help you do that because I've got that Grace." That is when I lost my fear. It was the very beginning of losing it. I tell you, this sickness has taken me places it would have taken me years to get to.

Yes, it is a teacher. It's like you live behind a curtain. It's like death is on one side and you are on the other most of the time. And all of a sudden the curtain opens up and stays there so you become aware of the other side, and soon you can see both sides all the time. Where you came from and where you are going, and then you have to live right here, right now. It turned around all my belief system, everybody or everything I hung on to in a righteous way, or because of a teaching. I had to go on my own experience only, to determine what was real or what was not.

We are all striving to accomplish that, you are right, but I wish we didn't have to be afraid. Fear takes you away from your own truth so you look for it in others. But you always have the possibility to get your truth back.

I am not afraid of dying anymore, I have reconciled with my death. At any moment I might receive something different about the situation, so each of us has to have the freedom to follow whatever it is. For me there is no holding on. It's kind of like a marriage.

In this community we have created, we are coming together in strength, not in weakness, so each partner has the freedom to have their own movement and growth without holding on to the old patterns, or imposing them on the other. I know there is some incredible growth coming.

I used to be afraid of living in isolation but now it's like wherever I go I won't be alone. I know that Subud people will be with me in any way that is right and if it is right. To me that's opening up. I let myself be guided.

When I was younger I had a vision. There was a waterfall coming through my house. It was like fluidity and God's grace. In the house were children, youths, so I understood that it was a place that would be opened to the youth, that it was my work to make it possible for that to happen.

From the very beginning of my adulthood I wanted to counsel kids, so I knew that it was my work. When I read Tom Brown's book (he was taught by Stalking Wolf Apache) I realized that he added a whole new dimension from which I could learn whatever was right for me, and incorporate it into my work.

After that my children and I will be going on a journey trying to incorporate as much as we can from his teaching, going to more and more support groups to keep getting more input. I cut myself off from the telephone, from a source of easy heat, from all my basic securities, and I did it knowing nothing about where I was going with it.

I am really eager to get my kids back into their strength and power. They lost their inner power when the divorce between my husband and me happened. I need to be in a place where I am free of reaction towards my ex-husband. I hope this will help them. Living like that will force them to learn about themselves and rely on themselves. I am going to give them a chance. I have a big van. I have a fifteen-passenger van and we are going to use that as our base.

We will be totally on our own, and we will learn not to be afraid of the world, not to be afraid of the rain and the cold. I have been afraid of the cold for a long time and I found out why. When I get cold it has to do with circumstances happening within the cold. I need to make the connection between this earth and the almighty without any ifs, without any fear in the way. That anyway is what I have learned.

PSYCHIC OPERATION

Resmiwati (U.S.A.) interviewed in L.A. (CA.)

Very few true words are exchanged each day; we may fall in love, or fall sick in order to begin speaking our true language, just as we begin doing the latihan in order to find our true self. At the beginning there was just that word, a sound without speech, the golden breath, the blue light of God. And then water, the flow . . . bubbles everywhere, the magnificent digestive power of bubbling water. Bubbles as echoes of the divine melody penetrating the material planes so they could be translated into language. She speaks and re-creates the beginning.

I left Aspen, Colorado in 1974 after finding out that I had cancer. In 1973 when the uterine cancer was discovered the doctor was practically going to wheel me out of the room where they did the biopsy and into the operating room. I said: "Ho ho ho . . . wait a minute . . . you are not taking my uterus out just like that." I remember walking out of that hospital and standing on the steps for a moment and . . . Woom! It came to me: "Go to Indonesia."

The money came easily and everything was made available. I wrote to Bapak and he answered that I should come. So I left my twin boys with friends, Laura and Saul. Paul, my husband, helped taking care of them also. The very first thing that Bapak said to me was, "Well, you're here, just surrender.

"He wants me to surrender when I am going to die?" I thought.

I was there seven weeks and really knew beyond the shadow of a doubt, after those weeks, that the source of the cancer had been purified. I also knew that if I went back to the doctor it could still show up in the test, but I felt confident that its source in the spiritual universe had been purified. It was gone. So I waited for almost nine months before I went to a doctor in Marin County. I had tested with five helpers as soon as I came back to see if it was necessary for me to go to a medical doctor and the answer had been 'no'.

Then Bapak wrote to me that if the latihan showed no results it was okay to have Laetrile treatment. "If the latihan shows no result?" I thought amused. It showed terrific results. I was so full of all those experiences I had undergone. I had not a doubt.

You tell me it was courageous to follow my receiving, but in that case, I can tell you that it was not courageous at all. It was exactly how it had to be. The blessing was that it could be no other way. It was amazing. I didn't have to decide about it. God! It was just how it had to happen.

Months later the testing showed that it was okay to see a doctor. They did all the tests. There was not a trace of cancer. But I tell you, those experiences, no one could really know how powerful they were. The stronger ones happened during the time I spent in Indonesia. Yes, it all happened there. It was during Ramadan and I was observing the Ramadan fast.

I mean there were nights when there were hands reaching in and around my ovaries and pulling them out, cutting things out. No one could have convinced me that it was not happening for real. It was a real surgeon doing it, a real one. I mean I will never forget; I can still feel it. A machine was brought in and pointed at my vagina, zapping it with radiation. I had experiences in which I was witnessing everything, everywhere, the past and the future all at once . . .

I wasn't in my body. My body was lying in that bed in the guesthouse and I was over there watching. What thoughts, what opinions, what attitude, what behavior had brought the cancer on, I had to see it all. It was like as if a film about my life was constantly projected on the walls, no matter where I was. I had to see how my attitudes and decisions had actually manifested that mass in my body and I had to tell my truth about it. I had layers upon layers of judgments.

For instance I would look at you and think, "Oh, that means this and this means that." I would see my father hurting my mother and that meant that I would never trust men . . . and I'll never this, or that. All that stuff had to be lifted off until I could see my father, or see my mother, just simply being, with no charge, nothing . . . and at that moment, blood would come. I would be bleeding profusely. So this is the type of thing that went on, night after night . . .

During the night I would see the men from Wisma Subud coming into my room, picking me up and standing me in the middle of the room, then doing a latihan around me. A latihan I could not even believe! And I would go to Rahayu the next day and ask, "Did this really happen?" and she would answer, "Oh yes, it really did. Everybody knows that men are the ones who can do a latihan for sexual purification."

It was all ancestral stuff. I was given the understanding of what a real man is inside a woman. To get to experience that without a man present I needed to surrender very deeply. It was a blessing, a state of grace.

When I came back here those experiences caused me to decide to have nothing to do with sex until I found the right man. I knew that if I went out and had sex with someone, just to follow my urges to give my body pleasure and sensation, I would have to experience the results. And I already knew what those results were. There was no way that what I truly wanted could come from doing that, so it was not even available as an option. It was not hard at all for me not to have the sexual in my life and I was celibate for many years until I met Ed. But that is another story.

I lost track of Resmiwati but recently learned that she died a few years ago of a different kind of cancer.

THE POWERFUL EXPERIENCE OF CANCER

Saul (U.S.A.) interviewed in Santa Cruz (CA.)

*I dreamt of Saul: a lanky wolf leaning into the storm,
eyes half closed against the sting of snowflakes lashing
him and challenging the thread of his intent. I dreamt of
transparent flesh over brittle bones like those of small birds,
his face borrowing astral radiance.*

*Deploying feats of perseverance, his love for life
renewed each day, he lets go of defenses and protections.
As he labors to bring his physical being back from the
spiritual, one more time, it's his openness we fear, for the
hand that dares touch him sinks right through skin and
flesh to the core of his being.*

The last few years have been very interesting to say the
least. Early in 1992 I was diagnosed with cancer, with a
condition labeled life threatening. Major surgery and
hospitalization followed. Several months of recuperation
afterwards brought great results. The cancer had been removed,
the prognosis was positive. Life went back to being as normal
as it could be, given the powerful spiritual and physical
experiences of the cancer scenario.

But then, after my visit to Stanford for my six-month check-
up cancer was detected in both lungs. After two surgeries and
lengthy recovery, things again have returned to normal.

*How has the cancer struggle affected your spiritual life? Has
it been a teacher?*

The cancer experience has totally changed my life. To
experience a doctor telling you that you probably will be dead
soon puts a really interesting slant on life. To be in (and survive)
that delicate balance between life and death brings a new
appreciation for life. The amazing grace, the psychic and spiritual
healing that then happens is incredible. Each day is a miracle
and nothing can be taken for granted.

To live in the moment to the fullest with love and compassion is what I learned. I woke up in the hospital room after the operation and the room was glowing, bathed in a golden light. The grace, prayer, compassion and love were so powerful it was like a physical presence you could reach out and touch. Certain areas of light were swaying and sparkling like a jeweled curtain. There was a physical feeling about my body, of warmth, and a vibration that brought absolute bliss.

So many lessons. Isn't it too bad that we can't really get life's lessons in an easier way? From a spiritual standpoint my life is much richer. I thank God everyday for the miracle of life and all its blessings.

Saul's description of the glowing room he woke up in after his operation brought back memories of a powerful experience I had as a child, waking up after an operation which saved my life. The similarity may be due to the fact that the healing experience is something we all have in common. It's like going through birth again but consciously this time. This experience, I believe, gave me a strong incentive to look for a spiritual path later in life and led me to the latihan.

During World War II, when Paris was heavily bombed, parents with small children were encouraged to send them to the country and entrust them to the care of farmers. It was safer there and food was more accessible. I was sent to a farm with seven other children and left, unbeknownst to my parents, in a very abusive situation. Eventually, an untreated ear infection brought me close to death. When my mother was finally appraised of the gravity of the situation she hurriedly brought me back to Paris, only to be faced with the distressing realization that medicines were unavailable, and that competent doctors and specialists were not to be found. Many were enlisted and had been sent to treat the wounded on the front lines, some had moved to the free zone, and others chose or were forced to work for the occupants. If they were Jewish, they were hiding or leaving the country if not already sent to concentration camps.

My father was fighting in the army so my mother was alone to deal with the crisis. She carried me, shivering and delirious, wrapped in blankets, from one end of Paris to the other because gasoline was unavailable for private cars or taxis, and subways were not running most of the time. Eventually she did find a surgeon who had been recommended to her, a Jewish man who had the courage to continue his practice, although by doing so he faced terrible danger. This man refused to be broken down, hide or wear the Jewish star. When he saw the condition I was in he didn't waste any time. He convinced my mother that I needed to be operated on that very day. He couldn't promise her anything he added, it might already be too late. If the infection had reached the brain there was nothing to be done.

My mother agreed to let me be operated on. The surgeon saved my life, a fact of which I became very conscious although I was just four at the time. I experienced him as a father, a god, a radiant and benevolent being I could trust more than anyone else in the world.

Before the operation, when I was about to be put under with ether, my beloved doctor told me what to expect. What I experienced was very different though. I felt myself expanding, then shrinking, expanding again, my body growing until it filled the entire room, the entire world, then reduced to the size of a tiny insect. This happened many times until it created an implosion of my whole soul. I became different beings in different times all through the operation. Like Saul, I remembered remembering, while I was being operated on. I also remembered the power that was with me as such a tangible force that it felt like I could reach out and touch it.

I remained between life and death for I don't recall how many days, but when I finally woke up to life, the intense feeling of being reborn thrilled my body with a vibrating bliss, while everything around me shivered and shimmered with the life force. I was fully aware of it all, more intensely aware than ever.

A fly buzzing and describing an arc of light across the room suddenly captivated my attention. The area of flight was sparkling with a magnificence that filled me with an intense feeling of love and gratitude. I could barely contain it. My brother, sixteen years older, sat by my side and I could see the connective filaments of pulsating light moving from my body to his. He pointed to the sky and from his finger sprung a fountain of light.

What he was pointing at was a formation of airplanes in the sky. To me they only appeared to expand the area of vibrating light that the fly had opened. Those airplanes were so tiny they might have been flies themselves. Like the fly in my room they trailed happiness and laughter. There were others beside my brother in the room: everything, everyone was connected with those filaments.

Suddenly I heard cheers, acclamations outside my room where people were listening to a radio. I was kissed and hugged by those around. Pleasurable currents rushed through my body. All things and people were living hearts that sparked fireworks of brotherhood and goodwill. I heard laughter again, and words of glee, inside, outside. I heard "Liberation. Victory. The Allies. The war is over. We have won."

The whole city, the whole country was celebrating. Radios were spreading the news everywhere; the poem everyone had prayed for while listening to the underground radio was read on the air. The whole country was experiencing the same rebirth as I was. I believed that everyone in France was celebrating my recovery.

The glow around my brother and the other family members in the room was like an endless source of warmth and security. The world was a benevolent place and the people in it loved me. They wanted me to live.

This was my true beginning. The flying beings in the room, in the sky were propelled by love and they moved me out of my old self. They obviously had the power to open everyone's heart." The belief that it was my recovery that France was celebrating that day stayed with me for a long time.

The war had given me birth; that's why people of my generation were called "the children of war".

Saul died not long after this interview, surrounded by family and friends.

PARTNERS IN SICKNESS

Laura (Saul's wife) interviewed in Santa Cruz (CA.)

A mother, at dawn, tending life. She leans on a sick bed as though it were a crib, her mouth forming a kiss as the light falls on her shoulders; she listens to the painful breathing, lending her own. She keeps nothing for herself. Her love a warm blanket with which she covers the shrunken bundle, the being who in dying is like a newborn.

The cancer struggle has been the spiritual teacher of my life also. Nothing has hit me deeper, with such force, so suddenly. Layers of self-indulgence have been burned away. Things that used to cause me great irritation or impatience or even fear are less likely to get me now. I feel more compassion where compassion is the right response, and less indulgence where I used to be an enabler. I am humbled by this experience, laid bare, stripped of arrogance I hope. More impatience has been burned away than in any other twelve-month period of my life.

From the latihan point of view I see that this has been a great spiritual catalyst for my husband and myself. Lessons we were too stubborn or unwilling to learn have been made imperative to learn if we were to walk through just one day. This life has no security on an outer level. If one clings to that, one is sure to be destroyed by death. To survive the threat of death or the actuality of death, one must learn to let go; let go; let go and accept this moment, then that moment, and let life flow. We can only pray for grace, allow and accept the generosity of life as it manifests. We cannot force it. A great learning time for me, beyond words really. It's all happening on a cellular level, like cancer. I wake up some days and realize that I am totally changed.

"If your cancer has caused you to stop, think, pray, and know God better, it has been a blessing to you. If your cancer has caused you to realize the importance and magnificence of this temple

wherein your soul dwells, you have been doubly blessed. If your cancer has caused you to look within and ask the Christ to dwell within you, you have been thrice blessed." Dr. William Donald Kelley

WHAT'S LETTING GO?

Laoma (U.S.A.) interviewed in Little River (CA.)

"In the final apocalypse of the self—the dissolution of the sole remaining duality, that of existence and non-existence—identity itself dissolves in universal divinity, and no individual consciousness is left to choose. The last step, then, is taken by God alone."

Dr. David R. Hawkins

Laoma and I had been planning to have this conversation and record it for weeks but always, on the day we had fixed, either an emergency would arise which took her to the hospital, or else she had exhausted herself and could not even talk. Finally, on one of the days I was on helping duty at her house, there was an opening. The doctors who had followed her case, also by the nurse who came regularly to her house, had just told her that her whole system was closing down and that she should let go, that she was entering the transition phase and should not fight any longer. They could not do anything for her anymore, so it was time for her to concentrate on her spiritual practice. But although she looked very bad on paper, in the flesh she was actually feeling pretty good.

She hadn't been practicing the latihan for a few years but still strongly felt she was part of Subud. I started by asking her about her opening in Subud.

I got opened in San Anselmo in 1972 and I did latihan regularly for about ten years. We moved from there when Dakota, my daughter, was four, and we sent away for both our names, which were Laoma for me and Leila for her. I practiced in Elk very regularly for quite a few years. Then I got involved in a Buddhist practice for a while and did the latihan only occasionally. I got back into it when my cancer was first diagnosed and then dropped out of it again, but I always felt like I was part of Subud and always welcomed the latihan whenever the group brought it to me.

I mostly wanted to talk about your sickness. You have been fighting very hard for your life and doing everything you could for years. Quite an involvement it has been, this journey to fight cancer. And now, especially today, you are told that you should let go because you are dying and there is nothing else to do, that you should be accepting the transition that is part of the journey. But I know you don't feel you are there yet.

In general have you been able to balance the spiritual and physical during this time of total involvement with the needs of the body?

Yes, I think I have. But I wonder what is supposed to be that letting go part? The more I look at it the more I see that there is not so much difference in the parts, that we tend to want to differentiate but it's all part of death, and death is part of life. That's really what I want to say. I have always been a very positive person and for the most part I am making this transition rather smoothly, and I am grateful for every day I am given. I certainly have dips but I find myself now looking forward to the next day. I am not at all looking forward to leaving, not at all.

So you live every day fully and intend to do this till the end and then naturally start the other journey, is that it?

Yes. People don't know me. They don't know how stubborn I am. These doctors, they prescribe and tell me I have to enter my spiritual journey. As though I have not been doing that! I find it very condescending.

Then the phone rings and Laoma answers. She talks to the partner of someone who was in her cancer group and is dying. She wants to go visit right then. She tells me that her husband and she had intended to see that person today but too much had happened.

"I think about her so deeply," she says to her husband. But he refuses to go; he believes that she needs to rest. She is very disappointed.

I try to get back to our conversation.

So Laoma, it sounds like you have experienced what Bapak described: "In God's eye there is absolutely no difference between life and death." You live . . . and then you live . . .

That's exactly it. You live as fully as you can and then you are not living anymore here.

Then you live the fullest you can on the other side, right?

Right.

What do you feel the nurse is saying when she tells you to let go?

Well, today I felt very angry because she was telling me to let go prematurely, because she doesn't really know me.

Yes, I suppose that you let go when you are ready to and you are the only one who knows that.

Yes, and what is letting go? What I have been working on in this last month is surrender and the willingness to surrender, which I have always struggled with because of my will. I have been exploring the depths because my will is so strong. I really don't think it's my ego.

I'd like to soften. I have been working on softening my will so I can just embrace what's happening and be willing to move to where I need to move, or be still. I had a long period of sitting last year, sitting in stillness, sitting outside and just being, watching the hummingbirds, but sometimes I feel that there is something that I am not doing that I need to do. I have always been such a doing person.

It might be that your main doing is learning to not do. That is the big task for all of us Westerners, especially in this country.

Yes, and watching everybody spinning around me . . . It's interesting from this place of quiet.

You have woven an amazing web of people around you. How does that feel?

It feels nearly like that has become my spiritual practice. I have been thinking that I would find it somewhere. What's my spiritual practice? I asked myself. I really think that it is the web of friends and family and love that is woven around me.

I tell you, having been working for all those years, so busy, hard working at the bakery, always having to leave the house, and finally getting to sell the bakery and be home, just at the right time. It was such good fortune, so precious!

So you are making peace inside of you and inside your house, no more rushing . . .

I want to enjoy every day and feel grateful for it. I was talking to Margaret the rabbi this morning about how this seems to be my practice, all those friends that come over! I want to keep everything as cleaned up as possible, because you may think that you clean up one relationship and will be able to shuck that other one out. Okay, now on to the next, (*she laughs*) but in the process more dirt accumulates. It's like the piles of mail or the dirt under the rug. I mean relationships are what's happening with me now. It's my life, and when I get into sticky places I have to look at this closely. Different personalities come over and some people aren't as easy for me to handle as others. They may have different energies for me to bump against.

And maybe see your stuff in it.

Yes, that's just it.

It's a constant cleansing of yourself and your stuff.

That's true, and seeing the parts of myself that I don't like, and trying not to be too hard on myself, not judgmental of myself.

It's a practice custom-made just for you, and people feel it. I can see that everyone is trying to get a little time with you. It's big for them, even people who call you on the telephone. They want a little piece of you. We all want to eat you up, we love you so! (We laugh and hug each other.)

There is no transitioning because you just do what you do and don't call it anything; you seem to be in a good place with all of that.

It's amazing. I didn't expect it to be like this because I was in so much pain for so long. When it went away it was like a new life

And now they are telling you that you are dying, but you don't feel it.

And "they" . . . put this little bug in my ear that says it could happen any moment and that is a little scary, I have that to contend with.

Could it happen that suddenly?

I don't know if it would be so sudden, but I have to watch out because it could be lurking right now. (*She laughs.*)

What do they want you to do when they are urging you do be prepared?

They, Daddy in particular, want to make sure that I am looking into my spiritual life.

Are you? Do you feel the connection between God within and God without?

I think so. I will have to look at that more, go deeper. It feels a little bit like maybe I am not doing something. It's that doing thing again. Do you think one needs to do something about it?

You don't really need to do anything when you learn to surrender—which is what you are doing now, and willing to go deeper each day. If I think about it for myself, I don't want to be stuck on this earth after death because I was unable to let go and surrender. To be stuck in confusion. So all I can do is to accept everything that comes, as it comes, good and bad news. If I fight I go into fear and denial.

Process things as they come, I tell myself. Learn to see everything you encounter every day as the next lesson that helps you grow. You are in the right place, always when you surrender to God. Everything, no matter how insignificant, is a lesson of life, a tool for finding my way.

I believe that when you make the passage it's very important to be clean and clear in that way; look at what's in front of you; take it in, and then let it go; go on to the next thing. Trust the next step, always, trust no matter what happens. If it is scary, look at it as something you have to go through for a while, only until you take that next step. Your trust in God is where your courage comes from and it propels you. That's what following your true nature really means in my mind.

You mean that this is what you have to do after you enter into the passage?

Yes, but before also. There is hardly any difference as you said yourself. You are on your journey and you have been for some time and everything is intense purification for you. You have to trust in order be guided in the right direction. You can't let yourself go into fearful imagination because it keeps you at a lower level of consciousness and robs you of the spiritual energy you need for the journey. If it comes, just let it pass.

There is really no work, no doing involved, quite the opposite, just trust. They are telling you to let go but they might use the word surrender. It's the attitude of acceptance and trust you have towards the events of your life that have a positive or negative effect on it. At this time every little thing that comes your way is meaningful and significant and I can see that you are doing the journey as well as you can and you are able to remain open to learning.

We all are on an adventure and the adventure is that we don't know. We all believe that we do know where we are going when we are healthy, but that's foolish. More often than not we are in survival mode, not yet the masters of our own destinies.

Let's say you had bad news today and people are telling you this or that, doctors, nurses make it sound scary and, as you said, you get angry. You learn to see that as part of the purification that brings you to your next step. Maybe something important is coming with that next step, some good news, an important understanding, liberation.

Yes, it is hard to trust the next step. I think that it's the fear of the not knowing that makes it hard. When we are on a journey that spells out familiarity it's not nearly as scary. Even getting into nasty places with myself is familiar. I recognize it and I think, "Oh that's Laoma, the nasty person," and I can stay with this for a while because I know it.

When you come to a place of fear, how do you handle it? Do you stay with it or do you try to push it away?

That's a good question. It depends greatly. If I am open I can just about welcome it. That's a big difference, the welcoming and recognizing that it's something interesting to look at.

Like an adventure?

Yes, but if you are closed, you tighten up. "The monsters are coming to get me!"

You know of course that these monsters are your friends. At least we are told so.

Yes. You just have to open the door and let them in.

Yes, and you are supposed to ask, "What do you want? I am ready to give you what you need." (Laoma laughs) I have learned to do that in dreams, to welcome my monsters.

I have a lot of curiosity about this process. In fact, there is something I want to ask you. What have you learned from all this?

You mean from being around you?

Yes, being around me, but also from being around Subud people. Sometimes I feel like being too much around Subud people who are "being Subud" colors my vocabulary. Do you know what I mean?

Yes, I know what you mean, I think, but I have been in Subud for so long that the vocabulary is beside the point. What the latihan has mostly taught me is to trust, and accept those I used to have a hard time accepting, people's trips that annoyed me. I still come up against my judgment—with Subud people even more than with people outside Subud it seems—but somehow, doing the latihan has opened me to having compassion for my faults and those of others. It has been a long process, however. It hasn't happened overnight. And though I still have a long way to go I trust that I can do it.

But as far as "being Subud" is concerned, I must say that I don't feel that way. So many of my friends are not in Subud, and they are doing many different practices. Some are not practicing at all but I feel them as spiritual people. I don't feel that I am locked in one vocabulary or interpretation. Do you feel that way about me?

Not at all.

I know that some Subud people might have a religious righteousness about them. They have some trip they are laying on others, or so I am told, but personally I don't meet many of those. There are always some people, in every religious practice, who need to do that. The latihan has opened my eyes to other things. Basically, I have gained a deeper level of acceptance. Of course I go through times when I fall from grace.

Do you really? Moi? . . .

When I fall I really fall hard. Two weeks ago I wrote in my journal: I am not a good mother. I am not a good writer. I am not a good wife, a good person, not a good gardener nor a cook. I am not good at life. I do not have any joy. I am not Riantee-the-one-who-laughs. I know only know how to cry, and complain. I am nothing.

From there you can start again. You have hit bottom. Here we go! Where is the bottom peg on this?

From there you can leap again. Once you have accepted the very worst, then you can go on towards the best of yourself without fear. I must tell you that it has been amazing being around you. You are so alive in this process. That's why you attract people. We all love you so much!

I wanted to ask you what helped you deal with the unbearable pain you experienced a couple of months ago. Was there any technique that helped you through, or did you just have to go through it with no help, like what you described when we were in the hospital together the other week. You said you just have to call it what it is. There is no fooling yourself.

Yes, no fooling yourself about the pain.

Is there any little trick that helped you through?

(Long silence) When I go blank, I sure go blank!

O yes. Dealing with pain is like this shield that comes over me. Nothing else exists. It is just pain. Big, black, dirty pain and it is a complete shut down. That's why it feels so good when it is over.

Do you feel like leaving your body then? Does it make you feel like checking out?

Yes it does.

Did you do a regular practice of some kind during the years when you haven't been doing the latihan?

Well, I did a lot of sitting meditation. What that seems to do is bring out what I couldn't do right. I learned a lot from that. It had to do with what I should be doing, about what I wasn't doing and comparing myself to others. A lot of comparing was going on, both between the best of me and the worst of me.

Did the sitting allow you to work on all that?

Yes it did, but it doesn't seem to be the best practice for me you know! That is what I liked about the latihan. It is not so mental. You let go and then it comes, like with the movements and sounds you make. It comes up and it goes.

A lot of people with cancer I have talked to, feel that their cancer is a teacher—an opportunity to do a lot of inner healing, also that in the end, death might be the healer necessary for them. That is, if they are open to that teaching.

I do feel that way. It certainly was an opportunity, but I didn't always take the opportunity. I see also that this process is so much about service and serving others, I see how different people's idea of service is, and how that affects me being on the receiving end. I get to experience both sides of it. People have been coming here and giving to me in all different ways, and some people are such naturals at service and do it with such grace. It's just beautiful, so natural. Others, on the other hand, try a lot. It's the same issue that has come up in life for me: trying too hard, trying to do it right, and having an agenda.

I guess to be a good server you just have to enjoy what you are doing and not call it anything. That's the best service. Enjoying yourself in it is the answer to good service. That's a great lesson because we are really on this earth to serve. It's a great process to learn the right place of service, not to have 'the shoulds' about it. If you do 'the should of service,' you kill it.

That's right! But we, it isn't final, we are not stuck, we always have choices.

Laoma was tired at this point and it was a good place to end our conversation. She and her husband Richard had talked all morning, first to the nurse about reaching the end of the process and having to let go, giving up all medication except for pain killers. Then they had met with the rabbi, planning the funeral, looking at the shroud, going over the ceremony, and choreographing everything. Laoma was a stickler for details.

I had a talk with Richard afterward. He also felt that it was enough of a letting go for Laoma to be doing all the preparations, to have picked up dry ice the day before in order to be able to keep the corpse for three days after the death. He said that he had been 'doing cancer' for ten years, that it might be a relief, as some people tell him, when Laoma dies, this along with the grief and loneliness of course. But although he is exhausted, he has the joy of keeping her alive as long as she wants to be, as long as she is enjoying it. Sometimes she asks him to be a super hero, like doing this cancer-death-funeral bit all morning and then wanting him to accompany her to the bedside of someone in her group who is dying. She pushes him because . . . that's Laoma.

The worst for her, Laoma tells me at a later time, is when she feels she is being a burden to Richard, when she knows he looks at her with exhaustion, thinking, "Oh, I have 'to do' Laoma again!"

When it was time, they both gracefully let go. Laoma had a memorial ceremony when she was still alive, saying good-bye, accepting and expressing love. Amazing, touching moments: Richard reading her a love letter he had written to her, the love palpable between them as they looked each other in the eyes, the sharing, the poetry, the tears, the laughter, the flowers, the food and all. Laoma held on for another few weeks, made it to some important events, friends' shows or openings, their daughter's informal wedding and then she died peacefully in Richard's arms.

"A patient cannot be cured or fundamentally healed until he or she invokes the power of compassion both for him or herself and others." Dr. David R. Hawkins

6

HEALERS AND HEALING

*"It appears that death itself is only an illusion and
life goes on unimpeded by the limitation of perception which
results from being localized in a physical body; consciousness
is the vital energy which both gives life to the body and
survives beyond the body in a different realm of existence."*
Dr. David R. Hawkins

In a talk Bapak gave in Cilandak in 1972 he stated, "Angels
do not belong to the human race. So if they strike people it is not
with a knife or a hammer or with their hands. The way an angel
strikes a man is not the way one man strikes another, but in due
course is indicated through a man's own fault. For example he
may suddenly fall sick or someone may unexpectedly injure him.
It is not the angels themselves who directly carry it out."

If this happens his experience might take the form of worry,
stress, anger or other negative pattern of emotions that impairs
the defense system so the whole system turns against itself; this
describes diseases of the immune system. It is as though the
invisible universe of thoughts and attitudes becomes manifested
and visible in the body's dysfunction, which happens through
the repetition of a negative stimulus.

I understand that health and prosperity are the natural state
of being. Anything less calls for inner examination rather than

projection and blame. A mind obsessed with a negative worldview will cause small changes in the energy flow to various organs and this eventually will result in sickness. On the other hand, if it isn't already too advanced and self-perpetrating, the disease can be reversed by changing thought patterns and habitual responses. We have proof that it is possible for a lifelong affliction to heal rapidly with a mere shift of attitude; but although this shift may seem to occur in a split second, it may take years of inner preparation.

It is essential to have compassion for oneself and all of mankind as we go through the painful struggle of evolution, to know and enjoy what we have instead of chasing after what we don't have or what we will acquire next. If we start finding benefit in what we have we free ourselves from the exhausting struggle of trying to make things conform to our standards, for this can bring on a sickness.

In our day and age angels might enroll the help of viruses to strike, viruses that defeat all attempts at cures. Dr. Hattori, a Japanese Subud member who received a revelation from God on Mount Kuramayana in Kyoto, in June 1965, tells us that diseases are caused by erroneous action. When people are exclusively moved by their desires and all their actions are motivated by desire only, they get sick. What is meant by erroneous action is to go against the sacred laws of life, of self and of God—those laws that are not written anywhere but that we carry, deep inside. Not giving ourselves the time and space to be in touch with our inner, with our divine nature, shutting off our true voice in order to fit in with someone else's picture is also a transgression against ourselves. When we pay so much attention to the material world that we ignore our spirit's needs a disease may eventually manifest itself in the physical body, having started in the psychological and the spiritual bodies.

I once had a dream in which I was told that there was a remedy for every sickness, right here on earth, often right within the body and mind of the sick person; if the remedy was not to be found it meant that the death of the person was a healing on another level.

Often, during the course of an illness, we are led through an endless labyrinth of specialists until the right combination comes and help is given to relieve the ailment. The long process of discovery is one of a continual broadening of the causes of the illness. At times the divine spirit heals directly, at others it leads us to the right doctor and will assist in the treatment. We must turn everything to the guidance of this spirit while making the effort to seek the most suitable help. The process of healing, however, transcends the cure of a bodily condition. There is a spiritual reason that the sickness occurred and spiritual healing teaches us something about ourselves that we didn't know before. We may ask, "What am I not seeing about my spiritual life that the sickness came to show me?" And if we assume responsibility for whatever is wrong, the inner forces can begin to heal us.

Learning to live with a disease and be taught by it rather than dying (daily) of it, can show a person what a teacher the disease is, and will be until the day of death. Working with and being in the presence of people with life threatening diseases is often a healing for the attendants. There is a danger however, for the part of us that is a rescuer, to become addicted to wanting to help. Needing to heal the person and being too attached to the results pushes caregivers into giving everything they have until they burn out. It's also easy to become addicted to the high provided by the proximity of death, that exclusive concern with the spiritual.

I understand better what Bapak meant when he said to an individual that the greatest obstacle to his spiritual progress was the desire to help others. How could he do business if he always gave away the reserves he needed in order to trade? The need to be needed may be the motivation for helping, also the need to feel good about oneself for doing good, the need to be useful. Any time there is a need involved in helping someone, there is dependency, which also means expectation; then the healing power is absent.

Most humans are afraid of an inner healing that would force them to change drastically. Hearing testimonies of many people with HIV for instance, I learned that the disease forced them to change their life, face things they never had before, resolve conflicts, speak their truth, explore new ways to look at themselves, and in general look at the bigger picture. They started healing their inner life and that ripple of healing traveled far, reaching many others, even those who didn't appear to be sick bringing their understanding of healing a little further.

A conventional doctor will fix health problems by dealing with symptoms, which is often temporary, but will not try to interfere with a spiritual condition he is not qualified to heal. Psychic healers on the other hand will often attempt to do just that and set up more causes to be worked out as more problems. From what I understand, the difference between psychic healing and spiritual healing is that psychic healing will not change the state of consciousness, and only temporarily relieve symptoms caused by an attitude we hold. Eventually the sickness will resurface with a new face.

In the meantime the healer is accumulating karma from all the people he or she heals with the psychic force. There is more to healing than removing the outer symptoms until the passion of the mind behind the illness generates the next symptoms. In the healing professions, people deal with forces that could overwhelm them, especially if they are not aware of what they take on spiritually. This is because they don't totally understand ancestral patterns and the purpose of the disease. Spiritual healing, on the other hand, changes the attitude that causes the problem so it can go away and not recur. The problem surrounding healing is karmic; often the sick person once broke a divine principle through ignorance.

I heard Ibu Rahayu, in answer to a question, explain that many people newly opened in Subud might be attracted to the healing professions because once the latihan starts working and one becomes conscious of the vibration of the life force, it seems so easy to use it for the purpose of curing sickness. It's like a natural extension of the latihan and is obviously something so needed, so useful! Besides, it is exciting to manipulate the forces and become aware of one's power.

When one begins to feel the prime vibration flowing through one's being, it seems like wisdom is only a hair's breath away. One feels so light and free of baggage, so close to being a clean slate on which what's needed for healing purposes gets written as one goes along. From that perspective it seems possible to help others attain the shift in consciousness that would reverse the disease process. Ibu, however, warns of the dangers involved.

She advises people not to hesitate changing profession when they receive that the one they are in is damaging to their soul. She also tells us not to feel satisfied—or not think that it is enough—if we just help other people. We must also make sure that we make progress. "Even when you are helping other people and you share an experience with them, within that experience you will receive for yourself what you need, and this experience will also have an effect of developing your own soul."

MY AIM IS TO SPEAK TRUTHFULLY

Lusijah (USA.) interviewed in Menucha (Oregon)

> *Things that are oppressive cannot be wrenched out of the self, for along with them they tear out the heart. The conflict within must be lived gently, for it is the training of the soul.*

I came into Subud when I was in College—I was twenty-one and now I am fifty-two. I didn't really have an intention. I wasn't looking for a spiritual path. My older sister Lorraine—she is a Subud member on the East Coast—was in the arts and she dabbled in a lot of different things, so I was not surprised to find that she was into yet something else. I, myself, was at the University of Iowa, which is a pretty conservative place.

Once, when I went to New York City where Lorraine was living, there was a gathering of women who met every Tuesday to make a quilt for raffling. I spent that Tuesday with them and I felt that there was a sort of calmness about those people, something I resonated with. I thought that they had some technique or something they knew. I didn't really look at it as a spiritual thing.

In my own family some of my uncles are ministers, my grandfather was a minister so I felt jaded on the God side. I felt that a lot of it was hypocritical and I was not looking for anything like that, but I was really interested in psychology even though I was studying nursing because it was more practical. I thought I would join this thing and get a good technique; learn something that would help my work.

The first time I was tested as to whether I could be opened the helpers got that I couldn't. That made me very angry. I couldn't believe it. Over Christmas vacation I went back and the helpers tested again, and this time it was yes. The helper read the opening words and during my opening I felt kind of nervous like, "What am I doing here?" I didn't feel a lot but then I didn't expect to.

I went back the next week and was standing in the room when I felt these huge waves coming out of my head. I had a very strong spiritual experience of receiving this connection, this life force going through my body and the top of my head. Then I thought, "That couldn't have happened." And it went away, but then started again. It happened about three times and I didn't know what it was, or where I was, or anything. It was such a profound experience, and if I hadn't had it, I would never have believed it could happen, and probably would never have stuck with the latihan.

I left the hall afterwards and got to my sister's apartment thinking that this did not really happen, that stuff like that is not real. And as soon as I started to think that, it started happening again. I thought, "Oh my God, what will I do now? This is part of me now." Ever since that time I have always felt that vibration inside of me in a very strong way.

I was in school and I started doing latihan by myself, although it was very difficult to do it on my own, going down to the basement or finding a room for myself. People would come in and I had to move elsewhere. Every night I had a very strong spontaneous latihan before I'd go to sleep. I didn't know if I was walking around or what was happening.

My plan at the time was to go to Vietnam, but I received that it was absolutely wrong to do that. It was very important for me at that time to check everything I did. So I got a job nursing in the Virgin Islands. The week before I was to leave, I dreamt three nights in a row that I had to go to New York City. So I canceled that plan and went off to New York.

Do you receive through dreams a lot?

Yes I do. Actually the project I am doing now came about as a result of a dream. It's a time when things are clarified and if I don't understand it the first time I'll have the same dream again until I finally get it.

Anyway, in New York I had the experience of the group and that was very important for me. My sister had moved by then, but other people in the group really took me under their wing and taught me a lot about Subud. I remember a man from Russia, the foreman of a window washing business, who showed me how to use the latihan in my daily work and stuff like that, such as doing a quick test in the bathroom. So I benefited from being around this group.

I ended up getting married and having four children in six years, which is a very powerful thing in my life also, a force that shaped me. The fourth child was one of those who came from Ramadan, after I had received the importance of being willing to have a child during the nights of power.

I never had any doubt that my receiving was absolutely right. The wonderful gift of receiving for me is that I feel such clarity; so that when things get very hard I can handle them. I was very involved with these little children who are, as all kids are, wonderfully all consuming.

When Hillary was two and a half I started receiving very strongly that it was important for me to go back to school, but I felt that it was absolutely impossible. I couldn't imagine how I could do that. My husband was a surgeon so he was gone all the time and was not available to help in any way, so it just seemed too hard. But I figured that if I had to do it, I would find a way.

It was a very hard path for me. I had to find a new way, doing cooperative care, making sure my kids were okay while going to school. This kind of life was a struggle because I really believed in the importance of the home, the home being the basic place of community. Women in our times, being mothers and going back to school to have careers while doing all the things that are expected of them, is a very hard thing.

So I did the schooling, got my master in nursing and became a nurse practitioner. As I did that work I felt very guided in different ways, a lot had to do with helping people believe in an inner healer and getting them to pay attention to that force within themselves that is the healing wisdom.

On one of Bapak's visits to Toronto I was talking to Subud brothers and sisters who were therapists. Somebody told me about naturalistic hypnosis. When I went back I began to study that. It's really a wonderful way of helping people, and being naturalistic means you are not controlling or giving people suggestions. You are just helping them find their questions and their answers. That work was easy for me from the beginning. It was like getting quiet and really being present with each person. I always began by asking, "Please God let me be with this person in the fullest way and let me be guided."

The work was wonderful. I loved it and felt my guidance. As I worked with people I began to get through my own stuck places and my conservatism, which came from my background. Things like hypnosis would never have interested me. I wouldn't have believed in it, just like I didn't believe in Subud at first, but my experience led me on.

The guide that's inside helped me work with people with illnesses and I began to see that there are all kinds of resources people have to help them heal. How different it was from the medical model that looked at the mechanical problem and cut out what it couldn't cure! So I went through my own biases and had some miraculous experiences.

When I first learned hypnosis I worked with people in hospitals with stress management. As I began to work with pain, I started to see what incredible images and stories people had, and how they found their own way through it all. One of my earlier teachers was a man who had been in a car accident and was paralyzed from the waist down. He was in pain a lot. While getting quiet with him and connecting him with the wisdom inside of him that could show him how to be with this, I asked for pain relief. Meanwhile, in his own experience, he saw his pain as something that made him a whole human being. It began to have a color, an essence and a texture, and he was amazed at the beauty of his pain that had been sent as a teacher to him. It was the first relief he felt since his accident. I saw him later and he had learned to not feel it as pain but as wholeness.

Because of this concept of people having such deep inner wisdom, I began to work with the physician Francesca Newton who got opened in Subud since. We have done a lot of work together exploring healing, finding out how to be with people, also asking for this inner guidance for ourselves and that other person.

It was like an awakening, an opening, and we felt that it was important for me to get a doctorate in order to get grants and do bigger work. So I went back to school to get my doctorate in clinical psychology and I wrote my thesis on looking at the images of people with chronic pain and their inner story.

For my doctorate I was using visualization and hypnotic strategy for people with HIV diseases and AIDS. I chose that because at that point there was not much happening with that illness and there weren't treatments to confound it. I didn't have a particular interest in AIDS, but when dealing with cancer there were so many different kinds of treatments. It seemed like a harder route to go.

So just before the Australian Congress I took a year to work with people with AIDS, doing visualization, exploring their dreams. When I work I enter into a world where I begin to experience the essence of the sickness and the healing that needs to happen. I never worked with a community that inspired me more. At the beginning I worked only with men, mostly gay men and I had never worked with people who felt so connected and opened.

This led to an awakening for me because they are young people who have gone through a whole lot of soul searching on account of being a minority group that is persecuted. This is my sense of it. The bigness I found so moved and inspired me, that once I started working with the AIDS community I couldn't stop. It has been my greatest teacher.

There is so much I wanted out of the Subud community like love, support and understanding for one another. But I have run into the fundamentalists a lot. In my own childhood, this kind of fundamentalism had been very painful. Working with this community has helped me to stay in Subud though. I never thought I'd question staying in Subud but so many times, early in my work, I was told I was "mixing" when I was doing healing work. I had a hard time with some Subud people's judgments. When you receive guidance and what you receive is greatly questioned it makes it difficult.

In the last five years I had to get a bigger sense of my own self and accept that it didn't matter what people thought. I never wanted to go underground or be secretive in my life in Subud. I want to be able to speak out as someone who feels graced for what they receive. I want our community to grow and be strong, have a place for everybody, including instead of excluding.

I have noticed this uneasiness around the subject of the healing professions. It seems like for some people, anything to do with the psyche and the subconscious is an area of mixing.

It's true but I have such a strong sense of my own self in this healing work with HIV patients! When I went to Australia I had a series of experiences when I felt that there was something opening in me; I had a bigger place and a bigger heart to do the work.

When I started the work, one of the initial persons I worked with was an ex-priest (he got opened in Subud this year.) He is one of our elders in the HIV community, greatly respected and loved. He is such a man of integrity that people in Subud immediately trusted him. So I feel very grateful for his opening because of his deep connection to our community.

You said that some of the young men in the community got opened also.

Yes they did. I began to work on finding this inner place of guidance in order to understand how to live with this AIDS experience, and the meaning of it. I did a psychodrama retreat. Lusana had done some work in exploring her own illness and she was going to lead a psychodrama around dying.

A man in his twenties, Lucas, played the part of the youngest son. It was a very moving time for him, putting him in touch with a lot of stuff. That night Lucas and I each had the same dream. Mine was about my own heart and a need for healing that Lucas could help me with. His was about healing also and that I could help him with that. Through this we decided to evolve a program of healing. I received that I didn't absolutely have to do this, but that it was a very good thing. So I was willing to do it. I instantly knew it would be hard. I stayed with the idea for a few days to feel my willingness.

Lucas was in a deep spiritual process but not yet in Subud. The week after our dream he went and asked to be opened. He did get opened very quickly, because he was having such momentous spiritual experiences that he needed support and help from the latihan.

We took this dream we had together very seriously but needed to learn whatever it was we had to do. We would get quiet and ask for God's grace and guidance. We had profound or quiet experiences, sometimes receiving the latihan together. This was the most shocking thing in the world to me. I had all these fears around it. "Is this right? Here I am doing the latihan with a man!"

I was told that the sexual segregation had to do with men and women having such different energies; the separation during latihan prevents an overpowering influence of the opposite sex's energy within. Bapak said that in our worship, our inner nature must be completely free from the nafsu or passions. If men and women do the latihan together simultaneously in the same place,

*it will easily attract the influence of the nafsu and this will cause
them to experience a turmoil of the nafsu asmara (passionate love)
which they will be powerless to prevent.*

Yes I know. It was like a crisis for me, but whenever we got
together I continued to receive that this was a very important
thing. We went to see a healer, Solihin, and he did work with
Lucas to help open something in him, also something in me.
Then we learned about healing from all kinds of angles and
people, homeopaths and acupuncturists, etc. We were deeply
immersed in understanding what the story was and what we could
know about it.

After a while it became clear that we should develop a
program using visions and images to help people with illnesses
be together. When you work with individuals they might get stuck
in certain places, but when we work together in a group that
doesn't happen.

People lie down in a room and ask that they should open to
their healing wisdom. They create a sense of safety that can guide
them and take them where they need to go. I remember a man
receiving this powerful healing symbol.

This healing process was an inner process, which brought
on dreams and spiritual experiences. People had images coming
to them and then had a sense of sound. So we explored sound
work. How to bring it about and have your body resonate with it.
Then movement work.

Not surprisingly a number of people ended up coming to
Subud and often, people being close to death would begin to
receive something like the latihan. I felt that it was right for me to
be present, just asking for God's grace and protection.

Most of the men I was working with were gay and because
they were vulnerable with an illness, they had fears about being
around a very straight group of men without me. The men in the
Subud group however, believed that I was a very intrusive person.
Why did I need to be there? So it became this very hard thing.

I tried it many different ways. I asked for a woman—a
wonderful colored nun who did diversity work—to come and do

a workshop. But the men in our Subud group felt that I was intruding again. Someone said, "In Subud, we don't do that. We are guided by God and that's it."

"So am I," I answered.

Lucas grew so much and found his voice as a strong person, but he often flew in your face about stuff because he was so scared. He didn't know how to be pleasant when being a strong voice. He was finally able to speak of things he hadn't up till then. It was hard for people, and he was judged as a difficult young man. That's why he wanted me to be with him in a loving way through his Subud experience.

I believe that it's what my teaching in the community is about now. The conflict we experienced, and having to deal with letters people wrote at the time, made me feel like leaving Subud. It was so hard; I was totally disillusioned with my Subud family. In building community there is a step you go through, a time of chaos and confusion, but if you can live through it, it takes you to a deeper place.

I never meant to be a controversial person, actually controversy is something I would rather not be involved in, but it has been necessary for me to learn, because the areas I am working in are controversial.

I believed at the time, along with Lucas and Ted, another young man involved with us and speaking for the gay community, that Subud could be more open and supportive. We encountered hard feelings again when we did the diversity training in Montreal.

However a number of people who had had reservations came up and said they wanted Subud to grow, that if gay people could act and look normal, they could accept them. Again there is a reconciling process that any community has to go through to deal with the ignorance and homophobia that is internalized in each of us. I believe that my dear beloved brother Lucas, who died in March, was a great helper and supporter in that process. He was there, not willing to hide in any way, and people were made to deal with him. He brought many young men to Subud and before he died people in Subud were willing to take him to their home and care for him.

I felt this incredible place of love and compassion awakening within the heart of brothers through all the struggle we had. It was like people learning about other people they had totally kept out of their experience. Because of my own past and the abuse I experienced in my life, it was hard for me to stand up and have a strong voice.

I had been abused in my Christian community by a neighbor when I was a child, but I could not tell my family because I could not speak of such things. It was an extremely religious family and the internalized belief that a woman was not an equal was an issue for me. And in Subud there is still plenty of that with older members.

When I first met you I experienced you as a strong woman with a powerful voice who could express clearly her opinions and show people their place of prejudice.

Well, thank you. I think that Subud as an organization, the latihan, the incredible people I have known in it, my brothers and sisters, the whole Subud community, have helped me to be empowered. My part in this is speaking my truth, so I have to speak of the fact that I have done latihan with men. I never planned to do mixed latihan but I have done latihan with gay brothers through illness, through dying, through getting quiet and through experiencing strong receivings.

I am not going to be secretive about that. I don't have any wish to create mixed latihans or anything like that. It just happened. I have seen more and more Subud men come forth who are willing to be present in a loving, strong way in our gay community. As people in our Subud community grow stronger from doing the latihan, their prejudices dissipate.

I have been guided through the process of setting up the project Lucas and I dreamt about: a non-profit class to teach empowerment skills to people living with life-threatening illnesses. We teach an inner process that people can learn and be guided by. Then we provide the experiences in the community to support that. Now we have a nutrition program and teach people healthy eating habits. We have a cooking program, a Subud sister is our nutrition teacher, and a woman from the Buddhist community offers a meditation group and a spiritual renewal group. We are connected to the medicine center, etc.

The aim is to provide people with the opportunity, in their illness, to be spiritual and become aware of the many different ways it can be done. Many people chose to be opened in Subud and that's great, but if they chose Vapashna meditation that's great also, if they chose to do Native American purification ceremonies that's also great. We have a wonderful man who works with dance and movement; he worked a lot in ecstatic dance forms. We have process classes, a sort of Jungian-in-the-body experience. One of the women is working on setting up a death and dying program, and there also is my own work with death and dying.

I studied Buddhist practices in order to teach support families methods they could use. I actually went and studied with the man who wrote the *Tibetan Book of Death and Dying* and I was trained in the practice of compassion. I always feel the power of the latihan coming through the families I teach. They are not in Subud, but I don't feel I am practicing mixing. I have been graced with the latihan and that is my path.

Over the years, since I started the practice, I have understood that there are many different ways for people to come to God and that I can't create all those programs by myself. I need the grace and help of God. Hopefully, with the support of the brotherhood and sisterhood, we can become more open about different paths, learning from them whatever we need to know. With the spiritual guidance I receive I can help people in whatever path they choose.

When Lucas died it was very hard for me. I loved him very much. It was a hard year. Actually, he moved and I went to Montana to be with him. Robin, who is a suicide therapist in Seattle, got introduced to Subud through Lucas and was opened. She and I do community-teaching workshops now. Our project is to teach people how to access the healing response. We are working to create a model, which I hope to write about and be influential with. If I want to be a doctor I ought to do something en route, base a program on the fact that every human being has a healing response, and that for it to be activated and grow, people need a community that can support that response.

Creating community has to do with the belief that we can live in harmony; and harmony does not come from suppressing strong feelings. It comes as a result of dealing with conflicts and going through the fire, experiencing anger and pain, staying with it from a place of integrity and truth. It's damn hard.

The project has become a Susila Dharma project (humanitarian wing of Subud). Illene Pevec helped initially to do the paper work. As we evolve it's important for more people in Subud to know about this project class, so that the prayers, guidance and gifts of all the people in Subud can be present. I feel that it's happening more and more and I so deeply want that.

This year several people from the project class got opened in Subud. They are artists who have a deep interest in using art as a healing form. We are working on starting a project that will support artists.

It seems to be coming together in a big way through Subud and S.I.C.A. (Subud International Cultural Association.) One of our members who is actually here in Menucha is a silver and metal smith who wants to form a guild so the people with AIDS can have easier access to working on their art and be successful in the world. Hopefully during the World Congress we can all come together in a strong way with our brothers and sisters, and the project can be recognized and appreciated.

I received that I must work with people whether in Subud or not, working with healing and with the healing energy, with images, and so bring together a lot of wonderful healers from many different spiritual paths and all learn to work together. I don't see us in Subud as having such a special gift that other spiritual paths do not have. The more we can work together the better. That is my wish.

A wonderful wish.

I am glad you taped this because I have been very controversial and my aim is to speak truthfully, make it safe for people who do healing work not to keep secrets whether they are gay, lesbian, bisexual, anything. The point is for them to be here and to be honored in their own richness, in any form it takes.

I thank you for your courage to push people through their limits.

I learned later that Lusijah happens to be Christian/Lucas' aunt, the one he talked about at the beginning of his interview.

I EXPERIENCED MY INNER OPENING GOING THROUGH THE CEILING OF THIS BARN

Solihin (England) interviewed in Menucha (OR.)

"The lower forces reside in human beings. They lead one in a state of confusion when they are left to take over. With the purification of the lower forces begins God's guidance. God is always working you (on you and with you) but He can work better when the lower forces are weak. Then we receive constant guidance and protection in daily life and what we receive eventually is total happiness in this world. That is God's wish for us."

Dr. Hattori

It was a Subud member in Weybridge, England who introduced me to Subud. I was about eighteen and he gave me some Pewartas (a periodical that published Bapak's talks and answers to members) to read. They were double Dutch to me, but I read them anyway. I was interested, but they didn't make any sense, and to be honest the man didn't really inspire me. Is that what Subud does to a person, I thought? At the time I was a sort of itinerant drop out, drug addict-seeker. I mean I was into everything. Not a very respectable human being.

I eventually went to Afghanistan where I met a couple who told me they had an Italian friend in London who was in Subud.

I acted as though I knew quite a bit about Subud. They were into Gurdjieff's work and I was quite interested in the work as well.

I spent eighteen months in Afghanistan wondering who I was, and what I was, and all that kind of stuff. This was in 1971-72. When I went back to England I had stopped doing dope. I had decided that it was the end of that for me. Something happened in Afghanistan. I had a series of experiences with Sufis and it was the beginning of an awakening on some level. Something was shifting.

I had used acid and dope initially to wake up and it did wake me up to start with, but it put me to sleep later, put me into a vegetative state. So I hitchhiked back with some carpets, jewels and trinkets to sell in order to go off to South America with the money. Instead, I ended up meeting this Subud chap again.

For some reason I bought a boat near Loudwater Farm, the big Subud place outside London. Loudwater was just being built at the time, or being rebuilt I should say. So, I suddenly found that there was this Subud group right down the road from me. Eventually I called. The Italian man I had heard about turned up and he had more credibility for me. He was this ex-banker, dry, droll sense of humor, didn't like my long hair or beard, and told me, "When you get opened you'll cut your hair and the earring will come off." I thought, "Well, God, if that's what Subud is all about!" But actually there was this quality about him, and he touched the upper middle class part of me.

I went to Loudwater for a first meeting and there was a man called Sachlan who was very involved with Anugraha (a Subud project.) I asked, "Well, tell me about Subud," or something like that, and Sachlan said, "It's simply the power of the Almighty, the very thing you read about in the Pewartas or in Bapak's talks."

As he said this I experienced my inner opening and going through the ceiling of this barn. I felt I was about two hundred feet tall; it was the most extraordinary of all my Subud experiences. I was totally present in my body, and totally huge at the same time. I had absolutely no problem with any of it. I knew then it was a *fait accompli*. I decided to be opened and I did the three months probation, but every time the three months were up I would actually get ill, or burn my feet, or something would happen to prevent it. And every time we tested it would be no, no, no. It was quite hard; I think nine months went by, before I got opened. The helpers would make excuses like, "You are not ready," or that sort of stuff, but I know I was put through the test.

Then I had this series of dreams. They actually were nightmares. In the first one the devil came to me and handed me a book with the word "chekon." It means devil in Hebrew—well the Jewish equivalent—but I am using it in Arabic. I knew what it meant and I knew that if I said it I would be captured, that the devil would get me. I couldn't move. I was catatonic. I was in a state of sleep and couldn't wake up, so I started asking for help, "Help me God, help me God," and eventually I woke up, a tight band around my head, with stars all over in the boat where I was living.

About two weeks later I had another dream. This time I was being attacked by the nasties and I thought, "I know what I can do. I can start to pray again." The memory of praying shifted the nightmare. Then I had a third dream and again all sorts of demons and nasties were attacking me, but this time I didn't even have to think. I just started the Lord's Prayer, "Our Father Who art in Heaven," and the nasties disappeared.

Then I got opened. Well my opening was absolutely nothing. Nothing happened. I stood like a lemon and some well meaning Subud member said, "Oh yes, that was a good opening, I saw your finger move." The arrogance of thinking he knew something more than I did! I had been opened but nothing had happened on the physical level.

About two weeks later I had another dream and this time instead of praying I thought, "Oh my God, I have the latihan." And the memory of the latihan came in and the bad things disappeared. I woke up. Then I had a fifth dream where I actually did a latihan in my dream and I have never had a nightmare since. Somehow my inner had absorbed it, but my outer hadn't, so I had to do it in the dream world.

I told Solihin of my experience with a very similar dream. It was the day after my mother died; I had just arrived in Paris. I was staying in my niece's apartment and woke up in the middle of the night to a flickering blue light, but I could not move. I was totally paralyzed by this dark, muscular entity sitting on my chest and sucking the life energy out of me. It was not a human, not an animal. It felt more like a gigantic octopus, all muscle, a spirit boa constrictor, totally black, a dense creature preventing my spirit from re-entering the shelter of my deserted body.

The harder I breathed in panic, the tighter it encircled me and the deeper it sunk into my chest. I couldn't breathe. I was losing my strength. The life force was leaving. I tried to call for help but had no voice. I could see the room I was in, the bedside table, everything was in place but I was powerless to move. I called out to my mother, then to God and was able to take enough of a breath to regain some strength and push the entity slightly off my solar plexus. Then the life force came back full force and moved through me. I was then able to shove the dark preying entity off me.

A few days later I was staying alone at my mother's house after the funeral to take care of things. I slept in her bed. One night the entity came back. Same scenario, the room, the bedside table, the flickering light, the catatonic state. My mother's house was located right across from the church. I knew that if I could get some light, the inner vibration would start and I would regain my strength. I stopped fighting and panicking. I tried to be quiet and unemotional. I asked for God's help and succeeded in moving the entity slightly off my solar plexus again, then, praying the whole time, I pushed it off. Too exhausted to stand up, depleted, I crawled to the light switch. Once the light was on I regained a little energy and I crawled to the front door facing the church. I knew that if I could open it so as to take a look at the church I would be safe. Once the door was opened the vibration of the life force flooded through. The entity never came back.

Interesting. I know that I had to wait for nine months to get opened because I am spiritually ambitious; I have a big nafsu. I didn't know that at the time, but my grandfather (who used to have a Masonic lodge in Scotland) was actually inside of me. He was in there until I was thirty-seven. I had a huge experience of releasing him. What I experienced is that my consciousness had been asleep because of him being in my vessel, because when he had died he had been unconscious, asleep. He died the head of the Masonic lodge, of prostate cancer, at the age of thirty-three.

I started having problems with my prostate and I recognized that I was dealing with my manliness because the prostate is the center of the human man. It had to do with my inner authority, my outer authority and my representation as a male, but I also recognized that it had to do with my grandfather and father's lineage.

At the time I felt like I was going to die. I was doing a lot of new work and felt unsupported, unrecognized. It was lonely and I was attacked quite a lot by Subud members who believed I was mixing. All that silly stuff. Then Alicia, my wife and I went off to Israel. For two and half years I had felt that I was going to die and that it would be in the Mount of Olives, at the Dome, on the rock, in Jerusalem. So I went up there and did my prayers and of course, I didn't die. That was at the big mosque where it's said that Muhammad went on his night journey and left a footprint. There is a little cave there. We both went in and spontaneously had a very strong latihan receiving.

From that moment on I never doubted myself. It was like what had to die was my doubts and lack of faith. It was not I doing latihan. The latihan came to me. I am a healer and that was really a big shift. After that my work started to come to me. I received all this new work, this handwork, and those *mudras*.

I also started getting a lot of attacks from people: them misunderstanding the work, me misunderstanding it; me talking my mouth off and them hearing what they wanted to hear, then passing it on to others. Also people would come away from seeing me and they would tell others a little bit of the story and then that story would be taken and magnified. So it was said that I was mixing and it's certainly true. I do mix, not really mix with dark powers, but I am following a very tight line between the power of man and the power of God.

Don't you think this is always true in healing work?

Sure, I am Solihin. I am a healer and I need to understand the forces. What I am doing is the work of a human being whose profession is to be a healer, but really the healer is the Almighty. When you asked me about telling my story there was a story I particularly wanted to tell. I have had a lot of dreams about Bapak. I feel really connected on an inner level. I had a dream of him dying just before he died. Never told anyone really.

We were in a very crowded room, lots of Subud members all talking among themselves, gassing, gassing, and Bapak was on a sort of dais, like, I suppose, in Subud offices. I was in the back. Either he told me, or I felt that he was going to die, and suddenly he collapsed. Everyone just kept talking and I was the only one who saw him. I threaded my way through and I picked him up and carried him out. No one paid any attention, no one saw. It was really an extraordinary dream.

I don't know exactly what it means. It might mean that this was a part of me, the part that is always gassing, does not see what's really happening. It could also mean that only one part of me recognized that Bapak was ready to go. Then about three weeks later, Bapak died. It was confirmation of my own inner receiving.

Later I was in Austria doing the life forces workshop. It consists of three workshops having to do with understanding the lower forces and understanding the higher forces. We had lots of non-Subud members attending. As a consequence of this many of them have come into Subud, really good quality people. We did this workshop where I came away feeling really disturbed. "Oh my God, am I doing something wrong?" I thought. "Am I introducing information to people who are not ready for it? Is this the work of the devil?" There is a part of me that is always questioning what I do.

I went home that night and I had a dream about driving Bapak around. He was sitting on my right and I asked him, "Am I okay?

Am I doing what I should be doing?" He went, "Yah, yah, yah," and put his hand out. I felt his hand on my cheek. I am sure people could say that he was just kidding with me, or compromising, that he was not saying yes, but for me it was the contact I needed. It meant that I was okay. Yes, I was growing. Yes, I was developing. I know we make mistakes because we tread a very delicate line between Said Anwas and Said Anwar. (A story told by Bapak about those two sons of Adam, one following the ordinary path of mankind and the other the extraordinary one.)

In our workshop we talk about them and about the part that is the power of man, and the part that is surrender to God. We bring it out and get people to recognize where they are with this. When they recognize that they are following the path of man, the work I offer has to do with the part that surrenders to God. I make them see that and help them change. I stop people from taking my teaching classes unless they surrender to God, and if they have gurus I actually tell them that they can't do that, that they have to hand back the authority to the Almighty and to no one else. We have grown with this work.

If I was an architect and I built a building, everyone would say what a wonderful chap I was. It's like Alicia's father, Lambert, who built Anugraha: people praise him for having built that beautiful building, a bit extravagant perhaps, but still . . . But here I am, working in a field in which I believe I am truly guided, but doing this is suspect because it is so narrowly intertwined with our inner development.

We are not forcing inner development. We are making a path free at the outer level to allow people to get in touch with what's calling them inside. You know, I used to have doubts, but I have less and less.

The source of spiritual arrogance is often rooted in self-doubt and the measure of one is often the measure of the other.

Oh yes, I do understand that. The doubts are my nafsu and they lead to the other. Now I recognize that my work was given to me. Unfortunately I filtered it through my own agendas, my own map of the universe, my nafsu, my own wound, and my wounded state. Thank God I tidied up inside.

You were going to talk about the changes in your work?

Yes. I had this experience in Vienna about inappropriateness. François (Solihin's partner) and I were doing workshops and I did something very inappropriate to him, something he was not expecting, this in front of everyone. It threw him off. We were pretending, and he expected me to do something to illustrate his point, but I did just the opposite. It totally floored him and he went into this dyslexic state. He couldn't think; he couldn't cognate; he didn't know what to do in front of one hundred and thirty people. You just can't do that! I bullshitted my way through, but we had been perfectly congruent until then, and the force of what I did separated us completely.

We went home and I thought I would never be able to talk to him again. I did some prayers and did latihan but I couldn't clear. Finally we sat down and started to talk but ended up bickering and arguing. Because we had done all these workshops, however, we tried to use them. I surrendered and I suddenly felt this swirling around my heart. What I experienced was that it was a snake. I suddenly understood that I had stung him.

I had this vision of a castle with a drawbridge down. I got in while the drawbridge was down and basically killed him. I saw that his ancestral pattern was to always have the drawbridge up, but because we were so close he let it down. Knowing that he was getting too close to me, to my heart, I bit his heart.

As I surrendered I felt the huge snake come out from the back of me, inside my body and out through my head. François and his wife Ilaina witnessed this process. This whole thing seeded in us the understanding of what Bapak's talks were about when he described the forces as material, vegetable, animal, human and beyond. We suddenly, graphically, saw and experienced the action of the lower forces, and we started to see our work in the context of forces. It was most significant for me.

We went into the hills of Vienna that night and we just talked, and received, and talked. It was really momentous. We saw that

I have this animal force like a horse, a big stallion and that his was a bear. It matches, him being a bear, like he goes to sleep after lunch while I gallop and I sweat and expect everyone to run out after me. Since then we took Bapak's model and we laid it into a Western context with a Western understanding. This is the base of our workshops. We do Life Forces workshops, Family Tree and Intimacy in Relationships workshops.

We teach all over the globe, and we see the caduceus as a bridge. It's an old symbol that physicians held out in their hands or put on the wall, on their visiting cards, but in reality it's a holy force.

Well, this did not germinate for me until a couple of years later when I started getting hot flushes. It took me nine months to understand what was happening, that the seed of this uprightness had not yet germinated. So all these years, I had just been pretending.

Eighteen years in Subud to have uprightness! But to mimic something is better than not have it at all. I kept straight lines. There were obviously beautiful people who came to see me, beautiful women, but I never was anything but straight. Then I started having these inner experiences and prying into that force which had never been investigated, *ever*. That was a biggy you know.

There is the wonderful story of Bapak and Muhammad who both had visits from Gabriel and got pierced in their chest. Muhammad's experience was that Gabriel took out his heart and Bapak tells us that he also had an experience when Gabriel took out his heart. In both cases Gabriel washed them out and put them back in. Bapak tells how his heart then felt like a big diamond in his chest, radiating, a jewel. What he truly experienced in that moment was that he was worthy in the sight of God. We teach people to manipulate forces.

We found, in our work, that the snake is very eloquent. I've written an article on the nature of the snake as the seducer. When people do this sort of work they get very close to each other, very familiar. There is a lot of touch-touch, feel-feel, good-good, and they start to misinterpret the sensory information, the feeling information, for grace. That is the seducer. We talk about this being the one-eyed trouser, seeing the penis as the snake on one level. But there is also the snake of the tongue, the snake of language, the manipulation of ideas. That's flexibility: the muse of concepts, ideas, philosophies that seduces people. I am really attentive in the work to make sure that the snake does not come in. It's also in the story of Adam and Eve, the fruit of their feelings.

That is why we have, at times, seen Subud members going with someone else's husband or wife. That's the snake. It's very important to put it in words because it's easy to mistake this good feeling-sensation if we are misguided. It appears to be holy but it isn't. A lot of what we do in workshops is to make people distinguish between mind and grace. It's not easy, particularly in this modern new age where everything is thought of as being grace. But it's just mind. It's just lower forces ninety nine per cent of the time.

What we have done in part is to actually develop a course called "Signals," where we open people to receive body sensations and inner sensations that they learn to interpret. There is a whole language of sensations that gives us the hidden message behind what's going on. We can feel the snake when it manifests itself because we get a signal. What's interesting is that it is a common signal, a signal that is similar for most people.

For instance, the snake is the tongue, and you get a tingling around the root of your tongue when the snake is there. We might get sensations in our left nostril or our right nostril, in our ear, a tingle, or we get a pain-in-the-heart signal, or a stabbing pain. We might get something around the head, etc. There are all kinds of signals. I think there is a catalogue of about two hundred signals. It's a language that might not be an inner language, a truly inner language, but it certainly is the language of the deep unconscious and that's okay because it's a form of communication.

Isn't the subconscious the communicator between spirit and consciousness?

It's the communication between the two, and you need it. The body is an ally. It is a piece of machinery. It is the only thing you have to tell you about your jiwa, and if we know the body it can be of full use.

I also received that the body is the ultimate tool, that we must treat it with the utmost care and respect, cherish it, and listen to it.

Yes, that is correct. So we also do a "Healing the Family Tree" workshop. We don't work much with Subud members anymore, mostly because they are so threatened, "Is this okay? Is it mixing? We will have to write to Ibu Rahayu about this."

I have been in Subud for more than thirty years and sometimes I get discouraged. I ask myself, "Are we really still doing this? Haven't we gotten over that yet? When are we going to grow up?"

But my experience is that after a period of intense questioning everything, there comes a time of great spiritual inspiration when you feel you have reached a new level. Then you start mostly coming across those who have grown to spiritual maturity and are doing amazing work.

Do you still get a lot of criticisms now?

Nowhere near as much. I think it has to do with my attitude. My teaching changed. My understanding changed. The language I use changed, and I now work with Alicia. That made an enormous difference. When I worked with François, although he was much more of a gentle man, more feminine in his quality, it was two men working. But with Alicia, there is a woman and she brings a completely different quality to the work. It feels right. She brings me back to earth when I need it, and I raise her consciousness when she needs it, so it's very good. There is a very good quality to the work, and the people who do the workshop with us feel very comfortable doing it with the two of us. If I am pontificating she'll say, "Hold on, I don't think we can deal with that!"

In a way I am the seed and she is the soil. When I become the seed I tend to scatter. Now that I am really touching this feminine part of my inner man—which is gentle, receptive, present—the seed is actually being put on the proper earth. I am thanking God that the latihan and the work have been given to us.

Since this interview in 1996 Solihin and Alicia have developed many other workshops and are very successful in their work.

THE WORK OPENED UP MY MIND BECAUSE I WAS IN A DESPERATE SITUATION

Heidi (English-Jamaican) interviewed at Amanecer (Colombia)

> *"A minuscule variation in a pattern of inputs can result in a very significant change in the eventual output. This is because the repetition of a slight variation over time results in a progressive change of pattern or, sometimes, in a leap to a new harmonic."*
>
> Dr. David R. Hawkins

Both my parents are from Jamaica and I am the only one of three children who was born in England. My brother and sister were born in Jamaica. We grew up very much as a nuclear family, which was unusual among the black community in England at that time. We lived in a fairly rough area. It was predominantly white working class people, an extended family sort of environment. We were the first black family in the area. My dad taught us all to box when we were young and going to school. He said he was not going to fight for us, that he would debate with adults but couldn't come out and fight children. So he made sure that we were in a position to be able to stand our ground.

I witnessed Solihin Thom demonstrating on you during one of his workshops. Do you think that the kind of childhood you had helped develop the tigress in you, which appeared during Solihin's workshop at Amanecer?

Yes, and it was very good, because as a family we never used to fight for each other. Each one of us could take care of ourselves. We had a reputation as a family not to be messed around with, which made life easier. In the end we didn't really have to do any fighting at all. There was a lot in that.

My dad was very sport-oriented and he used sport as an analogy for just about everything. He used to play a lot with us to teach us different sports, but it was really so he could use that as a metaphor and get us to deal with our environment in those terms. He used to talk about racism and things like that in terms of the side field, and side batting, one side refusing to go out, etc. He used the metaphors in terms of class and race, sport being used just as a diversion. He said there were two games going on, the game of cricket that belonged to one class, because only one class could economically score, and only one time, and then the game of football. In this way the social aspect of things was explained to us.

I understand that you are now a therapist.

I started doing massages when I was looking for a new way of life altogether. I became a certified therapist after I joined Subud. Previously I was in the police force for thirteen years and at that time I was doing undercover work. One morning I went out to work and my foot almost blew out, my right foot. I had an allergy that started as I went into the police force, and it became progressively worst until it came up to my waist, and even my respiratory passages. I had to go to the hospital with it, and they said there was nothing they could do for me except use adrenaline and steroids. I would have to carry those things on me at all times, or else I could choose to wear a brace.

My sister, at that point, was just starting to go out with the man who became her husband and he was in Subud but never talked about it. He had started to see Solihin for a physical problem, and that's how I began working with Solihin also. My physical problem seemed to be connected with ancestor stuff, ancestral misery, feelings of shame and other things. That's why the skin was folding in on itself. The irritation was so great that in an effort to try and hide, the skin was folding over. It makes perfect sense this explanation of it, and I myself had the idea that it had to do with ancestry.

It was such a relief to have had therapy with Solihin, because I had a sense that something was going on along those lines but couldn't put a name to it. Once it came out, I knew that was it. It was really important for me to understand that, because up till then no one really knew what I was talking about. To me the therapy was like a prayer to Mary, which is representative of the female energy. So the condition cleared and I never had it again. Just one treatment to get the story out, and prayer cleared it. It sure made me trust the process.

Up until then I was very black and white about what therapy was. I went to doctors, they gave me my tablets and I was off again. Alternatives were just for vege-type people. That had nothing to do with my life. It was like the group of people I would take the piss out of, because they were so nice all the time. They are the type to save the earth and all that sort of thing, and I was like, "Oh, give me a break. Give me my aerosol and my convenience and comfort and meat!"

So the work with Solihin really opened up my mind because I was in a very desperate situation. I was actually passing out with this condition. It was my airways and my throat that were being shut off. I was fortunate that the last time it happened I was close to hospital grounds, because had I been in the country on my own I would have died. So when my sister's boy friend described the work Solihin did I felt that I had nothing to lose. Although I believed that all this was nonsense, I tried it anyway.

When it came out, when I said that I could feel my ancestors around me constantly weighing on my shoulders and stuff, it made sense to me. When it came up in therapy I could feel a shift, a change in my relationship to those feelings. I thought I should keep working with this energy and get it moving.

The work was very much about surrendering, finding the right path in life, being aware of the light, being guided and all that sort of thing. But I had the feeling that I would have to give up so much to get there, to become this holy person. I was not ready for it. I liked to drink. I liked to fight. I liked my sex and all the good things in life. There was not really any control in my life. Although I told myself that I better do more work, in fact I stopped seeing Solihin for a while.

At that time I was in the central drug squad with Scotland Yard and I had been very busy, getting on very well. I was one of the youngest members there, so I was deliberately working as hard as I could not to spoil that and promote myself—because they can be very quick to cut you off. Besides, since I was a woman I felt that I needed to push harder.

Then an option came up to reorganize the crime squad for Scotland Yard, and I thought, "That's a way to really make my name. I should do it." That was the basis of it; make my name, nothing nobler than that. So I ran this squad and did all the undercover work. It was a bit ridiculous really, because we were doing undercover work one day and the next we were in the house and going back to the same area in our uniform. The danger was imminent, always there, but because I so much wanted to belong to the group I was ignoring it.

This went on until one morning, my foot looked like it was broken. I thought, "Well, shit, I must have twisted it or done something." I went out to the hospital and there was nothing wrong with it. They X-rayed it but found nothing, so there I was for about three months, hopping around with a stick.

Then I thought, "I can't stay off work any longer because I have made so much ground and now they are going to put somebody else in. All the work I have done and someone else is going to take the glory off it, so I must get back." I got back in to work and of course, they made me office bound, which drove me crazy. I got in arguments with everybody because I never liked to be confined. I knew already that I didn't have it in me to do that. I just couldn't do it. After about a week, everyone in the office just about hated me. I was getting on everybody's nerves, but I thought I should stay.

In the end I took time off and was excluded. It was made clear that if you were not exercising a function there was no place for you. It was really a disillusionment to me because I had worked so hard in order to belong to this group. I had gone through ten years of taking on the worst kinds of jobs, jobs that nobody wanted—if they did they demanded far more back up than I ever did. So they got it cheap from me, for half the price, and all the time I was buying into the idea that there was this big camaraderie, solidarity and everything else. But as soon as you were wounded and down, they were no longer there for you.

I felt as though the rug had been pulled from under my feet, that a big cloud that had been hanging over my head just crashed and there was nothing left you know. I went to see Solihin and he said, "Well this is about your right work and direction blah blah blah . . ." But it really was that I hadn't taken in any of the information that I got through working with him earlier. I could have done something about it and I chose not to, so there it was. The interesting part of this is that once you become conscious of it, it's there in front of your face and you have to do it. There is no avoiding it.

Most of the treatment I was having with him was about surrender, but I just couldn't let go of the idea that it might mean not to smoke, that it might mean that I couldn't do this or couldn't do that. I thought, "What am I going to do with my life? I'd have nothing. I don't think I can tolerate this." I would just be joking about what would be good for me, but not willing to make that commitment.

I went to one of Solihin's workshops, one of the first two he did. I realized that I could pick up the mechanics of it, understand how to get the process moving, but what I couldn't do was the interpretation because I didn't understand the life forces and that was the model that he was using.

I told Alicia that I couldn't afford François' workshop on understanding the life forces. She answered—I can't remember how she put it but she was doing a neuro-linguistic program which has to do with communication so she said it in such a way that I got into my mind that it was possible if I shifted my thinking. Rather than saying, "I can't afford it," and "it's out of my control," she reframed it in such a way that whether I could afford it or not, it was up to me. It made me very uncomfortable, but I rang up François and he allowed me to do it in installments.

I was just about to leave to go to America and I only managed to pay for my course because I had a refund on my electricity, which is interesting because it's the only time in my life that I ever had a rebate on anything.

Big change for me to ask in the first place, and to owe somebody something! Because I was told that you never go out that way you know, and if someone did you a favor, you, somehow, doubled it back to them. It got sort of exaggerated for me that way, definitely no debts were allowed. So this was a different space for me to occupy entirely, but I went on with it, and it was fantastic because I was already used to hearing about the mythical from my Dad.

THE BLESSING OF THE SICKNESS HAS OPENED
NEW DOORS OF PERCEPTION

Muchtar (Portugal) interviewed in Menucha (OR.)

"Searching for the place where God's power resides and for the means of coming into contact with the great life force that exists in every creature, including human beings is how it usually is. That is why, on these paths, someone with more experience is usually needed to give guidance to beginners."

Bapak

Being sick and facing the possibility of dying, also dealing with sickness, has changed my life drastically. It was so abrupt and brought on a lot of weakness. I feel frail, I tire very easily. Whatever were my activities and my interests it was all taken away or changed. I had been so much into all those projects; I loved to do this or that and so on, everything that involved a lot of action. All that has been removed from me. It is a really deep process of changing while everything is fading away. Still it is not clear what is coming next: it could be to leave this world and if not, to take a new step in a new way.

I have become more introspective, and maybe more sensitive to some fuel that I hadn't paid enough attention to before, something that relates to our life in all aspects. For instance, this interest I have now in these three houses: the House of Mind, the House of Heart and the House of Sex.

Bapak said that humans have to stand in front of God in these three houses and when we approach death—I might not be approaching physical death but in any case it's a spiritual death I have to consider. I want to know whether I am 'I' standing in these three houses in front of God or not. So I feel to explore them. I recognize that we need to share our experiences about these things because nobody alone can ever totally understand them unless we listen to the experience of others. Only then can we have a more complete perception. So I feel to open up those things.

You tell me that I am the first one, as far as you know, to open the door of the House of Sex so wide and that there is much excitement about this from Subud people, also some relief to be able to have that freedom to express that part of their life that is often so taboo. You think that I am a pioneer in this but actually Bapak talked a lot about it. He talked about it amazingly freely, but it's like we are a little bit shy to go into it that openly ourselves. When I read some of what Bapak said about it, it sparked my interest and I felt that it was time for us to explore this.

If you want to read about it, it's a talk of Bapak's called Communication. Bapak starts talking about communication and then he gets into the three houses, and it's only at the end of the talk that he starts again talking about communication. You can consider everything as communication actually.

Anyway, I am moved to do this, and because I travel a lot and get in touch with many members—also because of being an International Helper—many situations arise where people come to talk to me in private. I get a lot of understanding by sharing with people, and I also find this information inside of me. I know how important all this is and feel that it's time to release this information, but also to get more.

I have learned a lot even here with the workshop I started. Things people say during the workshop, things they say in private. Always, for me, it's a process of giving and receiving, which really is contained in the same thing, the same movements. Understanding the sexual from the inner point of view is the most wonderful exploration.

I can see also, not yet but in the near future—I don't know if it's in one year, in ten or twenty years—that we will have to open the door of politics, understand politics from the inner point of view. Bapak made amazing observations about politics, but we act as though politics is taboo because of course, being spiritual, we don't want to discuss that. We put it in another box, but it's essential that we get into it from an inner point of view because politics is what runs the whole world. So many disturbances are because politics are not received or perceived from the right place.

I hope that if it's not for this generation to do this it will be for the next, but I can see that at Menucha, in the future, we will be doing a lot about politics. Politics belongs to the human realm. You can't deny it. We can't put it aside saying that politicians are all bad, because they are people who have our care in their hands. And they need our care. Of course homeless and orphans need our care also, but politicians need it even more because they are struggling with very powerful forces. They are in the hands of those forces and they don't cope with that very well. They don't.

I had a little experience in Amanecer when I had to be in contact with the high officials. Lots of meetings. I could see how much those people needed the latihan, how much they were struggling with powers they didn't dominate, but by whom they were totally dominated. So I hope that for the sake of their healing we dive into that from an inner point of view.

My sickness is very much of a blessing because it has given me, after fifty-five years, another chance. Things crystallize as we get older and for me now, the blessing of this sickness has opened new fields of perception and better understanding. I am grateful. A lot of things have been removed and I believe new things are coming. I don't know if it's to prepare me to leave or to do some work here with it. It's a wonderful process of changing. Sometimes I see myself getting confused and lost because things that were my reference are fading away and I don't yet have new ones to replace them.

Of course the basic things, the love for my family, the love for Subud, that remains, strongly, but many other things are fading away. Then new fields are opening, but not always so clearly yet. That's why I feel at times a little bit lost. I believe it is a new stage in my life and I am enjoying it, enjoying each step. Truly I can't complain. It has been the most amazing time for me.

WESTERNERS HAVE LITTLE FAITH. THEY NEED TO ACQUIRE IT. IT IS NOT NATURAL TO THEM

Loretta & Alfonso (Mexico) as interpreted by Arifah (France) at the World Congress in Spokane

"The essence of beauty does not change through the ages, and people of high consciousness who see all life as sacred also see that all form is beauty."
Dr. David R. Hawkins

These are two of my friends from Mexico. Bapak once told them that if they were sincere and did their latihan very diligently God would show them the reality of the Mayan culture. They would be able to see the Mayan Gods incarnated. And they did.

They are from Puebla and have been in Subud for only three years but they have the feeling that they have been in it for at least twenty years. They have already attended three national congresses and they are here now at this international one. Puebla had the first Latin American Subud house. It was built thirty-five years ago. It is an important group.

Loretta and Alfonso were looking to deepen their connection to God through a Christian group that taught the Bible, but those teachings and the Catholic Church in Puebla were not enough.

They were not satisfied. They were required to read a lot; it took a lot of their time and intellect.

One day they were introduced by a friend to a man who was one of the pioneers of Subud Puebla, and in the course of the conversation Loretta heard the name Subud. She asked more about it and the man started explaining in a few words, but they said, "That's enough! That's what we want." And they got into Subud. They had a sense of Subud from within. As soon as Alfonso was opened, he immediately received a lot of purification (he actually calls purification: gift.) He understood that the story of his Saint's name was also his own.

He had cancer and had been losing a lot of blood for two days. The family thought that he was going to die. They asked for help from the Subud group, and someone said they had heard something about a tape from Bapak that could help. As soon as they put on the tape of Bapak playing the Gamelan, the bleeding stopped, and they all got into an extraordinary latihan.

Later they took him to the hospital where he was scheduled to be operated on for his cancer. Then he did chemotherapy and his veins didn't collapse, his hair didn't fall out. When they did a radioscopy of the heart there was no longer anything wrong with it. They analyzed his blood and they said that everything was totally normal. It was like he was given a new life.

Sometime later on, Loretta and Alfonso's daughter was suddenly losing a lot of blood from her legs. The helpers tested about it and said that she was finishing her father's purification. She was in latihan when it started happening and the blood spilled on the very clean wall-to-wall carpet. She was very ashamed. It started as a little pimple that opened up during latihan.

Mexican people are often very opened to the spirit. I lived there for four years. When I arrived no one knew me, but they immediately loved me as though I was one of them. Now they even call me their blood sister. I think it's marvelous, their soul and body. They have so much love!

In fact Bapak said that Mexicans were heart people. When I was in Cilandak before going to Mexico (I didn't know then that

I would go) Bapak asked us in testing to come up and dance like the Mexican ladies danced. Then he said, "So if one day you meet some Mexican, you must bow." Bapak loved them a lot. They helped Bapak during the Indonesian civil war. It's the only country that invited Bapak and Bapak's family, no matter how many of them and how much it would cost them.

Would you please ask them what is their experience of this International Congress?

Loretta—I live it intensely. It's a miracle that we are here because we didn't have the money to come. But I knew that if I had a sincere desire to, we would go. Fifteen days before the congress we didn't have the money. I said to Alfonso, "It looks like we are not going." But he answered, "If we have the faith, we will go. So, we *will* go." We had been doing the Ramadan Fast for three years in a row since our opening, to facilitate what good things were to come.

So, we thought we wouldn't be able to come to the congress and we were very sad, we were crying about it. Then we were called and told that everything was paid for us, that it was a present. It was a German man who works for Volkswagen in Puebla. He paid for the best hotel for us.

Arifah—This was because he loved them so much. He is dead now. They knew it would come because God is great and God gives many gifts. Since they don't ask for riches, only to live well among their family and friends, they will be granted what they ask.

The whole family is in Subud now. Loretta prayed so hard for them to get into Subud and now they are all opened. God watches over them and covers them with gifts. Myself, the greatest gift I was born with was my faith. Most of us in the Western countries must build our faith. I had this faith that was given to me, but since no one had it around me, I abandoned it.

Alfonso—My latihan on Monday was very good, a great peace and tranquility. Tuesday I felt it was so-so and I decided to do a test. I asked how it was for my inner to be here at this congress. When I felt how wonderful it was, the latihan came back full force.

Arifah—We do that kind of testing every day to find what is the meaning of this congress for people. Someone was not having a good time and we tested about it. It was because the attitude was not good; this, to the person's great surprise. When we asked what to do about it the answer was, "Go towards people, open, laugh, touch, embrace." She was very touched. Then everyone wanted to do that test.

Last year, at a Zone congress, there was a member from Puebla, Mauricio, who receives very well, and was in the same bedroom as Muchtar. They were just about to fall asleep when they felt a spontaneous latihan coming on. In the latihan they levitated and Montezuma appeared. He said to Muchtar, "I offer my power and my throne." Others experienced this also; Alfonso and Loretta saw Montezuma.

Later we all went to the volcano Popacatapetl. There was a Subud brother who had wanted to create a great center of worship of God for the whole world, near the volcano. I was there when it was planned. When we got to the place we all went into spontaneous latihan. This project was planned fifteen years ago and was given the name Eternal, Noble and Strong. Bapak wrote this in his own handwriting when the Mexican delegation went to see him. When Bapak was told how serious they were about this and that they had a place for it, he said, "Yes, it is a sacred place."

Now it's going to happen at last. Years ago I asked, in Anugraha, for ten thousand dollars to start this project, but they didn't even look at me. So I thought to myself, "It's not time." I had done everything, explained to them that Bapak thought it was important, related the group experience in testing about Montezuma. We asked from what time was Montezuma. The answer was that in the spiritual time does not exist, that Montezuma is still here. I told them about the volcano erupting the morning after Muchtar's experience.

My husband and I immediately understood that it was the purification of the volcano, that the volcano had spoken. Unfortunately many of our brothers in Subud said that none of this was true, just illusions and fantasies. Westerners have little faith. They need to acquire it. It is not natural to them. They need to touch. They listen but cannot hear. They look but do not see. They are partly dead.

But my two friends here have so much!

7

SUBUD AND MY OWN TRUTH

WOMEN IN SUBUD TALK ABOUT THEIR
SPIRITUAL JOURNEYS

I was originally opened in Subud in 1967 in a group composed mostly of newly married women whose husbands, for the most part, were individualistic men, reluctant to join any group, skeptical and averse to what they perceived as religious indoctrination. We were not aware of the requirement—which held at the time—that wives had to secure their husbands' written permission before they could be opened or we might have abandoned the idea of Subud.

The underlying message that in the spiritual realm women were to assist and follow men didn't sit well with me. I didn't like to be told what to wear or not wear during latihan, nor at what time in my menstrual cycle I was allowed to be present. These directives didn't seem much different from the religious rigor I had left behind when joining Subud. Even the word God was offensive to me. The concept was too big for words without the premise that the term was just a convention, that God was neither male nor female, that the essential ineffability of the divine lay beyond the reach of all logic and verbalization.

Once I understood that the essence of God within, through the latihan, was constantly guiding me, that what I received didn't come from Bapak but from a higher source, I became deeply committed. Whenever I stumbled upon concepts that troubled me I reminded myself that words were only an approximation, that they were just "good enough." I knew I would understand later, when I had the capacity through my own receiving, and I took Bapak's advice to think of it as "fairy tales." In the course of time, guidelines such as bathing before latihan, wearing dresses and skirts rather than pants, not being under the influence of any mind-altering substance, not attending during my moons, transformed from injunctions to festivities. Whenever I made this cleaning time before latihan sacred, the purifying water washed away the grime of the day, cleansing the space within, clearing the space without.

Every thing, every space, every body that I honor and take special care of is touched by God and becomes sacred, so I will respect my essential place of worship, my body. Skirts and dresses flow like veils around me emphasizing my femininity, expanding it. As the carrier of memory I suspend, for an instant, the masculine wandering and give it a home. My moons are solitary by nature and I want to honor this accelerated purification in quietness and silence, without interference between my divine nature and myself.

Bapak urged us to develop our inner capacity to receive for ourselves and gave direct advice only to those who asked. The guidance he received mostly pertained to the needs of specific individuals or groups at that time, furthermore he lived in a context of strong cultural and religious beliefs, which couldn't help but tinge his explanations. Whenever someone in Subud seems to be laying down the rules, it probably has to do with their own beliefs system and the stage of their purification. Ibu Rahayu tells us that right and wrong only exist between God and ourselves. There is no need for us to be right in the eyes of others. "If someone criticizes you, let it be; if someone praises you, let it be."

For the longest time it disturbed me that traditionally male guides, teachers, prophets or messiahs were the ones to interpret God's word and to define spirituality. I felt that little was known about how women developed spirituality, and as long as that realm was reserved to men an aspect of divinity remained unexplored.

Myths, tales, stories and fables fascinated women in our earlier Subud group. We discussed the fact that in the monotheist traditions the Buddha, Moses, Jesus and Muhammad's lives were full of heroic deeds achieved in God's name, but that there were no women sharing in that glory. Mary was present in the Catholic Church but mostly as an intermediary sufferer, and never, like her son, were her words thought of as those of God. The heroic journey, filled with trials and tests, was a journey of acquiring spiritual knowledge on the way to recovering a concealed sacred symbolic object. During this journey some great purpose that would transform a land of scarcity and misery into a prosperous and flourishing one was achieved. It was mostly men impelled by curiosity and a desire to explore the world who undertook the journey.

The same curiosity in women often led to the opposite result, releasing famine, disease and war on a land once peaceful and prosperous. It appeared that the transformation was for the better if the hero was a male, for the worse if it was a female. Women holders of keys unlocking doors behind which diabolic forces resided were common in tales. It was often because of female disobedience that people had to suffer all over the land. Women of all ages and condition were burned at the stake because of what they were accused of knowing. Even in present times educated women are locked away and hidden behind burkhas, even stoned because they dare being emancipated. The key women held was terrifying to men in power, as though it unlocked the place where everything that couldn't be controlled was stored away. In fact it was because they had been locked away, not because they had been released, that the furies were dangerous.

Women in the past often had to kindle spirituality in secret, taking the risk of being killed in order not to die inwardly. But it was women who were guardians of the spirit in pre-Christian times, vestals who kept the inner fire going; oracles who transmitted and interpreted God's words. I came to the conclusion that if females were often spiritual leaders at that time, it probably was because of their connection to nature: through the experience of giving birth; and because of the monthly bleeding that shaped their perception of reality. Their instinct to unite, sustain relationship, weave networks made them susceptible to the needs of others. Instinctively they accepted human nature as something to work with rather than against.

Women had been among Jesus' earliest followers because he offered them a new status in the society of the time, and during Muhammad's lifetime the strong egalitarianism that characterized the Islamic ideal included the equality of the sexes. Muhammad held dear the project of women's emancipation. The Koran forbade the killing of female children. It also gave women rights of inheritance and divorce. I was impressed to find this out because Western women had nothing of the sort until the nineteenth century. I learned that he encouraged women to play an active role in the affairs of the tribal community—where they could express their views openly and be heard. In answer to the women of Medina, Muhammad received a revelation that addressed women as well as men and emphasized the absolute moral and spiritual equality of the sexes. I learned that Muslim feminists are asking to return to the original spirit of the Koran.

I was attracted to Subud because in bringing together the path of devotion and the path of self-realization, it relieved me of the male oriented idea of spirituality. The life force flowed through all of us, Bapak explained, and whether we go with or against our true nature is a matter of how obstructed this flow is. Through doing the spiritual exercise of the latihan, seekers would come to the realization that there was nothing to attain by their own means, that it was only through grace that they received the gifts of the spirit. No hard work done with our own efforts was necessary for spiritual advancement.

When I find the quiet place inside myself a trust arises that my life itself is my teacher, that I am guided to my true destiny through the exercise. I don't have to behave a certain way in order to gain spirituality; no spiritual authority can challenge my inner knowing. Understanding that everything I do for my own growth benefits the rest of humanity helps me to value my progress no matter how slow. I do not have to save the world through heroic deeds, nor deliver earth shattering messages!

At times, to trust the unfolding of my life is difficult, painful work. It leaves me feeling uncertain, vulnerable, totally exposed. As my defective structures are taken away I often am left hanging until new ones appear. Spiritual crises were part of the process of purification when I first started in Subud.

During one of those, the idea I was given as a child was of a far away, unreachable God, located outside the material universe and having dominion over it, closer to some of us and further from others, with quantitative and qualitative judgments. This spiritual hierarchy which left much room for self deprecation and doubts dropped away and I understood that we, humans, were of the earth, made of the same stuff, and that we contained within ourselves the essence of God.

Traditionally the woman didn't seek but stayed behind to tend the fire, raise children, plant gardens, supposedly less important because less opened to the sacred. But Bapak indicated that it was through the ordinary gestures of everyday life and not by hard willful work that we would find God. In the daily enfolding of community and family relationships we would develop our inner capacity to receive. In this regard Subud seemed feminine, cultivating not the extraordinary but the ordinary; thus I was reconciled with my femininity. However, it disturbed me and many of my friends to hear some men in Subud say that it was not correct for women to make a place in the world for themselves, that they were to be sensitive to their husband's needs and nurture them because to fulfill those needs was a woman's most significant achievement. There might be a time and a culture in which this could be satisfactory, but women I had observed who attempted to carry out this role failed miserably, becoming alienated from their deepest truth.

During one of his visits to the U.S.A. Bapak talked on this subject, encouraging women, as maintainers of relationships, to become one with their spouse, but he quickly added with a chuckle that this didn't pertain to American women. They should go out in the world and have a career, start enterprises, because they were so good at it!

Many women in my village in France still entirely fill their time with tasks, chores and responsibilities because they feel selfish spending time with themselves. When something within them questions the belief that their role is to be of service to others, they feel guilty and disloyal. Since they can't clean up what they consider the dark corner of their soul they hide it. Unable to handle the anger and resentment within, they project it on others, not realizing that the disowned and unconscious parts of themselves (often indicated by charged reactions to people and situations,) are the keepers of great wisdom. But they cannot really be of service to others until they are of service to themselves.

Through this practice some women who had repeatedly made a habit of quickly putting away their own painful experiences, no longer felt separated from their emotional nature. They cried and cried during latihan. It's only when they are washed by tears that painful experiences break down and become a source of new life; through valuing our own grieving process spiritual maturity might be attained.

Some women were bitter towards men. They believed that it was men, throughout the centuries, who killed or paralyzed any spirituality and confined it within boundaries where it had no chance of developing, making it into such a rigid doctrine that it killed the natural flow. Slowly they began to get another perspective and were freed from the burden of anger when distinction between spirit and matter, sky and earth, mother and father faded, and they honored life in each of its manifestations.

We in Subud once used testing (as described earlier) to find out what the next phase in human development might be and received that it will be the reconciliation of the masculine and feminine principles within each individual, also their recognition of each other as equal partners in the outer world.

Women voices, young and old, fill this chapter.

YOUNG WOMEN RAISED IN
SUBUD FAMILIES

IN MY FAMILY, SUBUD WAS UNDERSTATED

Tatyana (French/American) interviewed in Mendocino (CA.)

*Contained within herself like the pit within a fruit,
holding the past flower and the future seed at the same
season* . . .

*I asked Tatyana, my daughter, what place she felt Subud held
in her childhood.*
Well, Subud was understated in our lives. We didn't have
any structure around it. It wasn't discussed a lot with us kids. I
feel that in fact, it played quite a minimal part in our early life
and even in later years, when it might have felt weird and
embarrassing to us, I don't remember it being a big thing at all. It
was sort of private and you didn't have to tell other people about
it. It was not something you felt compelled to share.

You, my mother, are much more involved now than when we
were growing up. You were isolated in Comptche and there wasn't
a group there. The major part of your life was being with us and
raising us. We were going to school. Also you were involved with
the school and doing whatever you were doing out in the larger
world with your writing. So Subud was not a big part of your life
except that you went to latihan in Elk once a week or so.

I can't really say that it had a big influence on my
development. I feel that the other psychological stuff, the Jungian
stuff you were involved with, was much more important in my
development. Whether the latihan enhanced that aspect of you
or not I can't really say, but when I went to college I definitely
had a core strength, a grounding most other people didn't have.

It was not really because of a spiritual training: I was a total
atheist and didn't believe in God. I still don't really, not in the
way other people do. I felt more like it was a strong grounding, a

connection to the earth, to my roots, the feeling that I was an okay person fundamentally—with all the layers of psychological malfunctions on top of that of course—but at the center, there was something essentially very strong and functional that got me through any hardship I had to go through.

And that might have come from the latihan: to be able to access the feeling of connectedness with everything. But I feel that it was much more the understanding of the psychological that helped me get the tools I needed, and that had a lot more to do with your psychological explorations and beliefs. I feel that the way I was raised in terms of ideologies has much more to do with Jungian models and archetypes.

When I left home I started to question why I felt that some beliefs were fundamental truths. Then I saw that it was because of your influence and the way we communicated, the language you gave us for communication. I don't know if the latihan had anything to do with that.

Your communication could probably be more defined in terms of Jungian psychology. I don't think you used the Subud lingo much—which is a good thing because if you had, like some of your friends, I would have been turned off and probably would have never been opened. One of the things you told me before I got opened, which I think most Subud people would not agree with, helped me. I was expressing my doubts, saying I didn't know if I believed in God, but I believed in something, a connection with the earth, an energy, a life force, maybe not from a unique source though. So you said, "Well, for now just think of it as a psychological exercise, clearing your mind, cleaning your channels, quietening your emotions, as a release. Later you'll see."

And this made it much less of a big deal, you didn't have to take Jesus into your heart type of thing, or for that matter Bapak, or God as the big father figure. It made it much more of an individual thing. It could start out on the psychological level maybe and then develop. I think that a lot of the time it's how the latihan works: as a release, a way to get in tune with your inner feeling and self. How it expresses itself in your body with movements and sounds might not impress you as so terrific and amazing, but that's okay, it isn't such a big thing. You don't have to have all this belief system around God, around the material, vegetable, animal forces, which I am not sure I believe in. You can appreciate the latihan for what it is for you, not have to take any of other people's stuff with it.

You start with what you have, with your capacity at the time of the opening, and you receive as you go along what you need to understand and know for your own life. Do you feel then that in a way it was a blessing that you were not more instructed about Subud?

I think that given my personality, if any dogma or ideology had been pushed on me, there is no way I would have been interested, especially the stuff about man being the leader, the woman being second in line, etc.

What was particularly difficult for me in all the literature I read was the word God. It disturbs me. I don't like to use that word. It has been too misused. Then the pronoun He, as relating to God, and *man*kind instead of *human*kind. I feel that in this day and age, when I read that kind of stuff it excludes me.

Those words obviously were translated in the sixties and there was not much consciousness around those issues at that time. If the words had been written in the nineteenth century you could get over those things more easily because people didn't know any better then, but now it seems like that big male God is a lingering prejudice coming from the Christian or Muslim religions. Spirituality is a much more abstract thing and it can be interpreted a million different ways. I am not comfortable having one interpretation and one word for it.

Many young women feel that there is a gender bias in Bapak's talks, but actually, I understand that there are no genders in the Indonesian language. It only comes in the translation, and reflects our Western gender bias. For instance the words Saudara, saudara, words with which Bapak always opened his talks, were translated as brothers and sisters when saudara actually means a person who is a member of a family even if not related by blood. When repeated it makes it plural. There is nothing in English to express that kind of close extended family connection and this leads to using the word "brotherhood" This is just one of many examples.

You feel that the word God has been misused. Is it because in your mind God is bigger that anything we can imagine and not to be defined?

Everyone is trying to define God, that's the problem. The point of having texts about it, is to try to define it for others. It's a vision of what the divine is or is not from a disciple or guru's point of view.

Does it mean that for you it is all of that and much more?

It is, but I don't know if everybody realizes that. The Christians believe they have the only God. The Muslims believe they have the one God. The Hindus and Buddhists believe they have the way to God and so forth. Everybody believes that everybody else is wrong and they are right. That's the point in belonging to one religion.

Subud is not a religion though, it is one's personal experience of God, of religion, of spirituality, etc. which includes all of it.

To define a thing is to substitute the definition for the thing. Don't you think that ideas and concepts in Subud change and evolve as people grow individually and also as a group? Things have opened up a lot. I think that we don't substitute the definition for the thing, but are willing to change the definition daily.

The Mendocino group has a very different perspective. When I talk to younger Subud members from other groups, I feel that I didn't have to go through anything like they did. I feel that in our group, although certain numbers have gone down at times—and conservative ways to look at things were expressed—no one ever imposed ideas or rules on me personally. Those who did talk Subud talk were obnoxious, but they never went as far as telling me what I should do. I feel that we have a very different vision here in Mendocino of what Subud is all about, so it's very difficult for me to judge.

The way I feel about Subud is that the general organization is far from being totally opened. It's pretty conservative. Right now there is more awareness about this in terms of people writing letters and expressing their disagreement on those issues of narrowness, dogma and rules. When you go to congresses it's an important subject of discussion. This is better than not being discussed at all. Those things can no longer be ignored and not dealt with. New people are questioning. The youth wants to be more relaxed about things and less dogmatic.

Do most young people you have talked to feel that way? I know that in general they don't read much Subud literature, so I wonder where they encounter those things that bother them?

It's true we don't read much of that stuff. Still, we feel the pressure. For instance at congresses, many older Subud members want to guide youth and direct you. Many young people's response is, "Listen, we are young but we may know something. We have wisdom also, in fact we may have more wisdom than you do!"

But I know that you also get support from older members, don't you?

Oh, of course, quite a bit.

I realize how important it is to hear the youth and support their choice of action because they may have come into Subud from a much more evolved place than we did. Not everyone starts from the same place. Some people are very aware of that. I have been made aware of it myself, especially in testing. Anyway, do you feel that through the young people's influence Subud is evolving in a different direction?

This is hard for me to say again because I feel that as a Subud family and even as a Subud group we have, up here, been very disconnected from the Subud organization in general. I only went to one congress in my life and never went to Subud camps. We haven't been connected, since we were born, to all the other Subud kids as some have.

Do you think that this is good or do you have regrets?

I think it's good. I feel that the latihan is a very valuable tool, but I also think that my work will be very separate from Subud. I am not like one of those people who want to be totally involved in Subud projects. If I can bring it into my work it is one thing, but

I am not sure about a lot of the philosophy. I want to make my own decisions and come from my own place, not be completely enmeshed in Subud ideas from the start. Only then do I think that it can be useful to me, only then can I be helpful in the world. I don't want to be involved with the structure. Only the latihan is valuable to me, all the other stuff is just more organization as far as I am concerned. I am glad to be helpful to some people, but Subud is a very minimal part of my life. The latihan is a big part of my life however.

You are saying then that it has been beneficial to you, given your nature, not to be raised in the thick of Subud. Is it because you had a chance to come to it on your own terms and establish you own beliefs about it?

I think that it has been beneficial because people who come to Subud on their own have made a bigger decision, and since they had to search for it; it was much stronger for them and they valued it more. It also depends on how it is presented to you as you are growing up. I feel that my sister Arianne, my brother Kyle and myself have an in-between thing, because we didn't have any of the pressure of growing up in a Subud family. I still think of Subud as an abstract thing and the people I talked to about it never really completely told to me what it was all about.

Also, I was never pressured openly or in any other way to get opened. When I did get information it remained somewhat abstract, which is why I was interested. On the other hand if we had had nothing, then we would have had to search. It is a big quest. I know I need to experience something more beside just the physical life. If you try many things and you come to Subud, then it is a pretty powerful thing. We, the second generation of Subud, do take it too much for granted.

It was a surprise to me when you told me you wanted to get opened. I didn't expect it. I made a point not to talk about Subud too much because I knew it would turn you off as I had seen it happen. Then all of a sudden, you announced that you were interested.

I don't really remember how it happened, except that I expressed some curiosity and exposed my misgivings. Actually it did take some convincing at that point. But I came from the place of feeling that there was a spiritual world and that there was nothing to take care of that side of my life. I was in college and getting more and more unbalanced with the intellectual stuff. It was driving me crazy. I needed some balance. I was feeling very alienated and disconnected from myself. That is the first thing the latihan taught me, being able to access spontaneity, being able to access creativity—all that stuff which was blocked and inaccessible to me, almost uncomfortably so. I needed to find a balance.

I think it came with time because I was not doing latihan while in college, only when I came back home on vacation. So it was slow. But I did get this balance.

Soon after this conversation, I had this dream:

Bapak has just finished giving a talk to a big crowd. Now six or seven of us are sitting with him in a small room. He is very relaxed and jokes with us as equals. He is soft and gentle, very willing to show his vulnerability and foibles.

Earlier in his talk he had mentioned something that puzzled me. It was during a question/answer session and I hadn't been able to get my question in because I felt shy. Now I am in a much more relaxed situation so I speak, "Bapak, can I ask you a question? I want to get some clarification about something you said earlier having to do with curiosity (of the mind) and isolation (of the heart)." Bapak goes quiet for a minute and is about to answer my question when he unexpectedly changes his mind and says, "No, I can't answer."

I understand that he cannot answer an important question privately so he would do it later in a public talk maybe. When I ask him if that is why, he answers that it is.

At this point my daughter Tatyana, who is also present and in a militant mood, asks him intelligent, philosophical questions about the absurdity of the masculine God image and all the pompous adjectives describing it. Wasn't God overly personified? She also has pertinent questions about theology, evolution, but mostly about Subud hierarchy and righteousness. She deplores that images of what is right or wrong have been projected as Subud dogma, with the effect that people hang on to those pictures and don't go on with their life as it is. Because of this they always feel they are not whole and they go through life with a feeling of dissatisfaction.

It is very heady and Bapak's answers seem to avoid the subject: "You will experience this for yourself at some point," and "You will receive the answer to that for yourself."

I am afraid that she will be extremely disappointed and angry at that paternalism. She does not seem to mind however, or experience any outrage. She calmly continues interacting and engaging as though exchanging observations and points of view with a peer.

All of a sudden I notice that Bapak has turned into an English woman—a woman who had been his wife during his life and took on the leadership of the Subud association after his death. She is very strong and powerful. When Bapak was still alive I had always thought of her as subservient, satisfied to walk in his footsteps and with nothing very original to say. I had put her in the category of meek older person of very noble character.

Now I become conscious that I had never really looked at her. Without the funny turban-hat she always wore and without her old-lady-glasses she looks rather young with smooth glowing skin. She is a vivacious, powerful and intelligent woman, a blond Nordic type. Depending on the angle, she seems to change race as well as age, back and forth, also change from the masculine sex to the feminine, from wife to daughter, to mother or sister.

Tatyana and I engage in conversation with her. We are part of her intimate circle of friends; she needs friends who have the capacity to be equals, not admirers.

At one point she is seized with bad cramps in one thigh. She explains that it needs to happen, not to worry. A man helper starts massaging the cramp away and she accepts his help gratefully, pulling up her skirt to make it easier. I also start helping and she casually takes off her skirt and then her top to have a full body massage. She is totally at ease. I notice that her body is hairless and boyish. It has a beautifully golden color, her skin tone is perfect, her pubis totally smooth like that of a young girl: a hermaphrodite's body.

I am told that she goes to the beauty parlor to nurture her feminine side so she does not always remain in her masculine side, which is Bapak. I wonder if those cramps are related to the changes. I am told they are a sign of very old age. But she seems to be such a young person!

The cramps are gone now and she is well. She ties her hair in a bun, then puts on her glasses and turns into an older, Indonesian woman. This is the image she needs to present at this time to the Subud world.

*   *   *

Ten years later Tatyana tells me that she does not have so much charge or judgment about Subud doctrine or Subud groups any longer, and that she sees people she knows trying to bring to Subud the best they have.

GROWING UP IN A SUBUD COMMUNITY

Petrice (Canadian) interviewed in Menucha (OR.)

The flamboyant vibration of the most daring color. A powerful movement forward.

I was raised in a Subud family in Canada. Mostly I experienced Subud camps, because my Dad organized all the Canadian camps. My parents were in Subud, but my Dad didn't do latihan, or rather he did it only until I was about five or six. But he remained very active in the organizational part of Subud, organizing the Subud camps, etc. It's only recently that he got back into doing latihan. He didn't do it for twenty years or so, but even so, when we were young kids, he was chairman and still really active in it.

I have my own theory about why he was not doing the latihan. I think he got scared or he ran into a block and wouldn't go further with it, so he convinced himself that he didn't feel it.

Do you think it was going too fast for him?

Yes, twenty years too fast I guess.

We grew up in a Subud community. It was really wonderful. We bought this piece of property all together in a small farming town, and it drew people from the city group, also everyone from the valley. I don't really know the details because it fell apart when I was about 8 or 10, but for the first ten years of my life I played on the farm with all those other kids.

It was like a dream, the ideal life. We had a lot of get-together parties, a big latihan hall and acres of playground. I had a big family, too, so I was never without playmates, never without things to do. We had horses, only one horse actually, but it sticks in my mind as though they were many. We had chickens and beehives and ducks. It was wonderful but when it fell apart, it was a hard adjustment for us. We moved to the city and once a year we would go to Christmas parties and see everybody again.

I still miss it and that is why I am a junky for congresses now. But I didn't always know I was going to get opened. When I was a teenager I would go, "Oh yuck, I don't think so. This is not for me. It's my Mom's thing." You know how it is. When you are a teenager you don't get along with your Mom all that well. Then, I went to the Australian World Congress. My Mom and I were supposed to go together, but she ended up getting sick so she couldn't go. I met people my age who were already opened and who were amazing. I kept thinking, "Oh my God!"

I got back home and I said to my Mom, "Momma, I want it." I was the first one who wanted to get opened in my family. I have an older brother and three younger sisters. My mom was very excited about it. My opening was very mellow. It was like saying, "Oh I know this." It was already with me. I wanted it to be a big exciting thing but it wasn't.

In general, I have the feeling that there is not going to be the great boom that there was at the beginning of Subud again. Not everyone is going to be rushing in the door. That has happened already. The growth will take another form; it will be slower.

RAISED IN A VERY ACTIVE SUBUD FAMILY

Manuella (Hungarian-English) interviewed in Mendocino (CA.)

A fetus, tenderly held within its mother's womb and pulsating with the great heartbeat does not wish to leave the place of trust and surrender. A child in the Subud Family, held within the Great Guidance, moved by the flow of the life force and rocked by the universal rhythm, has to puncture the lining confining her in order to find her true self.

I was born in England. My parents had already been in Subud for about ten years, and I was the fourth child born in Subud. We went to Indonesia when I was six months old to live near Bapak. My father was very personally involved with Bapak who often came to our house; for me he was sort of a grandfather figure. I remember I used to play *chu-chu* train in his house and he would be watching my younger brother and me play. We felt very close to him and as a child; I certainly didn't experience him as a god or anything.

We grew up with a lot of crisis cases around us and that made me a little embarrassed about being part of Subud. When I was in school as a child, I didn't want my other friends to know that I was part of that group. The kids of other Subud families felt the same. We sort of made a pact that we wouldn't tell any friends out of Subud, and we certainly were not going to be like our parents and join Subud later. So there was a feeling that our parents were a little bit eccentric and not doing things in the same traditional way that the rest of the families did.

We lived and we grew up with a lot of Subud dogma, which is not meant to exist but it does, especially in Indonesia where a lot of that dogma comes from. You find it in Indonesian culture, because that was Bapak's culture, so he lived according to certain principles that came from his Javanese background, his Islamic faith. Many of the families that went there, Western families, adopted his way of living.

My father became a Muslim and we did the Muslim prayers together. The kids did the Muslim fasting from the age of five. A lot of the ideas—like no sex before marriage, women being covered up, no alcohol—a lot of beliefs came from the Muslim culture. There also was a lot of talk about the material, vegetable and animal forces, which is part of Indonesian culture. You can find it in any spiritual group there. There are basic ideas that do not pertain just to Subud.

I remember that my friends and I used to peek and look at people doing latihan. We used to wonder about it and make fun of it, but there were also a lot of fears because our parents always said that it was dangerous for children to be around the latihan. So we believed that we would get sick if we got too close to it.

Growing up around Subud encouraged me to tap into something that was beyond the physical, beyond my physical senses. I remember my grandmother encouraging me to sit in contemplation every night before going to sleep. And I would do that. I remember that sometimes I would have this experience of light and be terrified of something supernatural happening. I also felt that I had a communication with something beyond. I would talk to this entity, I wouldn't call it God necessarily, but it was beyond our physical. So the belief in a beyond was very much part of my life at a very young age.

I think that Subud was somewhat restrictive as I was growing up, especially about sexuality. Somehow I don't know if it was just the Subud dogma or if it also came from the fact that my mother and father came from sexually repressed backgrounds—my father from a Catholic background, my mother from English Puritanism in which sex was not talked about, and nobody walked around lightly clothed or allowed themselves to be seen naked. I think there was a lot of tension around things having to do with sexuality and a lot of discomfort talking about it.

I feel in that way I was held up in my development. Also, there was this paranoia about drugs. Because we were in Indonesia there were magic mushrooms growing everywhere and there was a lot of marijuana. A lot of the kids we hung out with experimented with these. And I did also, not to a great extent, but there was the feeling that if you did any of those things once, it would damage you forever. It's a belief that creates a lot of fear, so I didn't experiment much until later, in my twenties, and then only a little, which may have been good. I don't feel that this has impaired my development. It was more like there was this religious attitude about being good or being bad, and I feel that it's only now that I am beginning to deal with that, take away this idea of good and bad from my mind. Still, there is a judgmental voice about what it means to lead a good life or a bad life.

There also was this idea that people are on different spiritual levels. People talked about what level you were on and how far you had developed spiritually. Besides, there was this idea that women were not as spiritual as men. I remember my mother getting upset about that, but I also remember that she agreed with that. I don't exactly know what the belief is, but it is something about women not being on the same level as men and being appendages to them, that the male is superior in the eyes of God or that he is meant to be the leader in a couple. Again, that is part of the Indonesian culture.

As Bapak said, "Whatever I tell you is going to come from my culture." He also told us that we each have to find our own truth, but of course, we who grew up with him and the people who went to live there to be close to him, took on his beliefs and his culture.

I find myself, wherever I go, looking for a master or a leader. My parents always were looking to Bapak for answers, whether they should do this or that, what work they should do, what name they should have. Most of the people who lived around him were there because they didn't trust their own inner voices. So they also looked to him for answers. A lot of people now try to put the same thing on his daughter, Ibu Rahayu, and she really does not want that.

More so than many other kids who grew up in Subud families in other parts of the world, away from Bapak, I had a tendency to give over my personal power to some male figure. It may be that those other kids also have a tendency to look to helpers for answers, but it couldn't be as bad as in Indonesia where people were always asking Bapak about everything. Of course people wrote to him from all over the world asking, also. I know because my father was always translating a lot of those letters.

The other thing about this spiritual level business, is that you are always thinking about other people in terms of categories. Are they as evolved as me, are they more evolved than me and so on. I remember once that a man asked Bapak, "Bapak what level am I on? What level is my jiwa on?" And Bapak answered, "Well, you haven't gotten one yet. Keep doing the latihan and you will get one." I remember hearing this and being horrified, thinking that maybe I didn't have a soul either. I still don't know what that meant.

I have talked to two women who were pretty shaken by such statements. In the end however, it turned out to be a saving grace. It might have been a form of shock treatment, a horse remedy. But it could also mean that we all have the possibility of having a soul but it is up to us to develop it. We have to choose to move to the vibrational level of the soul, not to act exclusively from our will but align with the highest vibration, or else it remains inactive.

Maybe!

THE WAY THE LATIHAN MOVES THROUGH A LIFE IS NOT IDENTIFIABLE AS CLEAR OR SINGULAR PROCESS

Arianne (French/American) interviewed in Mendocino (CA.)

"Anyone who surrenders to God with patience, acceptance and sincerity can receive the latihan kejiwaan. It is not the copyright of Subud. Nobody can lay claim to God."

Bapak

I asked Arianne, my younger daughter, what made her decide to be opened in Subud.

When I decided to get opened I was seventeen, a senior in high school. I was born into a Subud family and was the first of the kids to be opened. During all my childhood and adolescence I had always been attracted to religion, interested in magical things, but that made me also very susceptible to certain forces, very close to some kind of parallel world which lies below the surface of life. I could lie there in bed and feel it as palpable, a sort of positive or negative charge depending on my own mood or condition perhaps.

When you were very young you went through a time of feeling afraid of those things and I think that the other world you are talking about was opened to you, too opened maybe, with darkness and fear coming along with it.

I never lost the sense that this other world is close by and that it can be fearful. I think that as a child I struggled with the idea of loss. For some reason that idea of loss really influenced me, the fact that you could lose someone you loved at any time. Along with that I developed the sense that even when I was right next to my family, sleeping in a bed that was next to theirs, I could lose them. I felt very alone and had a sense of abandonment. All sorts of things that one could see as symbols of death became signs of abandonment to me. I developed a belief that they were bad omens, or premonitions.

I don't know if it had to do with being in France with my uncle's family when he was dying. I was seeing people grieving in a way that was confusing to me, and I didn't feel completely included. My association with visiting my relatives had always been very light—vacationing with my parents—and I couldn't totally relate to the tragedy.

Also it was hard to see somebody who was very close to death, somebody I had felt very close to, even though I didn't know him that well—only like a child knows an adult she is fond of and sees only occasionally. But I think it was a contemplation of mortality in general and of my own mortality, at an early age. I had a feeling that I could die at any minute, and the anxiety would become confused with foreboding, so that any worry about my parents being late—for instance if they were half an hour late it felt like hours to me—would become the certainty that something had gone wrong

Did you feel safer in the face of those negative forces after getting opened?

It didn't open up channels in an obvious way, didn't clear things out of my imagination. In some way it's more ordinary, or maybe more subtle. It takes a longer time to appreciate it. I don't feel like it has been a light in the pool of darkness, and it probably has some of both, lightness and darkness. It's possibly a way of dealing with the fact that spirituality is really made of both dark and light.

Do you feel some darkness in the latihan?

Yes and no. I feel that it can bring up darkness and bring out darkness. It does not only dispel it. The thing I don't really like about religion, or the way certain people tend to view spirituality, is the idea that there is something wrong in themselves, something dark that they try to dispel or put light into. That they need salvation. I don't really buy into that and don't think that it's so simple. It isn't as rich if you simplify it in that way. I think that you just have to find a way—a belief system or a practice—which allows you to develop a friendship with the whole spiritual realm, both the terrifying aspect and the more beautiful and transcendent aspect, the love side of it.

Have you been brought closer to your true self by doing the latihan?

I don't see it that way, especially as I get older. I have done the latihan for many years, sometimes more and sometimes less—sometimes not at all for as much as a year or maybe more—but I don't attribute all spiritual things that have happened in my life to the latihan. I don't see it as having permeated everything I do.

Even at times when I am doing it frequently, I don't get a strong feeling that the latihan is moving through my life like some people do. They look at their lives and can identify what Subud has done for them. They can specifically feel how it has moved through their lives, how it has changed them or helped them. "I can't imagine life without it," they'll say. That baffles me. I think it's your whole life that teaches you. There are many things that have opened up something for me. There are a lot of influences on a life. What the latihan has done for me is to open me up to the whole.

I had some kind of spiritual life before I was opened and I don't think that it has ended with the latihan. Maybe it's explored more through the latihan, in many different kinds of ways. Since each latihan is so unique, it brings the feeling of different types of spirituality, cultures, also different aspects of self, and those different aspects of self are not bounded by society or culture. Maybe it's because I was born into Subud that I don't have a strong sense of the latihan being the prime mover of my life.

I have heard this a lot from people who were born in Subud, that the latihan is not such a great moving force for them. Maybe it's because it's integrated so thoroughly into their lives.

I can't really separate what the latihan has done from myself. I don't see it as the guiding light but only as initiating part of the lessons I am learning in life and yes, gently diffusing light throughout my life.

Many people experience the movements and sounds of the latihan as a cleansing of the many voices that are not really theirs, voices that have come from parents, teachers, religion, culture, voices that have led them to do this or that which is not really what they want to do or is not in accordance with their own nature. Do you feel that this is true for you?

I feel that I am always confused by those voices. What are the important voices to listen to? Is it society's voice, or voices of people you admire for one reason or another, family's voices or the voices of one culture or another? Is it voices of the past, of the present or future? I feel that all those voices are very present, and I am not very good at weeding through them elegantly in my life. They tend to overwhelm me. It might be part of my personality, the fact that I have a hard time disassociating from those voices.

I do know what my own inner voice is telling me, but it's not necessarily at times when I am doing the latihan that I feel that inner voice or my inner guide the strongest. From the deeper place of my inner voice, I know that there are always many choices and there is always confusion in life. But I also know what I need to do. The other voices are not cleansed away; they just get put into perspective.

I don't necessarily attribute the guidance of my inner voice to the latihan. It would be false for me to do so. So then, why attach significance to it, because of the need to have something in my life that is sacred and elevated, something to which I can attribute my inner development? It could be that the guidance is so integrated; it could be lots of things. I believe in many ways of receiving guidance, also that other paths are valid.

Bapak has said that this receiving will happen any time anybody has a quiet mind and a quiet heart and is in a state of surrender to God. Then the spirit of the divine is able to move through him/her and that person's spirit will respond.

Yes, sometimes just the contact with nature will do it, being in a state of quiet meditation and being that opened. Has the latihan alone taught me to be that opened? Maybe it has helped, but it is not the only thing I rely on. It isn't the single cause. Sometimes even in the latihan you don't get that feeling of total surrender, and at other moments in your life, you might get high or whatever it is—I know that this is very controversial for some people in Subud, but for some others, getting stoned makes them feel closer to the spirit—something like fasting, or going on a hike by yourself, or sitting and meditating, and suddenly it happens. It's available to us in many different forms. But maybe I just take the latihan for granted.

You seem to describe a mystical experience. It's more like the latihan penetrates into every moment of your ordinary life, in a very subtle way.

I would say that some people definitely maintain that the latihan is about having a mystical experience. Surrender can be seen that way. I don't think that we know how the latihan works for everybody or how it is experienced. You don't know what an experience is until you experience it, so even saying 'mystical experience' is vague I guess. Being opened to something bigger than oneself, that is how I have often heard the latihan being described.

Why do you stop doing latihan at times?

I feel that the latihan is a choice. I don't want to do the latihan for any other reason than wanting to do it. And when you are born into Subud it's very hard to separate yourself from your parents doing it, from the group doing it. This sort of commitment to going to latihan often translates into obligation, depending on how close people are to you and how interested they are in you doing it. So it becomes more complicated for young people born into a Subud family to find their own rhythm with it. I advocate the most open and free attitude, the least possible organized version of Subud. It's my personal preference.

It has been proven over and over again that we are not really capable of handling the organization, trying to make something tangible out of Subud, something we can all agree upon. Everyone has totally different latihans and totally different approaches. Of course, there is convergence at times, and I think that's wonderful, but I don't think we should make too many assumptions based on the way we commonly experience.

We should get together and do the latihan, keep it light, open, fresh and alive. Just like that rebel group of Subud women doing their own latihan with no rules attached. Sometimes going to a new place to do a latihan can be a heavy experience. You can feel that there is something that is being played out, that you don't really fit in. Other times people want to impose something on you and you can really feel that. They want you to know how they feel about how things should be done.

I see more men having problems with this than women, especially among a certain generation of people. Certain things that bother me also bother men. The women don't tend to as much. Some men I know, even though they have been in Subud for over thirty-five years, have quite a sacrilegious attitude toward what they call the "Subud dogma."

I WOULD LIKE THE FREEDOM TO BE WHATEVER I AM

Muftiah (U.S.A.) interviewed in Spokane (WA.)

*"Denying basic biological needs and instinctual
drives is useless. Blocking normal sexual outlets results in
the creation of abnormal ones. To accept rather than
condemn is the way to find a solution."*

Dr. David R. Hawkins

*When I talked to her at the congress, Muftiah had just read a
book that was for sale in the gift shop and she was extremely angered
by it. I asked her for the name of the book and what offended her
so much.*

The book is titled *Subud Survival Guide* and it was published
in July *1997*. The author is a man named Harry Armitage. I
believe he is Australian because it is published in Australia.
The book is written in an A to Z format on different subjects.

The introduction does contain a disclaimer acknowledging
that this is the writing of one person who might be going through
a "purification" process, and to please forgive him. He also quotes
Bapak who said that you shouldn't believe anything until you
have experienced it for yourself. But who is going to look at the
introduction before looking up what concerns them? In a
bookstore people will open it up and flip through the pages without
seeing the introduction.

There are subjects you can look up and the book contains
some quotes by Bapak, the author's personal opinions, and some
excerpts from other Subud members' books.

Bapak was against making rules; he said Subud was not a
teaching. His words, taken out of context, are quite dangerous
because he was talking to one person or maybe to a group at a
certain time. I don't think he meant them for everybody as a
universal rule throughout all time.

I am disturbed by what the author has to say about sex. The
man really wants to drive it into the young people that it's better

to wait to have sex, that it's really damaging to "sleep around." Those are the words he used and I find it abrasive because the expression is a judgment in and of itself: "sleeping around." It implies all kinds of things. It may be better to wait to have sex till one is older, I don't know, but every time you put this in writing with Subud in the title it looks as if that is what Subud stands for.

That's also why I object to the things about homosexuality. It's under "Sexual Relationships" and there is Bapak's quote, which says something to the effect that having sexual relationships with members of the same gender is damaging to your inner. The author also says that homosexuals are welcome in Subud, that they should expect that by doing the latihan God may take away their desire to have sex with a person of the same gender. If I was not a Subud kid (born from parents who are in Subud,) and I heard that, I would never have joined Subud.

I have been dating women for the last six years. I came out when I was nineteen. I already know what some Subud people have to say about that; I have already experienced it here at the congress. Sometimes I feel ashamed that I am part of an organization that has members who say things like that about people like myself.

I am concerned about how Subud presents itself to the rest of the world. I feel embarrassed. I feel ashamed. I am afraid to tell my friends about Subud because they will find out about these negative aspects of Subud.

This only involves a segment of the Subud membership and things are changing fast even with them. Your parents are in Subud you said, right?
Yes. They have lived in Santa Cruz, California, for the last twenty-six years.

So you were born and raised in Subud. How was it for you as a kid? As a kid it was great. When I was a teenager, in California, there were lots of activities for Subud youth. That was a positive experience. My parents were really involved; we went to every California Subud congress—this is my first world congress. They were very active; Subud was a big part of life. We always had

Subud folks staying at our house, people passing through or moving in temporarily.

As a kid I didn't like the words "purification" and "crisis" (I think those words have changed since.) Someone just told me a nice alternative to the word crisis: transformation. "I am going through a transformation" has a different connotation. A purification was something sinful you had to change . . . and the way it was used so frequently!

When I was seventeen I was an exchange student in Honduras. There was no Subud there. I was there for five months, at the end of which I realized I was really missing being around the latihan, or just being around Subud people. So when I got back I decided to get opened. I decided I had to take responsibility for doing the latihan for myself.

I had my eight years Subud birthday here at the congress. The first few days of the congress were really great. After I got here I went walking around town and I could tell, walking down the streets, who was in Subud and who wasn't. We really do have something special and I can't say exactly what it is.

So the first few days were great. I got involved in the opening ceremony and that was a high. Then the issue of being gay in Subud started to come up for me. The activist and rebel part of me was saying okay, we have to do something about it. Then I came across the book and that was the clincher. First reaction was anger, then hurt and sadness over my struggle with this issue. I must say that coming out was the hardest thing I have ever done.

Did you feel you were inflicting pain on your parents?

It was hard on my parents, but they have come a long way. A Subud member approached me yesterday. She was very worried about me and full of judgment. I told my dad, "She is worried about me, and I am trying to feel her positive intent and not take on all the judgment." My dad said, "Oh, she just has expectations and you are not meeting them. She just has to go through an adjustment." He said that to me while I was waiting for you.

This gives me hope because I see that Subud people often will say judgmental things, but doing the latihan can move them out of their judgment. Of course there are those who cling to their judgment, very hard, but eventually they may be able to understand and have compassion. Both my parents have come a long way. My mom at first thought she had done something wrong. *Most parents do.*

I say I am a lesbian, I guess, because I need to identify and have a label, but I don't know what my future holds. I would like the freedom to be whatever I am, not bound by the gay community, nor bound by the straight community. Being bisexual can be hard because of pressure coming from both sides.

What was so traumatic at first was that I had internalized the "Subud belief." I put it in quotes because it is not really a Subud belief, but only a belief of some members. I had internalized the idea that being gay was detrimental to my soul. I wasn't too worried about being discriminated against socially because I live in a pretty open community. It was more that I believed I was doing something damaging to myself. For months and months I kept crying. I wanted to be in that relationship but kept feeling that I had to get out. I think I have moved past this; now I don't believe I am damaging myself.

We have to work on these kinds of issues. I guess it's mostly making people aware of the danger of generalizing and making rules when Bapak specifically asked us not to. I don't like to have to apologize about beliefs that misrepresent Subud to my non-Subud friends.

I am hoping, there are a lot of us who are hoping, to get a workshop going during this congress: "An Open Discussion of Gay, Lesbian, and Bisexual Issues in Subud." It would be open to everybody. I am meeting a lot of gay people here, so I am finding out that I am not alone, which is nice. We, as humans, have a tendency to want to look to somebody else for answers. That's why so many people end up following teachers and gurus. That's fine. In Subud, people want to believe everything that Bapak said. Bapak himself has said he was not a guru; he was not a teacher. He said not to believe anything he tells us until we receive it for ourselves. And yet we have made him a guru. It was put on him and still now after his death people hold onto that.

A friend I opened came to me soon after her opening with one of the Subud publications, saying she had been lied to. When I questioned why she felt that way she answered, "You told me there was no dogma or rules in Subud. Well, read this." She has left Subud since. There will always be people who need to fabricate rules for themselves and others.

The same thing happened in my group to a helper who had expressed her own beliefs that we, in Subud, didn't have issues about being gay (among other things.) So a friend of hers got opened and after receiving the first Subud Life publication she said, "What's this?" And she left. She stopped doing the latihan. That helper says she finds it difficult to be a helper because when she states the openness principles of Subud she feels she might be deceiving people. The world is opening about those issues, starting to understand and accept. If Subud does not follow it will shrink and shrink and shrink.

*   *   *

I have run across Muftiah at a regional congress a few years later and she was beaming. She announced that she was in a committed relationship with a man.

MIDDLE YEARS IN SUBUD

THE BEGINNING OF RECEIVING

Sabina (U.S.A.) interviewed in Mendocino (CA.)

There was once so pure a being that it couldn't plant its feet on the ground and whenever it tried to walk on the earth the foot bounced off so the next step was made more difficult. Human life on this earth is embedded in the worldly environment; so this being who wanted to be

human, became rigid in the effort to stay down. The hands,
however, kept flying like birds when the being talked. The
hands, a promise of flight . . .

I first heard about Subud when I lived in Aspen and as far as
I remember it was 1965. My husband Don and I knew this real
character, Steve G. I think we asked him to take care of our
house for a couple of months. He was a Jewish intellectual type
and he needed money. He was okay.

What I remember best is myself, standing in the backyard. It
was about noon. The sun was shining down on us and he was
describing this revelation from God, or something like that. He
got very animated and looked very happy about this. It was too
much for me at the time. It sounded hysterical, a cult, but in a
way I was interested to hear what it did for him. I felt that there
was no way I could be involved with something like that. It would
curtail my independence too much.

He mentioned Subud by name, but he also mentioned the
Gurdjieff connection as the way it had traveled to the West. None
of that meant much to me until later on. Then my other friends
started to join it, one after the other.

It felt like we were traveling diverging paths. My skirts were
getting shorter and theirs longer. My morals were becoming freer.
I was not interested in making babies. I didn't like keeping house,
and this "cult" sounded more and more repulsive to me. However
I loved my friends and they were still very much themselves in a
way, even more so than before. I watched them being more of
themselves, year after year. They were themselves even though
they didn't do the wild stuff anymore, and I never felt any judgment
from them. They were growing larger.

I was prone to depressions and I had a really bad one when
I was thirty-two. I lived in Mill Valley, California. I called my
friend, Lydia Rand, (you, now Riantee) to tell her how depressed
I was. During one other down moment in my life, she had sent
me the address of Subud in Athens, Greece where I was living at
the time. I remember walking and walking up and down the streets

on the outskirts of Athens. I never found the place. I spent four hours looking for it. It was like a kind of mirage. Like, it's there but I don't see it. Does it exist? Does it not exist? Is it on the astral plane? People were into those kinds of trips then.

Anyway, you were all my friends; and that was your trip. You still knew how to laugh and you seemed happier than I was, and although I couldn't imagine following in your footsteps as far as domesticity and relationships and other things like that were concerned. I decided that if it made you happy it could do that for me, maybe; I told you I wouldn't mind giving it a try.

There was this big center in Marin and you gave me the address. I went there as a probationer and waited for two months. Then Bapak was coming, so they tested and decided it was okay for me to get opened right before he came so I could have the benefit of his presence.

Oh, yes, I read all the Pewartas. I was fascinated by it all, even though I was also repelled by it. All that business about not doing latihan during periods, all the husband and wife stuff, the roles, women being the follower, women wearing skirts instead of pants, etc. were things to relegate women to a subservient level in my mind.

I was very busy trying to be intellectual, rational, because that was what had been given value in our society, so the softer benefits of being the woman at home tending the children, all that domestic stuff had no appeal for me. The housewifely virtues, the womanly qualities were not for me, no way.

How did I feel when I saw Bapak? Well, I barely saw him. He was up on the stage far away and there were many, many members of his 'court' all around him. All of Bapak's family, the people whose house he was staying at, and all the translators, International Helpers, important committee members and what not. To me, the idea of having to wait on all those Indonesian people who were so invasive, trying to feed them and imitate their Indonesian ways was very difficult. I couldn't imagine myself doing that and being one of the groupies. Unthinkable.

I attended the latihan off and on. I didn't receive anything.

Whenever I saw my friends Lydia and Lillia, when I occasionally passed through California, it seemed quite natural to go and hang out with them, witness the latihan, sit there with my eyes closed. But there was no feeling of my own, no movement, nothing. The obstacle was indeed my mind, the intellectual in me. Every two or three years I would pass through California to see Lydia and Lillia and one year, I was passing through on my way to Hawaii and they were doing the latihan in a church in Elk. I had just had a terrible grief with a relationship. I went in and started the latihan and . . . oh! It was so incredible! It was like an explosion of light and rainbows and visions. This incredible thing happened. It was like a psychedelic experience and this was the beginning of my receiving.

Sabina became active in Subud and was made a helper in Hawaii where she lived at the time, but she encountered hostility from two women helpers, which resulted in a sickness. She's left mainstream Subud since but still does the latihan occasionally.

*   *   *

A few years later Sabina, now Emmaline, left Subud for good. Since I was working on a re-write and asking people for addendums, she sent me this in March 2004.

"And what of your immortal soul?" a couple of people asked when I said that I was leaving Subud.

I sensed a smugness, a reproach in that question. "Our way is the only way," seemed the implication.

"God is bigger than Subud," I replied.

I knew this to be true, though my heart was broken and I was inwardly quaking. I used to say that the latihan was the love of my life, and I meant it. It took a long time to leave and I passed through many of the well-known stages of grief.

In my own fashion I kept on moving, exploring, trying to look behind the surface of what I encountered. I have an allergic reaction to too much hierarchy or ill-used authority. After an arid period, interesting individuals, forms or ceremonies began to appear in my life, physically or through the written word.

I now seek out that which flows, people who are willing to share parts of their wisdom, a caring spirit without too much duty or agenda riding on it. I am attracted to generosity and laughter: I give back whatever of this is in my nature when I can. The rigid or problematical aspects of my own personality trouble me from time to time without the latihan to lighten them up, but I have found that patient work and respectful discussion can often resolve a tangle. Inner and outer acceptance are important here.

I see that much of what appeals to me now are feminine characteristics, long dismissed by me because misconstrued by society and under-represented in all the major religions. Perhaps the time approaches, with the grand precession of the equinoxes, Harmonic concordance, etc., for the Divine Feminine energy to move freely and in honor about the earth once again—not to stifle or intimidate as patriarchal rule has so often done, but to heal the earth and its warring factions and bring us all into balance.

This is my current interest and I rejoice in whatever signs I see of it. I believe that my "immortal soul" will continue to witness changes whether in or out of physical form. It would be fun.

I was blessed in all I received from the latihan, and I miss some people in Subud. I continue to feel blessed by Source, though I know I understand only the merest fraction of what occurs in and around my life.

WOMEN ON THE SUBJECT OF
HAVING NO SOUL

IN THIS CRISIS YOU ARE NOTHING, NOWHERE

Rohanna S. (Peruvian-American) interviewed in Seattle (OR.)

Things are always evolving. There is nothing on this planet that represents the ultimate truth; our passage is only a chance to explore who we are and what we are after, to show us that we have the power to change things for ourselves.

In a conversation I had with Rohanna she recounted that at one point in her Subud life she was told by Bapak that she didn't have a jiwa yet, in other words that she didn't have a soul. I asked her if she felt damaged by this.

I don't know if it's damaging or not, but it worked for me as a real experience. Once you don't have the reality of yourself—when you believe you do not have a jiwa, you don't have a soul—you are just an imitator. You have copied yourself, split yourself into maybe thousands of pieces, for thousands of years. You do not have any identity. It came to me as strong as it can get. Nothing was real here, *(gesture pointing to herself, then laughing.)* I did experience that I didn't have a soul because if I had one, I would have been more real. I said to myself, "Well okay, I am one of those who do not have a soul."

So I prayed that I would get a soul, even just the soul of an amoeba. This might not make any sense because everyone knows that if you are able to speak, if you can also listen and see and think, then something has to be inside. But it is nothing authentic.

So I prayed to be authentic, even if it was going to have microbe size authenticity. I prayed to be connected to the reality of the power of God, directly, not through a thousand imitations, or monkeying, or whatever.

I do not know when it happened, I didn't notice when it happened, but I know now that I do have a soul. There was no big bang. I started having spiritual experiences, but I didn't know what they meant. I just experienced the reality of sounds, movements, voices.

It was valuable to be told I didn't have a jiwa because I became more humble and diligent. The whole thing was a crisis. A lot of people go into those kinds of crises. It was a crisis of truth. Truth. You don't have a truth. You don't even know what it is, or you think that one is better than the other, or you say, "This is the one!"

A crisis of being nothing. It's okay to be nothing if you are together with God, if you are somewhere. But in this crisis you are nothing, nowhere. A lot of my usual worries, unhappiness, disturbances left me at that point. I was erased. I had to start from scratch, from nothing. I had to accept that and from there I could begin to become myself.

MY JUDGMENT OF MYSELF WAS ENORMOUS

Mardiah (U.S.A.) interviewed in Seattle (WA.)

"The latihan is brought about by the power of God. It is a direct contact with God whereby the inner self is cleansed of the obstacles of ancestry, education, culture, etc."

Dr. Hattori

Mardiah had somewhat of a similar experience as Rohanna when she heard Bapak, during one of his talks, say that those who didn't receive anything when he tested them didn't have a jiwa yet. I asked Mardiah to tell me about it.

Well after his talk Bapak tested us. It was in New York, in a church, in 1968 or '69. I couldn't have been in Subud for more than a year or so. I was standing there with all the ladies for the latihan type of testing—I actually forget what it was we were testing—but I was very self-conscious standing there, very aware of everyone else and very distracted. After the testing I thought, "Where is the big Grace that I am supposed to receive?"

I went back to my seat. My judgment of myself was enormous. I had failed the test. At this particular time in my life I always put on an outer face and posture that was very often different from what I was feeling inside. So this experience just broke me apart. I was painfully aware and uncomfortable with the way I looked, how I appeared outwardly, how different it was from the reality inside. Then Bapak said, "And if you didn't receive anything in your testing, then you have no soul."

By the time the evening was over I was so uncomfortable, so upset with my reality as I judged it, that when I got outside the church I was ready to burst. There were some people standing around and I said to this guy who was standing there, glowing and having a cigarette, (I think his name was Maynard or something like that,) "I don't have a soul!"

And it came pouring out. I cried and cried. I had been pretending I was receiving, or acting like everything was okay, but I couldn't contain it anymore. Maynard just laughed and laughed, and you know, after a while, it actually dawned on me how ridiculous the whole thing was. I think that Redmond, my husband, was uncomfortable too, although what he did with it was different. He was more like, "Hey, let's go do something fun and get out of here." People were milling around in front of the church and they were just glowing, like they were in ecstasy. I thought, "Jesus God, what is this?"

That for me was a very profound moment, because I realized then what I was doing to myself, what I had always done. I realized that there was no such thing as not having a soul. It was actually Bapak saying it that snapped me into consciousness. It isn't like it changed everything for me right away. I went through a lot more years of pain behind my self-doubts, my denial of myself, my judgment, lots of years of being so uncomfortable, but it was the beginning of realizing what it was all about. It wasn't until I heard Bapak say that, that things got so uncomfortable I couldn't live with the way they were. Then, whatever was preventing me from feeling broke down, the obstacle to feeling who I really was and what I was feeling shrank away.

Your experience shows me that we are the makers of our own soul. Our soul will happen only if we are allowing it to be.

Right. The reality is that if you say you feel nothing then you feel nothing. And Bapak was not lying, it's a pretty hard truth, but I think it is necessary to hear it. It's very necessary to look at that, look at the responsibility you have to yourself, so the obstacles in your way to yourself have a chance to be broken down.

The first time you told me about not having a soul I remember laughing like that man in the hallway. It seemed so preposterous to me that anybody could believe that. How can anyone think that they don't have a soul? But I understand now that until you can regain your self-esteem sufficiently to trust that you have a soul in spite of whatever anybody says, you don't allow your soul to be there.

Did Mardiah only imagine having heard Bapak say that? It's not so important to find out. What's important is to know that it's the same with our latihan as with our life. It's our faith in our own latihan that allows us to receive its benefits. It's our trust in life that makes us aware of its gifts. As Bapak says, you have to prove to yourself what you believe. We get as much as we put into things, and it's only when we value ourselves—for our first duty is to ourselves—that we can start evolving, growing, and becoming visible in the eyes of God.

LATER YEARS IN SUBUD

IT'S EASY TO SLIP BACK, ESPECIALLY IF YOU HAVE A LOT OF ANGER

Lavinia (German-American) interviewed in Menucha (OR.)

> *Water, the irresistible current of the inner water that doesn't allow a person to be fixed in one place. The flow moves them, constantly cleansing them and pushing them on.*

I have a funny story related to me by a friend of mine. She was supposed to fix a coconut pie for Bapak and she had such a difficult time opening the coconut that she got mad and hit it hard in anger. After the cake was baked and looking beautiful she presented it to Bapak. He ate a piece of it and said, "Thank you very much, but next time, don't get mad at the coconut."

I live in Seattle now, but I came over from Germany in 1961. I got opened here. My husband and I used to go to the library a lot. We lived in Santa Monica. Once he went to the library without me and in the evening he said to me, "Look. I have a book for you." I looked at it and said, "Oh, what's Sa-u-boudd? What about it?" He didn't know anything about it but was prompted to take the book. I opened it and browsed through it. There was the address of Subud Los Angeles. "I have to find out about this," I thought. "This is the thing for me."

I have to tell you that I didn't wish to read anything about Bapak or anyone. I didn't want to know anything else about it. I just wanted to find out if the latihan worked for me. After thirty—five years I am still around . . . So it worked I guess. It must have.

I had a strong experience at my opening, even before I was opened, because in those days the applicants sat outside the latihan room once a week. Then the helpers would come and talk with them. Sitting there I started to giggle and do funny things. It was not like me. I didn't know I had been opened, but it really was something because I cried all the way to my home. I thought I must be disfigured. I looked in the mirror and saw that something was different about me. I looked different.

Something else was quite different. I had just learned to drive and driving from home into town was quite intense for me, terrifying really. But driving back home from the Subud Hall was so simple and easy. I was just gliding. So I knew that things were happening and they kept happening. I cried a lot, and I danced a lot, and whenever I looked in the mirror you couldn't see that I had cried. So I thought that it must be a different kind of crying.

When Harlan M. talked this morning I had the feeling that he was talking from a place of compassion for other people's suffering, but that he has reached a stage in life where he is no longer attached to the drama of his own suffering. Do you feel that way?

I am sorry to say that in spite of my age my suffering is not over yet. I still have a reaction to things happening, to unpleasant events. Right now I am in the process of not reacting by separating myself on the inner level. I realize that this is not an easy process. I just happened to recently see one of the tapes with the theme "Trials are a Blessing." Understanding that makes things easier. I hope it stays with me in the future.

About the future of Subud I see that in many groups in the West not much seems to be happening. I have just been in the Ukraine and seen all these new and young people. Their enthusiasm gives me a lot of confidence and hope. Subud only started in 1992 there. And their latihan! My goodness! They are practically where we are after such a short time. It's really wonderful.

I was there in September 1996. Before I went I asked the helpers to test for guidance about this trip, because going to Russia and Ukraine was a bit stressful for me. They received different things, but one of them said I should use lots of water inside and outside. It was quite surprising to me. I tried to drink a lot of water, that was for the outer water.

And here comes my friend Patricia again. When we talked about this, she told me that during her trip she was prompted to take three showers a day. Can you imagine that? To get this outer water is not an easy thing, because what they do there is turn all heaters off on the fifteenth of April, and turn them back on the fifteenth of October. So the hot water has to be heated by hand.

I remember reading somewhere that when a person drinks a lot of pure water the light encoded filaments in their body are reorganized to rejuvenate it. Water in the human body can be thought to be a gateway between the physical and spiritual bodies and to be around, or to use water enhances that function. Also the elements and balance of ocean water match the blood in the human body, so people are really like electrically charged water, made from the ocean rather than from clay or mud. Water helps us remain fluid I guess.

Anyway, if you were to sum up all your years in Subud and the essential messages you gathered what would they be?

I just attended a workshop today about "Doing and Being." There was much discussion about it and one of the ladies summed it up to the best of my understanding. She said, "To be in doing." It's not easy. Doing without thinking obsessively about how you are doing it, what you are going to do next, questioning whether it's the right time to do it, etc. My biggest stumbling block is not being with what I am doing but always thinking about what I am going to do next.

The latihan has helped me greatly with that. I definitely am a different person. I was a very angry person and there is still anger left in me. Once in a while it piles up, but basically I am not so angry anymore. My sister who knows me very well said to me when I went to visit, "You have changed so much!" She found out that I was in Subud and doing latihan when I went to Germany to the World Congress in 1985.

Later she visited me and said again, "You have changed so much. I would like to have what you have. I would like to join Subud." And it's the first thing she did when she got back home to Germany.

Bapak always said that the best way to attract people to Subud, was by our example, when people see for themselves what it has done for us.

It gave me confidence to realize that you can actually see a difference. It's so easy to slip back, especially when you have a lot of anger. You get angry again and again and again, and you almost despair. It's good to have another perspective on it, see that it is working slowly but surely.

I am so grateful to have had the latihan and its blessing. Life has been so gracious to give me this latihan. I see so much suffering in the world without it, and I feel so lucky. We have to be so grateful and careful not to forget, to do a prayer of gratefulness before we go to bed and when we first get up.

I would like to know what is your background? And I have been curious to ask, is there a secret about your great posture and perfect slim figure, about what makes you stand so straight and proud?

My father wanted a son, and since he only had girls he trained us as boys. He gave us a lot of pride. I guess he had to accept us as girls in the end. He had no choice, poor man. But I married quite late in life and my husband and I had no children. He died about ten years ago and now I travel a lot by myself.

Anyway, we were raised on a big estate in the countryside. We rode horses and sleighs and all that. My mother was an heiress and they had bought this estate in a place that was part of Poland at the time. A tutor taught us. At one point my father realized that one teacher couldn't teach us everything. He wanted us to have a good education so we moved to a small town where we could go to high school. So he sold the estate.

Interesting. My husband's mother was from Russia and had the same sort of upbringing.

Really! I was in Moscow on my way to Ukraine

What prompts you to go on those journeys?

Actually I only go to places when I am invited. In Amanecer, at the last World Congress, I met a woman from Ukraine. She is a very good interpreter and asked me to come and visit sometimes. I tested and the answer was yes. So, last May, after three years, I finally went. I always thought that I would like to go to Siberia. It may have to do with my sister's husband never coming back from there in the Second World War. Or it may be something else, but anyway, it did not work out to go to Siberia because the only Subud member we knew there had just left for Israel.

Off the tape recorder we talked about travels and ancestors and different ways of life, traveling being a time when we put ourselves in the hands of God the most sincerely and willingly, with trust, when we are not bound by habits and security patterns, by the musts and shoulds of everyday life. It's like a prihatin, a time of fasting, we become free to follow our inspiration and guidance, the movements of our inner. When we are on a trip the journey is never entirely our own. The spirit of the journey takes over and brings us to the people and the sight we would learn the most from at that time.

Lavinia talked about the fact that when we do the latihan we all become part of the same culture. It doesn't mean we lose our own, but, like the flowers that are part of wonderful beds in a perfect garden, we have our own individual identity, which is extremely precious, our cultural identity which is like the different beds, and our spiritual identity which is like the whole garden.

WOMAN AND MAN IN FRONT OF GOD

Arifah (French) interviewed in Spokane (WA.)

Translated from French

God cannot be held in any vessel without making it explode, fall apart, disintegrate. The immensity of God cannot be contained except for an instant, in passing, in the songs of small children, their games, in the disregarded language of the lowest of the lows, those seemingly abandoned by the world, in the blood of those who died for nothing, in the wounded bird freezing in winter, in anyone following the inner. God's presence can only be manifested within an open hand.

When you ask me to tell you, from my personal experience, what I consider to be the difference between woman or man in front of God, I want to say this: in front of God stands man, not woman. Bapak says that God wants to see the man in front of him. The woman must stay behind. That's why in Islam the woman walks behind the man like a shadow. She must push him while he is pulling her. She pushes him towards God. She is neither inferior nor superior, but different. They are both necessary roles. The man is the head and the woman is the heart. It has been a salutary lesson for me.

The way I understand it, everything is this world is supported, animated and maintained by its opposite. A man possess the positive qualities of power and action, but lacks the negative traits of love, affection and the emotional characteristics needed to return to the spiritual world. A woman can teach him to use his perceptive powers as a better way to God, instead of his reasoning faculties, and man has the chemical battery to draw the divine power to himself, which in turn woman receives from him.

There are many married women who complain about their husband not helping them with the children or other things at home. Bapak would say: Don't look for that kind of love in a man. The man will give you the physical pleasure of the creation of the child, then the peace and protection necessary to raise the child. He will be there in hard times, always protective. He is a guardian. At the end of life, when God asks man if he has a request, if the man has really loved his wife he will ask God to bring her along with him. God listens to the man.

I lived for years in Cilandak. My husband was very difficult to live with. He was very jealous, even of Rahayu. I spoke Indonesian and was always hanging out with the Indonesian helpers. I was mostly taking care of crisis cases. He started to prevent me from doing my helper's duty.

Our daughter was getting divorced and I received in my latihan that I should go back to France for that. I told Ibu Rahayu that I could only see darkness for me there and was afraid to go there. She answered that I shouldn't worry—that there also would be light, that it was my duty to go. Bapak also told me that I had to go. When my husband asked if he should also go Bapak answered, "She received to go, not you. You stay here."

When my husband took me to the airport however, he said to me, "It's over. A phase in our life is over. I feel that I am losing you." I answered, "You are joking! I will get everything in order and come back." But indeed, little by little we phoned each other less and less. I asked him to come to France because our daughter needed me there. But he didn't want to. Then he said to me, "This is impossible, me alone here and you there. We are going to divorce."

Before leaving for France I had an experience. It was like a vision during which Bapak received me in a palace and said, "This one will be your husband." Bapak showed me a man, but I could only see his back. I didn't want to get remarried. I had just had twenty years of a not very happy marriage experience. My affair with Subud, yes, it was grandiose, but in my married life I was unhappy. However, in Cilandak, everyone believed that it was not very important to God whether you were happy or not in your marriage. What was important to Bapak was that you'd be a good helper.

Anyway, Bapak pointed to the man and he did something to him and to me also. I thought to myself the next morning, "It must mean that my husband will change and become nice. Thank God." But later on that morning, on my way to work I received, "You are going to have another husband." I was still married but since my husband wanted to divorce, we started the paper work.

At one of the first big Subud reunions in France I met this man called Latif. I saw him first from the back and said to myself, "Oh! He resembles the man in my vision." Later he came to me and said, "The two of us will get married you know!" I thought to myself, "What cheek these French men have!" I told him I was still married, that my husband was in Cilandak, but he answered. "You will see."

After I got my divorce, it happened. All the people in the group told me, "No, it's not possible, you are not going to marry this man." But we did get married. My new husband and I went back to Cilandak to see Bapak, who blessed us. He kept us with him a few hours.

I know that usually Bapak was for sticking it out in a marriage, not divorcing. That's true but this was a different case I guess. When I went later to thank him and God, Bapak asked me, "Are you happy?" I was. I am very compatible with Latif.

My ex-husband didn't have much money and he was getting old. Latif sent money to help him. We talked a lot, the three of us. My ex-husband told Latif, "You don't have much work to do with my ex-wife. It's me who has prepared her for you." Latif answered, "Yes, I thank you." It's an example of the harmony that latihan brings.

Later my ex became very sick. My new husband started paying some bills for him, and the Cilandak brothers paid the rest of them—very expensive. One day, during Ramadan, I received God's grace and the message, "Your husband will disappear on the last day of Ramadan." In Indonesia nobody ever talks about death and you are never supposed to ask anything about it. Instead, you wait without speaking. So I just asked Latif if he wanted to go to Cilandak for the last of Ramadan. He said yes but didn't ask me why and I didn't tell him.

When we got there my first husband was in hospital, extremely sick. He had a cancer that had gone into the lungs. We paid for him to have a man come every day and take care of him. I went to visit him one morning and he was happy to see me. We talked, asked each other for forgiveness. More than anything he saw Latif and talked to him. It was very good.

While we were there he was taken in for X-rays because there had been a worsening during the night. As he was rolled away he put his arm up to wave a small good bye. We never saw him again: it was the end of Ramadan and we had tickets on the plane for the next day.

Since he was not dead when we left I believed that I had been wrong about the date of his death. I asked Ibu if I should stay because of my receiving about his death but she answered, "No, you have the tickets for tomorrow, so you just go." I took the plane at seven and he died at eight. We were in the air when my husband said, "You know, I am very cold." I answered, "Me too." Then we knew he was dead. God planned it so. Ibu Rahayu arranged for the prayers and dealt with the funeral, etc. All was perfect.

*   *   *

The following is an addendum in Arifah's own words, eight years later:

I want to add that Bapak gave in Barcelona a very important talk about sex before marriage, warning young people of the damage done to their inner by wrong behavior. He advised to have a correct sexual behavior before marriage so they can later create children with a good inner quality, instead of being the recipient of a soul of inferior quality, which will have to go through painful purification.

During the sexual encounter, the woman being the recipient, receives all the sexual impurities from the man she makes love to, especially if he has known many women on the same level as he.

It is recommended that the youth, men as well as women, take these questions very seriously and respect their bodies without adopting the New Age ways of modern society, often far from God, and looking for pleasure but not reaping happiness. The future mother must be prepared to live a healthy life so that her children do not have problems and suffer. These mothers, when they become helpers, will know how to advise younger women so that they may start their married life and motherhood on the noble human level. The children born from them will be the joy of their parents and a gift to society.

I have talked to many young people who were perturbed by the belief that sex before marriage, or any unconventional sexual relation, was damaging to the soul. They felt that it came from a Puritanism perpetuated by an older generation, belonging to a moralistic view from the past and that it didn't pertain to what people and the world were about at this time.

A youth explained that the danger was not in sex before marriage but in sex without discernment. If you have worked on yourself to gain self-respect and self-love, then to have sex with a partner who doesn't, considerably lowers your self-esteem and your level of consciousness. On the other hand, once you find the partner who does have this love and esteem of self, you do not want to leave them or find another.

"It is when sex is called sin that it becomes dirty," a young Subud woman told me. "Then the fun comes from breaking the sexual taboos."

8

RELATIONSHIPS AND MARRIAGE

"Our oldest dream: shared love, shared food and drink
and with each sip, with each bite, a certainty: I am loved.
Let us cry this oldest of dreams, let us laugh with it, shiver
and burn our fingers on it, let us dance with it and take it
on our lap this oldest of dreams: to be loved, without any
reason, with no merit, just like that."

Christiane Singer

The relationship of man and woman at this time seems to reflect the deep state of crisis in which humanity now finds itself.

We all have a longing for wholeness, the root of which is spiritual. The male-female attraction, an almost irresistible urge to unite with the opposite energy, reflects this desire to get to the end of duality and the sexual union is the closest we can get to it on the physical level.

When this unique relationship comes along, whatever was important to our sense of self becomes insignificant. The core feeling of incompleteness and fear seem to vanish as the partner becomes the single focus. For a time it looks like salvation, but then the partner falls from grace and starts showing some flaws, behaving in ways that disappoint us. We now perceive him/her as the cause of all our pain and we attack. This awakens our partner's pain and fear. He/she counter-attacks, and on and on.

This can go on for years. The ego hopes that the partner will change his/her behavior so it can conceal our own pain. If that happens the relationship might become what's called co-dependant. Addiction arises from an unconscious refusal to move through our own pain.

Feeling unloved can trigger the pain body, which in turn activates the partner's pain body, so both partners may be taken into a level of deep unconsciousness, which is like emotional violence. But at every stage we can avoid becoming unconscious by reading the signals. Hostility in the other can be a signal. There is a given formula: express your thoughts and feelings as soon as a reaction comes up, do not let a time gap of unacknowledged emotions fester and grow. Learn to express what you feel without blaming, and listen in an open, non-defensive way. Give space to the other to express him/ herself and be present without defending, accusing, attacking. In this way the relationship could become our spiritual practice.

Avoiding relationships in an attempt to avoid pain is not the answer; three or four unsuccessful relationships in three or four years are more likely to awaken us into consciousness than three or four years of contemplation in a desert.

There is a time for everything. A time of no commitment, a delightful wandering from flower to flower, diving into each pistil to taste the nectar, drunk with possibilities. But refusing to commit becomes a problem when the time for it is over and we hang on to something that is no longer alive. When freedom is understood as the abolition of all commitments and deep relationships, the so-called freedom leads to decay, cynicism and death. It's only under the power of limits that our spirit can get stimulated, inspired and rise. The true experience of life is not to run away from commitment but to dare it, for each time we truly meet with another we recreate wholeness and integrity.

From movies, novels and magazines young people often get the picture of love being a blend of physical novelty, attraction, eroticism, fixation, and the need to possess and control, all this creating an intense high. But this kind of love is often fleeting and precarious. When denied it can turn to hate and revenge. This is not love but addictive sentimentality.

A love that is unconditional requires a level of love and respect for oneself; only then is it unconditional and unchanging, not dependent on external factors to survive. That love comes from within and cannot be frustrated by the actions of another. It is a state of being that does not come from the mind and is pure of motive. When there is a problem it sees the totality of it and the solution. When this kind of love brings two partners together, it is illuminated. The lovers focus on the goodness of life and work towards inner contentment, relating to a world that is forgiving, nurturing and supportive. Their capacity for patience and compassion is augmented and their love has a positive effect on others around. They begin to experience joy not as a pleasurable turn of events but as a constant accompaniment to all their activities.

Love only aims at more love as each snowflake that falls aims at a new design, and through us it has one more chance at expression. The one we love might not remain the one we think we had seen when we first fell in love however. What's wedded together in marriage is only two beginnings, two attempts to move forward. We become two pioneers in a new land where the two of us make a third person. This third person finds its way amongst mazes to reach the wound we had covered over, the closet that couldn't be opened. To begin with we fiercely defend those strongholds, but later might realize that it's only when the secret closets are forced open that we can be released, heal and grow. The pain of it is not any worse than the one we withstand when we cover over.

There is a common fear that a deep commitment might make us lose face, but that face was only a mask and under it a truer face appears. Up till now we have only shown that one face to the world but we have many others. If we look at the word 'sincere' we see that it is made of two Latin words, sin: without, and cere:

wax. Sincere then means "without wax," indicating that there is no wax covering cracks and imperfections. Given a chance, our lover will remove the wax covering what we don't like about ourselves.

In relationships we find the mirrors that reflect the reality of our life, physical, psychological and spiritual. Bapak said that we attract the people showing us where we are at in our spiritual development. He suggested that we have a choice as to whom we attract. People that come to us are often the people we need in order to work on some unresolved issues in our lives. Every time we have a strong negative reaction to someone we have a chance to look at what's inside of us provoking the reaction, to see what part of us is threatened and why. Everything we encounter is part of our apprenticeship.

When we judge another we judge ourselves: most likely what we judge is something within ourselves we are not looking at because we despise it, something we cannot forgive ourselves for. It might be something that we are unaware of because it is so deeply buried in our subconscious, or a place where we became stuck in our emotional, psychological or spiritual development at an early age. The easiest and most common thing to do when we have a blind spot is to project it on others so we don't have to see it in ourselves. But it's our own humanity God invites us to work on, not others'!

Bapak advised us, when we feel attacked, to let it be. Learn to let it be. Put the distance of the latihan between us and the attack, between us and the reaction. For myself, whenever I am able to, I try to see in what way the attack might reveal a fault or weakness I had overlooked in my personality, in which case I can become aware of it and attempt to correct it. If, after looking sincerely, I can't find it anywhere in myself, I can let it go for it's probably not mine.

It is even more difficult to let go of praise because our ego has a tendency to bask in the acclamation of others. We may look to see if there is a base to that praise and continue to develop this quality in ourselves, if not, see it as flattery and let it go.

When there is harmony and good feelings between ourselves and others, when there is no jealousy or envy, no judgment or threat of any kind, we experience a little slice of heaven. It's like being held, along with everyone else, in the great hand of God and loved unconditionally; we experience the love parents have for a newborn child. I once had a dream that I was growing up under Bapak's direct tutelage. It was a complete feeling of being loved and protected, a total lack of fears and worries, absolute trust.

In this state of wholeness we only want what's best for the ones who share our joy of being, and we love them as we are loved, without condition. It helps to feel compassion rather than irritation for their difficulties, for the things that might make them difficult to be around. When we experience anger, this anger disarranges the world around us and creates disharmony so that we begin to attract more and more people who have anger. With the tool of the latihan and trust in God we can bring any difficult relationship to be of help in strengthening the very weakness that made us choose it. Our faults, once we become aware of them, can be the stepping-stones to our most important strengths and greatest qualities.

Leaving a relationship that is not to our liking often leads us to start another that will bring about the same problems and difficulties, the same incompatibilities, for those are things we have to work on within ourselves and we will probably be attracted to the person who will force us to do the work. It might be why Bapak advised most people who inquired to remain in their marriage, even when it was difficult.

I also understand that we choose our parents to complete some spiritual work, or to deal with what has been unresolved within us in another life. This possibility has freed me from blaming my parents for the faults I have inherited, the stuck patterns my upbringing has perpetrated. It allowed me to take responsibility for my life.

Our most important relationship, beside the one with ourselves, is the one we have with the partner we choose for our life and with whom we decide to start a family. We may pick that person for the wrong reasons, out of a troubled need and be disillusioned when he/she can't fulfill that need. Or we might have married someone we thought was a god and see that person turn into a villain under our very eyes, for passion rises out of nowhere, knocking us off our feet, exploding time, plunging the world into a delightful disorder before disappearing, leaving us empty handed.

Once we have come through the hell of failure and disillusionment we land on another shore, naked, lost, used up, empty, liberated from the armor in which dogma, morals and obligations had locked us, but terribly vulnerable. The metamorphosis awaiting us is the most violent adventure, as painfully difficult as the work of the worms extracting themselves from the chrysalides. An International Helper confided how wonderful her second marriage was and how she thanked God each day to be able to wake up next to her husband. She added that she also thanked God for her first husband—a man she couldn't remain married to because of the hell of disillusionment. It was him who had prepared her so well for this second marriage.

During our journey together we might go through countries whose tongue neither of us speak, where nothing we have learned will help us in any way. The only thing that will carry us through is fidelity, fidelity to our highest hopes, faithfulness to what we knew at the moment when we loved most. In marriage we are made to tip over the learned order and find our footing on quicksand. The one who is truly free is the one who undertakes the relationship journey, having taken a good look at the true face of love, with the highs and the lows, the victories and the defeats, without illusion. That one determines to live the adventure, whatever it might be, reading the signs along the way, listening to the beggar at the crossroads, refusing neither hardships nor bliss and ready to win, in the end, the most invaluable gift: the commitment honored without any deception.

I learned that on the physical level the man leaves energy lines inside a woman's body and that when conception takes

304 | R<small>IANTEE</small> L<small>YDIA</small> R<small>AND</small>

place those lines become merged with the make-up of the offspring. In this way the energy of the father merging with the fetus being conceived, enables him to sense that the child is his own. Many men have told me that they knew exactly when the conception had taken place. Sperm is a catalytic force of existence and every time a man releases sperm he is to some extent depleting his body. However, through the filaments he left inside her body, the woman feeds the man so that on an ephemeral level he becomes dependent on her. That is why a man returns to the same woman again and again to maintain his source of sustenance. Originally it was nature's way to ensure that a man, in addition to his immediate desire for sexual gratification, set up more permanent bonds with a woman. But too often, nowadays, men scatter their sperm all over creation and feel depleted and empty.

Sex takes, love gives. Unless there is love involved sex can be a miserable and sad experience, an unnecessary diversion on the road to God. The sexual union demands mutual responsibility because it is the deepest expression of love between two people, therefore sacred. Bapak talked quite freely and openly about the joy, freedom and playfulness of the sexual. He let us know that it was through sex that we could attain the highest level of humanity, that we came the closest to God. Through the sexual we rise above the illusion of separation and we can be one with another because there are no longer any barriers. We can learn compassion and unconditional kindness to all life including our own when we reach this place of oneness.

The biological mandate was translated into a social one when women raised girls to believe that their primary function was to find a suitable husband with whom to have children. There was a time when women became terrified to have the stigma of being a spinster. Some women believe that it was a way to trick them into conforming, and that to some extent most women are still trapped in this paradigm, even if they don't want to procreate. The belief that one is not whole if not in a relationship, and that the relationship is not complete if it doesn't bring descendants into the world, has many women in Subud (as well as men) under pressure.

Supposedly, it takes seven years of celibacy before a woman is rid of those filaments and the man of his dependency to that woman. I understand that it's very difficult to keep the commitment of celibacy because when it's just about to be accomplished the desire for a partner becomes huge. Psychic healers give advice on how to release old lovers' energy from our auric field: bless them and ask them to move out, giving thanks for the shared lessons. To keep talking about them reactivates them in our field even if they have been out of our lives for a long time.

If we truly believed that we inherit the ancestral blueprint of every person with whom we have sex, that beside our own issues we have theirs to deal with as well, we would think twice about having sex with no commitment, especially at this time when there is an acceleration of everything we take on. Sex is the most glorious gift we have been given, as humans, to discover our identity as God's creatures, but it is the love we have for a partner that prevents the shame and guilt—which our society and religions have tightly associated in our mind with the act as a tool of control—from damaging us emotionally and turning sex into perversity. We are still infused, in our culture, with the puritanical idea that sex is bad. It isn't bad per se, but without love and commitment it can be very harmful because one is kept in a low vibrational state that is degenerating rather than rejuvenating.

In latihan I once experience a total connection with all people, creatures and things. I knew all sins and all faults as though they were mine; I knew all perfections as though they were mine. I had total love and compassion for myself and others. There was no longer any separation, I was the subject and the object. It was a wondrous experience but I realized it would be impossible for me to handle the physical world in that state. Too much merging impairs our capacities.

Even in a married couple, harmony can exist without total blending. Attributing to the other, feelings and opinions of mine through over-identification can endanger the relationship. In the same way, when I over-identify with my children, I impair their development and prevent their wholeness. Harmony is to accept all our differences and not be threatened. The experience of unity does not require the other person to have the same vision as ours. It's automatic responses that are walls between people; true sensuality invites the intimate experience of all feelings, between all persons, regardless of gender.

There are, of course, many other kinds of relationships from which we can learn. Our relationship to food is a very important one since we work and create with it, take it in and savor it daily during our whole lifetime on this earth. When I cook, if I share a special understanding with the ingredients and remember to honor them, to handle them in a spirit of collaboration and intimacy, it allows those ingredients to guide me towards the combinations that will bring on the best possible taste, towards the preparation that will transform base metal into gold. This practice demands sincerity because handling food can be a spiritual practice, a form of worship. If I remember that I am working with living things and I do it in a sacred manner, it will bring out the best in myself and those who will eat the food. When we feed each other we partake in the transformation that sustains our lives creatively and we participate in the bountifulness of the world.

I don't want to be mindless when I cook and neither do I want to be unconscious about what I am putting in my mouth. When I feel the blessing each bite of food can be, I have the ability to be aware, as I taste, of the patterns the ingredients form, as they become essences in my inner. Having to depend on living things to sustain ourselves shows us our deep connection to them during our stay on this planet. Vegetables and animals, connected with earth, water, and sky are transformed by fire. As plants are the alchemists who transform the soil into food for us, so do we, when we eat in the right way, become alchemists transforming this food into energy and spirit. I once heard Bapak say something to the effect that we, humans, are the food of the angels.

He often asked the question, "Do we eat our food or does it eat us?" What did he mean by that? We are impoverished when we use food just as fuel, and if we do not eat in a spirit of collaboration food will use us, filling us with constantly frustrated desires as we stuff ourselves. But when I remember to let the spiritual reach into every aspect of my day, everything I do can become my spiritual practice. Even just eating an apple, opening my mouth and biting through the skin into the crisp flesh to overcome the initial resistance, and, as the delicious juice is released from the pulp, moistening my palate and running down my tongue, my own activated juices liberate the essence contained within the sweetness. The nature of the transformation taking place reveals itself as gratitude

Each of us are mostly who we are because others have released our juices, liberated our essence. Our life, in part, manifests as what it is because others have believed in us. When we are supported and nourished we grow and want to share the nourishment with others.

TIME WAS STOPPING AND I WAS ENTERING ANOTHER DIMENSION

Illene (U.S.A.) interviewed in Denver (CO.)

"In every love we recreate integrity and save the world from absurdity. Love knows only one aim: itself. It is reborn through you. It has one more chance through you. You are invited to love and serve, so that love and service can be of this world."

Christiane Singer

Prio, an Indonesian helper who was close to Bapak came to the Aspen group at the end of summer and talked about the purpose of marriage. As he spoke I realized I had to get married, like I wasn't going to grow until I got married. I understand this well now.

I never felt that way about marriage before. I had had plenty of boy friends in my life, not since I joined Subud though. Listening to Prio put me in a state so that I was ready to get married and I wasn't hesitant about it. And I did it.

I had already met Lawrence in Cilandak, but I had no idea that he was to be my future husband. I mean, we didn't have a romance. Our getting together is probably my most powerful Subud story.

We were invited to the same house in Cilandak on Christmas Eve because we were Christian and there were not many Christians there. He was working for a Norwegian photographer. There were maybe ten people who had spent Christmas Eve together and I had said hardly anything, no more than a sentence or two to Lawrence. We had no profound conversation or anything like that.

I went back to where I was staying. At the party I had been given a gift of an angel, but it was wrapped. When I put this object in my hand my whole body started vibrating. As I opened it up I said to myself, "What is this?" The vibration that was coming out of it was very powerful. It was a clay head, and the person who gave it to me said it was a Javanese angel. I exclaimed, "Whoa," because every time I put it in my hand I was getting these waves of vibration, then nothing when I was not touching it. Back in my room I put it in my suitcase and my whole room started vibrating. It was more than I could handle. It was actually rather scary, too powerful. So I went out to sit in the kind of verandah that they had in the bamboo houses.

I was sitting there; it was around midnight probably, when the Virgin Mary appeared in front of me. She was little, maybe about two-and-a-half-feet tall, and love was pouring out of her, so much love that I knew that the reason she was that small instead of life size was because my body could not possibly take any more love than that. I didn't have the inner capacity.

I don't know how long that lasted but while she was in front of me I heard a latihan going on. I heard singing, a really worshipful latihan. And then Mary was gone. I had no memory of how long that lasted.

Then I went over to the Subud hall to see if there were any men doing latihan but they weren't. I went to Sudarto's house. Varindra was talking to Sudarto. I didn't say anything, and I just sat there, trying to get a grip, trying to figure out what was going on. Finally I went back to my room and the room wasn't vibrating anymore, so I was able to go to sleep. It was so powerful and I had no idea what all of that meant, but of course being loved by the Virgin Mary is enough of itself, and you can draw enough significance from just that. It actually took me about ten years to start wondering if it was not connected to meeting Lawrence. Who knows?

Lawrence was staying in Indonesia so I didn't see him after that, but six months later in Colorado I went to a regional meeting. We got to the place at eleven in the morning. It was raining but then the sun came out and who should appear but Lawrence driving a VW bus. He opened the gate, and I just about fell out of the car I was so astonished. I had no idea he was in the U.S. No idea he was in the Sandia Mountains.

At one point he and I went for a walk. It was the only time we had together alone. I felt like time was stopping and I was entering some other dimension. It never occurred to me that there was any relationship between us, not at all. It had nothing to do with my heart, absolutely nothing nor with his, just this amazing experience of being together in some other reality. Then I didn't see him till September at the national meeting in Denver, and he invited me out to dinner one night.

I remember I was in this hotel in Denver. I was waiting for him in the lobby. He came walking down the stairs and I thought, "I could give myself to this man." Then I thought, "What a bizarre idea. We are just having dinner together." The funny thing is while I was having all of these experiences none of them touched my heart, none of it made my heart go thump, thump, thump. None of it made me long to be with him or think more about it.

After that Congress Mas Prio gave a talk about marriage. I still didn't get it. I think it was some sort of protection so I wouldn't let my mind or my heart get involved. Lawrence, on the other hand, was waking up. He told me later that when Mas Prio went from Aspen to Albuquerque he asked him if he ought to marry me and Mas Prio closed his eyes and said, "Yes, she is a good country girl!"

We saw each other again, three months later. We didn't phone. We didn't write. I mean nothing. In Aspen, there was a regional meeting at the Boomerang. My mother met Lawrence and he asked us out to lunch. She said "No thank you," because she knew the minute she met him that I was going to marry him and she didn't want to have anything to do with influencing me. She knew but didn't tell me.

That night we went for a walk and he tried to kiss me and I wouldn't let him. Imagine! I was twenty-four. I met him when I was twenty-three. It was like I was functioning in some different realm, out of the normal. After that he wrote me a couple of letters, and each one of his letters had a powerful impact on me. I was in Denver at the time, and I knew when I got the letters that I was going to marry him. I sat down to answer his letters and I didn't know what I was going to say to him. It was so clear to me that I was going to marry him that I had no idea what to say to him. He hadn't asked me to marry him in the letters. He didn't even say I love you.

I sat down to write this letter to him after work, I put the piece of white paper on the desk and took my pen and thought, "What am I going to say?" The sun came through the window. It hit an ice crystal and a rainbow went right across the piece of paper. "Oh no," I said.

I don't remember exactly what I said. I wrote him about a three-sentence letter and in the next letter he asked me to come and see him in Albuquerque. I got on the next plane. I just told him I was coming and got on the plane. He met me at the airport and we went to latihan that night. I had the most extraordinary latihan I ever had in my whole life, and I knew that he was my husband. There was no doubt. It was phenomenal, and for him also, but we didn't talk about it until later.

The next night I made dinner for him and after dinner he asked me to marry him. It was the first time he ever kissed me and when we kissed we were married. We both knew that it was the marriage. When he asked me to marry him I didn't say yes. I just asked when. Then he really knew he had awakened.

We got married in a week. I called my parents. My mother wasn't surprised. I told my sister over the phone. My mother said my sister turned white because she had never met him and all of a sudden I was saying that I would marry this man next week. Talk about crisis, this was the ultimate one. So in a week a Subud sister made my wedding dress.

Another made a cake and drove herself and it from Denver to Albuquerque. We had a lovely wedding in the Subud Hall. There must have been sixty people there from all over the place, it was just wonderfully planned somewhere.

The crisis I had been in earlier was indecision, right? There was no time for indecision there. It played no role in it. All happened in such a way that my mind wasn't involved. My heart wasn't involved. It happened totally on an inner level. I knew one hundred per cent this was the right man, but at times, it has been difficult.

We both had such a powerful inner connection that it pulled us through the hard times. When you have had such strong experiences, to go against them would be wrong. It was on the inner level that we got married. That is my most powerful twenty-years-in Subud experience.

THE MIRACLE OF OUR MARRIAGE

Marston (U.S.A.) interviewed in Menucha (OR.)

"Through this provoking authenticity so irritating and bothersome, the path leads to the mystery of being. A pale relationship, busy trying to avoid any conflicts, leads to emptiness."
                                        Christiane Singe.

A huge breakthrough for me was when my future wife came to Albuquerque. We met, had this whirlwind one-week romance, and became engaged. A strong inner thing happened with us, very bizarre. Within three months we were married.

She had gone to Indonesia and was very involved with Subud. She knew what it was about in a much broader way than I did in Albuquerque. Before getting married she asked for a commitment from me, "You can marry me, but you have to promise me you'll never leave Subud." To this day she can't believe that I said, "I am sorry, but I can't promise that." She ended up saying, "Well we'll get married anyway." This is just to show you the extent of her commitment to Subud. It had been like a miracle in her life and had totally transformed it.

I have, in my Subud years, witnessed this kind of miracle when someone's life is totally transformed by Subud. Some terribly difficult problem that someone has, some affliction, addiction or something is suddenly overcome by practicing the latihan. It's witnessing this amazing transformation when I first came into contact with Subud that made me decide to choose Subud as my spiritual path.

Yes, so our marriage became a Subud experience in terms of both of us doing latihan. We talk about it all the time, the miracle of our marriage and of Subud in our lives. It has been twenty-three years in Subud now, doing latihan regularly, twenty-three years together. The experience of that is just amazing. I am very grateful that I have been able to have that, grateful that I was able to find Subud when I was twenty-nine years old. I am now fifty-five. My wife Hadijah and I live in Seattle.

How did you meet your wife anyway?

I am a mime. Hadijah had nothing to do that evening and a Subud sister said to her, "Why don't you come see the performance in the park?" So she went, and her first image of me was of an eighty-year-old man in a cap and gown. I was made up to look as ancient and sick as possible.

We met after the performance and one member of the troupe, a woman, rigged it so we could be together. She invited us both for dinner and then left. It didn't work that well. We sat across the table from each other and were all embarrassed. You know how it feels. You want to leave but you don't know how without being rude. You know it's rigged and that feels stupid.

Suddenly my inner said, "This is your wife." I answered, "No it isn't, come on, get away from here." Meanwhile she was getting the same message, "This is your husband." It was a miracle because she was only going to be there two weeks. Then she was moving to Montreal. So there was this small window of opportunity for us to have this life together.

The story gets rough though, because the part of me that was saying, "Go away," really became very strong in me. So I started behaving boorishly towards her. I would totally ignore her. When I was near her, I would start to cry, so I would try to get away from her as fast as I could. My feelings were touched so deeply, and my inner was falling in love. A part of me kept saying that I didn't need this, that I had no space for this in my life. You know the feeling that comes when you have to take a risk.

Meanwhile she was going through the same thing because she had been married before and it had been a very bad relationship. Besides here I was, a mime. This was not a serious profession. When she called her brother and said she was marrying a mime, he asked, "Is it safe work? How deep in the mine does he work?"

But here we are.

YOU ARE MAKING A MISTAKE

Hamilton (U.S.A.) interviewed in Bali (Indonesia)

"The real tragedy would be not to attempt the impossible, to always remain within our limits. In a marriage we constantly show each other our limits, find each other in our most hidden places and bring each other out." Christiane Singer

I had been divorced fifteen years when I met Elfrida. I lived in New Jersey and retired from my job on August 1st. Then I went to Spokane the fourth or fifth, a few days after the World Congress had started. My first latihan was so great and special that I felt that anything after that was gravy. It was worth the long trip, just for that first latihan.

The first week was like that, very spiritual, latihans, testing in the kejiwaan workshop. At the end of the first week I met Elfrida. And then I was cut in half, two different halves that had no resemblance to each other. The first was a purely spiritual kind of thing, and the other was involving all kinds of emotions. It was a different ball game.

The first time we met we were not introduced. She was standing with somebody else and I was going somewhere else. I spoke to someone in the group in passing. The second time we met it was a brief encounter. We just spoke for a few minutes in a gift shop.

But on the first day I really spent with Stephanie, (now Elfrida) while walking together, a picture flashed through my mind of walking with my arm around her, so I said, "I feel to put my arm around you—is that okay?" She said yes. Usually, I would be too shy to say something like that to someone I had just met, especially at a Subud Congress, (*he laughs.*)

When did you realize that this was something very important for you?

Pretty soon. We had five days together and it was probably on the third day. It was enough for Elfrida to say, "Would you consider coming to Victoria for a month or so and stay at my house," for me to immediately agree. "Yes, I would consider that." When I went back home I found that what it involved was a lot of traveling.

When I retired from my job, I had said to myself that I would take maybe three months to decide what I would do. I would take things slowly, make the right decisions, and mostly relax. The moment I left Spokane I felt like a ball in the pinball machine. I had made arrangements to travel with a friend, Rafael from New Mexico, and stay with him for a few days. I went from Albuquerque to New Jersey, then went to Vermont to spend one night and drive my mother from Vermont to New Jersey so she could fly to

Florida. There was some more traveling, and after all that, I took the plane to Victoria beginning of November. I stayed there three weeks, after which I decided to pack up and move in with Elfrida for good.

It was hard to pack up, because the last house I had was a happy home and it's hard to break up a happy home. It felt like my home. Plus there was a lot of stuff, plus I wasn't sure about anything so I put a lot of stuff in the basement of a friend. I didn't know if I would come back or not. So now I have a basement full of stuff. Probably it will stay there. I never regretted my decision. I am happy. Only on the morning I was supposed to fly did I have a doubt. It was a hard job getting ready. I did it mostly by myself, working from morning till about twelve at night. The morning I was supposed to go I woke up with this dread in my guts, and this voice said, "You are making a mistake. This move is a mistake." I said, "Well I have a ticket going out tomorrow. I don't think I am going to listen to this."

I went to latihan in New York because they do latihan on Sunday. On the way out I was talking to Richmond Sheppard and told him about that voice. He asked if I had tested about it. "If you haven't tested, let's test right now." So we tested two questions: Is there any reason that Hamilton shouldn't go? Answer: No. What is the source of this feeling? Lower stuff. So that was it.

SOMETHING VERY POWERFUL WAS HAPPENING INSIDE OF ME

Elfrida (Canadian) interviewed in Bali (Indonesia)

"To enter in the service of life is a duty of honor. But who thought of telling the spouses that they leave for a journey without a return ticket, for an odyssey that will take them through dark forests, through desert steppes, that they may know weariness, the sensation of being strangers to each other and to oneself."

Christiane Singer

316 RIANTEE LYDIA RAND

I was fairly new in Subud when the World Congress in Spokane was about to happen and people started talking about it a lot. I kept saying to myself, "Oh I can't be bothered, I don't have the money, etc." But suddenly one day it became absolutely necessary that I go. I didn't know why but I had to go, so I went.

I didn't know where I would stay, if I would find a place to sleep, because everything would be full, so I was anxious. I drove there anyway, which was an experience, all by myself in my little black car.

I was there for about four or five days and attended the Selamatan, a ritual-celebration around the death of Mardiningsih Arquette. I had been in New York for the summer the year before and met some of the New York Subud people—amongst who was Richmond Sheppard. So I was at this Selamatan talking to a wonderful man called Yabo, when Richmond came along and joined us. Then this other man joined us and Richmond introduced him to Yabo, but not to me. I kind of looked at him. You know, being a single woman you are looking all the time. Just a little glance mind you, nothing insistent.

One of the good things about Subud is that you start understanding that if something is meant to happen it will happen, and that takes a lot of the desperation out of things. I still have to remind myself about that at times.

I want, in order to make some kind of parenthesis—to tell you something Hamilton told me later. He remembers thinking when he first saw me, "She is too young for that man," because he thought I was together with Yabo.

Then the next day I took some of my sculptures to the art shop and I went to see how they were placed. I saw the same man on the way, and I put on my most appropriately flirtatious act without being too blatant. I was just having fun. I didn't know if he was married with twenty children or what . . . so I asked him if he wanted to see my sculptures. He said he did so we went, and after a while I said, "I don't want to take more of your time!" He answered that he had plenty of time.

Something very powerful was happening inside of me, so I decided I better leave it at that until I knew what the status was. Eventually I went up to Richmond's room and asked sort of casually, "Richmond, you know, there is this friend of yours, Hamilton . . ." That's all I said and his answer was, "He is absolutely perfect for you." Then he added, "Call him up right now."

"Give me a break!" I protested.

The next morning I waited for Hamilton after latihan but he didn't come out, and didn't come out. Then I saw Richmond and said, "I am waiting to see Hamilton."

"Well I'll go get him," he answered. So Hamilton came out with Richmond who had told him I wanted to see him.

In my brazen way I said, "You know, I would like to know you better."

"Have you had breakfast?" he replied.

That's how we met. Then it was an intense six days of spending time with each other. One time it got pretty difficult because he came out of latihan and didn't want to speak with me. But then he thought to himself, "My God I might have sent her away."

Another time I wanted to have nothing to do with him. In my mind he was a kind of self-centered macho chauvinist pig. I swore I would never speak to him again. I was humiliated and angry. But we had made this arrangement so I felt obligated to call him up. I was not very friendly and asked him if he still wanted to go for that drive to the lake. He answered, "Sure." His voice sounded light so I went with him to Coeur d'Alene to swim on the day off from the congress.

We had this fabulous day. At one point he was sitting on the steps while I swam to the raft. When I turned and looked at him I said to myself, "Whoa, this is it! I could fall in love with this person." Something was very strong.

He was living in New Jersey. He had just retired and he was going to go to Japan. I said to him, "Would you consider coming to visit me on the way? and he answered, "Yes." Then there were three weeks of frantic phone calls and so forth. And then he came for three weeks. Before he left we were very much in love and knew we wanted to be together.

He was retired but I had a teaching job. So he went back to his home and packed up his apartment and everything. He left everything to come and live with me in Victoria in my house, which is a hard thing to do. It was pretty courageous and powerful, and he never felt panicked except the morning he was to leave, but he figured it was just normal fear.

At the time of the interview Hamilton and Elfrida were married and lived in Bali in a house they chose together. Testing had indicated that it was a good place for them, but they had various health problems, which brought them very close.

She taught in a village school for a few years and they returned to Canada.

THE NIGHT OF CONCEPTION I LEFT MY BODY

Mardiah (U.S.A.) interviewed in Los Angeles. (CA.)

"It's the intimacy of bodies and lives, shared nights and shared days that gives access to the truth of the beloved. Mixing our breaths and our juices, we, as a couple, are delivered to each other—body and soul—way beyond what we can imagine. What makes marriage so luminous is that it's the only relationship that truly puts us to work."
Christiane Singer

My friends Lariswati and Billy came to visit in Aspen. She had been in Subud for a long time and helped us a lot with understanding the latihan. She did a lot of latihans with us. She had brought this gamelan tape of Bapak playing and we used to listen to it, and then do latihan. One day we listened to the gamelan before doing latihan. Then we listened some more after. After that we went to Ferry and Don, some other friends near by, and we took a sauna, then rolled in the snow. I went home after that.

Redmond was working as a bartender and he would come home quite late. So I got myself all dressed up to spend some time with him when he came home. Later we made love in front of this funny old big stove in our living room and as we did I left my body and saw it from above with arms raised up, reaching to God. That was the conception of my third child. It was an extraordinary experience for me.

COMMUNITY IN ALL DIFFERENT FORMS BECAME A STRONG MOTIVATION IN MY LIFE

Lusana (U.S.A.) interviewed in Menucha (OR.)

Lusana, what made you decide to start a community in Montana?

I moved away from where I lived because of my divorce from my husband. I didn't want to stay in the place of hurt. I also realized that it's too hard to be part of a support system if you live miles away from each other. You can't be there for others because you have your own life to take care of, and you can't drop it just like that.

So community in all different forms became a strong motivation in my life. I knew it was the next step for me. It came, I think, with a lot of heart motivation. When you are attached to the end result, you are preparing yourself for a lot of disappointments.

Do you mean because the vision and the reality don't match?

They can't because a preconception is not real. God enters in there also, somewhere, and that is a totally different factor, moving in mysterious ways. I think that in the last four years I have had to let go of expectations and still know that the love is there. At one point I even wrote that I couldn't stop the loving, but I didn't know if I could live with the people in the community.

Then that shifted once more, that block of hurt . . . So you try to do it differently. Now we have gone to a place of separation. We are more autonomous. We don't depend on each other the way we did. We don't expect so much. None of those silent demands. It's more like accepting what the person is willing to give. I think it's going to be the next phase.

We didn't come into it with a big plan. We didn't sit down and discuss what the rules were and how we would do it. And we did come up against all kinds of different forces, particularly the material force, and the heart, which often operates from the wrong place. What it teaches us is that when we do something from the wrong place, there is nowhere for us to go with it.

We only had each other on the land, so we resolved to be guided from a different place, and change little by little. It has been very hard financially also: staying alive and making the adjustments. But I don't think I can move away from this community and the people I have committed to do it with now.

This learning process might not even be for you but for future generations.

Yes, that's right. But to me now, my whole life is today. Today are we going to go this way or that way? In the next three hours, am I going to go back home or stay in Portland? And I will know when the moment comes what I should do. So today is today and that's all there is. I just want to be in this moment, this moment when I am hanging out with you.

We talked about your cancer a year ago? How is your health now? Do you think you have the cancer under control?

For a long time I knew it was really gone, but now, because of the way I have been repressing and denying my emotional state I feel I am in danger again. Actually I didn't know until last night, but if I don't take care of myself first—and again I am coming up against my addiction to care taking—I will lose my life.

Now this opportunity that came for this young man, Rufus, to stay with us while he recovers from drugs, is going to teach me how to do it right I believe. To be moved by God as much as I possibly can, instead of me indulging in the passion of making everything right and doing it out of my own heart. It's not my will. It's God's and I just happen to be in the right place.

My biggest problem is my addiction to service. It comes from the fear of not being loved. I know that it comes from a need, and that's where the addiction lies. So I am trying to break from that, but I still don't know what my work is with other people.

Who knows how long this will last. At some point something will say, "Now you go this way." I don't hang on to things the way I used to. I don't have that passion. I realize that it is all a process, to put the forces in the right place within yourself. That's what Bapak said about working together and doing enterprises: it's to put those forces in their right place. It's the only way we can do it. If we live in isolation, we are not going to do it. It's easy to be saintly when you live in total isolation. You never come up against any of your issues, but right now the big issue in Subud is how to live with each other.

Yes, I was talking about that with Marius, one of your partners in the Montana community. He said that he sees cycles in the way things move, level after level of stuff getting worked on. Right now, we hear over and over from Subud members that their group is falling apart, that there is no Subud community anymore, that people leave to go back home right after doing latihan, always in a hurry, that there is separation between people, no more of that family feeling, etc.

But I believe, like Marius that it's because we are coming up to the next level of Subud. Many get discouraged and fall to the wayside—which always feels sad—but many others will come. It's like the way is being prepared for them. Some people have fears about what the closeness and intimacy may involve, about the issues it will bring up, and they'd rather not do it. So they leave. Subud seems to be coming to a stage, right now, when we will have to deal with all our fears and overcome our prejudices in order to get to the next step. This is being forced on us from all different sides.

Yes, you are right. And we have to come to that place of commitment to the process no matter what.

To a process, yes, but not to a result, because the result is not known. That's the problem. If we know where we are going in advance, we are not going to get there.

I feel that we are so result oriented in our Western society that it has become a sickness. It certainly is my sickness. Here I am, doing something, but I am not really with it. I already want to be finished so I can get to the next thing. Get it done. I never totally enjoy anything when I work and move that way because of the compulsive nature of my doing.

I do that too. I keep jumping to the next exciting part of my life. I think I am addicted to the idea of doing something, but the reality is nowhere near as much fun.

I am like that also. In fact, I'd just as soon be doing ideas and not living through them!

One of the ideas I have been excited about was doing an Art Center. For years I have collected things and now I am ready for it, but there is hardly time to work on it. When I do get to work on it, I am not so tense. It feels good.

I sometimes think that our attraction to ideas and the unwillingness to bring them to fruition might have to do with our impatience with incarnation, with our density and the slowness of moving through the physical world in our physical body. With ideas, you travel very fast, like in the spirit. In the flesh, however, things are rather slow.

We are dissatisfied with our limitations. We want an idea to happen. We want excitement for the heart and mind. We are so impatient.

The material world slows down ideas considerably, and we haven't totally accepted that. We are not willing to allow the time for the process of living on this earth to take place. Maybe we want to be in the spiritual realm already!

Or go back to it, fast. What I have done since I last talked to you is that I have started taking campground survival classes. That had a big impact because it took away fear, the fear of "How am I going to live if I am sick?" You go out there and use the skills you have been given on this earth. The blessing is that it renews my contact and claims my connection to the earth. It sounds stupid and trite but I didn't get it until I got it. Every time I go to the training something always happens because I am physically stretched, going past my fears and beyond my capacities. I come back totally in my strength; I do, except for my body breaking down at times.

When I was out there I had to do certain physical things. I was turned on to doing them, except that my body was not as strong as it needed to be. In other circumstances I would just have said that I couldn't do it. We limit ourselves with our thinking and what people tell us we can do or not do. Because I have been doing so much alone, it's like I don't have a community, or the strength of it backing me up. Right now we are not in support of our emotional selves.

It really hit me. I feel that there is no time to take care of myself because of the weight of carrying the financial part of the community . . . and a few other things. What I received last night is that the cancer might be coming back.

Did you get that in testing?

Oh no. Just that all of a sudden this place in yourself is not right again, so you will have to make another adjustment, find more support. I'll have to ask. "You see, I need help. You need to help me. I don't know how I am going to do this by myself so I need help." If I don't get help with Rufus I may not make it. I am not asking for money. I need emotional help so I can start having time for myself again. So we'll see how I can do that. I haven't got a clue.

Maybe you should start by stating with precision what are your needs, to yourself, to others.

That's exactly it.

FINDING THE RIGHT MAN

Resmiwati (U.S.A.) interviewed in L.A. (CA.)

"Desire is infinite and can never be satisfied. Who follows desire falls victim of it. The direct control of desires however is not a human task; the way to achieve it is to surrender to God. The latihan puts human desire under the control of God. Desires are necessary for living in this world, but left as they are they have a nature which makes

humans lose sight of themselves and of their inner, of their
true nature."

Dr. Hattori

Earlier you told me the story about how you found Subud in
Aspen, also how much the latihan meant to you. Did it remain
that way until now?

The only time this inner experience wasn't there is when I
stopped doing latihan from 1984 to 1985. I cut it out of my life.
I was just raising the kids, working hard and not having
relationships, when all of a sudden this man came along and I
said to myself, "He is the one!"

Then I had to start doing what a woman does, buy clothes, go
on trips, host social events and drink (because he drank.) He
didn't eat the way I did so I started pudging a little, thinking the
whole time that he'd come around to see the wisdom of my ways.
The latihan didn't have a place in his life. I compromised
everything I knew to be true for the sake of not rocking the boat.
I totally betrayed myself and I paid by suffering so much. So I
never will stop the latihan again, but I had to stop it once to
know, because I never thought I would ever stop.

You betrayed everything you knew to be true because you
thought he was the right one for you?

I thought my body was being made ready to be with the right
man. It was amazing to find out he was not the one, I was so sure it
was meant to be. You'll find out the reason for this, I'd tell myself.

I know the reason now. That experience threw me crashing
out of fantasy and into the real world for the first time in my life.
I was able to see how it really was instead of entertaining the
fantasy, instead of, "Somebody is going to come along and take
care of everything . . . take care of me." In this fantasy of mine I
would be the great hostess, plan trips, live a life I had never
been able to have.

But whom he had fallen in love with to start with, was this
incredibly independent renegade that I was. That was his fantasy.
When I went to live with him I said good-bye to that, to what he

THE MANY FACES OF SUBUD | 325

loved in me. There was no way we could make it. We were just destroying each other.

I crashed when I found out I was betrayed. I couldn't do the latihan. I couldn't do anything. I didn't care about anything. I was in a place where I couldn't pick myself up. It took me a good year to get out of it. It was like too much was happening already. There are times when it is not right for one to do it.

What was lifted, what was torn from me was the fantasy of a woman who was going to be taken care of forever by a man, and this woman would let herself be taken care of.

Such a fantasy seems to no longer fit our culture, the time we live in. The paradigm has changed.

What was the hardest, during that time, was that I couldn't do the latihan. What got me out of it was acknowledging that it was never going to happen again. I would not let anyone invalidate my whole experience of the latihan, of God. How could I have waited all these years while doing the latihan diligently and come to this? Why did that diligence not lead me to someone who was going to marry me so we could worship God together? To admit that I had been wrong invalidated everything I believed. So, I couldn't even say it, or think it. It was only about seven months ago that I could say, "I was wrong about Ed . . ." I couldn't even say the words before that.

How do you explain this? Do you feel that something came over you?

Something that was not God definitely came through this man. I had no strength. I believe that it was because we hadn't gotten married yet. In my being I was married one hundred per cent. As far as I was concerned, it was done the very first time we had sex, but there was no commitment on his part. He was saying all the right words, but there was no real commitment.

Anyway, when I finally went back to doing the latihan with this new way of seeing the world, I was different. I even think that what had to crash were some very mistaken superstitious beliefs, erroneous ways of thinking, even about the latihan, and God, and all of it.

Now I do the latihan in the car, in the hall, and I let it be what it is. And if someone asked I would say that I don't know anything about God, I only know that this is from God. Only God knows about God. I am supposed to know about me.

So all of it changed after that experience, and it changes everyday, everyday. If I tell you this right now, it's just for right now, and it might be different tomorrow. No point of view is available to me at all times.

I am still afraid of the relationship when I think of it. I don't know how it would be if he was standing in front of me, but I am not afraid of that fear anymore. Like, if I am afraid to talk I will go ahead and risk it; I will talk even though I don't know what I am going to say. This is making some changes in my ability to be responsible to myself in a more rational way.

Everything I did was from that irrational place: I knew from that place that I was going to be taken care of. So when I needed money I would wait till the last minute, then go to Las Vegas, smell the black jack table and win my rent. I never had this need to be stable. I always had to do so much myself. I was scrambling and frustrated and stressed out. "Where is the money going to come from?"

All that is changing now, even though I don't have a lot of certainty in my life about money, I don't care. There is no anxiety about it. That's a real gift. If someone looked at my life, they would think I was crazy. I haven't worked since October. And I am the one paying the rent!

Something significant in my growth in the latihan happened during the Subud World Congress in 1983. It was significant because I took advantage of some testing the International Helpers were doing. That correlated with one of the experiences I had in 1974 in Indonesia during the cancer purification. On my last day there, when I knew that the purification was over, this book all of a sudden appeared right in front of me. It was about four inches thick and it was opened so that about one-third of the pages were on the left, and two-thirds on the right. In the two—thirds part there was a big square cut out. In there were all those gems or stones in a box. On the other side were all those blank pages, and a pen. I will never forget what it looked like. This pen wrote: "Write your own script."

At the time I took it to mean write your own life, but that was not it. When I got to London in 1983, I tested what my true talent was because I didn't know what direction to take next. It took about three hours. The testing was amazing and it finally showed that my talent was writing. Nobody was willing to give up the testing until I experienced it. I felt it in my hands, which was interesting. I thought the writing would be in my head, but it was in my hands.

So you were doing the actual physical work of writing.

It was like Bapak used to say, "When your body goes into purification, your elbow will tell you about your elbow. Your knee will tell you about your knee . . ." I also understood that selling jewelry, which is something I already knew how to do, would support my writing. So I began selling jewelry to everybody in the entertainment industry, but I still was not writing.

I still have this fear that it is not okay for me to do something I love. With that much uncertainty about it, I never can figure out how to just sit down and say, "Do it for fifteen minutes." I have always been an all-or-nothing person. I know that the way to write is to structure your day, sit down, put your hand on the table. You have a story that needs to be told. I have had a story to tell since I have been eleven. I have to let it come through. Yes, let it come through rather than try to figure it out. That is where the hands in the testing come in, to show me how to let it come through.

GOD, WHY DIDN'T YOU TELL ME?

Osanna (Zambia) interviewed in Spokane (WA.)

"Love, when used properly, frees people; it should be like the oil that enables the machine to work smoothly and that is so when love is unselfish. When it is not used

in the right way it entraps people and often ties them to
the wrong person."

Dr. Hattori

You told me that you live in Wales now, but where are you
originally from?

I am from Zambia, Africa, and my husband is English from
Wales. We met through Subud. I was in England studying, then
working. I met an English chap, very involved in Subud, had
been for many years, and we became friends.

I only got really interested after a very long time. I thought,
"Well let me go to the Subud Hall and see what those wacky
people are like." I never was very impressed by the missionary-
looking types, which I had always thought spiritual people were
like. It was just not my scene.

So I went and it was quite extraordinary. There was a woman
there who actually didn't live in England at the time. Her name
was Alexandra, she lived in Lebanon. There were four other
women but it was she who impressed me. I looked into her eyes
and I was totally taken. I said to myself, "This woman really has
got something and I want what she has."

And really, it was because of her that I got opened in Subud.
When I left the hall I said to my friend, yes, there is something in
this Subud thing because I felt it in that woman and I want this
thing she has. It was a real strong calling. And I didn't see that
woman again but I got opened after three months and started
doing the latihan.

This was about 1986. During my opening I just had some
movements but it was more like I felt I had crossed a path. I felt
like I had been born again, although I hadn't verbalized this
until now. I continued doing the latihan and then I was coming to
the end of my stay in England. I was going to go back to Africa.
I thought, "Right, fine, but ever since I have joined Subud, things
have gone well. God has really been good to me." So I decided
that as a thank you I wanted to do the Ramadan fast in Indonesia.
I didn't really plan it, it just happened. It's just like the thought
came and I said, why not?

So I went all the way back home to Zambia. I took my luggage and everything with me because I was finished with England. When I got back, I said, "I have come back home, Mom, but I am leaving for Indonesia to go and say thank you and do my fast." So I went there and after two weeks, the same lady who drew me to Subud arrived with a friend, the man who is now my husband. This was her best friend and they came to do the fast together. I never thought about anything romantic at first. I was friendly with him, that's all. But it happened.

After Ramadan we were separated. I went back to Zambia and he went to Wales. Later I went to Wales to be with him. We probably had been with each other four months when we decided that we wanted to get married. So I took all the things that I had carted home all the way back to England. And I asked, "God why didn't you tell me? It would have saved me so much money!"

But anyway, I've got a husband and a nice one too. We live now in Wales. In the beginning it took me a while to adjust because it's such a different culture. I was very much a city person, not a rural person, and that's how it is there. The local people are farmers. But then I realized that what I needed was the country. I had been a city person and already had experienced the city. With my husband, I get the balance.

STEPHAN WANTS TO ASK ME FOR SOMETHING, THE THING IS ALREADY IN MY HAND

Rashidah, (Indonesian) interviewed in Berkerley, (CA.)

In 1971, Yanti, my friend who was a Subud member took me to Wisma Subud because she wanted me to accompany her and wait for her in the lobby while she did latihan.

In 1986, the second time I went, my friend Nurul pushed me into the hall and told me not to talk to anyone. So I did the latihan for six months without being opened.

One day Ibu Sujarwo went by and asked, "Are you a Subud member?

"No, but I do latihan."

"Were you opened?"

"No."

"Are you a candidate member?"

"What is the meaning of that?"

"Ah, I see. You have a mission in Subud."

"What kind of a mission?"

"You will know later after you are opened. Fist you have to become a candidate." She took my hand and took me to a room.

In 1987, before I became a candidate I dreamt of Bapak although I had never met him. I like to pray in the middle of the night so I was up doing my prayer and asking God to send me the right man to be my husband. I tell you, if you have difficulties in life, get up between one and three in the morning, go outside the house, pray and ask God for help. It takes one to two minutes, and your problem will be solved.

When I was in deep prayer at two in the morning I suddenly I hear a man's voice saying, "Come to Subud."

And I looked around but there was no one. "I need your help," he said.

"For what? Who are you?"

"I am Bapak Muhammad, Subuh."

"Why choose me, there are plenty of others?"

"God asked me for you."

But I like to argue, "I am not even a Subud member. I don't want this."

"If you accept this mission I'll give you a gift," Bapak said.

The first time at a candidates' meeting I got sick. I fell asleep and a Helper woke me up. I had a fever I was sick for three months. After eight weeks a helper asked if I wanted to be opened. I refused because the rule said twelve weeks. Testing showed that I could be opened but I didn't have permission from my mother.

Since I was not married, I was staying with my mother and needed to obtain her permission. The helper said it was okay without it, but I said no, I love my mother I have to get it. It was hard for me because strict Muslims have a lot of trouble accepting Subud. At the time I was sick a lot; I had seen ten doctors but none could find the source of illness. My mother said she would give her permission if her daughter could get cured of her allergies.

After the second meeting, I had a dream about this man with eyebrows meeting together into one eyebrow. He was wearing a white shirt and gave me a wedding ring. He said, "I am your husband." I argued again.

"You are too handsome and we never have been married. How come you say you are my husband? Go away." Then I woke up.

The next night the dream came again. "Please wait for me, I will come soon to pick you up. I am your husband." He put a wedding ring on my finger and I woke up.

At two o'clock I got up to ask God if this man was the right one to be my husband in this world and the life after according to my religion. "If he is," I said, "send him soon. If not take him away from me."

Four months later I was opened and he, Stephan, was in Wisma Subud. After latihan I was walking with Morris Peterson and Nurul out of the compound and into the street. Nurul asked me if I wanted to meet Stephan. My brother Mirza drove by with Prio's son and asked me if I wanted to go home with him. At the same time Stephan happened to walk by and Nurul introduced me to him. When I saw his face I was in shock. I knew he was the man in my dream.

The next week I invited Stephan to Mirza's wedding. I sent some poems to Stephan because I was a writer and poet. After that Stephan took me home from latihan six times, but my mother didn't like me to come home with a white man. Then one day she asked me to ask him to marry me, which is strange because usually it is men who ask. Before I had met Stephan my mother slammed the door on any man who wanted to marry me because she didn't trust them. Now I was wondering why my mother so readily accepted Stephan. To find a clue I took Stephan to my father's grave. Whenever I took a suitor to that grave before that, I wouldn't hear from him again. But this time it was okay.

Then I introduced Stephan to my brother Muhammad Akbar, but beforehand I asked him, "Do you want to be my friend forever?"

"Yes."

"Do you want to be engaged?"

"Yes."

So Stephan talked to my brother in the living room. My brother said, "You are old enough. If you love you don't need to ask my permission to marry my sister."

So Stephan told we could get married. "But I only asked to be engaged," I answered.

So Stephan wrote a letter to Bapak asking for his blessing and giving our birth dates. Bapak was sick but gave Ibu Rahayu a letter for us saying that we had to get married in two days, or else wait for three years according to our birth dates, for a propitious day.

Ibu gave the letter to Stephan and five minutes later Ibu Mastuti came to me and said, "Bapak blessed your wedding, but in two days you have to get married." We rushed to the government officials. According to the rule, Indonesian people who want to get married have to register at least three months before, but in this situation, the permission was granted.

So we got married on June 18, 1987. Four days later Bapak died. Often when Stephan wants to ask me for something, the thing is already in my hand, even before he asks and vice versa. So I went to Bapak Sudarto to ask what was happening, "I feel Stephan in the night even when he is not there." His answer was, "You and Stephan were husband and wife long before you were born. Because you mission was not finished God sent you back to the world. You have to continue to help poor people." Stephan works with Public Health.

A Subud member who liked Stephan asked him, "Why did you choose her?"

He said, "I am looking for a wife who can be with me in poor areas, a woman who loves to help people and who has a degree in health (I have a degree in pharmacy.) I want her to be able to stay in the bush in isolated areas." (Since I was a kid my father trained me to be in poor areas and not complain.)

In 1990 I came back from a pilgrimage in Mecca and asked Ibu to give me a Subud name. Ibu asked God for seven days and received that my name is Rashidah (Wise in God's path.)

YOUNG MEN TALK ABOUT RELATIONSHIPS

I MARRIED SOMEONE WITH WHOM I CAN HAVE A GOOD LIFE

Matthew (U.S.A.) interviewed in Menucha (OR.)

"Conjugal love is something we build, the work of patience and forbearance, through perseverance and slow growth. Often we fell the tree of a relationship believing it is dead. Had we waited a little longer we would witness the miracle of spring and sprouting leaves."

Christiane Singer

It was really before my opening that I received the biggest changes in my life. I had had a lot of depressions, in my teenage years especially. My parents were going through a divorce and that was one of the bad things at that time. So when I was sixteen I observed the Ramadan fast for the first time and I had one of the most profound receivings in my life. It snapped me right out of my depression, and after that I was no longer depressed. I really felt that it was the Qa'dar that they talk about. I associated it with Subud, like something that would happen to someone when they got opened. My life completely changed after that. So I hold Ramadan very dear and think that great things are possible through that fast.

My parents are both in Subud. During my opening everybody stood in a circle around me and the helper said, "Begin." I stood there for a minute or two and my hands began to shake and vibrate, then my arms. I don't remember in detail what happened but mostly I was sort of rolling around on the floor—not really rolling but somewhere between crawling and rolling, also jumping a lot I guess. But it didn't make a big impact on me. Some receivings can be quite astounding. But mine was just active. I don't remember vocalizing or using my voice.

However, I got really sick shortly after my opening. I was sick for two weeks, but whether that might have been a result of my opening or not I don't know. I guess an outsider looking in would say that things changed though, like, I dropped out of school and stuff.

I have always hated school except for a few years. Since I was a child I had always worked for my Dad, so after I dropped out of school I just continued doing that. I also traveled around on the West Coast, went to different Subud congresses and stuff. I didn't have the vaguest idea about my direction.

I got married in September 1992. I was twenty. Today I was just talking to my friend Rosabel about soul mates and marriage. For me, a soul mate is not really the issue. I would say that before I was married I was incapable of choosing a wife. I didn't have the tools or the understanding or whatever it takes, which I guess is the case for a lot of people. I feel sorry for those who have to choose a wife; if you get a directive from God it's one thing, but the way it happened for me is that I got lucky. I married someone with whom I can have a good life. We are compatible.

We met through Subud and lost touch for a couple of years. Then we met again. Just the typical sort of attraction. We had both planned not to have sex until we got married but then it didn't work out that way. I got her pregnant. So, we got married shortly after. We have two kids now.

You seem content. If you had the choice would you get married so soon?

Well, if I had the capacity of doing it differently maybe yes, I would do it differently, but considering my capacity, I would say that things worked out surprisingly well and they get better all the time. I feel blessed.

Some married people I questioned told me that you create your own soul mate, that it happens little by little as you work things out in your relationship. What do you think of that?

The idea of soul mate as the one person that might be ideal for somebody is theoretical for me, outside of my experience. If my wife is the one person in the world who might be best for me then I say I got very lucky. Left to my own devices I would have picked a worse situation, so I have a better situation than might have been expected.

You say lucky, but could you also call it inner guidance? Your mind might not have known, but your inner knew?

It's a combination of luck and guidance. The luck part could be grace from God. I don't think that I know a case in which two people have gotten married and have then arrived, living happily ever after. I know some good marriages which took years to get to that place.

What kind of advice would you give to young unmarried people who are waiting to find their mate?

Well, the best advice, most people have already been given I am sure. It's to be celibate, abstain from sex. It's easy to say of course, but I would say that sex just obscures things and makes them more difficult. It's not going to be of value in the long run. Other than that, I would advise to get to know the family of the person you consider because this is a great indicator. It's removed from the passion and you can trust it because you are impassive in it.

What I would say is the most important thing, is to continue doing the latihan. I would be afraid to stop the latihan. It's the only thing I have going for me that is substantial. There have been periods where I felt I had forgotten how to receive or something. These periods can last a while, but usually, I receive enough to make me think, "Oh yeah, it's still going on."

I have seen concern about the membership shrinking, but it seems to me that when someone gets opened in Subud and receives so that their life is turned around, then it's like an explosion of growth. It only needs to happen to one person to fill my heart with levity. To watch this go on seems much more meaningful than counting how many people we have or don't have. When the latihan starts to affect someone's life, it's enough to make you feel so good, and it becomes obvious that my own life is touched by it. That makes me feel secure and the concern disappears.

I think we have the responsibility to let people know about it. We shouldn't let it stay cloistered up, but beyond that there is no reason to get worried. I can't do anything right now, but I don't keep it secret from people I know. Those of us who want to and have ideas about the growth of Subud can do more.

WE ARE SOUL MATES ALTHOUGH WE DON'T HAVE A RELATIONSHIP BEYOND A FRIENDSHIP

Jaece (U.S.A.) interviewed in Menucha (OR.)

"If 'the other,' constantly shows me my limits, always finds the flaws in my armor, throws me off my haughtiness, pushes me out of my retreats, it's because he knows me in the biblical sense. He has access to the being that is my foundation."

Christiane Singer

I heard about Subud from a high school friend in Ottawa whose parents were in Subud. She didn't tell me exactly what it was but years later I ended up living at her mother's and I learned more.

There has been a lot of talk this year at Menucha about soul mates and relationships. Do you have any insights about that? You are very young, in your early twenties. How do you feel about meeting a person you would spend your life with? Do you believe that there is one person who is right for you?

I think that there is more than one person for each of us a lot of the time. If a relationship happens to be for ten months, then let it be for ten months. If it happens to be years then it will be years, but I don't think that there is just one relationship that is right. I don't really have a preconceived idea. It's nice to believe that . . . nice to think that there is this person you never have hooked up with yet, that is there for you, somewhere, but . . .

There is a danger in believing that maybe.

Yes, you start creating standards. You don't even know yet and you expect. You just have to meet who you meet and take them for who they are.

There was a discussion with people who had been married for a long time. They were saying that you create your soul mate as you go along, from within the relationship.

That's an interesting idea.

Someone, during that discussion, said that if you stay with it and in it, with compassion for yourself and for your mate, you begin to shape the relationship like a piece of clay. It becomes like a third person you are both working on. And this third person is made from the two of you and you have to begin considering its needs.

It's interesting because I feel this way about the good friends I have, especially the friend in high school who introduced me to Subud. We are definitely soul mates, although we don't have a relationship beyond a friendship, but it's a very close one, family like. It's interesting the definition of what a soul mate can be to different people and what that means. I definitely would say that I've found soul mates, but it's a very different thing from what is meant when one thinks of marriage

I guess there are different kinds of soul mates.

I like it better that way.

I FELT SOMETHING VERY STRONG, BUT SHE WAS TOO YOUNG

Rusdi (Colombia) interviewed in Mendocino (CA.)

"Obstinate, stubborn, equipped with a seeking mind undeterred from its purpose, marriage is nothing else but the quest, through another one, of one's own truth. It's the experience of a true relationship, a live one, one that doesn't avoid."

Christiane Singer

I am married. My wife is second generation Subud like me. We have three daughters: nine, seven and three. We met when I was working for a Subud project in Colombia and we were trying to raise funds. I went to a meeting in Colombia and I saw her among the public. I felt something very strong about her but she was too young, and I was in the University. I always said that I didn't have time for any relationship before finishing school. So we just met here and there and talked. But I kept having dreams about her, many dreams, really strong and getting stronger. So I said to myself "Well, there may be something there." So I tested and I felt, "Yes, she is right for you."

Then I thought, "This is crazy, how can I tell her?" But I had to call her. When I did, we started to talk and it was as though we had known each other for many, many years. Actually, right there on the telephone we started talking about getting married. And we did it two months after that. I had met her only four times before we got married.

We waited till the Ramadan month and observed the Ramadan fast before doing the wedding to see if this was a true soul connection or not. It passed the test and we got married right after Ramadan. This was twelve years ago and I am very happy.

I know how lucky I am, and I am so thankful that everything is coming to me, that I don't have a choice in it, that I trust and am not harassed by questioning, that I have no choice but to follow my inner guidance.

WE ARE SO SCRAMBLED, ATTACKED FROM ALL SIDES BY OPEN SEXUAITY

Harlan G. USA. interviewed in Mendocino (CA.)

I have been opened five years. In the last six months I have felt lots of changes in myself. When I was in college the latihan was put on hold, there was not much of a chance to open myself up to spirituality, but I have always been interested in it. I majored in comparative religions. I was on a spiritual search, wanted to study it. I did a research paper on Subud for my class in New Age religions.

When the time came I was ready to be opened and I had a very powerful opening. A lot of what Bapak talks about I can't relate to though. I can't really see that way, although sometimes, after talking to older Subud people or to my parents, I may come to understand it . . . most of the time a year or two later.

I feel that most Subud rules are crap. The lid needs to be taken off, especially since Subud is such an individual thing and you are supposed to follow your own receiving. At the end of the road your receiving might fit with the rules, but you can't force it.

I also feel that no sex before marriage is an individual choice. Not everyone can be that strong. Our culture, the way we were raised, where we live, all of that comes into play. And to make it a rule introduces the notion of guilt, so we are back into narrow Christianity. Although it may be right not to have sex before marriage, I feel that inside myself, but it isn't very realistic to expect that in this culture. We are so scrambled, attacked from all sides by open sexuality, by offers of sexuality; it takes a strong inner guidance not to fall for it.

I believe that the success of a good marriage comes from remaining independent; you can come together but remain your own individual, so I don't believe in the woman following rules of behavior towards her husband. As for the rule of not mixing I can understand it. If you get involved with very mind oriented stuff, you can become confused and sidetracked. For me the major obstacle to receiving the latihan strongly is my mind, the internal monologue. Now the guidance is beginning to override my mind and my intuition is picking up.

Recently I strongly received about this: I received that you should be able to put all that stuff aside because it just strengthens your mind. Of course it is very individual and depends on where you are on your spiritual path. Some people may be able to pick it up and not be so influenced by it. So it's not correct to make it a rule. Those kinds of receivings happen very strongly for me now.

About my life work, I feel that if I just keep on with what I am doing, a special thing will be shown to me and what I am supposed to do in life will become clear.

Harlan now has a thriving computer business; he is happily married and has three children.

9

WORK IN THE WORLD & IN SUBUD

OUR WORLDLY MISSION

Finding and doing the right work has been a concept very important to people in Subud. Countless hours have been spent in Subud groups and at congresses, testing about talent and the right work, not only for young people starting their career but also for older members still unsure that the work they were doing enabled their souls to develop and grow: some still looking for the work more fitted to their inner, others wanting to find out if they needed to leave a career they knew was a hindrance to their inner development and in what direction to go next.

When we understand that the thoughts and pictures in our mind all bring about outcomes in physical life, it becomes of utmost importance to feel right about our place of work where we spend most of our days.

At one point I was introduced to the idea of talent being different from right work. It can be understood as meaning that one might have a special talent for something—art, music, literature or science for instance—but that it is not necessarily the work that would enable one to fulfill one's financial needs in this world. This talent then could be used as a creative outlet, something to be pursued during one's free time that might lead to the teachings needed for one's growth and inner knowledge. It could also mean that talent is a more general concept; for example one person might have a talent with people and work successfully in public relations, or make a good therapist, or salesperson, etc. Another might have talent for communication, for organization, for business.

It's only when we become aware of our talent that we can start exploring the different professions available in which it can be of use. In fact, the advice often is to do what we like best and do it the best we can, for when we are not in resistance, God places us where we can be of utmost service. It is when we are an open channel for the holy spirit in our job, our home, social environment and all spheres of influence in ways that are right for us as individuals, that we come in accord with our mission.

There seems to be a tacit belief that once people are in Subud, their secret talent would one day be unveiled and that the right work would be shown to them as a kind of revelation. Everything would open up, fall into place and become easy because the right work for each person is decreed by God. At times, trying to find the right work might stem from the desire to be famous, to be acclaimed, and many people lose sight of themselves in this way. Dr. Hattori received that to seek fame or fortune makes one blind, that it is a hindrance to living a true life and meaningless in the eyes of God. It captures one but gives one no real power.

There is a fallacy in our culture that only the gifted ones are favored by the gods, that they are chosen to be the recipients of divine inspiration. Therefore their life, from the time their talent is discovered, is charmed. Their gift becomes the unique focus of their life, often to the exclusion of everything else. There is no longer any indecision because this talent is an obsession that leads them into a glorious career (and/or a miserable life,) but certainly into posterity. They are the ones blessed with a real mission on this earth whereas we, ordinary humans, are given to grovel in pale and empty lives.

We feel this way because most of us deny ourselves the right to our own creativity. We put our creative projects at the bottom of the list, forgetting that those are as necessary to our spirit as food to our body, that creating is a form of worship that reveals who we are to ourselves, healing our wounds and plunging us into our deeper knowing. In the process of creating, our energy merges with the Source, transforming our experiences, dreams and imagination into new forms that can be a gift of inspiration to others. We are altered in the course of bringing about this metamorphosis, just as we are altered by the creations of others. We can be active and enjoy manifesting forms as long as we are not totally identified with them, for if we are there is no longer room for God to come in. Those forms are not our life, only our situation.

What people are really seeking when they test for their true talent is where their own genius resides, for genius is within all of us, but it's only when we can recognize it in ourselves that we see it in others. True genius is a witnessing that bypasses the individual self. In a universe where everything is connected, no one is excluded from being a true witness. What is universal is available to everyone. The process of testing, formulating a question and waiting to receive in the quietness of heart and mind, stems from this belief. Then the answer appears in a flash. A question could not be asked if there was not already the potentiality of the answer, but at times the difficulty is to translate what is received into a form others can understand. It's often when we come to an impasse using reason that we need to test as we do it in the Subud latihan, because only a leap in consciousness can bring us forward. Posing the question activates our higher consciousness; the source of the answer comes from the divine as we leave the perspective of our habitual level. In accepting the answer we continue to receive clarifications over the next weeks.

Genius is not just talent; it values life, recognizes divine work in all its expressions and allows God to work through it. Dr. Hattori received that it is difficult for God to give guidance to those who are obsessive about their work. Most people live according to instruction from the outside, but to live a true life is to receive instructions from God and live accordingly. He says that we live as true human beings when we understand our God-given mission, which, he adds, is to guide people we come in contact with to their own mission.

To fulfill the spiritual purpose of life is to learn to give and receive divine love. How much love in service we are able to give is the measure of our wealth. But the compulsion to do and the tendency to derive our sense of self by identifying with external factors such as achievement, is an inevitable illusion when we are identified with mind. This makes it difficult to accept the low cycles, which are necessary for new growth to happen. Growth is considered positive but if it goes on forever it becomes monstrous and destructive. For new growth to happen, dissolution is necessary.

It's our mission that we must discover, and it might only be indirectly connected with our work. At the beginning of my years in Subud I received that my talents were many and my right work was whatever I was doing at the time when I applied myself to it. I would use a talent until it was time to explore another. There is nothing sadder than hanging on to something when its time has passed, so I would have to rely on myself to know when. Thanks a lot I thought, what am I going to do with that?

I realized later that work and career are not an end in and of themselves, as we tend to believe. They are tools for personal progress, a measure of ourselves in the physical as well as the spiritual world. All of our creations, projects, products, healings and manifestations come from a divine source inside ourselves. The way a healer put it, is that through our work with people we are guided to create thought forms that fire their own receivings and ignite the human codes of consciousness; this process evolves as we evolve.

Our work is a playground in which we learn the rules of this world, our tasks and responsibilities, how to make the right alliances and choices. It is a way to find the right frequency for us to operate in and maybe to discover our true mission. The work we do is not crucial either to us, to the world, or to God.

The right work for us can change once we have learned everything we need to from one career. In fact right work is any work that empowers us and doesn't harm anyone. We have been made to believe in our own disempowerment through the media and our educational system. We often feel insignificant and with no power to change things, even in ourselves, so we accept any job that will make us a living because we don't believe we can do anything else, or deserve anything else. When we let go of discouragement however, life becomes exciting and obstacles stimulate us. There is an opportunity in all things we create, in any job we take on. All we need is to trust ourselves and design our reality according to what we want to accomplish. The right work is the one that, as well as providing for our physical subsistence, helps us grow and experience ourselves as powerful beings. The purpose of testing about work is to show us what it is we want, to dare intend it, and to believe we deserve it. Sensing our own power we gain self-confidence and are not so easily intimidated.

I have observed that when people, in their job, take rigid positions, they create opposition and division, dissipating their energy. But when they are not driven to prove anything they have a more accurate appraisal of problems. As the need to control other people's behavior disappears, they also become more difficult to control, but colleagues and superiors find them easy to get along with and advancement is rapid. Through our job we find out what works and what doesn't for us. It leads to more understanding of ourselves through problem solving and conquered difficulties. We are told to avoid fierce competition however, because it kills the learning, and when the moneymaking proposition looms too big, it overshadows everything else.

A member working in a Subud function suggested that collaboration is an agent of change rather than a tool of change, because the process acts on the participants, changing them irrevocably. He believed that embracing life in all its manifestations and having the willingness to live the adventure

346 | RIANTEE LYDIA RAND

fully brought success in his endeavors, that learning to bounce back from adversity makes one more helpful to others.

As people become aware that they are the source of their own experience, they accept responsibility and gain the capacity to live harmoniously with the lower forces. The source of their happiness is no longer "out there" but "in here," they do not feel victimized and engage with life on its own terms, aiming at resolution. Nothing exists that the creator doesn't want, Bapak told us; God allowed all things on this earth because of all the different lessons that can be learned. But humans in general have a resistance to growing and finding new data. For that reason they turn away from the knowledge they possess within.

In our work in Subud as helpers, or in other functions, we can go through our personality difficulties with more ease and detachment than in our own family. The place of work is a place where all our abilities are exercised and we are shown capacities we didn't think we had for the job we were chosen to do; a space where we have a chance to touch others, lend them our eyes and see through theirs. When we are centered in it we don't pick up others' energy, we just share energy. Learning to push through our limitations it makes it possible for others to also do so. It's like an athletic record, which is accepted as humanly impossible to break, but once broken by one athlete it is followed by others.

Work is not an end but a tool. With that in mind we can stay light about it so that God may work through us. Our mission is the promise we made to God and to this earth at birth. We can try to remember this promise and be willing to change our direction when our work no longer fulfills it, even when this seems to threaten our security. What we hang on to as security is often misery. Once it's taken away and we accept this, we can put our trust in God. It is then that we start to blossom, aligning our goals with the highest power, dedicated to the highest degree of mastery.

According to Ibu Rahayu, "Once your soul can be penetrated and develop to a certain point, it will give rise to true human culture. It can manifest in the mind and then that person will become very intelligent and understand all kinds of things from within their own self. It can extend to every human organ, which is why human culture takes many forms. It can manifest through the voice, through sport and so on. All this comes from this inner power, which if a person is not able to use it, lies idle."

To follow the training of the latihan is our most important work, for it will reveal the latent powers present in every one of us. My most recent understanding about right work is that it was formulated within our true name, given as our mission, when we were ready to be incarnated on this earth. That is why it is important to have our true name. For instance, if I was given the mission, "Riantee," when I leave this earth I must go to the next as Riantee—as complete a Riantee as possible—in order to be recognized. This understanding came from listening to Ibu's words.

Aaron, (USA) interviewed in Spokane, (WA)

"We must not think obsessively or act compulsively when we are doing a project. Eventually life will be led in a better direction if we don't think too much"
Dr Hattori

In my case the decision was between fine art and construction work. They are two very different worlds and I embraced the construction for the first time in my life. I stopped telling myself that I was doing it until something else happened. I never believed that construction could be wonderful and lead to some happiness; I thought it was "just a job." I embraced who I was in it. I became healthier physically. I worked out more. I was much happier with who I was, what my achievements were.

Consequently the work has been going very well. Originally I did some testing about my talent and true work and frankly I couldn't figure out what I received.

So anyway, I did some testing with helpers. Some received that to stop construction was like shedding a very thick skin, and emerging. Those were someone's words. For years after hearing that I tried to shed that skin and emerge, but it never was in my nature to do that, to try that hard.

I agree with you that talent and true work could be two different things, but I have trouble doing both at the same time, and frankly, I have not had a strong pull to do artwork. My father is very much of an artist; he feels the art fully as a way of life. He has been very influential in my life, especially in the early stages. I did want to follow in his footsteps but my own art is different. I do think that there is a very nice thread of ancestral talent I enjoy, but I am not sure that now is the time to exploit it.

It may be later, but now is the time to really work and be in the world, develop my skills. I see myself living in the city, making money, buying a house and having enough to support a family. I see myself as a provider, as having people that depend on me. I want to be able to be depended on, being able to be dependable. As an artist it's not obvious. It takes a lot of courage to be an artist today, to be an artist with a family is an act of absolute faith and I feel that one has to feel that pull very strongly in order to do it.

I haven't felt that pull, but I have a sense that having a vocation is a noble thing. To tell you the truth, construction cannot be what I want to do forever, what I want to achieve, it's not the ultimate thing. It's something that I need to do, and I am hoping that I can achieve more artwork incorporated with it.

I remember something you told me. You once received that whatever you were doing at the time was your true work, writing or painting, housework or craft, that whatever it was, you had to do the best you could because *that* was your true work. And that's exactly what I have been doing. What you said summed it up and has been the best lesson because it will enable me to move forward with a sense of accomplishment. This has been a good year, many things were accomplished and I met many interesting people through pushing in that direction. In a sense the crisis has brought about some very positive changes in my life.

Since then Aaron had accomplished all of the goals from the above: making money, buying a house, remodeling it as a work of art, starting a family, being a provider etc.

FOR WORK I AM USUALLY DOING WHAT'S IN FRONT OF ME

Elias (Brazil) interviewed in Mendocino (CA.)

"We must live our life with a neutral attitude in order to let guidance come in."

Dr. Hattori

My name is Elias and I live in Brazil, close to Sao Paulo, south east of the country. In my case I probably don't have many stories because I am third generation in Subud and life seems to flow. The way my grandparents got into Subud is that they were searching for something but didn't know what it was. My grandma told me that at one point she said, "Stop everything, stop the search," because she had the feeling that something was coming.

Not long after, a friend talked to them about Subud and they didn't hesitate to get opened. One or two years later my parents were opened also. So I was born into it. Easy to find, easy to follow, and easy to know that this is my way, easy not to have doubts. Of course, it is still a long road. We all need to go through different things and we all have our own processes, but I never had any doubts that this is my way.

For work, I have been doing different things at different times. I am usually doing what's in front of me. At this moment we are starting an enterprise. A family enterprise with Subud members, six partners.

We are all in Subud and we use the latihan in our work, but there is always an enormous amount to learn when working together. Even though we were already very close and all in Subud, there was a beautiful process of learning, finding the role for each one of us so we could accommodate each nature, finding the best each could give to the enterprise. It has been a successful process and each one knows what to do to support the others. It was also compatible with my work in Subud when I was an International Helper, and any other Subud job I take on.

WHEN I WAS INVOLVED IN THAT WORK, IT WAS LIKE A WINDOW OF CLARITY

Rusdi (Colombia) interviewed in Mendocino, (CA.)

"In general, we are overly absorbed by our occupation. We can gain a great life force in this life from our occupation, but when we are too absorbed in work without a feeling of fulfillment we lead an empty life."

Dr. Hattori

My name is Rusdi and I am from Colombia. Coming to Subud for me was rather easy because my father was opened in Subud when I was eleven years old. He was a searcher, looking for something in his life. One day he had a dream about a particular person, a friend of his he hadn't met in the last ten years but who, in the past, had something to do with his search.

The next day he met this friend by chance in the street and the man said to him, "Look, I found something that might be of interest to you. Let's find out more about it." So they went to the Subud Hall and talked to what they thought was the priest. In fact it was a helper. Subud was very strange at that time in Colombia. The helpers decided to show the members that they could, using the Subud form of testing, fight in a latihan state. When the helpers finished boxing in front of the applicants my father and his friend left.

A week after that my father decided that he would like to go and see what happened next with these helper guys. He was more interested in the social aspect than anything else. So he had a meeting with the helpers and from that moment he felt that things were starting to change for him.

He had been a wealthy man but his business started to collapse, not such a good change. However, he realized that there was something very powerful behind this change and he wanted to find out what it was. So he got opened in Subud three months after that first encounter.

Meanwhile things had totally collapsed for him in the material world. Between the time he got in contact with Subud to the time he was opened he had nothing left. He had lost everything in three months. For us, as kids, what I remember is that our life changed drastically, of course, but also that our direction towards God became stronger. The business had taken all my father's attention, but three or four months after his opening he started to do Ramadan. It was immediately very powerful for him. So he was sure that the latihan was for him, that it was the thing he had been looking for. The rest of the family just followed. We trusted his receiving.

I can tell you my experience. I know it was the same for my brother who was eleven. I just accepted that it had to be like this. I started to fast even when I was a kid. The people around us thought that my family was completely crazy, to make their kids do that. For me, it was just about waiting for the time to get opened. My father wrote to Bapak and asked him to change our names. He wrote to Bapak about where we should study, and we followed Bapak's guidance. There was never any doubt about Subud. My mother was opened at the same time as my father.

My opening was not especially strong. I didn't feel anything very different but just did the latihan. I was opened at eighteen and I am thirty-five now. I have been in Subud for all this time, very diligently.

I was asked to test to become International Helper after being a deputy chair of the World Subud Association. It was not in my plan to do that because I didn't want to live on the North American continent, I wanted to return to Kalimantan where I had been living. But thirty men were tested for the position and none were right so I was asked to help. "Let's ask for God's help," was the helpers' answer to my protests. Then I remembered what I had told my mother the day before. She had been an International Helper and was tested again for another term. The answer was that she should continue doing that work. She was distressed when she came back to the hotel room because she was hoping to be finished with the job. I comforted her saying, "Look, if things are like this you have to surrender to God's will and you'll be given whatever strength you need for the job." I had no more objections. I tested and the answer was yes.

Earlier I was a civil engineer working in construction. Now I have become involved in this family business, which fits my schedule as an International Helper.

I do feel the latihan moving through me when I work. The strongest experience was during the building of the International Center at Amanecer. When I was involved in that work, it was like a window of clarity. I never had the feeling that I was doing anything but things were getting done. I remember the workers saying they didn't understand why it was feeling so special; the way things were getting done, the way I was giving instructions to them. We were discovering problems in the construction during latihan time. The contractor was surprised that at six o'clock in the morning I would arrive and tell him where the problems were. He would ask: "How did you figure that out during the night?"

THE POWER OF SUBUD AT WORK

N'Kanga (Zaire) interviewed in Spokane (WA.)

"There are two kinds of wisdom. The wisdom of knowledge, which you collect from different other sources and the wisdom of truth which is the direct ability to discriminate between right and wrong and leads to the enlightened wisdom."

Dr. Hattori

I am from I had a little sister who was very sick and I brought her to the hospital. The doctor was hesitant to do anything about it. But when I spoke to a colleague he told me about a brother he knew who could help me if I wanted. I went to see this brother and explained the situation of my little sister. He said to me, "I can help you, but it's not really me who helps. It is God. We are going to do a prayer while your sister is in the hospital for this very difficult operation."

As soon as we finished with the prayer, the brother said to me, "Okay, you can go to the doctor now and tell him that he can do the operation. There will be no problems at all." I left him and went to the hospital. When I saw the doctor, he said, "It was a very difficult decision whether to operate on your little sister or not, but at a certain time I felt that I could do it. I couldn't contact you so I went ahead." When I asked at what time he took that decision, it was the time of the prayer.

Afterwards the doctor said that the operation had been successful and that there was no more problem. He asked me why I had asked about the time of the operation. Had I done anything to make this possible? I told him I had gone to see someone in whom I confided and who prayed with me for my sister at such a time. He confirmed that it was exactly when he had felt confident enough to operate.

I went to thank the brother who had prayed with me and he told me that he was a Protestant minister. Outside of that, he also was a member of Subud. I told him I was a Catholic, but that I would follow whatever they were doing in Subud. So I started going, and in the third month he asked me if I was ready to get opened. I answered, "Yes," and that is how I became a Subud member.

Since I have started doing the latihan I understand the Bible much better. I am much more accepting, and I take everybody as my brothers and sisters, without any distinction of religion, race or tribe. I thank Subud because I am really understanding the Bible and the universality of religion now. There are even brothers who are not Catholic, who are not members of Subud, and they come to ask me about the Bible, even though I myself very rarely read it. I feel it inside. I perceive the significance. I explain it to them. Even my wife says to me, "Isn't there something you keep hidden in your pocket, you in Subud, to succeed in having mastery over the Bible? You even understand stories that are from other religions."

I have nothing with me. All I do is remain calm, and ask God to work through me. We, in Subud, only create a bridge between God and ourselves. It is our work. And now, the people who didn't want to enter any other spiritual movement beside their religion think to themselves, "Well, there is no evil there. We can come to Subud." And the membership grows. It is the way it happens in my country and through me.

My opening was rather quiet. While doing the latihan I found myself in a place with lots of people I didn't know and I had to speak to them because I was known throughout the world. I thought to myself, "But what does this mean, and how can I be known in the whole world? How can this happen?" I was totally amazed and at the end I asked the helpers. They told me that it was too early to say, but that with time I would probably find out. "And maybe even we, ourselves, will understand what you have been experiencing today," they added.

With time I was able to assume the vice presidency of the Susila Budhi Dharma Association, and two years later I was asked to take the presidency of the Association. So in 1991 I was invited to represent the Association in Spain. I said, "But I never took an airplane, how is it going to be? I don't know how I will do it." A brother answered, "Go there anyway. Here is what you must do." And we prepared something together.

So I went. I went to Belgium and Spain, presented myself and all went well. I spoke in the name of all the members of Subud and Somalia. Then I went home, did the reports for Subud and Susila, framed the Subud enterprises and social projects and something started to be born in me. I wanted to become independent instead of continuing to work for an enterprise, but I didn't know how.

Later in 1993, I was representing our country at the World Congress at Amanecer in Colombia, and I talked in the name of the fraternity. In 1994 I went to represent the country at the African Gathering in Johannesburg and it was there that the president of Subud USA told me, "N'kanga, I think you can do something for yourself that will allow you to develop even more."

"I don't know where to start," I answered.

He believed that I could do something as a computer programmer. I started with a friend who had computers. We worked together and I felt that if I could become independent by having my own computers it would allow me to work without problems, and little by little I would be known for what I do. Thanks to Subud, everyone accepts me: Muslims, Christians, Catholics or Protestants, Jews, they all come to me without any distinction, when I speak it is as though religions don't exist, only Subud.

My wife is not in Subud. I have been married since 1983. The first time I was to go to the States my visa was refused. My wife said, "You must try again." It was the 19th of June. We tried again on the 17th of July. It didn't work either. My wife said, "But why is it not working? Pray to your God and I will also pray for you." I said I would try again on the 24th of July and she decided to come with me. "You must be able to go, otherwise it would not be good. You have helpers in your group, why didn't they do a special latihan for you? There should be one planned."

On the morning of the 24th my wife and I and our child went to the group. I said, "Madame is insistent that there should be a special latihan for the success of this enterprise." They answered, "How come? She is not even a member. How can she talk about the latihan?" But they decided to do it anyway. So we went in to do a latihan and the National Helper asked, "Is Madame going to stay here?" I answered that she insisted that she should be right next to us.

After that we went to the Embassy with the National Helper. My wife stayed outside to find her calm and I went in for the interview. They immediately told me that they had verified if I really worked for the company I said I worked for. They found that it was true, that I was indeed a programmer for the pharmaceutical and perfume industry. They wanted to know if I was really married. "Yes I am married. My wife is in the car pregnant with a baby."

"Good. Can we see her?"

We went out and they saw her all big with the baby. They apologized and asked her how come she had accompanied me since she was not asking for a visa. "I felt that my presence was necessary because I could not understand why you kept refusing the visa. This is the third time." They told her not to worry, that I would get the visa this time.

So you see my wife is quite accepting of Subud. She is Christian of the Kubaniste denomination. At first, she believed that Subud was a religion and that I would ask her to give up hers. But I explained that not at all, that I was Catholic and never asked her to come to Catholicism, that I believe that each could stay in their own religion, but that Subud is the very essence of religion. So now she understands. That is why she insisted that I go to represent our country at the congress.

When we got back home my wife said that she understood why she had felt to come with me so strongly. "Now I know that it must be God who guided me." I have to thank God that Subud came to the world.

We received the Council of the Minister of Justice and we had to tell him what Subud was. After we had explained he asked, "But why don't you publicize it more?" When I told him that in Subud, we don't work that way he answered, "So you keep something that delicious for yourselves while everyone needs it?" I answered, "Our publicity is through our attitude."

"But," he added, "you could build something big that everyone could see and then they would come to it." I told him we would ask the Association at the world level, that if they accepted we would do it. I wrote them soon after. Today I can tell you that the financing for the construction of the International Center for Subud Africa at Kinshasa has been accepted.

The Center has since been built.

I WAS SURE THAT GOD HAD THE WRONG PERSON

Laura (U.S.A.) interviewed in Santa Cruz, (CA.)

"People should inform themselves of what they can get the most life fulfillment from, for it is the means by which humankind can make the world a better place."

Dr. Hattori

As I look back at my experience in the latihan and watch myself during that time I can see how I was growing in strength and capacity to receive for myself. It seems like I really had to start at ground level. It was not like I was one of those great souls who just got opened and immediately understood everything. I was really a slow plodder, learning gradually. The most profound experience I had was immediately after I left Aspen and moved to California.

At that time I was very involved in birthing and there was a large group of women in Carmel Valley who were all having babies. We all attended each other's birth. I think I probably went to ten births and at the time I thought that my life work was to be a midwife. So I went to see Bapak. I was ready, when he asked the question, "How do your hands move when you do your work," to palpate bellies or start catching babies. Instead I started painting. It blew my mind because I had never painted. I was sure that God had gotten the wrong person. This is for the woman next to me. This isn't for me. It was so completely and entirely unexpected it had to be real. In a lot of ways this revelation has been instrumental in shaping my life, my marriage and the birth of my child.

Did you start painting immediately?

No, because I couldn't totally believe the testing, and again, for me, it was something that unraveled as I went along, slowly. I started to do enamel work and did it for years. I saw myself as an artisan more than as an artist. It unfolded from there.

Eventually you went back to school to get a degree and now you are a very good artist making your living at it. You are very steady in your direction, even if you say you are slow.

That is true. When I find something that's fulfilling, I don't give up.

NOW I ACCEPT THEM AS THINGS PEOPLE IMPOSE ON THEMSELVES

Manuella (English-Hungarian) interviewed in Mendocino (CA.)

> *"Through the latihan we first receive a force in our inner not of our own doing. Eventually and gradually this force transforms people and leads them in the direction intended for them."*
>
> Dr. Hattori

One of the beliefs I grew up with was that you had to find your true talent and pursue it. So I remember that my father asked me when I was twelve if I wanted to know what my true talent was because we could ask Bapak. I said yes, I would like to do that. He said okay, but you must promise one thing, and that is that you will follow this, because otherwise you must not ask.

At twelve I believed that Bapak knew everything, so of course I promised to follow what he said. Up until that point I had been convinced that I would be an artist. I remember saying that to my father. But Bapak said I should be an economist, and true to my word I fulfilled that. I changed my whole focus in high school, then in college, and geared towards economy. Every summer vacation, every school vacation I got jobs in the field of economic development. When I graduated I worked for the U.N. and the World Bank as an economist.

Did you like it?

No, I worked for one year after finishing school and then I quit. I have not worked in that field since and I don't feel any regrets. Already in college, I sensed that it wasn't for me, but it became like a game almost. I could be very good at it. It probably was because I was convinced that it was my talent. Bapak had said that I would be a very good economist and become an adviser to government. And I was.

My first job in Indonesia was to advise different local governments on how to prioritize their different development projects. I was good at it, but I think my life would have been very different if I hadn't asked Bapak when I was twelve. I was good at sciences and probably would have been more attracted to the medical, but my father also influenced me.

Anyway I think that this thing about one's career, one's lifework, one's true talent was part of the Subud dogma. It does not allow for the idea that we are many things and we bring who we are to every situation we are in.

Often, when Bapak was giving personal advice, many people made his advice into beliefs that started to act as superstitions. It kept people from totally experiencing and accepting what they had to work with.

I once received that my talent was whatever I was doing when I was doing it in the right way and without compulsion. I had a tendency to be obsessive about projects, and if I had received what my life work was, I might have been totally absorbed by it.

I used to get so angry at those things I believed Subud imposed on people! But now I accept them as things people impose on themselves. Even if people choose the way of judgment and righteousness, as long as it does not hurt or impair somebody else, it remains their stuff to work on. They may have to go a longer way, that's all, but it might be that the longer way is their way.

I think the focus should be on the practice of the latihan and people should not read anything for a long time, take it solely on personal experience . . . unless we can produce more liberating literature.

NOT CONSCIOUS EFFORT,
I WAS JUST FEELING IT AND DOING IT

Heidi (English-Jamaican) interviewed in Amanecer, (Colombia)

"The life force works best when there is no intention, nor emotion, nor knowledge. The person feels that there is something beginning to happen in their inner self. The changes spread through the whole body, reaching every part. Eventually the body is enveloped by the force."

Dr. Hattori

Before doing the work with Solihin and later, after getting opened I read a lot. I heard a lot about Bapak. People were making him into a god, but to me he was just a man. All that blah blah was getting to me, so I stopped reading any Subud stuff. But I needed more of an explanation about things and the helpers were very patient. I had so many questions. I read on the fasting and understood the truth of it. My complicated questions were answered and to me it was an indication of truth. Some of it I can't believe, but perhaps it's like a collage of different things.

It was during Ramadan that it came to me: to keep my intentions in line as much as I was able to at that time. Lack of food and liquids was a hard thing for me to do without being totally controlled, so I knew that I had to clear my intentions in order to become more spiritual and less material. In the years past it was too much to take on. It was so hard just to deal with things materially.

Every time I ate outside a meal I knew unequivocally that it was wrong, I couldn't have amnesia about it. I started to refrain because in the end it was not worth the aggravation. I stayed within the fast, but again that strictness in myself was about my will, strengthening my will. Again I got face to face with what was feeding that will. But last year I was really able to surrender.

I find that it doesn't have as much to do with the stringency of the outer fast as an observation of ourselves leading to a stronger inner fast.

That's right. Between doing the latihan and the yearly fast I have changed a lot. First I changed my line of work from being an undercover agent to being a therapist. Then my idea of what sexuality was started changing. I wouldn't call myself promiscuous, but I did enjoy sex with a collection of dudes, and it became so connected to my self-image.

After my opening I was in bed with the man I was going out with at the time. I knew that something was going to change because I was dissatisfied. I thought, "He never did this. He never did that." Anyway, we were in bed and I couldn't touch him. The actual contact of him was disgusting me. It was very difficult because how can you explain that to someone. For me that was the end of the relationship. In a way I wished that I had had the language skills at the time, because I don't know how it affected him. I suddenly understood what I had been reading about the sexual. Before that, the way I read that stuff was: yeah, okay, good for you! I would never have taken it on. It really sent me into a terrible space.

My sister was not into talking about things like that. The friends I had were quite happy to talk about any aspect of religion but that's all, and the House (Scotland Yard) was only talking about work and sports. It was really difficult. I was feeling it for months, carrying it around, in the evening even more so. It really hit my feelings and I was floored by it. I felt ashamed, debased.

Then I felt movement in the latihan. I wouldn't move before, I think, because my head got into it. It was very difficult. I suddenly had a feeling that a certain kind of energy was penetrating me. It hit me at such a deep tissue level. Since the thing happened with my boyfriend I have not had a period. The inside of me has become solidified, like a cyst. Around the egg those threads form like a cocoon, and the lining is not clearing. So the problem is that any tissue that increases in the body can then become ground for cancerous cells.

Solihin is working with me here at Amanecer. I found that I had been very much in my animal stuff and that allowed me to utilize people. When the more spiritual side of things started to emerge, I could say that it was a healing. I realized it, but I didn't know what to do with all of it. I needed to feel it, so it took me a long time. I did my fast, which I thoroughly enjoyed. I didn't have to work for money for a while and I enjoyed that because it was not any kind of conscious effort. It was just feeling it and doing it.

I was supposed to work out what my criteria was for the work that was right for me. So I listed five main purposes: what I thought was important for me as a person. A large part of that was about respecting my own life and needing work that wasn't going to be in conflict with that. I was going around and around the subject. I needed something traditional and flexible.

I ended up with massage, acupuncture, hypnotherapy and something else. I listed the study criteria and I was really lucky because the course that I chose should have taken two and half years, but I did the academic part very quickly. I can't stand fooling around, so I majored in a year. I still got to go and do the practice. And here I am.

BECOMING A MINISTER

MY HEAD WENT THROUGH THE CEILING AND MY ARMS THROUGH THE WALL

Rohanna L. (Canada) interviewed at Menucha (OR.)

"Jesus Christ represents the female principle among the prophets. That is why Jesus is always referred to as the son of Mary, 'the meek and gentle' Jesus. Muhammad represents the male principle. The word Muhammad means Man. In perfect Man both those principles are balanced."
Bapak as reported by Varindra

Rohanna, could you please tell me how and when did you come to Subud?
I came to Subud when I was twenty-six in 1969. I was doing

an intentional search for a spiritual path in my early twenties and I met the man that I married. He was a student of Gurdjieff and I was very attracted to Gurdjieff's teachings when I first met Marcus. I had read all the books and also John Bennett's book, which had that last chapter about Subud. It really touched me but I didn't think that it was accessible as a practice. I thought that something that far out must be on the other side of the world.

Marcus said, "No, there is a Subud group here in Vancouver." "Why don't we look into it?" We went and met some men and I didn't feel the connection. I let it rest for a while, but felt like we were not getting anywhere with reading books and talking. It was pretty limiting. I decided to look more into Subud.

Our friend Latifah was a member. Just when we were about to go to Vancouver and find out about it, two Subud couples moved to where we lived on Vancouver Island. They were helpers so we were able to become candidates. The timing was just perfect; before that time there wouldn't have been anybody close by for us to do latihan with.

Right away I felt that it was something for me. As soon as I met the people, there was something about them, something about their energy. When I looked into their eyes there was something different which made me think that what these people had was what I wanted, even though I knew that they had personal problems and they weren't saints. They were real people.

I believe I was opened before the opening. They had us sit outside in the early days. We were doing a small picture frame business in this community where I grew up, had gone away from, and then had come back to. I had my first child when we moved there. When we started doing latihan we did it in the back of a picture frame shop, with janitors cleaning around in the hallways.

I remember there were only two women doing latihan at first, and one of them was a helper. I was sitting in the other room as I had been invited to. I had been doing so for two months, when I had this experience of something in me expanding. It was like my head went through the ceiling and my arms through the walls.

It scared me. I never had quite experienced anything like that. I had always been a pretty pragmatic person, coming from a fairly non-religious family. The generation before had been very religious, but my father was a political activist and fairly cynical about spiritual phenomena. So it was only something I had read a little about. I was not too opened to this happening to me.

It really got my attention though. I hadn't expected anything like that. The opening itself was joyful, I remember singing. One of the women had been singing a melody and that stuck with me. Soon I was moving into my own sounds. Right from the beginning I was making sounds and moving, which to me meant that the latihan was a pretty neat thing. Because it had quite a strong effect on me I kept up with it quite regularly. I was not one of the people who had to wait there for six months before having an experience.

There hasn't been any time in my life when I was not doing the latihan. During my first two years of ministry, I was in a very rural location where nobody knew I was doing the latihan. Because of the isolation I wasn't as diligent, but I spent a lot of time just sitting quietly when I felt off center. I would just sit and receive. But sometimes it was hard when I was doing the latihan alone. I would sit for half an hour and nothing would happen, sometimes I'd fall asleep. It took a long time before the latihan came.

When I am with other people it's there right away. When it did come though, I would have a great latihan, but often I didn't have the patience to wait, would get bored and go do something else.

How did you come to ministry work?

I started when we did talent testing, but even before that I was feeling as though what I was doing as an artist wasn't satisfying me. It wasn't as much fun anymore because I'd reach a state where I was getting known, I was exhibiting and selling my work, and I felt that people expected me to continue doing the same kinds of images. I just didn't seem to have any extra time to be experimenting and growing as an artist. I had to earn a living from it, I had a few commissions and ongoing exhibits, but probably there were other things in me that needed to grow and demanded attention.

So I received that I should know more about the holy books. I had images of myself serving communion to people, mostly Christian images, which was the religion of my ancestors. I hadn't been very involved in the church until the recent years and this mostly because I wanted my children to go to Sunday school. Then I started going to church pretty regularly, taking the children to Bible study groups. But I never had a thought about becoming a minister.

When this came to me, I was pretty surprised and I ignored it for quite a while until one night, when we started doing testing about other people's work. I asked myself, "Should I be focusing on that also? What does God want me to do?" So one evening I did some testing about it with a woman along with another helper. This was in Vancouver and I was still living in Salt Spring Island, so I ended up staying overnight.

I was about to go to sleep, but during that time between waking and sleeping—which is a time when I have had a few other phenomenal experiences—I heard a voice inside of me that said, "Rohanna, you are supposed to be a Christian minister." So I said, "I don't want to be a Christian minister, thank you," and I just turned down the volume. I didn't even tell anybody about that right away, I thought I had just imagined it but I hadn't. It was a real experience. I still don't really know where it came from, maybe it was a trickster, a joker . . . I think it really came from a part of me that needed to grow and maybe it's a difficult way, but it was a way to grow in the direction I needed to.

I had to explore the whole thing, it looked impossible. I went to my minister at the time, this really nice guy. He crossed his arms and sat back in his chair saying, "Well you are already a minister. You don't have to go back to school. You have three kids and a husband and a job. How are you going to do that?" So he tried to come up with ways to do it without going through the process that he had gone through, because he knew how hard it was, let alone the time, all those books and papers and stuff . . . But it seemed that I was meant to go through that.

I was teaching at a college part time in a suburb of Vancouver, and while teaching I started to look in the career files. I went to talk to the career counselor and told her I was considering looking into ministry. She gave me all the information she could and I started exploring.

Are you pretty satisfied now being a minister?

Being a minister? I think it was more fun in the doing, like a lot of things . . . I am not that much of a scholar. I may have that potential but I am too right brain to be a scholar. I could write books and teach, but it's important for me to come from the heart. Not that I always do, but that's a goal that I have, at least to integrate the heart and the mind. I don't consider myself a scholar, but hopefully I am a reasonably well-educated person that can connect the heart, mind, spirit and body, becoming more whole.

I think that the latihan is always with me. I feel it when I am writing, speaking, doing my art. Of course there are times when I get heavy and out of touch and I am not so aware of it, but it's at the center of everything. Everything else could go, but the latihan will remain. The church is a big part of my life, but the latihan is more important because it is the content. The church is a structure, and sad to say, I have never felt anything in Christianity that came close to what I have in latihan.

I have been doing Christian meditation, been around beautiful liturgies. I've felt the spirit quite powerfully during Communion particularly, and sometimes when I am baptizing a child. Then I really feel this power from God. Baptism and Communion are the two sacraments of my Protestant Church when I feel God the most strongly; also sometimes in large group gatherings, when there is a lot of beautiful music and prayers. Then it comes close to the latihan, but it's a different energy, different quality, not anywhere near as intense as in a large group latihan like here at Menucha. That's the best it gets for me.

Have you had any part in the Subud organization at any time?

No, I am not drawn to that. Five years after I was opened I became a helper. I was not a helper for many years before I became a Regional Helper for four years, then a National Helper for another four years. When I went into ministry I stopped being an active helper because I didn't have time. It was hard to do both. I regretted not being a helper, but a lot of my job in ministry feels like helper's work. I go to the hall to do latihan and the last thing I want to do is to talk to people about Subud or go to a meeting. My energy rebels totally. I just want to do my latihan, have a cup of tea and go home. It may sound irresponsible but I have to look out for myself, too.

Do people in your church know you are in Subud and are they interested?

Some of them know about it and they think it's fine for me to do that, but it doesn't draw them. I recently heard that a woman who was part of my congregation in another community, a woman I became friends with just got opened. So it can happen. There was also an elderly lady in one of my congregations who got opened. I suggested it to her as something that might help because she felt very far from God. I gave her literature to read and she decided to get opened. But she didn't feel that she received very much and didn't stay. She was in her seventies and not very open to new experiences, and the church had always been her way. Those are the only two examples.

I get a sense of who people are before I tell them anything about Subud. If they hear negatively from someone else about it, they never come to tell me. Some of my colleagues told me directly that they were a little skeptical about the things I was into. They said it very politely. I suspect that they think I am way out there. They don't come out and say that because I am very confident in what I do and they like what I do, but I can see from the way they interact with me that I am a bit of a threat to them.

They probably have some label for me, maybe a bit flaky. It's like the Subud people who always are worried about mixing. They probably think that I am mixing, too, because I do other things like going to native ceremonies, because of my interest in world religions and my talking about it pretty freely. Anyway, my colleagues have no good reason to try to get me fired because our church takes the stand of being inclusive of all people and all paths to God. Christianity is not supposed to be the only one. Subud takes the stand of being inclusive of all religions also, so I think I am okay.

Rohanna was made an International Helper at the Bali World Congress)

10

PROPHETS, VISIONS & INSPIRATION

"If the whole power and reality of God were to enter into man, the earth itself would disappear, for his Power is incomparably greater than anything he has created."

Bapak

It was late, another warm evening by the bank of the river, lights dancing on the water, Leonard sitting at a table finishing some business with a man from Zaire. I had crossed paths with him before, in the jungle in Colombia, in France somewhere, maybe even in London, here and there, I had heard that he had stories to tell. And he was willing to sit and tell them in spite of the late hour. When I transcribed our conversation later, I felt compelled to seek information about the different prophets of the monotheist religions. As I did, it dawned on me that each had a different experience of God because their personality influenced their conception of the divine. It was suggested in one of the books I read that on Mt. Sinai, each of the Israelites who had been standing at the foot of the mountain experienced God in a different way.

Throughout history the gods have been a reflection of humans at a certain period, then as needs changed, a messenger of God would come and add a new vision to the old one. At the very beginning there was the universal mother, mostly pregnant but remaining a virgin at the same time, the mistress of the heavens. She was worshipped as the goddess of fertility and good crops. Sometimes a god would appear who was vengeful, angry and jealous. This god of righteousness, justifying cruelty and punishment, allowed followers to disclaim any responsibility for their own negativity. When new territories became necessary and coveted, an ageing and tenebrous god took over, and humans started to fight. When times were chaotic it was a punishing father who was worshipped. In monotheist religions prophets shaped the image of God, each a little differently according to the times and circumstances, bringing new messages, which represented what was required for humans to move forward.

The one God that remained true for all of humanity however was the spirit of love, the life force or Holy Spirit that filled everything and made it alive. Prophets seemed naturally to remain in contact with that Holy Spirit and with the original awareness most humans lose at birth. I heard Bapak explain that prophets are complete human beings and that there is no separation between their soul and the power of God. I believe that by doing the latihan diligently we come close to that state, for as we allow the life force to penetrate us we are part of God. It corresponds to a preparation within our whole body. Bapak made sure we understood that the latihan did not come from him, but from God.

Although the prescribed way to God varied over the ages, most prophets seemed to agree that one had to put mind and heart aside in order to find it. Abraham was said to have laid aside all ideas about God and "espoused a faith that was unmixed and pure of any concept," that for Moses "the true vision and knowledge of what humans sought consisted precisely in not seeing." From the Koran we learn that God told Muhammad to listen to the "incoherent meaning" carefully, not to rush to find words or put a particular conceptual significance upon it until the true meaning revealed itself in its own good time. Muhammad was opened to receive "the terrifying otherness of God" no matter how painful the revelation; as a result, his words, preserved in the Koran, are said to have a beauty that reaches through hatred and prejudice to the kernel of receptivity. Early philosophers like Philo stated, "We know our God by his operations, but we do not undertake to approach his essence." Plato as well as Philo saw the soul as in exile, trapped in the physical world of matter and in order to ascend to God, its true home, it had to leave passion, the senses, and even language behind, because those bound humans to the imperfect world.

As a result of their greater faith prophets would often have a vision in which their frail and mortal life would be metamorphosed by the power of God. It was like an annunciation that broke down their cautious self and commanded them to change their life, after which their house was no longer livable in the way it had been According to the Bible, prophets foretold the day when God would pour out his spirit upon mankind, and everyone would have visions and dreams. This is sometimes interpreted as meaning that anyone who has a total belief in God could be a prophet, for the divine inspiration fills those who are opened to it. Old sages viewed human beings as God made manifest. Ancient writings suggest similar wisdom, "The kingdom of God is within you, and whosoever knows himself shall find it; you shall know yourself that you are in God and God is in you."

Ibu Rahayu tells us that the power we have been introduced to in Subud might be just a drop that God puts into us, but it can develop, grow and become one with the great power that envelops everything. The prophets spoke the words of God, this because whatever they did was moved by God's power. She also says that when we sing in latihan, it is actually our breath being released—something very deep. And we might begin to feel as if we are no longer standing on the earth, as if we are floating above the floor. That means that we are no longer under the action of the lower forces, and when we are able to think with a mind that is already clean, we will be able to understand things and know things that we don't know *a priori*. We all have moments when we are graced with great insights, but the difficulty is to sustain such inspiration, not letting doubts undermine it. To be in the vicinity of those who keep an unshakable faith is an inspiration with strong influence.

Bapak told us that at this time, humanity no longer needed intermediaries between themselves and God: all the teachings that humankind needed had already been given by the founders of the great religions. What was needed was to understand and follow better their message. At a previous stage of human development however, prophets, spiritual leaders and teachers were needed, maybe because people believed they were too unworthy to receive God's revelation for themselves. The common belief was that man was basically bad because of his humanness, unable to manifest godliness. He needed salvation. Prophets, on the other hand, only followed that voice from within which spoke so loudly others could hear it also, often experiencing the divine tapping their buried aspirations. This offered such consolation to ordinary humans with all their questions, such a balm on the wounds a lifetime was not long enough to heal.

Prophets were said to be born of virgin mothers, or mothers who drank milk that fell from the sky. Their personality traits were expunged as a consequence of a mystical experience or revelation and they were liberated from the consequences of the past, freed from cultural concepts and worldly standards, from the time and space paradigm. They no longer apprehended from within the confines of language; they were conscious without the interference of words, moved solely by the life force.

As fascination with the outer world entices us from infancy's inner awareness, we lose touch with our inner self. Our being slowly develops, rocked with ancestral lullabies, immersed in conditional love, trained in traditional professions and crafts. We inherit the ancestral flaws along with its qualities and the family's material possessions, and forget to remain true to our inner self. Past the tumultuous rebellion of the early twenties, sons often appropriate everything back from their fathers, even the lines on their faces. After that, all they do is get old. Plants and animals have no difficulty living up to their own nature but men and women find it hard to be fully human. Not prophets though; for they have the great freedom of no choice, their faith being such that they can't deviate from their inner guidance.

In other cultures prophets may be referred to as self-actualized beings who are said to have attained God-consciousness and are granted visions of ineffable peace. Dr. Hawkins describes the experience of enlightenment as that which is witnessed and that which is witnessing taking on the same identity. Enlightened beings do not feel separated from others and they put themselves at the service of those who are willing to seek the true freedom of the spirit. When they reach nirvana they know with certainty that earthly life is but a tiny drop in a wide ocean and with this knowledge they are as big as the universe. Since they no longer identify with the physical body, its faring is of non-concern to them, they no longer have any fear. They have a sense of complete oneness, because there is no localization of consciousness so their existence transcends all time and individuality.

This is the level of non-duality; in that state, everything is reported to move in slow motion, suspended in time and space, radiant and alive, continuously evolving in a choreographed dance. There is an infinite silence in the mind, everything is connected to everything else by a presence of infinite grace and power.

Unfortunately listeners often distort the universal statements of the prophets. There is much misinterpretation by followers vested with authority. There also is a hazard to the teachings when prophets and enlightened beings are venerated like idols. People want to talk to those envoys of God, touch them, caress their feet, kiss their hands, be in their circle, happy just to brush their sleeve: everybody wanting a piece of them. They become like a book that has to be read in order for people to obtain knowledge but instead, they start worshipping the book itself.

Not unlike Jesus who repeatedly denied being the Messiah, Bapak kept the worship of his followers from being diverted from God, reiterating that he was not a teacher, not a prophet, not a spiritual master or visionary, that he didn't have any special powers. He spoke to us because most humans beg for guidance even if they seldom follow it. They thirst for a master to show them the way, for someone to translate the words of God for them— convinced as they are that they are not worthy. He explained that he gave talks because we asked him to, but that at this time we no longer needed a teaching because the latihan made it possible for us to have a direct connection to God. We shouldn't believe anything he said until we experienced it for ourselves, in our inner, as our own truth. His background was the sacred Muslim tradition, which emphasizes God's immanence in the believer, the divine presence being incarnate in the devotee. Because of the divine nature of the Koran each Muslim is provided with the means of direct contact with God, with no need for mediators, and is therefore responsible before God for his or her own fate.

In fact the Koran is very empathic about human responsibility: God does not change humans' condition unless they change their inner selves. Bapak also stressed the continuity of the religious experience of mankind, he said that each new prophet confirmed and continued the insights of his predecessors. It seemed that in order to acquire a complete inner understanding, we would have to integrate each one of the world religions. In Judaism as well as in Islam there is no formulation of a special doctrine about God. Instead God is felt as an almost tangible presence. Each believer experiences the divine according to his or her own nature. It is as though God adapts himself to each person, in accordance with his or her comprehension. The futility of using one's mind to try to understand God is stressed in many religions, God being too big a concept for the human mind. Even praising God too frequently is sometimes discouraged for words are bound to be defective. The whole point of the idea of God is to encourage a sense of the mystery and wonder of life, daily.

Bapak didn't perform miracles, did not heal the sick but remained as ordinary as could be. According to some he even succumbed to temptation and although that thought disturbed me, it also freed me from the trap of idolizing the man. I now believe that the story, whether it had any reality or not, came out for just that purpose. Subud is the miracle of the ordinary. If we had to wait for a spectacular miracle to honor the Almighty in our heart, there would have to be a miracle a day and a Messiah for each generation. Maybe there are, but we have eyes that do not see. It's only during times of inspiration that we become aware that everybody we meet, every book we read, every conversation we have is not random. Faith is the one daily miracle carrying the sacred in everything we do. The definition of a miracle is that it comes exactly when it is needed. To me, that is the latihan in my life.

We are responsible for keeping our inspiration going, doing the best we can in all circumstances of our life. The latihan also helps me find that inspiration. I looked for the definition of inspiration and found that it was the action by which we bring air into our lungs; but it's also something that gives birth to a thought or a feeling in someone's spirit, something that suggests a divinity. Inspiration is the state of the soul when it is under the influence of supernatural powers. We are all inspired at one time or another, we are all capable of being filled with divine inspiration—for every human has the potential to be a messenger of God, but part of our socialization is the notion of sin. I believe that what is called sin is the compost that allows the seed to grow. Bapak tells us that by sin he means something that leaves a trace within our being, that whenever we speak badly about someone or something—it needn't be a human being, it could be anything, an object, a material thing—it means that we have committed a sin because whatever we are speaking about was created by Almighty God. We stop the process of creation when we label things.

"To make a table we have to kill a tree, we have to kill animals and plants for food, all things whose existence are decreed by God. No matter what man does in this world he cannot avoid committing sins." (Bapak, 1977.) So a person without sin would not be of this earth. "The one who claims to be spiritual and clean is the one who is dirty. It is the one who no longer claims to be clean who is really clean, because there is no longer any dirt within him that wants to claim." (Bapak 1982.)

Christianity describes a material world that is satanic and fated to destruction, whereas the spirit is good and destined to eternity. However Jesus repeatedly said he was a sinner. The good and the bad are in both levels, what we accomplish in the physical is food for the spiritual and vice versa. It is a constant exchange, the spiritual being the metaphor for the physical and the physical a reflection of the spiritual. I am reminded of Varindra's words that "Everything is about something else," and those of Jesus, "Nothing is everything."

To quote Bapak again: "It is not as people say: that the satanic force is the 'enemy' of God. How can the devils become the enemies of God, and how can God seek for an enemy? If God has enemies, antagonists, of course there would be a balance: and thus, if the satanic force were regarded as an enemy it would be equal to God, because it would be in opposition. If it is not an enemy, it cannot possibly be so. God has no enemies, for the One Almighty God also created the devils. All the life forces are enveloped, occupied, filled by the power of God." (1977)

We never know anything from the mind. Truth penetrates through the heart and the flesh into the inner. Our spiritual truth can be read in our earthly situation. Ideas come and go if they are not integrated in our blood, our guts and our organs. They fascinate, are stunning like a burst of sun on a mirror. It's our job to keep that inspiration going during the cloudy times, to find the sun coming from our inner. We must cultivate the voice inside that fills the night with music and dreams, that makes the day shine with a brighter light. "With us everything is reality—there is no story, no pretence. You can see from your own life what your situation is. It is always said that if you want to meet an angel, you have to be an angel. Everything depends on reality. There is no chance that you can go to heaven after you die, if you have not experienced heaven before—even if it is only a taste, a sample. So whatever you believe is true, you have to prove it to yourself. It is this ability to prove that is the fruit of the spiritual exercise (latihan kejiwaan). (Bapak, 1982.)

Religion is influenced by the culture of the society where it is practiced. It is a product of the land we live on, an approximation of the truth. It cannot really help the development of our soul, nor find what is truly ours, but Bapak advised to keep practicing our own religion because it was important for our heart. As the old gods died when their earthly mission was accomplished and returned to their celestial abode, all national representation of God will die one day and all cultural concepts of what is sacred will die with it. The divine cannot be locked within the confine of a country or a continent because the creator is universal and accepts all religions, all human beings. When that notion is entirely integrated it will be the end of a world, the beginning of another. It will probably happen when humans start operating on a higher frequency level, which is, I believe, why the latihan was given to us.

Was Bapak, as some people think, the Second Coming? Was he Adam, Abraham, Moses, Jesus, Muhammad? It may be that even the Messiah never knows himself that he is the Messiah, for he is like a secret messenger whose power will only be revealed when the time has come.

HOLY TRANSFORMATIONS

Leonard (French—English) interviewed in Spokane (WA.)

There is no mature love, no reasonable love, only the spirit of childlike abandon which does not reason or construct, but with each gesture, each word, recreates the beginning of the worlds. The child like person has nothing to accomplish but to satisfy the unending curiosity that is a state of grace and fearlessness. Taken out of self, it is reborn with each thing, each plant, animal or person it comes across. Adults may die within their life, but those who give up adulthood to run on the paths of childhood are children of God, prophets and visionaries who receive the divine inspiration and are filled with the gigantic breath; they hold the deepest aspirations of their contemporaries and give substance to their dream.

Leonard, would you be willing to share stories about your life in Subud?

Yes I have many stories. Some day I'll write them. But for now I'll tell you a few. The first that comes to mind is when I was young, in my twenties, and I was driving Bapak around. We arrived at our destination—and when you drive Bapak you have to come out of the driver's seat, run and open the door for him and then rush right back and park if you don't want to miss any of the talk. Finding a parking place in Leicester is not so easy, and I didn't know the place well, so I had to go out of my way to find a spot. I rushed back in, expecting to be late and the only place I could find was right in front. I was out of breath.

In fact Bapak was just coming to sit down. He was smoking a Kretek, which is an Indonesian cigarette, and while he smoked and talked I was beginning to wonder if I didn't need glasses to see well from where I was. Then I remembered I had brand new glasses in my pocket. So I put them on.

Bapak talked and it was fascinating, but I was a bit dreamy and floated as I listened. Suddenly I looked at him and said to myself, "Who is that? This is not Bapak on the stage." I thought there was something funny or that I was really tired so I took my glasses off and put them on again. It was even clearer to me that the man on stage was a different person. He was very good looking. He was young, strong, athletic, very relaxed as he talked. I thought to myself, "My God am I delirious, do I have a temperature? I was trying to figure it out but I couldn't. So I went deep inside myself because obviously, from the outside, I couldn't understand. I asked, "Please God, help me out. What's happening to me? Who is that character out there? I thought it was Bapak talking and it's not. Who is it?"

And then, like a resonance in a cathedral, the answer came, "Adam!" and I started to cry. There was Adam. I was taken over by an immense inner understanding that it was Adam. Then Bapak went on talking and suddenly, between tears, I saw that it was not Adam any longer. I took my handkerchief out and dried my eyes. I asked God, "This is extraordinary. Who is that now? It's not the same man as before." There in front of me stood a man with a very large nose and curly hair, very big curls, black hair turning gray. He was thin but very tough, very wide and muscular, square, a big man. The word Abraham came from inside. I was seeing Abraham. Tears came out again. I was very emotional. It was too much you know!

I am an artist and I could have drawn those men, painted them they were so clear in front of me. Extraordinary. As the evening went on Bapak continued talking and again I saw another man when I looked on the stage. He was a bit pudgy, also quite tall and big but had lighter skin, blue eyes. Abraham had dark eyes. This man had a very big forehead, white hair but shorter than Abraham and a different type of hair. It's almost like he could have been a red head but he was white. He was a man in his sixties and I knew, I didn't have to ask this time. I knew it was Moses. I remember his hands were very wide, short fingers, very, very gentle but very pudgy. I really noticed all the details because being an artist I learned to be very observant.

I looked carefully at the clothing. With Abraham it was very roughly fashioned. He had very little on. You could see most of his body. Moses had a long robe, white, it looked like an Egyptian garment. I was very moved. Abraham is a man I adore.

Suddenly as the evening went on I had another shock. I saw Jesus. Bapak became Jesus in front of my very eyes. There he stood, very feminine. His movements were supple. His hands were long and thin. His voice was clear like crystal. There was such love coming out of this man it was wonderful to be in front of him. He was neither a woman nor a man, an extraordinary character.

By that time I was really in a terrible state, crying in my chair. I would barely recover and then the feeling would come back and I'd cry again. I said to myself: "Come on, get hold of yourself!" So I wiped my eyes, blew my nose and went through two hours of Bapak talking and transforming. I was exhausted.

Suddenly, I saw a little man in Bapak's chair, with a thin black mustache. He had a little round face. He was slight of built, very quick, very agile, talking very fast with lots of movements. I knew it was Muhammad, I just knew. He had beautiful almond black eyes, fascinating eyes. While I was looking at him there was a kind of explosion in his face, like a star bursting, and then I saw Bapak roaring with laughter . . . the Kretek he was smoking had exploded. Sometimes these early ones would explode in that way . . . and Bapak was laughing because the thing had exploded.

If you remember when Bapak talked there was this phenomenon happening. You felt that he was talking to you personally. As he laughed he was looking straight at me and inside I said, "Thank you Bapak, I know who you are now."

It was the sixties and I experienced that Bapak was actually all the prophets in one. That was why he knew the Bible so well. He knew more than anybody could know, and people often wondered where he got his information. Well, he lived it. He was a pure soul from God that had taken different forms, had accumulated knowledge, a colossal thing. That was why Bapak said there would be nobody after him. He had integrated them all.

This was an amazing experience and I never told anybody about this for years and years. Something inside me said I could not tell anybody except Melinda, my wife, and I asked her not to tell anyone, this until an extraordinary thing happened about a hundred days after Bapak's death.

I was in Anugraha, the International Subud Conference Center in England. I had been a director of Anugraha and I was a National Helper in England. For some reason they asked me to talk, "Leonard, it's one hundred days after Bapak's death. We are going to have a big Indonesian Selamatan at Anugraha in memory of his death. Could you talk about Bapak this evening?" I felt so-so about it, but since I was asked I decided to try. I was a bit nervous to be honest. All week long I was preparing myself. I was gathering bits of feelings here and there about Bapak's death. It was very momentous for all of us, and I was trying to feel my way around.

When I got to the big hall, there were spotlights right on the pulpit; three other brothers were on my left and I was the last one. There was an Imam who came and talked first, then there was an English priest, then an Israeli brother who did the Jewish prayer and after Sharif, who could not be there so we would hear a recording of Sharif's talk at Bapak's funeral, it was me. The whole place was dark, and then they announced us. I hadn't heard Sharif's talk before. His lovely voice on the microphone filled the hall. I was very close to Sharif. I have always been. We met in Coombe Springs and I lived in his house for a time. We are close friends. I heard his voice and one after the other he said all the things I had planned to say.

I felt everything had been taken up, taken away from me. When he finished I was left naked in the chair, with nothing to say. "Oh my God, what am I going to do," I asked. "I prepared myself and knew just what I was going to say but now I can't say it. What do I do?"

"Just go up there and you'll see," was the answer. So I heard myself being called and I felt my heart beating in so many directions I could barely keep it in my chest.

When I got to the pulpit I put my hands on either side and became completely quiet. I remained still. Everybody was waiting. I heard people shifting around in the room but I just stayed quiet and suddenly—the hall of Anugraha was quite high, you know, with the big dome up there, and everything was dark in the room—I saw this enormous being filling the place. I saw Bapak, very, very big, taking up the whole place. He said to me, "Leonard, why are you wondering what to say?" I answered, "Well Bapak, I don't know what to say. Sharif said it all." But Bapak answered, "Bapak told you already, you must talk about your experience."

"You mean the one where I saw who you were?" And Bapak said, "Yes, you must tell that one." So I told the experience I just described to you. Because I was very filled with the feeling of the experience I saw that many people out there were crying.

Later, when I went out, an English priest came and said to me, "Leonard, you have switched on the light. Now I understand who Bapak is, and this has helped me to understand all the prophets and what this is all about." He was so moved!

And what is even more fantastic—and this is a story very few people know because most of the people who experienced it are not here anymore, I know of two guys left, one is an electrician, I always forget his name, Raymond? The other is Laurent Hennessey living now in France. The experience took place at the Alexandra Palace in London.

It must have been early seventies in a huge hallway, a palace, but very uncomfortable at the time, very dusty. Bapak had given a long talk and at the end of the talk Bapak said, "Now Bapak wants twelve helpers." He chose twelve of us and he said, "Come with Bapak; I want to do a latihan with you." So we went out. There was Lambert Gibbs at my right and Laurent Hennessey on my left. Bapak put us in a circle with him standing in the middle. He talked to us and then said, "Now Bapak is going to show you how Bapak receives," and he started to move.

He moved and became extremely light and fast. He moved like the man I had seen who was Muhammad. He told us that Muhammad used to move very quickly and that he spoke quickly. He was very masculine. What he said made me feel tremendously peaceful inside, total peace. He added that Muhammad spoke the words of God that actually touched people.

After he finished this kind of acting—Bapak liked acting a lot, he received this but acted it as well—he became what he was acting. Then he suddenly changed and started to move differently. His movements more feminine. It was extraordinary how he moved. And we all saw Jesus, I remember even the oatmeal robe, the beard, the face and all. Bapak then said "Bapak is going to show you now how Jesus cured people through touching then." And he went around, one by one; my heart was going boom boom boom as he came closer. I must have been in the middle, the sixth or the seventh in the circle.

He put his hands on someone two places before me, was it Simon Sturton? And said something to the effect, "What is your profession," "Banker" was the answer. He then said, while keeping his hand on him, "Banking is not good for you, find other work." It was a bad hall for hearing, I couldn't hear so well when he was at the opposite side of the circle, but as he came closer to my friend on the left he put his hand on him and said, "Oho, calm down, you're flying too high, be more grounded," and added something to that effect: "Can you feel Bapak's hand? It's cool. When the soul acts on the feelings it's always cool there. The hot means activity of the nafsu. It's burning inside, that's why it's so hot there." And I thought to myself, "Oh God what is he going to say when he comes round to me?" I was trembling all over inside, and then he stood close in front of me, put his hand over my heart and said, "Yeah, yeah, quiet, quiet now." And I felt his cool hand, soothing. All my apprehensions, fears and panic disappeared, a state of deep peace and a feeling of quiet oneness took over my whole being.

He explained, "That is how Jesus was passing the contact to people, by touching. He had to touch people." Then he talked about the heart and actually he was Jesus at that moment. I was in tears, overwhelmed, completely soaked, and this confirmed my previous experiences, in the hall at Leicester.

Later I received a letter from the north of the Congo. The letter said: Dear brother Leonard Lassalle, I write you because I had a dream. I was asleep at night when I saw a gigantic man, very tall, who came to tell me that I must find God. In the dream he said that there is someone who can help me. So I asked this angel-like being where and how was I going to find that person. And the angel told me, "Look on your bedside table. There is the name and address."

When the man woke up he lit a match and found my name and address on his bedside table. So he wrote me, but he didn't speak about Subud. The angel had just said "someone who will help you get closer to God." So I answered that I was surprised by his dream but that God knows everything. I added that if God was mentioned and my name was given in connection to Him I believed that it was because of Subud and I wrote him what I knew about it. I gave him the addresses of the closest groups but I don't know if he followed through. He said he was amazed to see the address of a French man on his bedside table, but you know, in Africa, there are many more stories like this than here, things that we think of as impossible or miraculous, because we ourselves are not used to them.

I came to Subud through Gurdjieff. Until 1955-56, I was an art student. One morning, I came to the class and I saw a very beautiful woman sitting on a chair, our model for the day. I told myself we were very lucky that morning, and as I began drawing her I realized that she was not like other models. Most of the models have a tendency to fall asleep. It's very tiring to sit there perfectly immobile. She on the contrary seemed very awake. I had the feeling that inwardly she was doing something. She had that kind of look.

When we took a break at eleven o'clock we had a cup of tea, and I asked her what she was doing when she posed. Since I insisted she finally said, "Well, I am doing Gurdjieff's exercises."

"Oh Gurdjieff, I am also into that," I retorted. This was Melinda, who later became my wife.

We began talking. Then we started going out and became friends. It was in May 1957. I had a student room with a window on the street. At three o'clock one morning I heard something down below. I was not too happy to be awakened since the street was usually rather quiet. I went to the window and looked down— it was hot I remember—and I saw Melinda and Lambert, (an architect who worked a lot for Anugraha, quite a remarkable fellow, a very good friend of Melinda's) who had come in Lambert's little convertible car and were honking. I hushed them. "What is this? Be quiet, it's the middle of the night and everyone is asleep. What do you want?"

They came up and told me that there was something extraordinary happening in Coombe Springs. Everything was turned upside down. There was an Indonesian who had just arrived and started something called the latihan. "We don't understand anything about it. We don't know what it is but it's rather extraordinary," they added. I told them to go back to sleep. I thought they were nuts to wake me up and tell me such crazy things!

So they left but later Melinda told me about the experiences she had. She had become my girl friend and I went to see her in the night often, like the fox in the poultry, jumping in her bed and leaving very early in the morning because I was not part of Coombe Springs and had no business being there. I never wanted to commit to Gurdjieff's work entirely.

But now I felt that there was an atmosphere of renewal, of big changes, and I started asking myself questions. One of Gurdjieff's exercises was to look at oneself and watch to find out how long one could remain conscious. I could never last much more than three seconds. Impossible for me to remain conscious. The question that came to me from the very depth of myself was, "So François, (that was my name in those days) how would you know which of the François will die at your death? Which part of yourself, of your consciousness will be there at the time of your death? Because when you are with your mother you are one François. When you are with the woman you love, you are another. When you are with a cop another yet. If he arrests you, even another. A different one for the person you buy a paper from, etc. You are never the same. So how can you know which is the real one within yourself." I was seized with a terrible panic then. I felt that if I died and didn't know how to present myself, I wouldn't know where to go, nor in what being to put myself.

I went through a terrible crisis, and my friends who were anti-Subud told me that it was all caused by Melinda's bad influence. "You must absolutely leave that woman," was their advice. The crisis lasted about three months: May, June, and July. I was in a total fog. When people asked me something, I answered I didn't know. I was stupid. I felt I knew nothing. I was at the very bottom.

In October, I felt I was so stupid I didn't even know who I was. "So I might as well do this latihan to see what it is," I told myself.

I went to meet Pierre Elliott in Coombe Springs on my way to see Melinda. He said that if I wanted to be opened I should be present that night because they would open people in the hut.

I went that night and I was shaking like a leaf. There was Icksan, Sjafrudin, Bennett, Bapak and myself. I was standing up like this and they told me to close my eyes and begin. Before I closed them I saw Mr. Bennett, a very respectable handsome man, very tall, way over six feet, a very intelligent looking man with a high hairline, gray hair, dancing in front of me like a monkey, trotting around like a female baboon. Very strange. I also saw, in another corner of the room, Icksan laughing and doing weird things with his arms. I couldn't see Bapak because he was behind me somewhere. I thought that they were totally nuts, and I felt like running for my life.

This lasted for a long time. Then, from behind me, I suddenly heard an enormous burp, very loud, and I thought, "On top of everything else they burp on my neck. It really has gone past the limits. They are real pigs. They talk about God but really!" Then as I was voicing all those objections to myself, I heard another burp. I was only nineteen you realize. I was very down to earth, brought up around goats in France and all . . .

Anyway, there was this other burp that went on and on until I said to myself, "What a beautiful burping that is. I wouldn't mind being able to burp like this." It was like listening to a rolling coming from the very bottom of the earth, to a volcano beginning to erupt. It was coming out with such freedom, so graciously! I was so awed by this I wondered who could burp this way. So I turned slightly and just there—Bapak was standing with his head right next to me. I suddenly felt entirely stupid. I was so small, so humble, so dumb.

I saw myself at ground level, and then, as soon as this enormous burst of humility came upon me, my arms rose up and I felt carried like that (flying movement.) I was totally centered and felt this very delicate, fine vibration inside. Then a few movements came and I heard, "Finish now." I was furious. How come it finished so soon? My first latihan had only lasted a minute. I was not happy when I put my shoes back on and left.

The next morning I asked myself a question, "François how do you feel today? If you did die, what would happen now?" And the answer was, "It would be okay." I was connected. It was extraordinary. I knew then where I would put myself if I were to die. After that I entered life head down. It was a fantastic end to my crisis.

Since then I have done the latihan three or four times a week without fail. I had the luck not to go through a period of doubts because it felt right from the beginning, like an entirely natural thing. I had experiences very early on that were like lighthouses, to show me that all was well.

To answer an early question you had about my background I was born in Nice, France, in 1937, and raised by an English mother who escaped from England at age seventeen to live an artist's life in Paris. She had rejected all of the English ways.

She came from a very aristocratic family who descended from the royal family, and she wanted to break away from all that. My grandfather was a priest who read her the Bible with a stick in his hand. She needed to escape such a very stern man. She came to Subud later, so did my grandmother. We were five generations at one time: my grandmother, my mother, my children, my grandchildren and myself.

My grandmother, the mother of my mother, died in my arms. That was a divine experience, but I had so many of those I don't know where to start. You are right, I'll start with that one. My grandmother was a very soft and gentle woman who suffered at the hands of her husband. He became a Colonel in the English Army after having been a priest. He died in 1914 while picking up corpses from battlefields, Germans, French, English.

He felt his work was to go to the front and fight, so he was always gone to war somewhere. My grandmother was very lonely. He was a very handsome man. He looked somewhat like I do. He was long and thin. He had a big mustache and a strong charisma. Women loved him, and since he didn't have the latihan, he didn't know his nafsu well. So he had many temptations and my grandmother suffered from this also.

She was a very religious woman, Anglican, very gentle. And she always loved me very much. When I started the latihan she would often make me sit down next to her, give her my hand and remain quiet. And I felt the latihan and she felt it also. She would tell me she felt an enormous peace about me. Really, she loved me enormously this grandmother, a very important person in my life.

I started doing the latihan in 1957, my mother in 1959 although she was anti-God, anti—religious and all that stuff. She had never talked to me about Jesus or the Good God when I was little, and I had to discover it all by myself. She never said anything about it, neither good nor bad, just never talked about it. She was very close to nature, a naturist. She didn't want to talk about religion. She was also in rebellion against the rich Parisian life. She had been married to a lawyer who was one of the biggest art merchants in Paris, very well known, and she got sick of that scene. She left him, escaped again and went to live on an island, the Ile du Levant.

But this is another long story—just before the war, an island with no water, no electricity. She lived twelve years with two children on this island with no school, no shop, nothing. It's incredible when you think of it. She ate fish like the locals. She was a painter, an artist.

To get back to my grandmother, her mother, it's a rather extraordinary story. She was ninety-seven years old and wanted to die, but she was in good health. She had decided to live close to us, so we put her in a nursing home close by. She came to see us regularly during the day, and one day she told Melinda that she would like to start doing the latihan. My mother was there for a visit at that time: she had come from the Provence in the South of France (which is where I was raised, my culture) for the occasion, and so Melinda and she opened my grandmother.

Melinda had been doing the latihan with my grandmother for fifteen days when we had this celebration at home one night, a birthday. Many Subud members had come to our place and toward 12 o'clock or 12:30 I told Melinda I felt that my grandmother was not well at all. I had to go to the home. Melinda retorted that at that time it would be closed, that I wouldn't be able to get in. I decided to go anyway and I left on foot. It was about a twenty-minute walk. When I got there the place was closed but I saw a window opened so I climbed in like a thief and I went to my grandmother's bedroom.

I could see that she was in very bad shape, and as I sat next to her I noticed that her stomach had become very round, very big. She was awake and told me that she was in pain and if she died it was okay. What she didn't want was to be sick and hang on so that people would have to take care of her.

She was always very clean, took care of all her stuff herself and was always impeccable. For her it would have been humiliating to be crippled. I asked her if she wanted a priest since she was Anglican, but she answered, "No, I just want you to stay here." I asked if I should call a doctor and she said no, she just wanted me to stay right there.

So I sat next to her and I did the latihan. I sang and sang for about two hours. At one point she said she would like to pee. I took her chamber pot and helped her with it and then I put her back in her bed very delicately. She was round and a little heavy. A few minutes later she said that she would like me to pretty her up, to powder her face and put a little perfume on, so I did. I put a little lipstick. I perfumed the air around her. She felt better.

I took her hand. I looked in her eyes and in them I saw her whole life, like in a film. I had heard of this phenomenon but never experienced it. It was as though a film was playing backward, all the emotions could be seen, love, doubt, fear, etc. It only lasted a few minutes. It came at an incredibly rapid rate. I saw all this in her eyes, small blue eyes with lots of love, but I also saw some very painful moments, hurt, anger. Then she did a little good-bye sign with her hand and when I looked at her chest to see if she was still breathing I saw that she was not.

While I was looking at her I felt a little vibration, very delicate, very fine, musical even. I had felt that before with other people who had died in my arms, but this time this vibration rose through my feet from down below and went up my body. When it came into my solar plexus a huge "Allahu Akbar," came out of me. Very powerful. I actually yelled it, and then I felt her soul coming out as it passed through me, making my hair rise.

When I looked at her body again, I saw that her blood was spreading in spots on her hands. There were still a few spasms and then she started to stiffen. I covered her up and stayed with her a little while. It was three o'clock in the morning. Then I went to the kitchen where I knew there would be someone at that time. The nurse was furious, "What are you doing here?" she asked. I answered that I came because my grandmother was dying and that now she was dead. She answered that I couldn't know if she was dead or not, etc. She went to look at her and examined her, and finally came back to tell me, "Well she's dead."

I went back home. We had a little sitting room with a big couch and there was room to walk in the back of it. I did a short latihan so as to cleanse myself before going to sleep. As I started going around the couch, to my utter amazement, I saw my grandfather sitting there on the couch. He had been dead twelve years but I saw him sitting there, mustache and all. He looked at me sternly, angry. I asked him, "Why aren't you happy? Grandmother is dead and will join you soon and she is happy." But he was still grumpy and that was so funny to me I burst out laughing. I laughed and laughed to see this grandfather furious with me. Him sitting on that couch with that stern look was so incongruous!

He looked up at me standing there laughing, then started to smile and then joined in. We laughed together, wild laughter, and as he laughed more and more I saw him taking off, rising, and then I felt the same sensation as with my grandmother. I knew that he was liberated. Then he was gone. I really felt that he was opened at that moment, that he received the contact. So I was very light and happy when I went to our bedroom and lay down next to Melinda.

She asked me what happened and I told her that my grandmother had died. Melinda adored my grandmother so she started crying and sobbing, heavy sobs. While she was crying I felt the beginning of an erection coming on. "This is crazy," I told myself. "You are really a weird fellow. You are sick. You'll have to wait. It's not the time." But it came on stronger and stronger as Melinda was crying more and more in my arms. I asked God, "Why do I have an erection right now. It's not the time." And the answer was that I had to satisfy this.

So I came on to Melinda and she said, "What? Now?" I told her, "Yes, I know. It's weird, but I have been like this for half and hour, and in my latihan my inner says that I must follow this."

"Let's follow it then," she answered. And of course it was a perfect union. We both felt it, at that moment we had one soul. What was most extraordinary was that during that union I saw my grandmother dying. Then I saw the universe and the opening of the Milky Way, which was like the feminine sexual parts. Then there was a firework of light and my grandfather and grandmother were projected into the heavens through this opening. It was amazingly beautiful.

Melinda fell into a deep sleep. As for me, I was in a state of ecstasy, total union with my soul and with God. I do have that now, but then it was a much stronger experience, and because of it I felt liberated.

The next day we arranged everything for the burial. We celebrated with champagne and everyone was so happy. It was a deliverance. Even my uncles, who fought all this spiritual stuff and kept wallowing in regrets, changed their attitude after a while. They said they had never experienced such joy. And after that they both got opened in Subud.

After my grandmother died, my mother inherited some capital. She lived in Cannes at the time. She had a very difficult life. She was sixty. She had a shop that was not doing well. She was very alone. She had great difficulties because she was not a businesswoman. She was an artist. So I invited her to my own shop. I had a five-storey store in the very center of Tunbridge Wells, in UK. She accepted and came to stay with us.

She died at the age of eighty-nine in 1992 at my home in Provence, in my arms, like my grandmother. Death is an important moment and if you can assist someone in being totally relaxed it helps him or her, especially if they have anxiety about it. She was such a wonderful grandmother, so gentle with the children. I have seven children, three girls and four boys, the youngest is now twenty-five. We have eight grandchildren.

In my early years I had good luck and bad luck. The bad luck was to have suffered because of my father. Lassalle couldn't have children, so my mother had me with another man because she wanted to have a son. My older brother had been taken away by his own father. So Lassalle raised me until the age of six or seven when he died in the war. My real father was a Parisian Jew, a rather well known artist, but he rejected me because he didn't want his family to know about me.

I suffered a lot from not having a father. All the men with whom my mother lived, I was unable to get along with. I suffered a lot from this, so I swore that if I became a father one day I would be a really good father. I would be there for my children and I would, (and I will) take care of them till the end.

The good luck was to have had a mother who was interested in education, who knew A.S. Neil, and to have gone to his school. It helped me enormously. It gave me self-confidence. He was like a father to me. He understood me so well. When I came out of Summerhill I had acquired quite a stability. I was ready to face life. A very good school.

I am lucky with my children. All my kids are good kids. They work. They raise their families well. They all started the latihan. They are very devoted to each other. They help each other a lot, and if one is sick everyone else chips in. It doesn't mean they don't suffer. They go through difficulties. Sometimes you wonder why, after being raised so well, do they have to go through all this?

But I think that suffering is necessary to have compassion. A human being who never suffered doesn't understand others. Suffering opens the door to compassion, comprehension and love of God. It is an extremely interesting thing, a double-edged knife. One side of it can be very negative and totally stifling, but the other side is totally positive and makes one leap ahead in the spiritual world.

These experiences have much contributed to my awareness of souls. I understand more and more about human beings. I see that every being is like a universe, a whole universe. Like the solar system is a being, and every one of us is a system. Sometimes, when you look into the eyes of people, you see where they come from in the galaxy.

I see the earth as a place where all human beings come together because the souls need to experience the physical world, the physical suffering, the physical happiness, and the lower forces that are in the universe. Is it only on the earth that the soul can understand and integrate its deepest learning? Is it an education about the forces so humans can bring them back to their rightful place? Is it a little like the dragonfly that takes a little drop of water on the lake, the planet, because she needs it to go on with her flight?

In the same way human beings have to come back to earth more than once because they miss their opportunity. I told someone very close to me who believed that she was dying, that it was not time yet, that she was not ready because her soul still had the need to express itself on the earth. "It needs to express your love for God, your adoration for God. It is very important that you do not leave right now because you are still young and if you do you will frustrate your soul and it will have to go through a very difficult process in order to reincarnate and start over again. This time now is an incredible opportunity, especially since you have the latihan," was what I said. The next day that dear person told me she had decided to live.

AN INNER JOURNEY

Sylvia (U.S.A.) from her own words.

In 1972, I attended the Subud National Congress held in New York City. Members from all over the U.S. were there and somehow, I linked up with a group from California. After the congress, the Californians were going to Montreal for the Canadian Annual General Membership Meeting, and they invited me to go along with them. Being a practical, task-oriented person, I said no at first because I had to do my laundry. But they talked me into going. I had just accepted the job of Subud National Secretary, so I was able to justify going in order to learn about the national concerns of our organization in another country.

The next morning we set out in a van driven by a man called Sjarifudin. The rest of us took turns sitting next to Sjarif or sitting on the floor in the back of the van. After a while, we closed our eyes and became quiet. I was sitting near to a woman, Illia, when I began to feel a very strong electric charge in my body, starting in my feet and legs. Slowly, as we drove, it spread upward throughout my body. I was able to open my eyes and chat for a while. Then I closed them, and the current resumed. Unlike the even path it took as it rose through my body, I noticed that the charge was scattered and diffused when it flowed every which way around my head.

Finally, just as we arrived in Montreal, the energy passed through my head and entered a quiet channel above it. This channel, which was to continue to grow throughout the weekend, was a narrow cylindrical column that rose from my head and went straight upwards. Inside, it was hollow, unless it was filled with my inner being. I discovered that my inner could move up and down the channel in accordance with whatever inner or outer situation was at hand.

We were now at the meeting. There were many people to greet. I was a young, insecure thirty-year-old who was intimidated by helpers. The first sign I had that something was indeed different was that I was able to clearly see, by listening to the words and witnessing the behavior, the shortcomings of a woman who had been a Regional Helper. My, I thought, this is interesting.

Most of the people present attended the first part of the Canadian annual meeting. I took avid notes. Every once in a while, however, I would have to close my eyes, for my inner was calling on me. During one such experience, I felt strong vibrations in my head that lasted quite a while. At the end, an inner bandage was wrapped around and around the targeted area, like a mummy casing. I opened my eyes and became aware of the channel above me. Instead of being just above my head, it was now about a foot higher, filled with my inner being and consciousness.

Evening came. The group from California and I went to have dinner, and I moved down the channel to chitchat and dine with them. After dinner, I alone returned to the meeting. Very few people, aside from those committee members and helpers who had official functions, were present. I continued my note taking. Suddenly, a big argument began among the officials. The more people talked, the louder it became, and the more conflict ensued. The dispute went on for some time. Although I did not understand the nature of the controversy, I remained quiet and continued to close my eyes on and off.

During one such eye-closing period, I felt the inner presence of Hanafi von Hahn, a Canadian National Helper, calling to me. My own inner joined his, rose above the fracas, and landed on a man sitting among the rest. The next moment, that man rose and spoke. Whatever he said was the antidote to the disagreement.

A number of other similar and also personal experiences occurred during the two-day event, before the group from California and I got back in the van to return home. The channel above me had continued to grow and was now higher than the clouds. I sat quietly in the van with my eyes closed. Then, the energy that had been so high dropped all the way down to my stomach. I felt a war going on inside of me. There were demons of all shapes and sizes battling each other inside my abdomen. I knew only one weapon to fight back and that was saying the name of God over and over again. God, God, God, God, please help me God. Eventually, the war ended.

Slowly, my inner began to rise again, up the channel through my body and above. It rose even higher than it had been. Then I heard Bapak. He laughed and told me I would always be a little spacey. Then he left. My inner had only a short distance more to go before it reached the sun. The sun was a vast body of light. My inner being seemed to merge with the light.

After some time I was dropped off at my apartment in New York. The California group invited me to continue on with them to the West Coast, but I declined, this time because I needed to attend classes.

The next day, as I sat in an education class at New York University, I felt the tiredness of my teacher. I also heard an inner voice tell me that now I needed to fill in all that had been shown to me by living my life.

It is now almost thirty years later. My outer life has progressed with hard work and the blessed guidance of the Almighty, but it is much more difficult to speak about inner progress. I am grateful that I still have years left on this inner and outer journey.

EPILOGUE

"If real words and meaning in each language were
taken and with them one language was created, it would
not be necessary to go to school."

Gurdjieff

This book could go on, there are many more interviews I
haven't used, many more topics I haven't approached and the
process of sharing stories is still fascinating to me. People often
start by saying that they have no story, that their life is not
interesting enough, but through telling their story they come to
see themselves as the heroes and heroines in their own myth.
However, this book is long enough and I believe I have learned
what I needed to learn from this process. Obviously, everything
contained in this book, beside the interviews, comes from my
own receiving which is from the perspective of my level of
consciousness and influenced by the purification that is mine at
the time, although I also believe that in Subud we have the ability
to receive above our level.

I want to thank all the people that have so graciously
participated and apologize to those whose interview I didn't use.
It was only through lack of space or because it didn't fit the
topics I explored, but in no way did I make a choice based on
the intrinsic value of the interviews; I just had to follow my
guidance. Those interviews may be used at a later date.

The most important lesson I learned through the unraveling of
this book is that there is a right time for everything and if I let

myself wait for it I will receive help, especially when I remember to ask. There are always helpers and guides by my side. When I acknowledge their presence they respond. I remember one occurrence when I was totally overwhelmed, looking at more than a hundred pages of notes taken at different times over the years and unable to find what I knew was there, (or did I even know exactly what I wanted for the chapter I was working on?) I became conscious of a fluttering around me, some invisible activity wanting to be noticed. I remembered that we all have guardian angels, so I went inside, found my inner quiet and let my hand be guided. Out of the pile I pulled two pages. It was exactly what was needed for that chapter, much better than what I believed I was looking for.

I have used those helpers ever since and give them much thanks also. After that experience I learned to trust this way of working more and more, letting my hand be guided and my choices be made for me. Whenever I wanted a piece of information I didn't have, I just asked.

I also came to understand that language, in the same way it helps develop taste and understand feelings, also teaches me to recognize spirit. Writers—and there are quite a few in our Subud group—often feel that writing is their spiritual practice because the transformation of sensations, feelings and ideas into language is like the distillation that extracts subtle essences from fruits, transporting those who drink the resulting liquor into a higher state.

Writing, like all art forms, is a commitment to perfection and beauty: it ennobles one. There is no art without love; through the touch of mind and spirit the one who creates comes in contact with grace, expressing it through beauty of lines or elegance of style. All creative endeavors bring us to the place where we join the divine.

But we are often naïve and trite in expressing this first inspiration. The logical and rational must follow, and that is the process of editing and refining. For this, first Christy, a sister in writing and in Subud, then Ilaina were a tremendous help in weeding through my overgrown garden to uncover the edibles.

To perceive our godliness, our field must reach a higher vibration. No matter how hard we try to receive spiritual guidance, we can't until our field matches frequency with that higher vibrational order. And that is where the latihan comes into play. Through the latihan I am taught a new dance, which cancels the dance of obstruction, evasion, mimicry, and scarcity in which I have been trained. It forces me to let go of every belief and assumption, dismantling the model for living through imitation that has been implanted in my genes, allowing my higher self to build new structures forever to be improved upon. Under the impulse of the life force I go deeper into personal exploration and the meaning of identity; this connects me with a larger view of life that stretches my human boundaries.

From this perspective I understand that my actions affect all others. Every choice I make is of great consequence. Bapak said that everything is written within. Every thought is known and recorded and we have to accept responsibility for it. We are accountable for every deed. The universe does not forget. On the spiritual level we are naked for everyone to see. As we choose our path moment to moment, life watches in anticipation, for we are connected to everything else, and everything we do that supports our life also supports all life. Even the isolated wise man in his cave influences the thoughts of others. So we will experience whatever we have caused, and the positive ripple we create will return to us.

Separation from our true self has allowed tyranny to set in, in this world, but the latihan will bring us back to our authentic nature. Some say that the latihan came to us so we could survive the reality shifts that are taking place at this time. The ability to change reality within us is ignited by the practice, because we get out of the mind structure and stop basing our experience on paradigms set up by our society. I once heard someone say that civilization began when humans started to believe what others told them, rather than listening to themselves. In that case we can say that the latihan de-civilizes us. As I get more and more de-civilized I see that the process of creation is happening right now and if I trust this, I can partake in it. In this creation I have free rein to invent new forms. I will create for myself whatever I believe I can create, as long as I remain within the divine order. I also know from Bapak's clarifications that the process of purification never ceases, even after death.

Although there are many teachers on this earth at this time, all offering clues, no one has the total answer for me, I have it for myself when I can be quiet enough to hear the voice of God within and trust in my own receiving. In that way I can prove my own beliefs to myself. My body is one of the most valuable things I have during my time on this earth, and when I develop the body of my soul the divine dispenses information to me. I honor this body as well as the body of my jiwa (soul), which is constantly modified and can take many forms. As this soul body changes, my destiny is altered along with it. The latihan sees that I am not stuck on one image of myself but that I keep all my images opened to movement.

Our only possibility of survival on the physical and spiritual level is cooperation: a sharing of knowledge between all the species. It is needed to create harmony on this earth. We are slowly becoming aware of the existence of humanity as a whole, even if we are far from living as complete human beings on this earth. When this happens we will be able to live as a single unit, sharing a consciousness and fulfilling a task much greater than our earthly task, but before this comes to be true I have been told that the world may have to go though an enormous crisis. We must be prepared to surrender and accept a new state of being.

GLOSSARY

SUBUD—A combination of three Sanskrit words:
>   **SUSILA,** associated with the qualities necessary to develop nobility in humans
>   **BUDHI,** associated with the inner force inherent in all humans leading one to one's true path
>   **DHARMA,** associated with surrender and the willingness to put what one has received into practice in one's daily life

LATIHAN KEJIWAAN—Spiritual exercise (of Subud)

INITIATION OR PROBATION—The period during which the interested person inquires about Subud before getting opened.

HELPER—A person experienced in the practice who is witness at the opening and helps new members with their understanding of Subud.

OPENING—The witnessing of the new member's wish to begin the spiritual exercise.

RECEIVING—Being opened to a state of surrender and acceptance of what is received.

TESTING—Doing latihan and receiving in latihan the answer to specific questions.

CRISIS or METAMORPHOSIS—A time of transformation, during which former habits and belief systems are changed for the better.

JIWA—The Indonesian word for soul or spirit.

NAFSU—The tools we need for life on earth (mind, senses, feelings and emotions) otherwise known as passions.

PRIHATIN—Privation—A fast, either from food and drink, or an inner fast from some form of wrong thinking.

BVG